BOOK-WOMAN

SON

OF A

GRIFTER

A Memoir
by the *Other* Son

Kent Walker with Mark Schone

SON

OF A

GRIFTER

The Twisted Tale of Sante and Kenny Kimes,

the Most Notorious Con Artists in America

ωm

WILLIAM MORROW

75 YEARS OF PUBLISHING

An Imprint of HarperCollins*Publishers*

ISBN 0-06-018865-0

for

Lynn, Kristina, Carson, and Brandy

SON
OF A
GRIFTER

1

LIAR

I make my living as a vacuum-cleaner salesman. I've met a lot of good liars in my day. None of them are as good as my mother.

When people lie, the story goes, some tic gives them away. They blink or break their gaze or touch their noses with their fingers. Polygraph machines operate on the principle that these physical signs are inside the body too, and involuntary. Breathing quickens, heart rates jump, and the needle on the lie detector skitters over the graph when run-of-the-mill humans try to deny a criminal truth.

Who can beat a lie detector test? Swamis, maybe, with pulse and breath control, or con artists, or cold-blooded sociopaths. My mother claims to have relatives among the first category, and most observers probably think she belongs to the other two.

I agree that Mom would have no trouble fooling a machine. I've seen her walk into parties filled with little clumps of people who each know her under a different alias. Instead of fleeing in panic, she works the room, remembering what fake name she used with each mark, never slipping, never breaking a sweat. A few electrodes and straps on her arms wouldn't faze her.

But it's too easy to say her skill stems from the sangfroid of a grifter. Her gift for lying comes from passionate conviction. She never blinks or stutters in the midst of the most ornate fibs, because she believes what she's saying without reservation. A good liar always starts with a germ of truth and builds from there: that's Mom. She can't distinguish between what's real and what she's invented, which makes her preternaturally persuasive.

I can make a more educated guess than anyone on earth about when she's lying, though there are no outward symptoms. I just know when and why she does it, and about what. The hard part is reaching backward through decades of fabrications and embellishments to find what she started with, the first hard kernel of reality. Even when I think I've found it, I don't always trust it.

If you ask me where Sante Kimes came from, then, I can't be sure, nor would I swear to anything under oath. All I can tell you is how the story evolved.

AT 9 A.M. ON WEDNESDAY, July 8, 1998, I pulled my white Corvette into a parking space and killed the engine. I unfolded a cardboard sunshade and spread it across the dashboard, just like all the other morning commuters in Greater Las Vegas, and then walked to the service entrance of the low cinderblock building on Decatur Avenue that housed my business. I'd been out of town over the long holiday weekend and had a lot of catching up to do.

As soon as I was inside, my sales manager approached me. I heard Greg chirp "Good morning," but what struck me was the pained expression on his face. "Your mom and your brother have been calling here," he said. That's why he looked uncomfortable. He knew I wouldn't consider this good news—I hated having my fifteen employees know anything about the antics of my estranged mother and brother. "They've been calling nonstop for the last two days." There was a backlog of sixty messages, most of them aborted collect calls—the kind people in jail have to make.

Already I was embarrassed, but I played it nonchalant. "If my mother or Kenny calls again, tell them I'm not back yet. I really don't want to talk to them."

The last time they'd phoned so often was fourteen months before, when Kenny got arrested in Florida for shoplifting and aggravated assault on a police officer. His story was that he was with a "girlfriend" who happened to put something in her purse with every intention of paying for it, but the police got the wrong idea and he had to defend her, and so on.

I knew who the so-called girlfriend was: Mom. She not only liked to steal, she liked to dress conspicuously. A security cop with an eye out for shoplifters couldn't help but notice a senior citizen in fishnet blouse and bell-bottoms, wearing her trademark black wig and trailed by her gawky twenty-two-year-old son. On this occasion, at the Federal Discount store in downtown Miami, a plainclothes detective had stopped my sixty-two-year-old mother as she waltzed out of the store, her bag filled with stolen lipsticks. While Kenny "defended" his "girlfriend," swinging at the detective, Mom slipped out the rear door and went into hiding at a motel. Kenny went to jail.

The phone calls that ensued were almost comical. The first came from Mom. In her breathy, high-pitched voice she fed me the usual stew of manipulative half-truths, lies, anger, and actual concern. "Kent, you have to help your little brother. He didn't do anything." False. "With my record, I can't help him." True. "You're all he's got." I often thought that *was* true.

"What happened?" I asked.

"Oh, it's just silly, no big deal. He was trying to cover for his girlfriend, and the cops roughed him up, and I am so worried about him."

"His girlfriend wouldn't wear big black wigs, would she?" I joked.

"I had nothing to do with this, Kent," she lied. Her voice changed from pleading to demanding. "This is your brother, for God's sake, and he really needs your help!"

I explained that I was two thousand miles and three time zones away from the Miami lockup and there was nothing I could do for either of them in the next fifteen minutes. The conversation ended, but in the time it took to pour a cup of coffee the phone rang again. Kenny, calling from jail. I'd never heard him so panicked. This was his first real experience behind bars.

"Kent," he barked, "have you talked to Mom?" His voice was even more hyper than usual.

"Yes, we just hung up."

"If she calls back, give her this message for me. Tell her to go, go, go! I'll be all right, but if those assholes get their hands on her, it'll be the end of her."

So much for the girlfriend story, I thought. Aloud I said, "Kenny, get a lawyer, and do what he says. You haven't been in any major trouble before, and I'm sure they'll go light on you." Part of me still held out hope that this would be the long overdue event that finally shook him. I wanted him to know there were consequences to the way he and Mom had been operating.

The Miami calls poured in hourly for another three days and then stopped dead. I found out later that Kenny had pleaded guilty on two counts and received probation, and as soon as he was released he and Mom had fled the state.

So when Greg told me on July 8, after more than a year had passed, that the calls had started up again, I assumed something similar had occurred. Mom and Kenny were in another misdemeanor of a jam and hadn't yet scratched their way out. They wanted, "needed," my help, as usual.

But things were different now—*I* was different. At least I hoped so. I'd tried to stop caring. Asking Greg to cover for me wasn't a momentary impulse. Avoiding Mom and Kenny had become my policy, and I was praying I could stick to it. After Greg gave me the unwanted news that they were once again burning up the phone lines, I tried to put it out of my mind and get on with business as usual. At nine-thirty the whole staff assembled for our daily sales meeting. Then the reps went out into the field. I settled down at my desk to deal with stacks of accumulated paperwork.

Almost immediately, Greg poked his head into my office. "Line one is for you," he said.

"It's not them, is it?"

"No, it's your friend Carl." Carl was a pal from my brief stab at college.

I picked up the phone. "Hi, how're you doing?" I was hoping he was going to buy me lunch.

"Kent, have you seen today's paper?" He sounded as wary as Greg.

"You know I don't read the paper." It wasn't part of my routine.

"I really think you should look at today's."

"Well, just tell me what's in it." I was impatient, and his tone perplexed me.

"Go get the paper," pressed Carl. "There's something about your family."

"Okay."

"It's on page four. I'm sorry. Call me later."

I walked into a coworker's office and hijacked a copy of the *Las Vegas Review Journal* and saw my mother staring back at me.

She's going to be pissed at that picture, I thought, almost laughing. She was dressed in her jail uniform, without her big black wig, scowling. It was a photo, circa 1986, from her trial for enslaving illegal aliens—Mexicans she worked to the bone as unpaid "maids." The headline was also pretty familiar. WOMAN WITH 1986 CONVICTION LINKED TO N.Y. CASE. My mother had made the papers often in her forty-year criminal career. I figured she'd stolen something again, only this time it was extra big.

Then I saw the first line of the article and I think my heart stopped. "A woman previously convicted in Las Vegas on charges of enslaving four Mexican women is now at the center of an investigation into the disappearance of a New York City millionaire."

I had to tell myself to breathe as I read the story: A wealthy Manhattan widow named Irene Silverman had vanished and Sante and Kenny were being held in connection with her disappearance. "Who in the world is Irene Silverman?" I wondered. But further down in the article there was a name I recognized, and when I saw it I went into shock. "Investigators in Los Angeles want to question the pair about the fatal shooting of David Kazdin, 64. Kazdin's body was found in an airport trash bin earlier this year."

Dave Kazdin had been a friend of the family, and of mine, for years. I started connecting the dots. Dave's name was on the deed of the house on Geronimo Way where Mom had lived off and on since we moved to Vegas. His body had turned up in a Dumpster not long after Mom, desperate for cash, had told me she wanted to take out a loan on the Geronimo property—and not long after the house had burned to the ground.

I read the article over and over, my spirit sinking a little lower each time. But the shock was mixed with an odd sense of relief. The fear of what Mom and Kenny would do next, and the waiting for it to happen, were over. Then I chastised myself silently. *Your mom and brother are arrested for murder and you feel relief?* Then anger and confusion came in waves, a different emotion every few seconds, as I sat behind my desk dumb-founded. I had known this day might come, and now that it had, there was nothing I could do about it. The word was spreading among my employees. I'd noticed them gathering outside my office before I started reading the paper. Ten minutes after I finished, the phone began ringing, and it didn't stop

for two days. This time it was the media. Now I was going to
have to relive the past whether I wanted to or not.

OVER THE LONG FOURTH OF JULY weekend,
when I'd packed my wife, Lynn, and our three kids into the car
and headed for California, I'd been flooded with memories but
had tried not to dwell on them. We'd attended a friend's wedding in Temecula on Saturday the Fourth, then driven to Newport Beach. It was there, long ago, that Mom and I had moved
from Palm Springs to start our life with my stepdad, Ken
Kimes, and it was there that my half brother, Kenny, had been
born when I was almost thirteen.

We pulled into Newport just as the sun set. The cool ocean
breeze was a welcome relief from the oppressive heat of Vegas
in July. There was a carnival atmosphere down by the Balboa
Pier, the streets full of people celebrating the holiday.

The excitement my wife and kids felt just being a family by
the sea helped bury my memories of that other, earlier family
for much of our four-day trip. I recall thinking to myself, *So far,
so good.* I wanted to make some new memories.

The vacation was just what we needed. The kids played in
the surf and fed the seagulls. Lynn and I enjoyed some roman-
tic dinners and watched the sailboats in the harbor. On our last
night there, Monday, July 6, we went to the Studio Café, a little
club at the base of Balboa Pier that's known for live jazz. It's
also known for the Adios Mama, a concoction of gin, rum, and
every fruit juice you can imagine. Drink one of those blue mon-
sters, and you're relaxed. Two, and you're done for the evening.

Lynn and I were sipping drinks at the Studio when she
asked, gently, about a subject she knew was sensitive. She
wanted me to show our kids where I'd lived when I was young.
I got a sinking feeling, but I thought to myself, *I can do this.* So I
said, "Tomorrow," and ordered a second Adios Mama.

Tuesday morning we drove south down the Pacific Coast
Highway through my childhood.

We passed restaurants where I'd eaten as a kid. The sight of
some of them made me smile. Others I remembered because I'd
once hurried out the front door ahead of an angry manager or
waiter after Mom had said or done something. Mom's favorite,
Chuck's Steakhouse, had vanished. That was where Mom and

Ken had the first of their serious public arguments, the first where Mom had to be physically evicted from the premises. She was drunk, and in one of her incandescent rages, a sort of altered state that was frightening to witness, she'd flung a full tumbler of bourbon at the wall. Glass and ice had showered the other patrons.

Soon we neared the condo that had been my first address in Newport, the first home that Mom and I shared with Ken Kimes. We were there only a few months, but they were good ones. Not once did the police come knocking, and no one tried to serve Mom with a summons. We didn't hide when the doorbell rang. It wasn't like the way we'd lived in our old hometown — in Palm Springs, Mom and I had always been on the run.

But soon after the first place in Newport, the old pattern had resumed. In two years we lived in five different houses and changed our phone number eight times. We bounced between addresses in a master-planned neighborhood called East Bluff. As I piloted my new family through East Bluff twenty-five years later, I was reminded of what it felt like to lose friends. I remembered how the halls of my elementary school had buzzed with talk about Mom and the ring she'd stolen from another student's mother. Parents wouldn't let their children play with the son of someone like that.

Whenever there was a problem, we'd move, and as I drove around East Bluff with my own kids, I realized just how many problems there had been. We passed the convenience store where Mom had bluffed and shouted her way out of a shoplifting arrest. We passed some more former homes. I realized that I didn't want to show my children more than one of my old addresses. They'd become accustomed to stability; they'd lived on the same suburban street for years. I didn't want to have to explain to them why their dad had moved so often.

So I picked one address out of many, a Spanish-style ranch house on a cliff overlooking the Newport Back Bay. The setting was beautiful, a hundred feet above the water, and there was a twenty-foot-wide, mile-long greenbelt along the bluff that the whole neighborhood used as a backyard. I could take the family on a stroll there and show them at least one place where I'd lived, and if I was lucky the kids would think it had been my only home instead of one among dozens.

I pulled over to the curb on Vista Entrada and parked. We

walked out onto the greenbelt. "This is it," I said, pointing to the rear of the house. "That window there is my old room."

"Cool," said my daughter Kristina. "You must've loved living here."

"It was pretty neat," I agreed. It had been, some of the time. While Lynn played in the grass with the kids, I looked out over the marsh-fringed bay, now a nature preserve. Then I looked down at the ice plants on the cliff, and an afternoon from 1973 came flooding back.

I was in the fifth grade and had just gotten home from school when the phone rang. I picked up the receiver. I was alone in the house.

"Hello," I said.

"Hi, Kent." It was my stepfather, Ken. Mom hadn't yet worn away his health and his fortune, but that day there was strain in his voice. "Kent, I need you to do something for me, and it's really important that you do it right now, okay?"

"Sure, Ken." I never called him anything but Ken for the whole quarter century he was my stepdad. "What do you want me to do?"

"Do you know those big brass scales your mom and I brought home a few weeks ago?"

"Uh-huh." I could see them on the living room coffee table. They were antiques, heavy and ugly.

"I need you to get rid of them." His voice was growing more nervous and hurried. The only time he sounded like this was when he knew Mom was itching for a fight.

"What do you mean, get rid of them?" I asked.

"You have to get them out of the house right now." Ken was insistent. "I don't care what you do with them, just get them away from there, and don't let anyone see you."

"I can put them in the trash." That made him yell. "*No!* Put them someplace where no one can find them. Do it *now*, Kent. It's really important."

And then he hung up. I looked at the scales again. They were grotesque, but Mom and Ken had seemed so proud of them. When friends dropped by, the two of them would brag about how valuable the scales were. Now they wanted this prize to vanish; it didn't make sense. But Ken sounded scared, so no matter how strange it seemed, I obeyed orders. I ran to the closet, grabbed a sheet, and wrapped up the scales. They were even heavier than they looked. I slung the makeshift sack over my shoulder and stepped outside onto the greenbelt.

Ken's urgency made me nervous. I looked around to see if anyone was watching and then crept to the edge of the cliff behind the house. I grabbed the ends of the sheet and swung. When I let go, my bundle sailed out into the abyss as if propelled by a slingshot. The scales bounced once in the ice plants and disappeared.

When Mom and Ken got home that night, the air crackled with tension. Typically, I didn't learn the truth until much later, long after the scales had vanished, when I overheard one of my parents' drunken fights. Mom, it seemed, had stolen the scales from an antique shop. Weeks after the theft, she'd sauntered brazenly back into the same store, and the owner had summoned police. That was when Ken called me. He thought the cops were racing toward our house, sirens squealing, so he'd asked me to dump the evidence.

Before I could start cataloging all the other times I either watched or helped as expensive items were "disappeared," my wife's voice brought me back to the present. "We should be going now."

I was ready. Touring my old neighborhood had awakened too many memories. It had been four years since Ken died, months since I'd spoken to Mom and Kenny. I'd worked hard to leave the bad stuff behind me and had almost succeeded. I thought about it less and less and felt that much stronger. But as we walked back to the car for the ride home to Vegas, I realized that the visit to East Bluff had kicked up old doubts about myself. Why had I let myself, even as a grown man, get sucked into so many of my mother's schemes? I still didn't know whether it was because I loved her or because I was like her. I renewed my vow to keep the past out of the present—for my own sake and for the sake of Lynn and the children.

I had tried to shut the door on my past in Vegas the year before. By then, there had been a hundred reasons not to let Mom and Kenny come around anymore. But it was hard to deprive my children of their grandma, or Babish, as they called her, especially when Babish always brought gifts and excitement with her. The problem was, she also brought trouble, and with Kenny as her lieutenant she had only gotten worse.

My daughter Kristina was the first to get burned. In the

summer of 1996, when Kristina was twelve, Mom and Kenny convinced me she should keep them company on a trip to the Bahamas. The three of them were in the Vegas airport watching their carry-on luggage squeeze through the X-ray machine when the attendant saw something strange on the scanner. There was a stun gun in one of Kenny's suitcases. By the time the attendant had called the police, Mom and Kenny were gone. They left Kristina next to the pile of bags, holding the bag, so to speak. The police interrogated my terrified twelve-year-old daughter for hours before calling me, and didn't release her till I convinced Kenny to return to the airport and take the blame. He must have conned his way out of a bust, because I heard no more about it.

Neither Mom nor Kenny ever apologized. Yet after a brief interruption I not only resumed speaking to my mother and brother, I even let them live with me. Ever since Ken Kimes's death in 1994 they'd had a cash-flow problem. A year after the stun-gun debacle, Mom and Kenny left their house on Geronimo Way and moved in with us.

Trouble erupted immediately. There was a chasm between the way we lived and the way they lived. My household was fairly average, until Mom and Kenny appeared with their "maids." Up through the mid-eighties, the "maids" were usually Mexicans and Central Americans without papers. After the feds put Mom on trial for slavery, she switched to white vagrants. She'd troll for them at the local homeless shelters, and soon they'd be scrubbing her floors, taking orders in exchange for nothing but a place to sleep. Now these scruffy maids were bunking at my house.

The verbal abuse began within hours of each maid's arrival and continued till the victim decided that homelessness was preferable. Sometimes Sante treated my wife as if she were a mop pusher too. After ten days, Mom had gone through six maids, and Lynn had seen and heard enough. She didn't like the strife, and she didn't like another woman running her home. Meanwhile I feared that one of these ex-servants would file a lawsuit. When I asked Mom to stop bringing them home, she agreed.

The very next day I walked in the door and found yet another strange woman on my couch. "She's from an agency," Mom insisted. "Are you sure you're not from the Shade Tree shelter?" I asked the woman directly. She said she wasn't.

A few hours later she ran down the stairs crying. "Take me home!" she wailed.

"Why do you treat people this way?" I shouted at my mother. Kenny began cursing at me. As the conflict escalated, the latest ex-maid blurted out the truth. "Please," she begged, "take me back to Shade Tree."

I decided it was time for an ultimatum. I wanted to sit down with Mom and Kenny and stipulate that there were to be no more vagrants in our home. Lynn and I would hire a legitimate housekeeper who was answerable only to Lynn.

I invited my wife, my mother, and my brother to lunch at the Macaroni Grill in Las Vegas. When everyone seemed to be getting along, I raised the issue of the maids and Lynn's unhappiness. A bitter, profane argument broke out.

My mom has never been able to handle the idea that someone else might be more important to me than her. We were in the foyer of the restaurant, about to move the fight into the parking lot, when Mom began talking about my wife. "I can't believe," she hissed, "that you put that cunt in front of me."

In a flash my hands were around her throat. I don't remember whether I lifted her off the ground, but I could have. I'm a big person, six-foot-three and 220 pounds. Mom had used me as her muscle in the past, and now I'd turned on her. She'd finally pushed me too far. "You and Kenny," I spat, "are moving out."

She looked scared for a second, but I could also see the steely resolve in her eyes. I let go of her neck, wheeled, and escaped to the parking lot. Sante followed. She grabbed at my arm as I opened the car door, but I pushed her away. She fell against the side of the car. As I backed out she stepped behind it, daring me to hit her. I swerved in her direction. Anyone watching would have thought I was a criminal, brutalizing a little old lady. My own feelings were mixed, as they always were when it came to Mom. I was disgusted at myself, but I also felt justified, and free. I'd finally made the break with Mom and Kenny. When Lynn and I got home, we piled their belongings in the driveway and vowed to cut off all contact.

During the next year I backslid occasionally. I let Mom and Kenny deliver Christmas presents to my kids. I called them when I received water and power bills in my name from the Geronimo property. They should have known better than to scam *me*.

But for the most part I kept my no-contact promise — and I felt like I'd had my heart cut out. I missed Kenny, but the absence of my mother destroyed me. She was the superhuman force that had sustained me all my life. Sante Kimes loved me with an unconditional, all-enveloping, fearsome, enormous love. Nothing compares to it.

"I've loved you the longest, my brown-eyed boy." Mom has said that to me as long as I've been alive. Maybe, as a sociopath, Mom couldn't really tell where I ended and she began, but that meant that if I stubbed my toe, she felt the pain — she'd do anything to make it go away, anything to make me happy. In her presence I felt invulnerable. For whatever reason, healthy or unhealthy, she exalted family above all else, and that meant that she praised and exalted me.

I gave a speech at my high school graduation, and from the podium I spotted my mother in the crowd. She was mouthing, "I love you," her face streaming tears, pride coming off her in waves. "You're so lucky," said a friend who'd been standing near her. "Your mother loves you so much." I smiled, having heard similar things before. You would never have known I'd lived with a classmate that whole school year while my mother ran from the law.

"I've never been a cookie-baking type of mother," Mom would say, with epic understatement, "but I did the best I could." She was right. On her own terms, she was devoted. Every year when I was a kid I had a birthday party so lavish that it spooked the adult guests. Mom buried me under expensive gifts, all stolen, and plied the grown-ups with caviar and top-shelf liquors.

Mom continued her over-the-top tradition with Kenny, one birthday surprising him with a pony. It was stolen, shoved in the back of an RV, and then hidden in our garage, but it was a pony. As Kenny grew up, Mom kept the party going with her grandkids. She collected pumpkin seeds the day before Halloween when my daughter was seven. She scattered them in the grass and told Kristina they were magic. After Kristina had gone to bed, Mom covered the lawn with jack-o'-lanterns, so that when my daughter woke up there was a magic pumpkin patch outside her window.

Babish became a hero to my kids. But adults found Mom's presence still more enchanting. It was exciting simply to be near Sante, and to soak up her enthusiasm and the good times that followed her around. She was the center of attention in every restaurant or hotel or casino we entered. "If you could bottle all that positive energy," a friend marveled, "you could fly a rocket to the moon!"

Once Mom and I were flying to Hawaii when she decided that the rest of first class should help us celebrate Ken's appointment as an ambassador (another story in itself). Within thirty minutes, all the passengers were out of their seats and partying like the home team had won the Super Bowl. When the grumpy captain left the cockpit to quiet the ruckus, Mom went to work on him too. Before long he'd joined the party. The drinks poured, the in-flight movie was cancelled, and the pilot accepted an invite to dinner at our house. In the months that followed, whenever he flew over our property he'd flash his landing lights.

It was exciting to be with Mom when she was good, but it was more fun when she was bad. I watched speechless as a woman approached our table in a restaurant and, thinking Mom was a movie star, asked her for an autograph. Mom took the pen and signed, and a crowd gathered. She wrote "Elizabeth Taylor" on two dozen napkins and menus, never breaking character.

It was even more thrilling when she was *very* bad. Getting Away with It can be addictive. I remember racing through the streets of Manzanillo, Mexico, in a cab, minutes ahead of an angry hotel owner whom Mom and Ken had stiffed. We owed him for a week in a luxury suite. We got on our plane, breathing hard, pulses racing, and as the wheels left the runway and we knew we'd escaped, it was like being high.

There was a price for all the love and fun. Sante demanded total loyalty in return. She never ceased her mantra of family, family, family. In her mind, everything she did was for the benefit of her children, and she never let me or Kenny forget it. In later years, as her legal troubles mounted, she'd invoke the higher good of family to summon me to her aid. "Those sons of bitches are trying to kill us," she'd insist, and she expected me as a good son to do my duty and help her.

By that time I was trying to resist her pull, but it was difficult. Mom and I had too much in common. She'd passed on to me her temper, her love of luxury, and some of her quirky tastes. Every time a new science fiction flick hit the local theater, she and I had a date, and we shared a geeky obsession with *Star*

Trek. I'd tape episodes of the original series and *The Next Generation* and take them to Mom's house. We'd watch stacks of tapes at a sitting, driving everyone else from the room.

Ultimately I pulled myself free of my mother by relying on one of her virtues. Her willpower had always enabled her to outlast her foes. I'd inherited that toughness. Everyone else would back down from a fight with her, but after my early teens I never did. In the end, I *was* able to resist her, no matter how much it hurt. Kenny, thirteen years my junior, didn't inherit that strength. He's now suffering the consequences.

As I drove back from Newport Beach on the night of July 7, I had another twelve hours before I'd learn how tragic the mixture of Mom's love and Kenny's weakness had turned out to be. I still hadn't heard the name Irene Silverman. But I was thinking about my mother and brother all the same. Try as I might to focus on other subjects, as I followed the highway through the empty spaces to Vegas my mind kept spinning back to Sante Kimes. *I miss Mom so much,* I thought, *and I'm always wrestling with whether or not I'm like her, yet I don't really know who she is.* I'll *never* know. My mother is a woman without a verifiable past. All I have to go on are the creation myths of her own making, and even those are constantly subject to change.

2

THE HINDU AND
THE WHORE

During her enslavement trial, part of Mom's strategy was to come up with a pitiful tale about her early years. What she "revealed" was intended to evoke sympathy. It doesn't jibe with what I heard growing up, but that's to be expected.

The Sante Kimes who was on trial claimed that she was born in Oklahoma City on July 24, 1934, to a thirty-four-year-old mother of Dutch extraction, Mary Van Horn, and a forty-four-year-old farm laborer father with a background thought exotic in those days. Prame Singhrs was an East Indian. Sante Kimes was born Sante Singhrs, an Okie with a twist. She said she had an older brother, Kareem, and an older sister, Reba. Before the slavery trial I'd never heard Mom so much as mention siblings.

Like other Okies, the Singhrs family supposedly escaped the Dust Bowl by migrating to Los Angeles in the mid-thirties. My alleged grandfather abandoned his son and two daughters when Mom, the youngest, was three. My grandmother, claimed federal defendant Sante Kimes, turned to prostitution to support her kids.

By the time she was eight, Sante was allegedly a street kid in Studio City, just over the hill from Hollywood in the San Fernando Valley. According to what she told a court-appointed shrink, she scrounged food for herself and her siblings while my alcoholic grandma turned tricks. A bubbly, eccentric woman named Dottie Seligman, who owned a movie theater on Ventura Boulevard with her husband, Kelly, apparently saw the little girl hanging around and began to buy her meals.

Noticing that the mother of the dark, vivacious kid seemed very scarce, Dottie Seligman hatched a plan.

Dottie's brother-in-law was another Okie, an Army National Guard colonel who had put down roots in Carson City, Nevada. Forty-eight-year-old Edwin Chambers was a stern, well-respected man with a noticeable stutter. He and his wife, Mary, were unable to have children, so Dottie provided some. She had decided that Sante and another L.A. kid, a chubby, reserved seven-year-old named Howard, needed parents as much as her sister and brother-in-law needed children. My mother arrived in Carson City as Sante Singhrs, a name the other kids ridiculed, but within a year she was Sandy Chambers. Papers had been drawn up that said so. An instant family was created.

Several knowledgeable people, among them Mom's best friend from high school, Ruth Tanis, have come forward since July 1998 to shore up this version of the truth. This camp holds that "Sandy" was a liar and a thief while still in high school. They say that my grandmother, Mary Chambers, referred to her daughter's "Hindu" background long before the "maids" trial, and that Sandy admitted her real mother was a whore. There is a birth certificate with the right names, dates, and places on it. Who can argue with that?

Documents, to me, are the least reliable evidence of anything in the life of Sante Kimes. She has always finagled alterations in official records by befriending a dozen clerks till she identifies a suggestible person willing to break the law. She promises so much, and has such a good reason for the change she wants, that it seems a small favor. I have, on tape, a conversation in which my mother dangled a fake trip to the Bahamas in front of a sucker to get him to do her bidding. It worked.

I look at the birth certificate that says my mother's name is Sante Singhrs and rearrange the letters. Maybe Singhrs was Sanchez. S_N_H_Z. It wouldn't take a whole jar of Wite-Out to pull it off. Sante is a Spanish-sounding first name; Sanchez would explain why Mom's skin was semidark and why her Spanish has always been so good. Or if she was born in Oklahoma, maybe she *is* an Indian—the Native American kind. In 1934 there were hundreds of thousands of those in Oklahoma, and fewer than a hundred Hindus.

The Hindu/prostitute story rings false for other reasons. For instance, Mom told the shrinks that Ed Chambers had raped her repeatedly in Carson City and that even earlier, during her Studio City childhood, she'd been molested by other adults. Given the way Mom used sex as a weapon in her later life and the fact that she did seem to be a runaway when Aunt Dottie met her, I wouldn't be surprised if there was truth to her tales of abuse in California. Young girls often leave home for that reason. Her sexual behavior and her terror of poverty fit the profile of a kid with a desperate past, as does her appetite. Like many ex-street kids who never really believe the next meal is coming, Mom binges. But I seriously doubt the stuff about Grandpa Chambers raping her. Mom leveled those charges in 1985. Not only was the man dead, but sex-abuse claims had become a newly popular means of seeking mercy from the court.

Because of Mom's mysterious roots, and because she changed her story so often, my own ethnicity is an open question. I'm happy that way. It's hard to be prejudiced against anyone when you don't know what you are. I might be Latino, East Indian, American Indian, or plain old vanilla. For a while my mother was more French than de Gaulle—until she became East Indian. In my lifetime, she's called herself Sandy, then Santee, then Sahn-tay, then Shawn-tay. Mom's maid's tale may be the one moment of unguarded truth in her life, but it's equally likely that it's just another fiction. I'm sticking with the version I heard when I was young, which is as good as any other.

As a kid, I was well acquainted with Dottie Seligman, who moved to an apartment near us in Palm Springs after her husband died. She also visited us later in Newport Beach and Hawaii. I can confirm that she did procure two children from Studio City for Ed and Mary Chambers. But the rest of Dottie's version of events, as presented to me and my father, was nothing like Sante's. According to Dottie (who died long before the maids trial), Mom was a wild child from a respectable family. She wasn't the daughter of a prostitute, but of parents who simply didn't know how to control her.

In the early eighties, when my real father was living in Carson City and working as a plasterer and Mom had become Sante Kimes, dashing from one gilded town to the next with my millionaire stepdad, my father got a phone call from a woman who claimed to be Sante's sister. She said that the siblings had been separated in 1947 when my mother was adopted, and now—as my dad recalls it—she wanted to come by and talk.

She had accompanied her husband on a business trip and was calling from a Reno hotel room. Dad thinks her name might have been Reba. She knew that Sandy, as she called my mother, had wound up in Carson City and that my father was Sandy's long-divorced ex-husband. In lieu of her sister, whom she hadn't yet tracked down, Reba wanted to meet my dad. He said yes.

Dad says that the woman who appeared on his doorstep was a carbon copy of Sandy Chambers, aka Sante Kimes: same dark hair and olive skin, round, pretty face, buxom figure. And she'd brought photographs of the two look-alike sisters and their solid middle-class family, including their mother, who didn't look like a whore. Nor did Reba make a single reference to hard times. As Dad remembers it, the woman explained that the family had come from back east, maybe Pennsylvania, and that they'd been prosperous and happy in Los Angeles. She also said that Sandy—the woman never called her Sante, the name that appears on Mom's supposed birth certificate—had been a girl with peculiar habits. Reba laughed as she told Dad how much young Sandy enjoyed putting matches between the toes of sleeping people and lighting them. The fire tales were eerily believable. Childhood pyromania almost guarantees adult criminality, and Mom grew up to be a crook with a special interest in arson. She'd rather burn a house for the insurance money than sell it.

Before she left, Reba gave Dad a phone number in Reno. Intrigued, Dad rang her the next day to talk some more and was bewildered by her response. "Why are you calling this number?" she hissed. "Never call here again." She slammed down the phone. The woman who claimed to be my aunt seemed to share her sister's mercurial nature.

My dad is an honorable man, not prone to hallucination or invention. I believe that this encounter with Sante's sister occurred, especially since he told me about it soon after it happened, years before the disappearance of Irene Silverman and even the maids trial. Already there were plenty of cops, from Honolulu to D.C., who knew about Sante, and plenty of department stores and car dealers and carpet warehouses and furniture emporiums and ex-friends who'd been burned too bad to forget her. But she wasn't known to the world at large in the early eighties. There was no reason for anyone to pretend to be

Mom's sister, call her ex-husband, show him a bunch of old photos, and then disappear.

Ruth Tanis, my mother's high school friend, also claimed that Mom had a sister named Reba, though in Ruth's version the sisters didn't look at all alike. According to Ruth, Reba and Mom's real mother came to Carson City while Mom was a teenager, and tried to drag her back south, but my mother wouldn't go. After the two women left, Sandy told Ruth the prostitute mom/Indian dad story, adding that her father, Prame, had been some kind of Hindu holy man, which made her a princess.

I wasn't convinced by Ruth's story. By the time I heard it, Ruth was an ailing sixty-four-year-old alcoholic, and Mom was locked up on Rikers Island. I knew that Ruth hated Mom for breaking her heart. She died in the fall of 1998, only a few months after my mother's arrest, so I'll never be able to question her more closely. If my mom hit Ruth in high school with the same spiel she gave the judge thirty years later, it was either true or it was a story, and Mom has always been able to keep her stories straight.

Who Sante was before Dottie plucked her off Ventura Boulevard is a matter of speculation. It's after that point that the mostly true history of Sandy begins. She was Sandy Chambers by eighth grade, when her new parents deposited her at school in Carson City, Nevada. She grew up there during the forties and fifties, when the town was a couple of blocks wide and a mile long. People still hitched their horses to posts on the main drag.

My father, Ed Walker, had entered the same school a year late because of whooping cough, so he was a thirteen-year-old seventh grader when Sandy Chambers appeared in his life. There were only forty kids in each class, and she was the new girl, a dark-haired and outgoing (if quirky) transplant from the far-off cosmopolitan realm of Southern California. She was willowy then, though often her weight would soar upward and she'd wear a girdle to disguise it. She had a beautiful face and a full bust, the raw material that she would later force into a Liz Taylor mold. She had already started caking her face in white powder to conceal her olive complexion.

It was a tiny town, and everybody knew everybody. By the time she started Carson City High School, my mother had attracted an admirer in Ed and a best friend named Ruth Thom, while alienating many others. Sandy, a B student, joined club after club: Spanish, 4-H, Future Homemakers of America, the Girls' Athletic Association, the school paper. She was full of energy and involved in everything, as everybody was; there were fewer than two hundred people in the whole school. But the new girl from L.A. seemed to want to control whatever she touched, to run every activity, and that put some students off. Twice she ran for school office. Both times she lost.

Her only close friend was Ruth, aka Boobie, a doctor's daughter who seemed to thrive on Sandy's energy. Short and blond and as busty as Sandy, Ruth could be silently stubborn when she wanted, but she was an enthusiastic and loyal participant in life Sandy's way. They went skiing and horseback riding together, and Ruth moved into the Chamberses' house during her senior year because of trouble at home.

Like Ruth, my father was bewitched by Sandy. She barked and he jumped, though all the while she had her eyes on other boys. Ed was tall, handsome, and rugged, sort of like James Garner with a crooked grin, and he just hung in there till Sandy decided to let him be her boyfriend. By then he was in tenth grade and a basketball and track star. She was a year ahead of him.

"We had plans," my dad has told me, suggesting that when Sandy graduated in 1952 and he was about to start his senior year, they had some kind of understanding that they'd be getting married. It seems more likely that *he* had that plan, and she had another.

After graduation, Ruth and Sandy, who were inseparable, took a six-week course at a Reno secretarial school. Then they lit out across the Sierra Nevadas for the big, or bigger, city of Sacramento, the capital of California.

The two girls attracted a good deal of male attention in their new hometown. Jim Tanis, a Naval ROTC student at the University of California–Davis, sixteen miles east of Sacramento, met them somehow, and one night he and a buddy went over to the girls' apartment. The guys brought their acoustic guitars so they could impress the ladies. They strummed their instruments as they sang folk and country songs.

Tanis was somewhat taken with the big-breasted blond girl. He figured she'd be somebody he could go out with for a while. As for my mother, "she just wasn't my type," he recently told me, and he wasn't talking about her looks. "I'm a pretty good judge of character, and she impressed me as bossy and pretentious. She put on airs. She came on like she was King Farouk's wife."

By then my mom was already a skillful liar, dropping hints that she knew famous people and generally had a window into a life more fabulous than what was possible in Carson City or Sacramento. People who loved her accepted her tall tales as a side effect of her early unsettled life, which had left her with a desperate need to be important and adored. She was an imaginative person, with ambitions to be a journalist or novelist, and like everything else about Sandy, her writing style was imperial: she talked while Ruth Thom typed.

Jim Tanis knew better than to criticize Sandy in front of Ruth, but he failed to see the charm in my mother's penchant for twisting reality. "To Ruthie," he said, "Sandy could do no wrong. I never mentioned her name, and I tried not to run into her."

Mom's ways didn't deter my father one bit. After Ed finished school, he got a summer job in Sacramento and moved in with relatives so he could be close to Sandy. Mom promptly relocated to San Francisco. Her sidekick Ruth tagged along, while Jim Tanis kept making the trip from Davis to see her. Soon he and Ruth were engaged. My father continued his long-term, long-distance pursuit of my mother, sometimes double-dating with Ruth and Jim. When Mom got restless again in 1954 or early 1955, she moved to Santa Barbara, Ruth in tow, and took journalism classes at the local branch of the University of California.

Jim Tanis's father managed a ranch near Gaviota in the Santa Ynez Valley, inland from Santa Barbara. One weekend Jim brought Ruth and Sandy to the ranch, where the three young people attended a barbecue. Then Sandy went back to Santa Barbara alone.

A little later Jim's dad got word that a dark and pretty young woman had used his name to open an account at the I. Magnin department store in Santa Barbara, charging more than $400 worth of merchandise. Now Mr. Tanis, who earned perhaps $250 a month, was in debt, and Sandy Chambers had disappeared—justifying Jim's suspicions about his fiancée's best friend.

Jim married Ruth in January 1956 and shipped out to Pensacola for navy flight training. Though his pay was barely enough to cover rent, he sent money regularly to his dad to pay off Sandy's debts. Ruth and Sandy kept in touch by phone after that, and Ruth rarely told Jim what her friend was up to because she knew how he felt. Ruth still believed, however, that Sandy could do no wrong, and that the I. Magnin scam was a youthful indiscretion.

Ed Walker, meanwhile, was now attending college in Seattle. He wanted to be an architect. Some say this was Sandy's dream rather than his (she'd later demonstrate an odd edifice complex, chasing after builders, developers, and major property owners). My dad denies this. He insists that the desire to build was all his own, in place since freshman year in high school.

Ed's other plan was to marry Sandy as soon as he graduated from college. She was getting farther and farther away but still let him visit her, especially during his summers in Carson City. He'd drive down to Santa Barbara, rent a hotel room for the weekend, and on Sunday he'd make the long haul back to northern Nevada.

One day in the summer of 1956, my father knocked on the door of the Chamberses' ranch house in Carson City. He hadn't heard from Sandy for months and didn't know where she was. Mary Chambers had to give him the bad news, knowing that he'd be deeply wounded. "Ed," she said, "Sandy is married." On May 9, in the Chamberses' living room, Sandy had exchanged vows with an army officer named Lee Powers. He'd flown in from Fort Benning, Georgia, for the ceremony, and she'd driven east from her latest address, the University of California at Berkeley. Ed was crushed. That whole year, while he was making his epic treks south to spend a few hours with his beloved, she was two-timing him.

Powers, like Ed, was tall and handsome. He was a jock who wanted to teach high school phys ed when he left the service. He also happened to be Jim Tanis's lifelong pal. Tanis had been a small kid and would have been an easy target for bullies if not for Powers—who was Jim's bodyguard in grade school and his crony through the end of high school. Sandy and Lee had met through Tanis, but somehow Tanis hadn't warned his best friend about her, and now it was too late. Sandy was Lee's wife.

My mother had landed her jock dreamboat with a lie, an old-fashioned, unimaginative one. She told Lee that she was pregnant, and like a good soldier he did his duty. They married on May 9, 1956, four months after Boobie and Jim. Powers left the army and signed on as a graduate student at Cal State in Long Beach. Mom became a housewife.

I can see my mother enjoying the Suzie Homemaker gig for a week or so. Maybe less. Peace and quiet always bored her, and the thought of being a schoolteacher's wife must have mortified her. She tried to talk Powers out of it. He wouldn't budge. He was doing what he wanted to do and ignored Mom's entreaties to take up some more lucrative occupation. She was at the interview when he got his first teaching job, in the northeastern suburbs of L.A. in the spring of 1957, and I'll bet her mind was racing as she sat in the chair smiling at the principal. She could imagine where she and Lee would be living in thirty years and she hated it. Images of entrapment and penny-pinching virtue and high school basketball games and a measly pension made her sweat the way no polygraph could. It was the fight-or-flight instinct. She picked flight.

My mother went to plan B. Plan B was good old reliable Ed. He would be better husband material because he would do whatever she said.

Sandy left Powers after a year of marriage and called him from the road to say she wouldn't be coming back. She wrote to Ed and told him Powers was history. The letter was really a royal summons. Sandy knew that Ed would come running at a crook of her finger, and he did. He quit school, walking away from his architecture degree, and reported to her side. They were wed on November 9, 1957. After six years my father finally had his wish. Dad may never be sure that he even knew Mom's real name, but we're both certain of one thing—when she came back into his life, it was the worst thing that ever happened to him.

3

SANDY AND ED

y dad was driving. It was 10 P.M. on Christmas Eve in 1969, and we were heading south between mountains on a two-lane highway outside Reno. Snowflakes fell into the beams of our headlights and seemed to bend as the big Lincoln raced through the high desert darkness. Air from the car heater hit my legs. I started to drift off in the cavernous passenger seat, my stomach full of restaurant food. I was seven years old.

Bang! There was a sudden sharp noise from the Ford in front of us. I bolted upright in my corner of the vinyl bench seat and peered over the dashboard. We had reached the swamps of Washoe Valley. The sedan ahead of us lumbered over onto the shoulder. Ed hit the brakes and eased in behind the parked Ford. There were no other cars on the road.

My father and I had just finished eating a sort of holiday meal, a civil, unremarkable, even happy dinner that we'd shared with my mother, who'd divorced my dad a year previously, and her boyfriend Clyde. Mom and Dad had reached a sort of weary détente or, more accurately, my dad had enforced a de facto truce by moving four hundred miles north of Palm Springs, which had been our hometown for several years. He was back in the part of Nevada where he and Mom had grown up, and she was still down in the California desert doing whatever. She couldn't cause much trouble for him anymore. I was visiting my dad for Christmas, and Sante had flown up, and somehow Clyde had appeared, and we'd driven from the Reno airport to have an odd, ad hoc family get-together in some semifancy place. There hadn't been any yelling. All three adults had acted like adults.

Afterward Mom had gotten into Clyde's car, and Dad and I had jumped in the Lincoln, and we'd set out toward Carson City. We were a two-car convoy, with Mom and Clyde in the lead.

Now those two had pulled onto the shoulder and were outside their car looking down at the right rear tire. My dad, a buff six-foot-three, ambled over to them. He left the motor running and the headlights on, and I stayed in the warmth of the Lincoln. I could look out into the circle of brightness and see the three of them wrapped in their winter coats as if they were actors on a little stage. My mom had a fur hat shoved low on her head, and her hands were in her pockets. The snow was thin but steady.

My dad crouched down for an instant to look at the tire and then straightened up and started talking to my mother with a quizzical expression on his face. They seemed to be arguing, but I couldn't make out what either one was saying. Clyde had already walked back around his car to the driver's seat. Maybe he planned to pop the trunk, so he could pull out the spare, or maybe he planned to stay warm, like me, and let my dad fix the flat. It wouldn't have been out of character for Mom or her boyfriend to expect Ed to do the work.

Then my mother, standing two feet from my father, pulled a revolver out of her coat. She pointed it at my father's stomach. He took a step back, raising his arms and extending them halfway out from his sides with palms open.

Sante started yelling, jabbing the gun at my dad, and I could hear a little bit of it. "You turned us in! Admit it!" He was shaking his head: no. She kept shouting, and he kept shaking, but he held his ground.

When she pulled the trigger the shot echoed in the valley. I saw orange flame in the narrow space between my parents. Mom kept firing, but my father never fell down or backward. He pawed at his stomach, looking for blood or powder burns. Somehow Mom had missed from point-blank range.

I was in awe when my dad reached out and yanked the pistol from her hands. He threw the gun into the blackness, and that's when he finally started to run. He was sprinting south along the highway toward Carson City, unthinking, perhaps hoping to race all the way home to the safety of his father's house.

Clyde had never cut off his engine, and now he peeled away from the shoulder in pursuit of my father. When he caught up to Dad, he rolled down the driver's side window, stuck a long black tube out, and fired. My dad kept running. Either he was very lucky, or Clyde couldn't drive and shoot at the same time. Clyde fired again, and I wondered why none of the bullets had found their mark. Then my father wheeled and grabbed this gun, just like the first one, and flung it into the swamp.

Two headlights were coming toward us. Dad stood in the highway and flagged them down. Clyde jammed his car into reverse, grabbed my mother, and sped away.

The driver heading toward Dad didn't want to stop, but Dad blocked the road. When the vehicle slowed, he beat on the hood and pointed up the road toward Clyde's taillights. "My wife and her boyfriend just tried to kill me!" he yelled, and told the poor, scared strangers to call the police. They gaped at Dad all dish-eyed and hit the gas.

Dad paced back and forth in the oncoming lane and peered into the snow, hoping for another set of lights. None came, and he gave up. We drove back to Carson City, Dad stunned and grim, gripping the steering wheel and staring, me in a fetal ball, shaking and speechless.

Mom and Clyde didn't show up the next morning to open presents. After the adrenaline had subsided, my dad decided to let it go. Mom may have tried to kill him, but she'd failed, and now she and her henchman were gone. We were okay, and we were having Christmas together. It was a great day. My dad gave me an awesome toy crane.

MY FATHER WAS AN ambitious, intelligent, handsome, and very honest man, but from the first day he met my mother he was in her thrall.

Mom, in marrying someone she later said was more a brother than a husband, had wagered right. She wanted a mate who'd honor and obey her, for richer, not poorer. Something about tangible property—real estate, houses, apartment buildings—inflamed my mother. Mom gave Ed Walker a mission: build.

They lived in Sacramento during the first years of their marriage. Mom had real jobs for a while. She was born to hype, and she dabbled in public relations and promotions. She launched something called Hi! Welcome to California, a Chamber of Commerce–type welcoming service that existed mostly in her press releases.

It was my father who succeeded. In 1960 he scraped together eleven thousand dollars, bought a lot, and designed and built his first house, a cottage at 4931 Hemlock. He'd become a developer, as Sante wanted. Soon he had a reputation as an up-and-coming young contractor, with a stack of projects throughout the metropolitan area.

But it wasn't enough. Those who think my mother is a garden variety sociopath, driven by nothing but dollar signs, can't explain what she did over the next eight years. Nor can anyone unfamiliar with Mom's power over men explain why my father went along with it. In order to understand what you're about to read, you should know that around Sante, all men behaved like fools. She was beautiful then. Nothing felt as good as basking in the charged warmth of her love, nothing hurt as much as having it taken away. I remember one of Mom's suitors sleeping in a chair by our pool for three nights, begging to be let back into her bed. My dad had it worse than anybody, since she was his first love—his high school sweetheart. He took otherworldly abuse for years just to stay close to her. He couldn't begin to admit how much he'd endured, or let himself think about why he'd endured it, till long after the torture was over.

Mom's adult criminal career really began when the Hemlock cottage caught fire a week before Christmas, 1960. It seemed innocent at the time, a blaze begun by something forgotten on the stove, but my dad and I both now think that my mother torched the place. It bore her imprint. Meaning, the job was botched—the fire only destroyed the kitchen. Dad got ten grand out of the deal and hired a carpenter to refinish the kitchen. He sold the cottage soon after for forty thousand dollars. Mom's first arson would have been a financial success after all—if she hadn't spent thirteen thousand on Christmas gifts.

Suddenly, at age twenty-six, something had changed. She was busted two months after the fire for stealing a hair dryer, and then she launched a lawsuit against the insurers of the Hemlock cottage, trying to recoup six thousand dollars for imaginary property "destroyed" in the blaze. Mom had shoplifted before, set small fires, but now she was playing on a bigger scale. She even changed her name—Sandy became Santee, with two *e*'s. Her first arson, first lawsuit, first five-figure debt—all of it threatened Dad's hard-won success.

My father rationalized my mother's bad behavior as quirks and compulsions. In the early days he told himself she didn't mean it, she just couldn't control her random destructive impulses. Besides, she was trying, in her own fashion, to help Dad. She hunted down business contacts and dragged them back to my father's lair.

Her biggest score was a blowhard named Everett Earl Wagner. An ex-oilfield roustabout with properties in Canada and California, Earl Wagner hired my dad to construct three houses in the Sacramento suburbs. Dad had just finished building Wagner's houses when I was born on September 27, 1962.

But now, in addition to stealing and setting fires, Mom was being unfaithful. She was screwing her "business contacts," and in early 1963, it made the papers. Adultery was news in those days. When Wagner's wife filed for divorce and named Mom as the other woman, the *Sacramento Bee* took notice. June Wagner charged that Mom had been having sex with the oil-man at my parents' house and Dad's office since September 1961.

The scandal was compounded by the fact that Wagner, who'd screwed my father's wife, had also screwed my father. The big-talking developer hadn't coughed up the cash to pay Dad's subcontractors. Dad had to sue him for nine thousand dollars.

Wagner agreed to a meeting. Dad showed up for it with brown canvas gloves on his hands. He didn't want to break any of the bones in his fingers. Wagner was bulkier, but my father was faster. He couldn't knock the big man off his feet, but he broke Wagner's jaw and nose and gave him a concussion. It was clearly not just about the money. No charges were filed, but Wagner stayed indoors for several weeks.

As Mom's ambitions increased in scale, she got Dad into more jams. She ran up fifteen thousand dollars in debt at department stores around Sacramento, and Dad paid it off in full, though his credit union threatened to drop him. "I'm going to get those sons of bitches," said my mother, meaning the department stores that had dared to ask for their money, and she charged up eighteen thousand dollars more on mink coats and furniture. To ward off the creditors and pay off the legal bills from my mother's court cases, my dad began to sign over the deeds of his properties. He lost four houses and seven duplexes.

Sometimes Mom went behind his back and did it for him. Dad and a mortgage broker named Ed Schroeder were partners in a number of properties, including a forty-eight-unit apartment complex. Mom went to Schroeder and offered him Dad's half of that building for eight thousand dollars. The complex was worth seven figures. Naturally Schroeder accepted, and Mom pocketed the cash.

Finally she destroyed my father's last and most-prized asset, a modernist castle he'd built in a canyon at the end of a dirt driveway on Winding Way. A huge wall of glass, perhaps twenty feet tall, covered the front of the house. My earliest memory is of headlights from cars on Winding Way shining through that outsize living room window.

On New Year's Eve, 1963, Mom and Dad dropped me with some friends and went out dancing. I was fourteen months old. Throughout the evening, Mom would rush to the pay phone, telling Dad she wanted to check on me. Dad wrote it off to a young mother's worry.

Past midnight, my parents retrieved me from the sitters and drove back up the canyon. When they reached the clearing at the top of the drive, they were greeted by a pack of fire engines. The house was cinders. This time Mom had gotten it right.

Between the fires and the bum deal with Wagner and the scandal and the attorneys' fees and the bad credit, my mother had busted my dad out with the single-minded skill of a mafioso. After six years, my parents left Sacramento with nothing and headed to Los Angeles.

Thirty years after Aunt Dottie had found a little girl hanging around her theater, Sante was back, living just a few miles from the streets of her youth. We had moved into a condominium in Burbank. I was not yet two years old. My dad was twenty-nine and starting over.

But some kind of motor was revving up in my mother. She'd been an annoying, grasping, lying narcissist as a high school girl, and then she'd graduated to outright criminality.

Before we got to Burbank, she'd kicked Dad out of her bed. He knew she was being unfaithful. Yet my dad, still in love with the woman who was now the mother of his child, wouldn't give up on his marriage. He hung on, even as Mom began to pursue her own brilliant career in earnest.

Dad's sole contact in Los Angeles was a good one. Lionel Leon was a big-league hotel developer who owned up to six hundred units at a time. He grew them and sold them and made some more. We lived next door to Lionel's daughter Marilyn in the Burbank condo. We seemed to have new friends and business partners, and my dad rebounded quickly.

But Mom sabotaged the relationship with our new benefactor by feuding with Marilyn, so Lionel stopped steering business to Dad. My father rebounded yet again, scrounging up more building contracts across the northern fringes of the L.A. sprawl. He pursued his own visions too. He bought an "unbuildable" hillside lot on Laurel Canyon Drive, and designed a unique split-level home.

Recently I visited the place. I pulled off Laurel Canyon and parked on a concrete pad suspended twenty feet above a ravine. A walkway crossed the ravine and connected the parking pad with my dad's dream house. Sleek and modernist, the quirky glass-walled structure was divided into two parallel sections. One sat lower on the hill, while the other, which contained the master bedroom, rested a full ten yards higher. I was looking at a creative solution to building on steep terrain, and at the sum of my father's ambitions. He couldn't finish architecture school because of Mom, but he could still draw blueprints and turn them into reality.

Mom would sabotage that house and this phase of my father's career as well. Something about the proximity of the glamour capital of the world, just over the hill to the south in Los Angeles and visible in the studios that carpeted Burbank, inflamed her itch to live beyond her means. She started up the credit scams again.

We kept living in the Burbank condo while Dad worked on the Laurel Canyon house. The condo had a garage on the first floor and stairs that led up from the garage into the living room. One afternoon, Dad returned from the Laurel Canyon job site, mounted those stairs, and opened the door to a phalanx of cops.

A detective sat at the kitchen table, combing through a mountain of charge slips. Meanwhile, other cops cleaned out the apartment, taking everything except the furniture. Santee had spent twenty thousand dollars on tape machines, mink coats, virtual wheelbarrows of luxury items. My father had eight thousand dollars in the bank, enough money to satisfy the whims of a reasonable person, but this was Mom. She'd used credit cards in a variety of aliases. "I'm not going to arrest you," the detective said to Dad. "I don't think you had anything to do with this." He'd seen Mom's growing rap sheet, and perhaps he also sensed whose will held sway in our home. When Dad drove down to spring Mom, he took me along. It was the first time I visited my mother behind bars. I wasn't yet in kindergarten.

My mother faced seventeen charges of grand theft, and Dad couldn't afford a good lawyer. Ironically, one of Mom's boyfriends came to his financial rescue. Bob Prescott, the owner of Flying Tiger Airlines, a shipping service that was a precursor to Federal Express, was Mom's richest "patron" yet. Though he'd guessed the nature of Prescott's interest in Mom, my cash-strapped dad was happy to let him pay the attorneys. Prescott's high-end counsel saved Mom from prison time, allowing her to walk with a petty fine.

My mother was once again free to pursue her complicated lifestyle, and my father was free to watch. Dad kept coming up the stairs of the Burbank condo, opening the door and seeing things he didn't want to see. When, for the first time, he actually caught her under the sheets with another man, he finally either wore out or gave up. "I can't live with you anymore," he told Mom. He rented a flat a half hour east in Arcadia, where he had a contract to build an apartment complex. He thought he'd be close enough to see me and far enough away not to wind up in jail with my mother. I also think that thirty minutes was as far away from her as he could steel himself to move. After he had seen her in the act with her boyfriend, self-respect demanded that he "leave" her, but he couldn't, not completely.

It was only an informal separation, meaning that Dad remained the breadwinner for his wife and toddler, and Mom let him know it. It was pay for play—he had to fork over grocery money if he wanted to see his son or if he wanted to have any time with Mom. Once she called and asked him for fifty dollars, and when he arrived she was on the couch making out with a boyfriend. He still handed her the cash.

And she had other ways of reaching across the San Fernando Valley and into his pocket. Near the end of 1965, Dad finished the Laurel Canyon house, his pet project, and became a partner in a bar out in Arcadia. On more than one occasion, a bank clerk called my father at work. "Mr. Walker," the clerk would say, "you're overdrawn." My dad would transfer some of his dwindling funds from savings into checking, trying to convince himself that he'd done some bad math and that Mom wasn't stealing from his account. His short-term solution to my mother's embezzlement was to ask the bank to call him *before* he was overdrawn.

Eventually the bank had had enough and closed the account altogether. This time Santee Walker had squeezed Ed Walker dry without even living with him. He ran farther from her, another hundred miles east of Arcadia, to Palm Springs. It was 1966. He was thirty-two, and starting from scratch yet again.

For the most part, my father characterizes events after Sacramento as the marriage being over in carnal fact, but with him trying to make it work for my sake. Denial is something all Mom's victims have in common. Starting in Palm Springs, I have my own increasingly clear memories of Mom and Dad's relationship, and I think this business about the marriage being over is something Dad discovered only in retrospect. He clung to an illusion in the face of pure humiliation. He knew the names and faces of all her boyfriends—Mom began to *introduce* them to him—and with her rap sheet he had ample grounds for divorce, yet still he wouldn't file.

In Palm Springs, Dad lived in a house on Twin Palms Avenue. My parents were sometimes together, sometimes apart, and I was shared between them on a haphazard basis. Most of the time I lived with Mom at various addresses in L.A., but she also let Dad care for me on the weekends in Palm Springs. I remember "helping" him carry lumber and nails as he converted the garage of the Twin Palms house into a studio.

What he was really doing, however, was baby-sitting me while Mom gallivanted around with her latest boyfriend, the same shady guy named Clyde who would wield the shotgun in Washoe Valley. As for the house, it seems that Clyde had hired Dad to fix it up for Mom as a second home. The studio was meant to be a bedroom for Dad. Mom and Clyde would sleep in the master bedroom in the main house.

Mom and Clyde had apparently talked Dad into caring for

me and their Palm Springs house while they pursued mysterious business in L.A. Mom and Clyde would come to Palm
Springs and leave with lamps and end tables and bric-a-brac
heaped in their big backseat, concealed under a sheet. Dad sur-
mised that they stole the items in Palm Springs, carted them
back to L.A., and then either fenced them or, more likely,
torched them. According to his theory, they'd set up the stuff in
some house for which Clyde held the paperwork, set the place
on fire, and collect insurance on the house and its contents.

Mom spent more and more time at the Palm Springs house,
but most weeks she'd still go back to L.A. We began living at
the Laurel Canyon house; once finished it had become Mom's,
thanks to Dad's inexplicable generosity. In giving it to her, he'd
made a terrible mistake. She and I drove up to the house one
day and — surprise! — the upper half was a charred wreck. Mom
burst out crying and then made a phone call.

Mom's greatest gift as a con artist is that she believes her
own lies. She commits a crime and then convinces herself she's
innocent. She invents a fiction and replays it in her mind till it's
reality. Even though we all knew who was behind the Laurel
Canyon fire, no one said so, because the culprit was more
shocked and upset about the damage to Dad's dream house
than Dad himself.

Dad put up with the betrayals, the crime, the destruction.
Mom played my father like a yo-yo, banishing him from the
Twin Palms house, letting him back into a spare room or a
couch — or, on rare occasions, into her bed. There were enough
joyous reconciliations to keep Dad hanging on, and to keep him
from facing how much time, money, and emotion he'd wasted.

During those periods when Mom and Dad were together,
in whatever manner they were together, it was violent. Or
rather, she was violent. I remember her gouging a car key into
the shiny red paint of his Camaro, and bending the doors back
until the hinges snapped. She threw a Pentax camera at him,
shattering it on the wall behind his head. Once I was sprawled
on the living room carpet watching *Davy Crockett* on the tube
when my mother winged a butcher knife at Dad. It stuck in his
forearm and quivered. It seemed just like a cartoon to me, till I
saw the blood running from his hand into the rug.

Dad's response to her abuse was, remarkably, to plead for
calm while asking such inappropriately rational questions as
"Why do you do this?" He must have channeled his anger

somewhere else, like maybe into the nails he pounded, or Earl Wagner's cheekbone. Sometimes he drank. But he never so much as clenched a fist at Mom—and he refused to ask *himself, Why do you do this?* I'm sure he couldn't have given a satisfactory answer anyway.

Toward the end of 1967, when I was five, Mom threw Dad's clothes out the door of the Twin Palms house. He carried them away in paper bags, crying. She served him with divorce papers, and his illusion was officially dead.

Though Dad says they had already been separated for three or four years before the divorce, it didn't seem that way to me at the time. I guess my dad needs to exercise a little spin control on his memory, since in the eyes of any objective observer he'd behaved like a lovestruck puppet. Instead of separation, I remember him hanging on as Mom shoved him to the edges of her personal life. Until he was standing in the driveway with the paper bags in his hand, he didn't want to accept the fact that all Mom needed from him was money and baby-sitting.

For a while after the split was official, he stayed in Palm Springs. Every few weekends he'd pick me up from Mom's place and take me to his, and he'd always ask about her: What was she doing? With whom? Never did he say anything derogatory about her. My mother, on the other hand, trashed him without end as a weakling, a failure, and a drunk, and in the future she'd lie and say he was bisexual and that the two of them, throughout their marriage, had been more brother and sister than husband and wife.

In the aftermath of the divorce, Mom lived in Palm Springs full time, moving from house to house with me in tow. Dad was always nearby. He was entitled to see me on weekends, but my mother wasn't the sort to obey a court order. She'd stuck him with a twelve-grand-per-annum alimony, but she didn't think he deserved to see me at all. I had to sneak over to his apartment during school lunch periods.

My mother didn't want to see Dad any more than she wanted me to see him, but she didn't want anyone else to see him either. When my father acquired a girlfriend, a red-haired bookkeeper named Vicky, Mom developed an annihilating jealousy. Dad was her castoff, but Mom wasn't about to allow a new woman anywhere near him, especially since that woman would be spending time with me.

So one day, when Dad was permitted a rare visit with me at his drab little studio apartment, I heard a knock on the door, then another quick, hard rap, and saw a shape rush past the curtained windows. My father had been in the shower. He appeared in the living room with a towel wrapped around his waist, but before he could answer the door, a five-pound rock came crashing through the window, bouncing harmlessly on his couch. After the rock came my mother. She leaped over the couch and attacked Dad, her fists flailing. She was looking for Vicky. A few weeks later, she found her. As Dad and I watched, Mom grabbed her rival by her long red hair, called her a whore, and dragged her around a parking lot. We didn't dare interfere.

In 1969, my father finally left Palm Springs for good. What did it was the hailstorm of summonses beating on his door, as many as five in one day. My mother was committing fraud constantly, and half the time my father's name got dragged into the cases. The documents said that a woman who represented herself as his wife owed thousands of dollars and that he was responsible and was expected in court. Restaurants, hotels, stores, and contractors all wanted Ed Walker to pay the debts of Sandra Louise Walker.

Dad liked Palm Springs and still had work coming in, but he had to get out. I stayed with Mom in California, visiting my father infrequently. For a short period, my mother would appear unannounced in northern Nevada and stalk my father. There was the stunt in Washoe Valley, and the time he could only shake her by roaring into the desert in a four-wheel-drive truck, but eventually she left him in relative peace.

After eleven years of marriage and a parasitic divorce, she'd destroyed every project he'd ever worked on. He didn't own anything he'd built; he owned barely anything at all. There had been times when, through his diligence, he'd built up a paper value of close to a million dollars, an impressive sum in that era, but because of her he could never keep it very long. If Mom was only about greed and sociopathic guile, it didn't explain why *she* never ended up with much of anything either. As a con artist, she was more about destruction than profit, a point I would later try to make to my brother, Kenny. Mom had a desperate need to rub up against affluence and an equal compulsion for excitement and control that wrecked everything she touched. The combination of forces defeated Dad. At age thirty-six, he was back in his Nevada hometown working for his father, even sleeping in the very bedroom where he'd grown up.

Thirty years later, my father still lives in Carson City. He married Vicky and divorced her, then married and divorced again. He joined his father in the plastering business and then became a contractor on his own. He eventually earned his certification as an architect, but never achieved the kind of success that was within his reach back in the sixties. Now he's on his fourth marriage, and this time I think it will last.

Recently, while his wife Mia was down at the corner store pumping nickels into the slot machines, my dad and I talked on the phone about old times. I have a big advantage over most people when it comes to recalling my past in that so little of it was uneventful. There were few of those banal, contented stretches that make it hard for normal folks to remember more than scattered scenes from their childhood. That's why I was stunned to realize that I'd forgotten about the shoot-out in Washoe Valley till my dad brought it up.

When he described what happened, in his deep, slow, aw-shucks voice, it came back to me in vivid detail. It certainly wasn't a bogus "recovered" memory. I remembered, suddenly, the bright muzzle flashes, like tiny bolts of lightning aimed straight at my father's gut.

My dad is such a calm, gentle man that it's hard to imagine him ever married to Sante Kimes or beating the hell out of Earl Wagner. Describing the gun battle, he was as placid as ever: "I said, 'Oh shit, what did I walk into?' "

I laughed. I couldn't help it. When people tell me what Mom has done to them, I often respond strangely, from some combination of embarrassment and nervousness, awe and chagrin. I apologized for laughing, but Dad didn't mind. He was amused himself. From the dull safety of his retirement, where he worries about what to watch on TV and whether his six cats are fed, he can afford some black humor.

"I said, 'I'm the dummy on this one,' " he continued. He'd yanked the guns from Mom's and Clyde's hands because he'd realized they were both firing blanks. "They had this all planned out. Somebody ratted on them for something they did in Los Angeles, and they wanted to know if I was the one."

Then my father said something that floored me, despite my

intimacy with our family history and the painful knowledge that he simply couldn't stand up to Sante. He told me that he'd handed me over to the woman with the gun the very next day, right after Christmas dinner.

"I went *back with her?*" I blurted. My dad couldn't really explain why. He was ashamed, as he often is when thinking about his time with Mom.

"I feel like an absolute jerk. She used me from day one, you know. From the first day in high school all the way through . . . It makes me feel stupid, now that everything has come out." *Everything* meant Irene Silverman.

He also feels guilty about leaving me behind in Palm Springs with Mom, and this is astonishing to me. He hung on for so long and endured so much, imperiling his life, health, and freedom. He can't imagine the empathy I have for him. Or maybe it's pity for him and anger at Mom. I know what it's like to love the woman, to have her make me feel like the most important man in the world, for as long as she needed me to feel that way. But I'd sure never had it as bad as he did.

"You really loved her, Dad."

"Of course I did. But she didn't love me. She's a sociopath, and sociopaths have no conscience and no sense of love." He sounded as if he'd read a few psychology texts on the subject.

"What did you love about her?"

"I couldn't really tell you. When you love somebody, you can't categorize what's good or bad. It's chemistry." And despite pounding on this question over and over, asking it a dozen different ways, that's all he could or would tell me. It was frustrating, because it was the very reason for my phone call. Why? Why did we love her, any of us?

I think he knows but won't tell me. In that word *chemistry* are buried other words that a father doesn't want to share with his son. Lifelong sexual infatuation. First love. Masochism. Mom made sure Dad knew about her other men, since the competition and jealousy rendered their reunions all the sweeter. Anger itself is an aphrodisiac for some people. Dad could admit to himself and to me that he'd been a sucker all those years ago, which after fifteen years and a million dollars wasted is a lot to admit, but not that the reason was the strongest love he would ever know in his life.

"I felt until recently," I told Dad, "that you held a candle out for her." The "until recently" part was meant to soften the blow; I believed the candle still burned, and that it had helped break up marriages two and three.

"No," snapped Dad. "When I leave, I leave." There was no point in mentioning that it had taken him a decade.

"Did you miss her?"

"I was depressed about it," Dad conceded. "But there was no way in the world I could get involved with her again. It was like committing suicide." A little later, though, we were talking about birthdays, and I noticed that while he stumbled a second before recalling mine, he recited Sandy/Santee/Sante's without missing a beat.

He does something that's common among Sante's prey. In hindsight, he paints himself as tougher than he actually was. Whenever I hear a story about Mom—and there have been many—that begins, "I told her, 'I'm not gonna . . . ,' " I listen with a great deal of skepticism. Very few people stood up to her except in their own memories.

To me, Dad insisted that "your mother and I couldn't get along because she couldn't control me," which was far from the truth, unless you don't count the first fifteen years of their relationship. When people ask him why he put up with her, though, he does have a few good answers.

At first, when her behavior wasn't quite so bad, he tried to adapt to it because in those days people were more hesitant to divorce. "She was my wife," he explains, "and you accommodate your wife as much as you can." Later he practiced denial because he couldn't accept the gravity of what she was doing. Dad told himself that if he could just make her happy with money and success, the fire inside her would stop burning. I told myself the same thing for years.

By the time denial was impossible, he had a son. He thought Mom was a likely candidate for prison, and he wanted to protect me from winding up in foster care. "I couldn't forsake you," he said. "You were just a little boy. I worried about you all the time. If it had been just me, I would've walked out in Sacramento." Maybe.

Now that he's accepted the fact that he was Mom's first and greatest mark, time and distance have given Dad some perspective on her relative skills as a con artist. Through the years he's run into a few in the real estate business, and in his assessment, she's the best ever, bar none. "She had the gift of gab. She was a first-class promoter and manipulator. She was a pro at using people's greed against them. She'd win their trust and then turn around and zap them. She had the charm, she had the looks, and she knew how to manipulate men."

It's weird to discuss your adulterous mother with your father, even when they've been divorced for more than thirty years. I know that her infidelity still hurts him; I was surprised that it seemed to hurt me just as much. Until our long-distance talk, I hadn't known how compulsively and extensively she cheated on him.

My dad was pretty matter-of-fact about it. He said that when people weren't going along with her schemes out of greed or naïveté, they were doing it out of lust. "Most of the people she dealt with were men. And most men are gullible. They think they're God's gift to women, and a lot of them are cheating on their wives anyway. She'd get them into her enough where they'd fall for her and give her anything she wanted. Then she'd do something that she could hold over their head, and once that happened, they were stuck."

Dad was exactly right. It's what she'd done to my stepfather, Ken Kimes, and it wasn't that far from what she'd done to Kenny.

"She calculated that," I said.

"You bet. There wasn't anything she didn't calculate. She always preplanned everything. I've seen what she did to me and Wagner and Clyde and other people. She manipulated us. She had old Clyde turning cartwheels. He was practically bankrupt when she got through." I could almost hear him smirk. At least he could find it funny now.

He was also tiring of our conversation. His cats were running under and around his legs, and in the background I could hear Mia, home from the corner store.

"I'm going to make a sandwich and watch TV or some damn thing," said Dad. "I've been dealing with this stuff for forty years. It's time to give it a rest."

"Get your rusty butt to bed, old man," I joked. But before I let him go, I had a final question. I needed to learn if after all this time he'd come to terms with his past and forgiven himself for loving Sante. My motives were selfish; I wanted to learn how many years it might take for me to achieve the same thing.

"Does it give you" — I hesitated, grasping for the right word — "closure to talk about it?"

"There's never going to be any closure," he said, sighing. "Now you, you've got your whole life ahead of you. You can't let this hold you back.

"You've got to look at it this way," he concluded. "It could've been worse. I could've been a dead man."

4

ME AND MOM

ello, sir, my name is Kent. Pleased to meet you."

The man in my living room seemed charmed by my formality. I was wearing a suit jacket and doing what my mother had told me to do when male visitors came to the house. I walked toward this one and held out my hand. I was almost eight years old.

The man smiled, smothering my hand in his. "Kent, nice to meet you. I'm Rod." There had been Clyde, Glen, Bob, and Paul before him. They all looked the same—a little older than Dad, more well dressed than handsome, faces crinkled from the Palm Springs sun. My mother would bring a man home (that is, to whichever house we happened to be calling home at the moment), and I was supposed to behave like a little gentleman. Or was *butler* a better word for it?

"Can I get anything for you?" I asked Rod. He grinned. "How about a screwdriver?" He was testing me, trying to figure out how many tricks I knew. "Yes, sir," I answered, and headed to the bar cart by the fireplace. A screwdriver was the first drink I had learned to make. I filled his order and made myself scarce while Mom and her date sat on the couch, nursing their tumblers. Soon they got up and headed for the door. As always, Mom was dressed to the nines, in a seductive way that played up her resemblance to Liz Taylor. It was the late sixties, and she had the same big black hair and curvy figure as the Burton-era Liz.

It was important that I perform to Mom's expectations. She had a job and I was her assistant; the goal was to marry a millionaire. She'd been sleeping with them throughout her life with my father, ever since Earl Wagner in 1961. By 1970 my parents' divorce was two years old and Dad had decamped to Carson City. It was just the two of us now, me and Mom, and I lived in her new world full time. In it, there were no half measures. Landing and keeping a millionaire had become her career, which meant it was also mine.

She'd explain it to me over and over again in hour-long speeches. They were often delivered in the bathroom as she applied makeup, preparing for a date. "There are two kinds of people in the world, Kent," she'd say as she gazed in the mirror and penciled her eyebrows into thick black arches. "The haves and the have-nots. The have-nots aren't really people at all." She rubbed gobs of pancake into her cheeks to lighten her olive complexion. She had plans for me too, similar to her own. "You're good-looking," she'd say, swiveling away from the mirror to appraise me. "You can probably find someone rich to marry yourself."

She made it seem like a necessity, the natural and expected thing to do if you really cared about your family. "Kent," she'd say, "you're the one I've loved most and longest, and I've got to look out for you. For both of us." She knew I missed Ed, and did what she could to belittle him, often noting that he'd failed to provide what we needed: "We have to find someone who can give us the things we deserve." Once she nailed the right guy, everything would be okay. I could contribute to the cause by wowing her beaus with my politeness and maturity. Later, when I had my own children and understood what it meant to be a parent, I saw my role through the director's viewfinder: if I were the perfect son, she'd come across as the perfect mother.

And Palm Springs was the perfect place to go prospecting. At the time it was a lively resort, despite being heavy on senior citizens. There was a lot of money around, and Mom was in her mid-thirties, a young hottie by local standards. Her vivid wardrobe and over-the-top personality drew a lot of attention when she did the town, but then meeting people had never been her problem.

Santee the glad-hander and Palm Springs the glitz magnet were made for each other. Mom had some uncanny gift that allowed her, in those pre–Sonny Bono days, to spot the well-known. Within seconds she'd be at the famous one's elbow, flattering, gushing. She dragged me onto the Canyon Country

Club golf course so I could shake hands with Vice President Spiro Agnew. We were on the tee with him as he waited his turn. It wouldn't be the last time she charmed her way past the Secret Service.

Fame was really just the scent of money to my mother, and money was what mattered. She cut right to the chase, literally, with the last real job I ever knew her to hold. She talked the publisher of a local magazine into making her a reporter, because the magazine was called *Millionaire*, and those were the people she wanted to meet. Her early flirtation with journalism — the high school paper, the college courses — had been consummated. More significantly, her association with the magazine gave her entree to the nearby country clubs.

I remember flying to Acapulco first class with Mom, courtesy of hotel magnate Teddy Stouffer. The whole way down she schmoozed the other high-rolling passengers, hoping to make some kind of connection. Stouffer put us up in one of his resort properties. He was gray and creaky then and is surely dead by now, but nothing deterred the millionaire-hunter from chatting him up at a Palm Springs tennis club and trying to land him. Recently Mom has floated a different story about this long-ago trip. She claims she was sent to Acapulco by Hugh Hefner — not on assignment for *Playboy* but to pose for a centerfold. Somehow things didn't work out.

The job with *Millionaire* apparently didn't either. I remember seeing the owner, a white-haired gent with a black eyepatch named Kelly Preston, in a witness box in a Palm Springs courtroom. I think he was testifying against my mother for something or other. I'm not sure whether Mom ever published a single item in the magazine or received one check, but the connection served her well for a time.

She never had a job after that. People wondered how she supported herself; some whispered that she was a hooker. When Mom did land her millionaire, Ken Kimes, his daughter would be among the whisperers. Certainly no one would ever accuse Mom of being a Palm Springs matron. She'd added implants to her already hefty bust during the early days of silicone, and made a habit of strutting her stuff in sheer tops. That plus her heavy makeup, her none-too-subtle manhunt, and the fact that she lived so well without a visible source of income suggested she was either a prostitute — or a criminal.

Some of her cash came from the alimony she was granted in

the divorce settlement with Dad, twelve thousand dollars a year. The rest she made either through fraud and theft, or via an ancient form of genteel sexual barter with the men who wandered through her life. She had serial boyfriends, one at a time with an occasional overlap. The boyfriends didn't live with us, and we were never in their homes (at least I wasn't), so I don't know if they had wives or if they knew about Mom's illicit hobbies. A couple of them were developers, real estate types like Stouffer, or local brokers like Rod. They were usually businessmen who owned something Mom had heard of.

When the candidates for millionaire husband came to visit, I put on my show, and Mom did her own. She projected glitz and excitement, though there was rarely anything but peanut butter in the refrigerator. Perhaps Santee's dates didn't realize that her address was always temporary and that everything in the house was either stolen, on long-term unintentional loan, or obtained via nonexistent credit. It was all grifted, from the furniture they sat on to the liquor they consumed.

In return for sex, the men paid some of the bills, kept Mom in dresses and jewelry, and took her out to eat. There were periods when she qualified as a kept woman, if a personality as strong as Sante Kimes could be kept. Her major demand from each boyfriend was shelter—in the style to which she was accustomed. When faced with providing this for herself, my mother would persuade a real estate agent to "rent" her a spacious ranch house, ideally with a pool and near a golf course. She'd stall on the rent, or write a bogus check, or direct the bills to someone else. But much of the time she lived in homes custom-built for her by her lovers, like the place her boyfriend Glen constructed and Bob Prescott underwrote at the corner of Sierra Madre and Santiago in the shadow of the Canyon Country Club. We were there for more than a year before the creditors started taking the house apart, piece by piece. The landscaper dug up and trucked off the entire front yard, after Mom conned him into making it look like the Las Vegas Hilton, a lush jumble of cacti and other desert plants, and then stiffed him.

Mom's men would always be left liable for debts in the thousands, but she never ran out of suckers. Except for Lee Powers, every man who was ever in love with Sante Kimes is either still in love or dead. My father was only the first victim. Mom was brilliant at playing the men against each other, keeping them jealous, angry, and sexually obsessed. She enchanted them. She had some kind of sexual hold on them, but I don't know how she did it. She could be whatever her man of the moment needed her to be. Decades later, Mom and I watched an episode of our favorite show, *Star Trek: The Next Generation*, featuring an alien seductress who could adapt to any man and become his perfect mate. Thinking back to Palm Springs, I told Mom, "That's you," and she responded with a laugh.

In order to pursue these men, Mom needed freedom of movement. So she would dump me for days at a time—on my father, her friends, even on people I barely knew. Finally Mom found a neighbor who would take care of me for weeks without complaining. In 1969, we were living next door to Evelyn, a childless woman in her thirties who was married to a retired L.A. cop. She invited me over to help her make some puppets and decorations for a party she was planning for the kids in the neighborhood. I went back day after day, and Mom realized she'd scored free child care. She also seemed to think she'd acquired a new maid; once, while Mom was out "shopping," she called Evelyn and ordered her to run to our house and check on the turkey in the oven.

From then on until we left California in the mid-seventies, Evelyn looked after me. She became my surrogate mother, or "godmother," as Mom dubbed her. She'd take me in as often as ten times a year, usually for just a weekend, so that Mom could free herself for some man, but more than once Mom didn't bother to pick me up on Sunday and Evelyn would take me to school the next morning. I rode horses with her, played cowboys and Indians, went to the movies—normal kid things. I cried when it was time to leave.

A few years ago, before Irene Silverman disappeared and my mother and brother became infamous, I tracked Evelyn down. It had been fifteen years since we'd spoken. I thought she could help me make some sense of the way I'd been raised, and maybe I'd recover something wholesome and stable from my past.

She was still in the Palm Springs area, and we arranged a visit. I wanted to tell her in person how much she'd meant to me. What I said was this: "You always did what you said you were going to do. Everything was the way it was supposed to be." In her presence, there had been serenity and honesty instead of chaos, conflict, and deception. Life with Mom was, to say the least, unusual, nothing like the happy nuclear families on TV, but with Evelyn I got to live that TV life for days at a stretch. She was a beacon of normalcy and gave me a model of a settled, decent existence that I carried with me into adulthood. During our reunion, I explained to Evelyn that she was one of the big reasons I had turned out okay.

She remembered me as a nice kid, polite, quiet, bright, and agreeable to whatever activity she proposed. She said I was strong and well coordinated. She taught me to water-ski. When we first met, I tried to impress her by reciting my multiplication tables.

Evelyn had wanted a child to care for, but she sensed that I needed a mother too. Almost from the outset, she knew something was wrong with Santee. "Your mother was so interesting and flamboyant," recalled Evelyn. "She'd dress really sexy but thrown together, like wearing a baby-doll nightie as a blouse. She'd tell me about how she used to date William Holden and Trini Lopez and all these actors. She was always very busy with these projects that she'd talk about, always coming and going. But we were very careful around her once we got to know her background."

Six months after our Christmas party, the phone company had called Evelyn. They wanted to know if she'd met the lady who lived next door. "I thought it was a little odd, but I answered their questions," said Evelyn. The phone company was poking around because my mom hadn't paid her bills. Not long afterward, Evelyn's husband, Keith, happened to be talking to a carpet installer who mentioned that Santee Walker hadn't paid for the wall-to-wall job in her house. Keith, the ex-cop, had an instinctive distrust of my mother. Now he began asking about her around town.

A man at the local racquet club told him that Santee had been banned from the premises—something about missing property. Keith's friends in the Palm Springs Police Department had a list of incidents, most of them involving shoplifting. But Evelyn and Keith didn't reject me because of my mother's rap sheet. We simply didn't discuss her. Our policy was don't ask, don't tell about anything regarding Mom—with one memorable exception. I wanted to know if it had stuck in Evelyn's mind as it had in mine.

"You were very disturbed," said Evelyn. She remembered

the incident as I did. During one of my visits, I had told her, "My mother burns down houses." When Mom came to pick me up, Evelyn blurted, "I think Kent may need to see a psychiatrist. He told me some crazy story about you burning down houses!"

"I do," beamed my mother. "I do burn down houses." Evelyn was slack-jawed as Mom merrily provided details. "I've burned down two. One was my ex-husband's house in Los Angeles." It was the bi-level Laurel Canyon spread, to me a dim memory of blackened wood and teary phone calls. Evelyn could never figure out why Santee was so proud of what she'd done or why she seemed to think Evelyn could be trusted not to tell the police. Santee embellished the tales of arson with another story about stealing a tiara from a man in Nevada, but she never corrected her own math. In Sacramento alone she'd set at least two fires.

Evelyn's ability to distinguish mother from son made her exceptional. Palm Springs isn't a huge place. I moved from school to school and house to house a dozen times or more, in the early years going back and forth to L.A. as well. With each move I'd meet a new group of kids and make some friends right away. Sometimes Mom would try to help, and I loved her for it. When I was six and seven she got me amazing playthings, like a golf cart, a minibike, and a horse, that impressed my peers. For my birthday or no reason at all, she'd throw lavish parties and invite my entire class. My parties would have been the envy of any kid—professional clowns, ponies that drank champagne, games, huge cakes—with Mom in the middle as the bubbly master of ceremonies, making sure the other kids knew I was special and important.

But then the rumors about Mom would make the rounds of my latest neighborhood. Within a few weeks, no one would invite me to sleep over, and in some homes I wasn't even permitted over the threshold. Once the parents made the connection between me and the woman they'd heard bad things about, my friends evaporated. Mom's compulsive, ceaseless larceny was in full bloom when I was a child.

There are different kinds of firsts. There's the first time I was aware of something, the first time I witnessed it, and the first time I participated.

One of the earliest, clearest memories I have of how Mom operated is of a car dealership in Palm Springs. Mom and I were in the lot, squinting through the sun at a big car, talking to a salesman.

"I really like this one," my mother purred. "We should definitely take it for a test drive."

We pulled into traffic, Mom driving, the salesman in back, and me peeking above the dashboard on the passenger side of the front seat. Mom went to work. She started name-dropping, talking about the places she'd been and the people she knew, creating an image to fit the car. An hour and a half later, we were still tooling around, and Mom's rap hadn't flagged. The salesman had, though. "Couldn't we head back to the dealership?" he pleaded.

"No problem," said Mom, and spun the wheel. When we got to the lot, Mom stayed in the driver's seat and left the car running. "I definitely want this car," said Mom. "But I don't know if I can parallel-park it yet." She gave the salesman a coquettish smile. "Why don't you pop inside and get the paperwork, while I practice parking?"

He ran to get the contract, and she drove away. Parking practice took place in our driveway. It was that easy.

I was a toddler when I solved the mystery of where things came from. The car thefts were simply shoplifting writ large, and most of the items in our house were shoplifted. A furniture store had to be tricked into delivering a new sofa, but lunch meat and jewelry and makeup and clothes fit nicely in her purse. Petty larceny was therefore a daily occurrence, and it was the first of her criminal activities that my mother shared with me. I was there, I watched, and eventually I was complicit. Before Kenny went "shopping" with Mom, that was my job.

My most vivid memory of shopping with Mom dates back to grade school. We had driven to a dowdy little strip mall on South Palm Canyon Road in Palm Springs. Mom was inside a dress shop, picking through the merchandise, and I was outside, perched on the hood of our car, bored. I knew what she was doing without having to see it. She had a huge shopping bag with double string handles, and she was filling it.

Suddenly Mom burst out of the store, walking fast across the asphalt with another woman in pursuit. "Stop!" yelled the lady. "Stop! Come back here!"

Mom didn't stop. She reached the car and tossed the bag through the window. That's when the woman caught up to

Mom and grabbed her arm. "You stole something!" she
shouted.

"What?" A switch flipped in my mother's brain. Her voice
was pure outrage. "Take your hands off me!"

"I saw you!" The woman's grip tightened, and my mother
began to flail. "What are you insinuating?" Mom yelped. "Take
your hands off me! I'm going to call the police!"

That's when we heard the sirens. The woman had called
them herself.

In that instant my mother had a flash of inspiration. It
wasn't a plan or even a thought. It was pure instinct. She balled
up her fist and hit me as hard as she could in the mouth.

Blood filled my mouth and ran down my chin onto my
white shirt. She'd driven my lower lip into my teeth, and the
flesh was torn. I nearly blacked out.

Even my mother seemed shocked, but only the three of us
in the parking lot knew who had swung. Mom started screaming, "This bitch hit my son!" On the mall's covered walkway,
heads began spinning in our direction.

She was still screaming when the cops arrived. One cop
gripped my mother, a second held the other woman, who was
actually the store manager. My mother jerked herself loose,
hammering two more rights into the face of her foe.

All the while she was still bellowing about "that bitch," and
the cops bought it. The manager burst into tears as the cops
cuffed her. Before they could do the same to Mom, she
announced, "My son's been through enough. I've got to get him
to the hospital."

The hospital was a left turn out of the parking lot. Mom
turned right. She drove slowly and never looked back. She
brought me to the private residence of a doctor she'd been "cul-
tivating." I received the sort of off-the-books health care familiar to any wounded holdup artist. I got stitches and a few
lingering symptoms: for years afterward I had moments of
numbness in my lower lip, and there's still an odd ridge on the
inside of my mouth. If my lips get too dry, they always split in
the same place.

Even as I experienced them, these "situations" tended to
blur together. There were so many of them, yet they rarely varied. I was always at the end of my mother's arm, looking up at
the adults. Except for Mom, they were all in uniform, and Mom

was talking her way out of something with a mixture of bluster, charm, intimidation, and sham. Half the time the cops put their cuffs away and walked off laughing.

There was a code in our household that my mother instilled in me until it became a way of life. Most kids are taught not to talk to strangers. To Mom the most dangerous strangers of all were cops.

One afternoon I was playing in the front yard of our tan house on the Canyon Country Club golf course, the one that Mom had procured with Monopoly money and Bob Prescott's name. A man in a suit walked up to me. "What's your name, son?" he asked. "Kent Walker, sir," I answered. He pulled a badge out of his jacket pocket. "Is your mother home?"

I told him I'd go and see. He stood at the front door while I ducked inside and searched the house for Mom, but I couldn't find her anyplace. "She's not here," I reported back. "Is there any adult taking care of you?" asked the detective. I was getting nervous. "Well, the maid's here," I offered, "but she doesn't speak any English."

The cop gave up and left. I went inside. As soon as I'd shut the door, Mom appeared. She'd been hiding in a closet, and she had entered one of her angry altered states. *"Don't you ever give out your name!"* she screamed. *"Don't you ever talk to the police!"* She hit me with her fists, an extension cord, and a wire coat hanger. That was the code. I learned it well.

When we drove somewhere in the huge new sedans she favored, half the time I was hugging the floor. "Get down," Mom would say, and push me out of sight. "Don't get up until I tell you." It was usually after some beef at a store where there was a suspicion or a charge of shoplifting, and I guess Mom was afraid there was a warrant out for a woman with a small boy. The small boy had to become invisible.

As I got older, bigger, and smarter, Mom stopped hiding me. She decided I could be part of the plot. At first I was cast as a decoy during shoplifting. Then she wanted more from me. My father had declined to become her accomplice. He'd ignored her behavior, endured it, and finally escaped from it. I was too young to say no and just old enough to say yes. I crossed the line from observer to accessory and became the partner in crime Mom had always sought.

I was in the passenger seat of a Lincoln, parked by a curb in

Newport Beach, not long after Mom met Ken Kimes and we ditched the desert towns for good. Beyond the curb was the house where Mom and I had been living, one of our first addresses in Newport and distinctive for its harsh red carpeting and jet-black furniture. Mom had grifted the Lincoln from some dealer somewhere. Suddenly the door on the driver's side opened and my mom jumped in. She plunged the key into the ignition and was about to shift gears when she stopped short, sagging, with a look of frustrated panic in her face.

She stared back at the house for a second, then turned to me. "Kent, I need you to pick up something Mom forgot. Can you do that?" I said I could. "Good," she continued. "It's a manila folder next to my bedroom window. Run in real quick and get it."

The Lincoln idled while I ran into the house. I found the folder and went out the front door. I was skipping down the steps when there was an explosion. The next thing I knew I was on my face on the lawn, the wind knocked out of me and the house on fire behind me. I picked myself up and got into the Lincoln. Mom peeled away without a word. I was aware that our houses had a habit of burning down: I had seen it happen in Laurel Canyon and again in Palm Springs. But this was the first time I'd played a role in one of Mom's arsons, and I'd done well.

I'm not sure why Mom sent me into that house. Maybe it was instinct, like the right cross to my mouth. I now know what she's capable of, but that doesn't mean she was trying to kill me. She needed that folder. It may have been the title to something, or some stolen letterhead she'd been hoarding so she could forge letters from doctors and lawyers. She might have been too scared to go back herself, or thought our getaway would be quicker and safer if she stayed behind the wheel with the motor running.

Trying to supply the Why was a luxury when I was a kid. No matter why Mom was the way she was, whether she was evil or crazy or both, the consequences were the same for me. I simply had to cope, and I coped by going numb during the scariest moments and trusting Mom's love during the rest. I knew that she loved me fiercely, and that my comfort and well-being were vital to her, however warped her sense of what comfort and well-being were. She might not have seen me as anything more than an extension of herself, but whatever she wanted for herself she wanted for me too, and to this day I believe there's nothing she wouldn't do for me.

In Newport Beach, for example, I got in a fight at school. It wasn't much of a fight. I was all of ten, and my opponent was a few years older. He picked on me and beat me up, splitting my lip, and I came home crying. Mom saw my face and asked what had happened. She took my hand and led me to the car. As we pulled out of the driveway, she said, "Show me where this boy lives."

When we got to the house, she rang the doorbell. The boy's father answered, and he was soon joined by his wife. Mom explained that she was upset and called the man's son a bully.

"Well, boys will be boys," he said, chuckling, or something like that. He didn't notice that Mom's eyes were blazing. While he talked I could see her looking around intently till she found what she wanted. The man was still smiling and talking in a neighborly way when my mother picked up the last six feet of a garden hose and began whipping him with it.

The hose lashed him in the head, but he looked more bewildered than injured. His wife, who'd been standing behind him in the doorway, tried to intervene. Mom grabbed a handful of the woman's hair and let rip.

Triumphant, Mom issued a threat. "Now I'm going to the police," she hissed, backing away as the couple cowered. "I'm going to get your son expelled."

She never went to the cops, but the bully never bothered me again. It would have been impossible for any ten-year-old not to feel warm and safe within such a feral, unconditional love. She proved again and again throughout my childhood that she would annihilate anyone who so much as slighted me.

She would do anything for the two of us, for "the family," and her first order of business was to add another member, so we'd be safe forever. By mid-1970 in Palm Springs Rod the real estate broker was her boyfriend, but his days were numbered. She'd met a new, wealthier man, who owned motels.

Rod was over one night arguing with my mother about the other man, Ken Kimes, when the phone rang. Rod was threatening to answer it because he thought it was Ken. I picked up the receiver. Rod was right.

"Hi, Kent," said Ken. "Is your mother around?" He could probably hear the argument in the background, despite the hand I had cupped over the mouthpiece, but maybe he couldn't. "She's taking a bath," I improvised. "She can't come to the phone."

"Is she really?" said Ken. I said yes, and he didn't push. He hung up. I'd done the job for which Mom had trained me. I'd helped her corner her quarry.

Rod was soon history, and we left Palm Springs for Newport Beach to be closer to Ken. Within a year we had shacked up with him, and the deal was closed. Mom had landed her millionaire.

5

THE MILLIONAIRE

Nearly everybody in our family drama is an Okie, or claims to be. Ken Kimes really was one, twang and all. Born on a cotton farm in 1917, he fled with his parents and five siblings to California in 1933 when Oklahoma became the Dust Bowl.

They traveled west in a flatbed like the heroes of a John Steinbeck novel, and with thousands of other hard-luck Okies, they became itinerant crop pickers. They lived in the labor camps that fellow Okie Merle Haggard made famous in a country song. At sixteen, my stepdad was following the crops in the Imperial and Central Valleys, stooped over in the fields, picking peas and melons under the hot sun for less than twenty-five cents an hour.

The family settled in Salinas, on the central California coast. They saved up their pennies and bought some property. By Pearl Harbor Day, twenty-four-year-old Ken had already started his career as a developer. He had built three houses on those dearly won plots. But Ken's pride in his accomplishments had a twist. Like Mom, he considered beating the system a special sort of triumph. As he told it, his military career was about getting away with things.

First he convinced the U.S. Army to delay his induction so he could finish his accounting classes in San Francisco. Next he talked his way into the cooking school so he could become a mess sergeant, safe from flying bullets.

Ken got shipped out to the remote, desolate Aleutian Islands of Alaska, where Japanese invaders had seized a wind-scoured lump of rock called Attu. Ken would sometimes brag, especially when he was drunk, about killing Japanese with his bare hands or a bayonet, and when we lived in Hawaii, he would claim to hate it "because of all the damn Japs." He laid this hatred to the experience of close combat. But while there was, in fact, a grisly battle for Attu during the war, I could never decide if Ken really had been in the thick of it.

The other tales he told and retold about the Aleutians sounded much more like him. He relished recounting the money he'd made as a mess sergeant. He traded army rations to the native Aleuts for caribou meat, fresh fish, and giant Alaskan king crabs, auctioning off the best cuts of steak under the table. He bought a car and operated a lucrative cab service. He leased out the Quonset-hut mess hall for nightly card games.

He was a flag-waving, John Wayne–loving, only-in-America patriot, a pro-business conservative Republican who was proud of bilking the government. His scams weren't confined to his three-year stint in the service. He got some kind of federal check every so often as a registered member of the Pottawatomie Indian tribe. His mother and aunt had attended an Indian mission school back in Oklahoma, but they both looked like blue-eyed Anglos. Aside from Ken's huge Roman nose, which resembled an eagle's beak, I couldn't see anything Indian about him either.

Ken was especially smug about the way he divorced his first wife, Charloette. After his military discharge, Ken had staked his wartime profits on a new career as a developer. He and Charloette had lived in a trailer when necessary to be near his construction sites and to save money.

He'd built his first motel in 1952, when California's postwar boom and the rise of the automobile made the motor lodge a no-lose proposition. Ken's properties were monuments to a certain prechain, owner-operated era. There were special bathroom tiles with Kimes Construction logos in the shower stalls at his Tropics Hotel in Palm Springs. Several motels sported a Polynesian tiki motif of the sort popular in the fifties and sixties and now considered kitsch. By 1965 he'd amassed an empire of ten motels and one restaurant in both California and Arizona.

But success made him paranoid. He thought everybody was after his money, including Charloette. He complained that she badgered him for cash. He said he used to put a hundred thousand miles on his car annually trying to get back from his job sites to their home near Disneyland, just to stop her nagging. In fact, he was probably making the drives to spy on her, since he'd forbidden her to leave the house.

Charloette filed for divorce in Orange County, California, in 1963. Though he was the unfaithful one, Ken went on the attack, portraying her as an adulteress and a jealous, greedy nudge. His lawyers stretched the divorce out for more than two years, at the time a county record, and left Charloette with almost nothing. Ken kept most of the million dollars in assets the couple had accrued in their eighteen years together — along with the kids. A Cadillac convinced his sixteen-year-old daughter, Linda, to file an affidavit on his behalf, and other gifts prompted fourteen-year-old Andrew to echo Linda's preference for living with Dad.

Ken's ability to buy off his own children only confirmed his dark view of human nature. Maybe he liked my mother because her greed was so up front and obvious. When Mom met Ken in 1970, she really did go after his money. She'd read about him in *Millionaire* and decided he would be the One.

Ken was building a hotel in Palm Springs, the Tropics, when Mom made her move — through one of her nicer boyfriends, Glen. He drank milk with ice in it and whittled little tiki idols. He also worked for Ken.

When the hotel in Palm Springs was done, Ken moved back to his condo on Balboa Bay in Newport Beach. He needed to stick close to a couple of projects under development in nearby La Jolla. Mom had been throwing herself at the tall quiet man with the thinning chestnut hair for a year, and he'd left town. So without exactly being invited, she followed him. We moved to a cheap apartment on Balboa Island, and Mom ransacked the grocery and clothing stores of the funky beach town to make ends meet. Ken's fate was sealed. He finally realized she wasn't going away. She was relentless.

Ken was then at the peak of his success. The centerpiece of the Kimes Construction Inc. empire was the Mecca, a hundred-room motor lodge with Arabian minarets on South Harbor Boulevard in Anaheim, across from Disneyland. Ken had been smart enough to buy plots across the street from the theme park when it was still in development. He was worth at least twenty million dollars at the beginning of the seventies.

Twenty million bucks and a real estate czar: Mom's biggest score ever and one she'd been working for, in her bizarre fashion, since she left high school. At last she could cast off the old desperate grifter persona in favor of the grande dame. Everything about her changed.

Carson City's Sandy had become Sacramento's San-tee; in Palm Springs, after she met Ken, Mom was suddenly French and calling herself Sahn-TAY. She spelled her name Santé, with an accent—what she called "that little thing over the *e*." In Newport Beach, she dropped the accent, and changed the pronunciation to SHAWN-tay and her roots to East Indian. Ken never got it straight. He referred to Mom as San-tee till he died. To her face, though, he called her Mama, and she called him Papa, because that's what she wanted. The two of them were a unit, and the three of us were a family.

Because Ken liked white, Mom dumped almost everything in her wardrobe that wasn't. She kept up her bosomy Liz act, but now she did it in monochrome. Because Ken liked gardenias, Mom restricted her perfume "shopping" to that scent. She would stick with that palette and that smell for the rest of her life.

In high school Mom had boasted about her distaste for alcohol, and over the years she'd used booze as a tool, getting people drunk and compliant while she stayed sober. Ken drank, which was all the better. But it was necessary for her to pretend that she was his drinking partner, pouring her cocktails into the plants when Ken wasn't looking. After a while, she stopped pretending. She believed that rich, sophisticated people of leisure drank, and Mom desperately wanted to be one of them. She even started talking differently, affecting a haughty, breathy tone that she thought was upper crust.

Sandy was history, except when Mom needed an alias. Sandy's friends were history too. Once we moved to Newport, she never spoke to anyone from her past.

Only Ruth Tanis was hard to shake. Ruth would get drunk and call my father, Ed, to talk about the most important person in both their lives. Dad got sick of it eventually and told her to leave him alone. Ruth called Mom too, though Mom never called back and rarely even mentioned Ruth's name. But in 1990, perhaps in a momentary fit of nostalgia, perhaps because Ruth was so persistent, Mom invited her to Vegas for a visit.

On the night she arrived, Ken and Kenny and I listened to the women reminisce. Ruth would start an anecdote and Mom would take over, adding vivid and suspect detail. Ruth just nodded, too happy simply to be in the same room with "Sandy" to contradict her. I could see that Mom had always run their relationship.

Ruth had become an alcoholic in recent years, and by the second night she was getting on Mom's nerves. "Why didn't you keep in touch?" Ruth demanded. "Why didn't you send me one fucking Christmas card?" Ruth, stuck in drab Carson City, was obviously jealous of Mom's luxurious, exciting life. Drinking had already cost Ruth her husband and her job. All she had left was a grudge.

By day three Mom wanted Ruth gone and told her so. Ruth was wounded; Mom couldn't resist rubbing in the salt. "Boobie," she said, "it's been a long day. Papa and I are going to go out and get some dinner. Kent will take you to the airport. Why don't you hurry up and pack?" No hugs, not even the comforting lie of "I'll call you." At that, Mom and Ken left for the restaurant. Twenty minutes later, Ruth was packed and ready. She was also cursing.

"That fucking bitch!" she spat.

"I'm sorry it turned out this way," I said. "Give Mom some time. Maybe you guys can make up." I didn't think it would happen, but I wanted to make her feel better.

"You don't understand!" howled Ruth. "That bitch, your *mother*, stole my wallet!"

6

THE AMBASSADOR

In 1986 a federal prison van took my mother from the Clark County, Nevada, lockup to a prison in Pleasanton, California. She had been sentenced to five years.

"Now's your chance," I told Ken Kimes, who by then had been my stepfather for fifteen years. "Divorce her. End the relationship. No one would think badly of you."

Mom had cost him millions of dollars in legal fees. He'd been in jail — something unthinkable in his pre-Sante life — more than once because of her, and was currently on probation for a felony conviction directly attributable to Mom. He had avoided prison by agreeing to three months of daily visits to a halfway house for alcoholics. His bottomless thirst for booze, like his criminal record, was a product of his relationship with my mother.

"Divorce her," I urged again. To my knowledge they were married, though others doubted it. Ken had been introducing her as his wife since 1975, and there might have been a ceremony in Vegas in 1981. At the very least they were common-law spouses. Ken would have to fight her in court to get rid of her, but he'd win. Her record was far longer than his.

He had raised the issue with at least one of his lawyers. After dancing around it a bit, he'd asked, "How do I get out of this? How can I free myself?" But the questions were rhetorical. When Sante's own son recommended that he cut and run, he said nothing. He never left my mother. He loved her too much.

It seems remarkable that someone who'd amassed a fortune of twenty million dollars as a legitimate, hard-working businessman would fall for my mother and stay with her. People well acquainted with my stoic, low-key, and very formal stepfather and my excessive, glad-handing mother couldn't figure out the attraction. They saw her skimpy outfits and heard her frank talk about sex and figured she must be a marvel in bed. Given the way men have always obeyed Mom, I don't doubt it, but it was more than that. She gave him manicures and poured his drinks and praised him in front of his friends. She massaged Ken's face and body every day, and in moments that were meant to be private I saw her spoon-feeding him like a baby. It was the same mix of maternal and erotic that would shock observers of Mom and my brother, Kenny, a quarter century later.

A few friends of my parents decided that Mom must "have something" on Ken. Besides her sexual hold on him, they figured she kept him in line with blackmail. There's undoubtedly a grain of truth to that theory, since Ken was party to twenty years of arson, insurance fraud, theft, and worse.

But he stayed because he loved her, and he loved her because they were made for each other. Behind the off-the-rack suit and tie was an insecure, cheap, loving, kind, and fiercely proud man who liked to be thought of as humble. He shared Mom's suspicious nature and her obsession with money. Fueled by alcohol, his paranoia and mania for control came to rival hers.

Ken's money was his whole self-worth. He measured himself by his bank balance, and he was proud of the fact that he'd earned it with his own sweat. He knew Mom would try to steal his assets. He wouldn't tell her what he owned, and he ordered his bookkeepers never to answer any questions about money from the woman he called Santee. He wouldn't give her even a nickel of cash. She had to steal money from his jackets and pants while he slept.

Ken was happy because he'd found the ultimate cheap date. He had divorced his wife in part because she resisted his will. He wouldn't let her leave the house, and he wouldn't give her any money. Mom, on the other hand, generated her own money and stole her own luxuries. I almost never saw Ken buy her a dress or jewelry or anything nice.

From their earliest days together, when he hired a detective to spy on her, Ken knew where Mom got her cars, furniture, fur coats, and knickknacks. Not only did he not mind, he approved of her larceny. He drove cars he knew were hot, and laughed about it. And he admired Mom for her sheer ballsiness. He enjoyed the battle.

I remember driving home from a restaurant where I'd shared a chaotic, uncivil, drunken meal with Ken and Sante, nothing out of the ordinary. My car was a few lengths ahead of theirs. We were headed back to the house so they could resume their quarrel over a few Seven-and-Sevens, with me as referee. In the rearview mirror, I saw their Lincoln swerving from the centerline to the shoulder and back. Mom, in the passenger's seat, had both hands on the wheel and was trying to jerk the car into the ditch. I had seen her do this before, as I cowered in the backseat, and I'd heard Ken complain about it on other occasions, but framed like a postcard in my rearview mirror, their struggle struck me as the perfect metaphor for their relationship. That's it, I thought. They don't care if the car crashes. They're fighting each other for control, and they love it.

Mom gave Ken what had been lacking in his settled, successful life, what she'd given Ruth long ago—excitement. It can be serious fun to be bad. Adrenaline is an addictive substance. Ken loved beating the system, and so did my mother. For both of them, Getting Away with It was like air and water.

Ken Kimes was transformed after he met my mother. She talked him into doing things that the old Ken, the boring developer, never would have touched. Ultimately the schemes cost him millions. But first they cost him his reputation.

THE PRINCIPAL OF LINCOLN Middle School in Newport Beach looked like a linebacker crossed with boxing referee Mills Lane. Mr. Woolsey had Lane's imposing scowl and bald head plus forty pounds and four inches. He was in his fifties, I think, and would retire at the end of the school year, but everybody in the sixth grade was a little scared of the chrome dome in the suit.

My class was acting up one morning. The teacher couldn't calm us or make us stay in our seats. But we all raced back to our chairs and zipped our lips when someone spotted Woolsey through the classroom window, marching our way.

Woolsey entered smiling. "Ms. Jones, what a well-behaved class," he said, beaming. "Good morning, kids!" The man must have been deaf. We answered with a weak chorus of "Good mornings," still half expecting some form of punishment.

"Kent, may I see you for a second, please?" Woolsey couldn't lose his grin. I slunk out of the classroom with the dread of any eleven-year-old summoned to the principal's office, but with a difference. Whenever I got pulled out of class, it had something to do with my mother.

Woolsey and I went to his office, and he shut the door. I sat in one of the chairs facing his desk, ready for anything.

"Your mother contacted me a few minutes ago," said Woolsey. Nothing new there. "She told me that you were going to be visiting President Nixon at the western White House next week, and that you were to select three friends to accompany you on the trip."

Sometimes Mom could surprise even me. I tried not to show my embarrassment, and I think I recovered quickly, giving Woolsey a weak smile and nodding. I'm lucky he didn't ask me how Mom knew Nixon, because I don't know what I would have said.

Living with Mom meant thinking ahead. You had to do a sort of calamity forecasting, because whenever you suspected she was leading you into some sort of legal, social, or financial disaster, you were probably right. In Woolsey's office, I was already formulating a plan for how I was going to sidestep the inevitable, which was that there would be no visit to the president's vacation home in nearby San Clemente. The best I could hope for was that the "field trip" would be delayed and then forgotten.

Woolsey, however, had his own plans. "We need to think about who you should take with you, Kent. It's a great honor to meet the president, and you'll be representing Lincoln."

"Um, I figured I'd take my friends, Jim and Jeff and Mike."

Woolsey pressured me to take the school's top students instead. As a compromise, he proposed that he pick two delegates and I pick one. Somehow I got out of that office with Woolsey parked in wait-and-see mode. Soon enough, he'd figure out why.

The rumor got around school before the end of the day. I know the kids were impressed by my close personal relationship with Richard Nixon, but they were ribbing me about it, calling me Mr. President. I still hadn't lived down the last time my mother called the principal's office, near the beginning of the school year, when Mom informed Woolsey that her son should be treated well because he was Indian royalty. I don't recall the specifics, but I was supposed to be something on the order of a maharajah. I had also become the godson of an important UN official from India. My classmates teased me for a long time after that, mocking me as the "Indian prince" and trying to draw dots on my forehead with red markers.

It was 1973, the year my mother discovered that she was now and had always been a proud East Indian, the same year my stepdad became an ambassador. Both transformations occurred with the mostly unwitting assistance of C. V. Narasimhan, a sixtyish gentleman from India who was an undersecretary general of the United Nations. In a completely uncharacteristic move, Ken Kimes the penny-pinching racist had dug into his own pocket to fly this kind, upbeat, dark-skinned Asian out from the East Coast and house him in the Balboa Bay Club for three nights. The Balboa is a private yacht club on the Pacific Coast Highway, and Mom and Ken had used their connections to rent C. V. a room.

While he was in town, they rarely left his side, and I was under orders to be on my best behavior. Mom gave me a script. I was supposed to tell C. V. that I'd already been accepted at Oxford, though in fact I was only about to be "accepted" into the sixth grade at Lincoln. I balked because the lie was so damn dumb. At ten years of age, even I could tell that. Yet my new stepdad agreed with Mom. Ken also wanted me to peddle this fib. Was he crazy too, or simply spineless? That was the first time Ken asked me to lie.

C. V. and Mom chatted on the phone fairly often after that. By the time school began in the fall, he'd become my godfather, and Sante had once again rewritten her personal history. During C. V.'s visit he'd been pronouncing her name Shawn-tay.

The new name stuck. As an East Indian princess, Mom could drop her French pretensions and cut down on the champagne. I received my own retroactive baptism as an Indian when she called Woolsey that September. I kidded her about it soon afterward, and she blew up. "Kent," she sniffed, "you *know* I've always been proud of my Indian ancestry."

Mom met C. V. because of a company she and Ken founded in April 1972 with the unusual name of Kiosk, Forum of Man, Inc. You can see Mom's influence in the name itself. Ken, who was close to sixty, had always done business under conventional tags like Kimes Construction Inc. But this project was entirely different from anything he'd done before. Mom seems to have talked him into a career in public service, as she conceived service. They were going to celebrate the Bicentennial and make some cash in the bargain.

I think that Ken had good intentions. By then I'd already memorized his anecdotes about enlisting in the army during World War II and suffering through the brutal cold of the Aleutians. He was a proud, patriotic, self-made man. He had realized the American dream of working hard and getting rich and truly believed the red-white-and-blue stuff, he said.

Forum of Man printed and sold two kinds of posters. One had pictures of every flag in the world on it, while the other was dedicated to American flags, state and historical. My parents contracted to print a total of two million. Ken wanted the posters in schoolrooms across the country in order to "educate the public and restore patriotic feeling," or some such. There would be a worldwide celebration at the UN in 1976, and every nation with a flag on the international poster would be invited to take part.

Forum of Man had offices in Irvine, California, which were staffed by "the assistant to Mr. Kimes," aka Sandy Singhrs, aka Mom. With "Sandy" handling publicity and Ken as the front man, the Forum hoped to get various governments to endorse and subsidize the poster project. Ken and Mom planned to sell the posters for fifteen dollars a set, plus shipping. If they had pulled it off, they would have made a fortune.

Their first coup was landing a meeting with C. V. at the UN in New York. I don't know how Mom did it, but once they'd had their photo taken with him, they seemed legit: Forum had an apparent endorsement from a top-ranking UN official. It also helped that Mom had nabbed a handful of letterhead from C. V.'s office, with which she generated a flood of forged letters of introduction from the undersecretary to U.S. officials.

Mom and Ken began jetting to D.C. quite often. The ruse was working. During this period, Mom started wearing a fake rock the size of a Concord grape on her ring finger, telling people it was her wedding ring. I think she got the idea from seeing Liz Taylor with an authentic version on TV. I remain amazed by the number of people who thought it was real. Had it been a diamond and not five carats of glass, Mom would have needed a full-time security guard.

Though they would later try to distance themselves, the country's official Bicentennial body, the American Revolution Bicentennial Commission, seemed to take to Mom and Ken right away. In a single afternoon the ARBC conferred upon my stepdad both legitimacy and a title. Ken and Mom met with the director, Hugh Hall, in Washington. Cameras flashed as Hall stuck a Bicentennial pin on Ken's lapel. The commission published the photo in its newsletter, making the mistake of repeating some of Ms. Singhrs's press release copy in the caption: "His extensive travels and outspoken enthusiasm . . . have led Mr. Kimes to be widely known, although unofficially, as an Honorary Bicentennial Ambassador." From then on, Kenneth Kimes would be Ambassador Kimes.

The picture went on the wall of the Kiosk offices, soon to be joined by a welter of others. On April 18, 1973, Mom got Ken an appointment with the First Lady to talk about the posters. She'd set up the meeting with a phony memo from White House communications director Herb Klein. Perhaps suspecting that something was amiss with the pushy lady in white from California and her consort, Pat Nixon declined to have the official White House photographer commemorate the meeting. Never at a loss, Mom whipped out a camera and did it herself.

The framed photo of Ambassador Kimes and the First Lady hung on the Kiosk wall next to a thank-you note from the president for Ken's work on the Bicentennial. There were other notes from the White House, almost all of them fake. Mom had somehow secured a stash of White House stationery. The only letter that might have been close to real was a thank-you for the flowers Mom and Ken had sent Nixon during his recuperation from pneumonia. I think it started out as a real note, the presigned kind the White House mailroom sends out by the thousands to well-wishers, because Mom had altered the generic salutation to read "Honorary Ambassador K. K. Kimes."

The Irvine office filled up with framed letters and celebrity snapshots, and Ken loved it. He was a public figure all of a sudden and reveled in the attention. His attempts to play humble clashed with his big ego, which required him to make sure that everyone knew of his accomplishments. You couldn't walk past the scalps hanging on the Kiosk wall without hearing the story behind each and every one.

Mom, the consummate promoter, used the faux photos and letters to get Ken still more attention. Using the Nixon connection to open doors, she parlayed each success into another. Ambassador Kimes started off small. I once watched and laughed, cruelly, as he presented a poster to the host of some animal show on an L.A. TV station. Ken froze as the host kept lobbing lines at him. He wanted my stepfather to say something, anything. All Ken could do was gape and smile and nod his head.

But he quickly lost his stage fright. Mom, still using each media coup as a down payment on another, bigger moment, had gotten him onto the program for the Rose Bowl. It took her weeks of phone calls, but come New Year's Day of 1974, Ken was at the mike on the field in Pasadena, and I was in a suit and tie in the press box with Mom. It was exciting to see the sportscasters up close and watch my stepdad, Mr. Ambassador, lead fifty thousand football fans in the Pledge of Allegiance in front of a national television audience.

That was the pinnacle. Mom used the Rose Bowl to leverage Ken a final shot at glory, a cameo at a nationally televised prizefight. I can't recall who the combatants were. It wasn't Ali, Foreman, or Frazier, but it was a big deal. Mom had thought she'd arranged for the Ambassador to hand a flag poster to Muhammad Ali in the center of the ring, right before the main event, and she learned her lesson. She was a bullshit artist, but in the prizefighting world she was a lightweight bullshit artist. Maybe the moment had never really been arranged in the first place. In any case, when Mom and Ken arrived at the fight, someone in Ali's camp had nixed the deal. All Ken got from the champ was a quick handshake in the locker room. Ken slipped through the ropes and was on the canvas for an instant before a preliminary bout, trying to say something above the din, but there was no Ali with him. I saw Ken on TV weeks later; he'd made it past closed circuit onto the delayed, edited network broadcast, sharing a screen with audio by Howard Cosell. I was impressed, even if it hadn't worked out as planned.

But Mom and Ken were furious. They flew back from the fight spewing venom. They referred to Muhammad Ali as "that fucking nigger" and everybody at the fight as "those fucking niggers." But as soon as there was a picture of Ken shaking Muhammad Ali's hand on the wall, Ken and Mom were telling people that their "friend" Muhammad was a big backer of the Bicentennial poster idea.

Not long afterward, the family project fell apart. Mom and

Ken went to D.C. at the end of February 1974, and when they returned there was no bragging about who they'd met in Washington. Instead they bickered about whose fault "it" was. Within a week or two I found a copy of the *Washington Post* in the house with Ken's picture in it. When I read the paper, I found out what "it" was.

On the night of February 26, Mom and Ken had dressed up and gone party-hopping on Embassy Row. Ken was in a pinstriped business suit. Mom had slathered on makeup and wore white as always, with a wide lace fringe over her décolletage and a white fur hat warm enough for Siberia. She'd emptied the jewelry box, accenting the gaudy wedding-cake effect with a rhinestone pasted into her right ear.

Mom and Ken were all dressed up with no place to go. They had no invitations. That didn't slow them down. Their first crash was their most audacious, a soiree across the street from 1600 Pennsylvania Avenue at Blair House, hosted by the vice president. Mom and Ken worked the room, ignoring the stares and upturned noses. Mom in white swam in a sea of dignified black. Guests asked her about the bauble stuck to her ear, and she said, "My father is East Indian. It's customary." Ken parried a who-the-hell-are-you query with "I'm self-employed, honey."

My parents melted into the official receiving line and landed another photo op worthy of the Kiosk wall. For a minute or so they made small talk with Vice President, soon to be President, Gerald Ford and his wife, Betty. The Secret Service did not intervene. Before anyone could detain them, Mom and Ken were gone.

Their next stop was a party at the Renwick Gallery, where Dillon Ripley was celebrating his tenth anniversary as director of the Smithsonian Institution with a black-tie dinner. One of Ripley's underlings quickly rejected the man in pinstripes and the woman in the snowbunny getup.

Then Mom and Ken hit the diplomatic circuit. They stepped out of a taxi at the German embassy, interrupting a cocktail party. The German ambassador's wife asked them if they had the right address. "Is this the Belgian embassy?" asked Mom, playing dumb. Rather than call a cab, the Germans whisked the interlopers away in a chauffeured car and delivered them to the Belgians' doorstep.

The driver waited while Mom and Ken rang the doorbell. A

butler answered and said—surprise—that there was no event at the embassy but that the ambassador was hosting a private reception and dinner at his home. Undaunted, Mom and Ken ordered the chauffeur to take them there.

Assuming that the two strangers in the German embassy limo were guests of his wife, Ambassador André Rahir let the pretenders into his house. My parents ordered drinks and were noshing on party snacks before Rahir realized his mistake. Perhaps too much the diplomat, he permitted them a second round of drinks but said they'd have to leave before dinner. Mom, who by now had sampled free beverages at four parties, decided it was time for a speech. She offered to enlighten the assembled Flemings and Walloons on the meaning of the Bicentennial. Rahir declined her request and showed Mom and Ken the door. Loath to have these two party crashers hanging around while they waited for a cab, Rahir provided them with their second chauffeur of the evening. A Danish diplomat squired Mom and Ken back to the Statler Hilton.

The next day Ken made a speech to a group of disabled veterans, a gig Mom had arranged for the Honorary Bicentennial Ambassador. But it was Ken's last act in that role. Mom had huffed and puffed and inflated Ken's résumé until she'd blown down the doors of the White House, and though many people suspected something was fishy about the arrivistes from Orange County, she was getting away with it. She had the ARBC's approval for Ken to play ambassador, and with a little more of her Ponzi-style networking, Kiosk might have been looking at a profit. But she couldn't stop herself from pushing too hard. Mom had sabotaged her own most successful scam—the morning after her party-crash binge, all of Washington was snickering.

She and Ken were mocked in both Washington dailies over the next few weeks. With a little probing, reporters discovered that Ken's credentials were fake. The White House disowned the note from Nixon with the ambassador salutation on the top. Ken offered to prove it was real and flew to California to fetch it. Maybe Mom had altered it without his knowledge, or maybe Ken had made a sucker's bet with himself that the *Post* wouldn't check it out, but they did. Experts spotted the mismatched typefaces right away. The First Lady's office, meanwhile, realized they had no carbon in their files of the purported invitation that had brought Ken and Sante to the White House in April 1973.

Lawyers for the ARBC, which had permitted my parents to stamp their posters with the official Bicentennial Commission logo, now demanded its removal. On the West Coast, alerted by the forgeries and the crashing of Vice President Ford's party, FBI agents paid visits to associates of my parents, asking lots of questions.

Mom professed ignorance in several interviews, insisting that it was all a big mistake. The ARBC had told her to drop some posters off at the Renwick, she claimed, and the Belgians had invited her. "We're just confused about this," she whined. "Mr. Kimes has only the interests of America at heart. We are not political people. We are not sophisticated. We just care about unity and getting rid of cynicism in the world."

The long, detailed article in the *Washington Post* about my parents' deceptions made me feel awful. Ken had been called a fraud in a national newspaper, and there were hints of criminal charges. He'd been disowned by the Bicentennial Commission. His attempt to become a famous and respected figure had failed, as had Mom's sprint for the limelight. It was the Earl Wagner scandal and the *Millionaire* mess in reruns.

When Ken came home that night, I made the huge mistake of mentioning the *Post*. "Ken," I said, hesitating, "I saw the article in the paper. I just wanted to say how bad I feel that you had to go through that." I meant it. He and I had lived in the same house for several years now, and I thought we understood each other. We were members of a fraternity of two. We caught all the fallout from Mom's behavior, and Ken had just swallowed the biggest dose since Ed Walker.

But Ken didn't react the way I'd expected. His eyes became slits. He yelled, "What article, in what paper?"

Mom heard him and came rushing into the room. She looked scared. I got it right away: she'd forgotten to destroy the evidence. Ever resourceful, she tried bluffing. She grabbed one of the old, positive articles off the wall. "He meant this one!" she said.

Ken wasn't buying. "Kent, don't lie to me," he thundered. "Is that the article you were talking about?" He pointed at the framed clipping in Mom's hand.

There was no point in lying. I shook my head no.

"Then what article are you talking about?"

I told him I'd go to my room and get it. I returned a minute later empty-handed, having scoured my bedroom to no avail. "It's not there anymore," I quavered. "It's not where I left it."

"What do you mean it's not there?"

"I put it down on the bed, and it's not there anymore."

Ken looked at Mom, his face deep red. He kept looking at her as he asked me slowly, "What did it say?"

It was obvious what had happened to the article. "Mom, just show it to him," I begged. "He's going to find out anyway."

"I have no idea what you're talking about, Kent. What article?" she lied. Now I was getting mad. Mom had left me no choice.

"The one that says you guys are frauds and that Ken was never an ambassador. You know, Mom, the real big one."

As soon as the words were out of my mouth, I ran to my room and shut the door. I could hear the fight that ensued, but I didn't have to watch. At some point Mom mysteriously "found" the article, and once Ken had had a chance to read it, the screaming got worse. They were still arguing as they went out the door to dinner. I had a break for a couple of hours. The maid cooked me something, and I ate in grateful silence.

It didn't last. They came back through the front door still snarling at each other, and the volume increased again. Mom and Ken's fights were remarkable for the sheer stamina they required. It's an athletic feat to argue from cocktail hour to bedtime and, as often happened, to resume the dispute as soon as you open your eyes and keep at it for another full day or more. It helps if you're drunk.

When I got up for school the next morning, the living room looked like it had been ransacked by a burglar. There was an empty bourbon bottle broken on the kitchen floor. The article that had started it all was in the fireplace waiting for a match.

Mom couldn't keep C. V. from reading the paper either. I was home sick from school not long after the Bicentennial blowup when I heard Mom talking on the phone with my supposed godfather's secretary. The assistant was refusing to put Mom through. All I could hear was Mom's side of the conversation, but it was apparent that the person on the other end was saying that someone had been using C. V.'s letterhead without permission and that the someone was probably Mom.

My mother got angry. "You know that C. V. is a personal

friend of the ambassador's," she said in a cold and condescending voice, "and I can assure you that they *both* will be very upset with your accusations." The secretary wouldn't budge, and Mom hung up after a few more minutes of threats.

She redialed immediately. She was no longer Sante. The officious, affronted anger vanished from her voice, which was now warm and sunny. "Hi, honey," she chirped. "This is Sandy Singhrs. Is C. V. there?"

Kiosk, Forum of Man went away, and the Bicentennial was never mentioned again. Ken had sold a grand total of 5,000 posters, leaving him with 1,995,000 in storage. We couldn't give them away. Nearly twenty years later, right before Ken died, I found the last of them in a storage unit in Vegas and trashed them. If you believe what Mom said that Ken had invested in the project, he lost at least a quarter of a million dollars, perhaps as much as half a million. It was the first of many financial bloodbaths that Ken would suffer because of Mom.

It was funny, though, how Ken kept his title despite the newspaper exposé. Until his death, Mom would invoke the name of "Ambassador Kimes" whenever it was needed. It must have worked, because we always got good tables in restaurants and good service. I think we met the owner of every restaurant we ever entered.

I LOVED THEM BOTH, but Mom and Ken, two matched souls, brought out the worst in each other. My stepdad was good to me. He always helped me out in a jam. Cheap as he was, he'd lend me money when I needed it, and he set me up in business. He adored my children and showered them with affection and gifts. When I was a child, he was—relatively speaking—the voice of reason in our household. As I grew older, we became best friends.

But as time passed, Ken's reason flagged. My mother had found his worst weakness, alcohol, and exploited it. Before he met her, or so he swore, he didn't have much of a taste for booze. Afterward, he did his business in the morning, started drinking in the afternoon, and went out for cocktails and dinner nearly every night. Mom kept him in that vulnerable, suggestible state just before shitfaced. She'd pour his drinks and then repeat her crazy theories until he believed them. She turned her millionaire into a fake ambassador, a laughingstock, and a hollow-legged, paranoid alcoholic.

But living with Ken brought out something awful in Mom too. Being the mate of a rich man wasn't what she'd expected. It didn't fill the emptiness inside of her. It didn't stop her from stealing, scamming, and setting fires. Instead of being satisfied, her hunger to manipulate and accumulate grew stronger. Ultimately, unfulfilled by the wealth she'd always sought, she began to work on a bigger scale. With the backing of Ken Kimes, Mom graduated from fraud and theft to outright murder.

First, however, the money warped her in ways that didn't kill people, just injured and humiliated them. Cash plus paranoia brought a heightened mania for control. She took it out on the women who worked for her, her so-called maids. And having money made Mom fearful of losing it. She became obsessed with Ken's relatives, her supposed rivals for the Kimes fortune. She decided she needed to produce an heir to protect her stake, since that heir wasn't going to be me, the stepson.

7

SHOPPING
FOR MAIDS

I t was Sunday, and our tight little family unit was out for a
drive. It would be a very long drive, the sort that required a
big air-conditioned Caddy for maximum comfort. I had the
wide plush backseat all to myself. Mom was in front on the passenger side, dressed in flowing white. Ken, who wore a suit
even on a day of rest, was behind the wheel. To a casual
observer, we might have been on our way to church, an affluent
accountant with his glamorous wife and well-behaved ten-
year-old son.

We weren't going to church, of course, or to pursue any
other conventional family activity on a conventional Sunday.
The three of us were headed south, to Mexico. Mom needed a
new slave.

It took hours to reach the border, and once we'd passed the
Customs checkpoint we drove on for hours more, stopping for
gas a few times in Baja. When Mom stepped out of the car,
locals would gather around. They probably thought the *gringa*
in white was famous. Mom would chat with her admirers in
Spanish, which she said she'd learned in high school, and Ken
would sit in our car like a *patron* while some lackey pumped the
fuel. I would stretch my short legs and lean against the car
drinking orange soda out of a glass bottle with a straw.

At one of the stations, Mom's conversational skills won us
an invitation into someone's home. We pulled the Caddy down
a rutted dirt road, parked in front of a shack, and went inside.
Light poured through gaps in the mud-and-plywood walls

onto floors made of dirt and cardboard. Kids of six and seven poured through the door.

A mother and her two teenage daughters, all with heavily Indian features, sat in the half-light. Mom focused her charms on the mother, and before long they were bargaining. Mom clutched a wad of bills. As they talked the woman's eyes locked on Mom's hand.

Within fifteen minutes the stockier girl had bundled up her few belongings and slipped into the backseat of the Cadillac next to me. Now we were four strong. As we drove north toward home, Mom leaned into the backseat, smiling wolfishly at the timid young girl. I recognized every fourth word in the ceaseless stream of Spanish issuing from Mom's lips. The girl was *linda*, beautiful, she was saying. We were lucky to have her with us. She was joining a *familia*. Mom promised she'd be treated like a daughter.

We stopped for a soda, and this time my new sister got one. As we were getting back in the car, we heard a little boy screaming.

Ahead of us on the highway, a dog lay convulsing, hit by a car that had torn it in half. The animal's guts glistened on the pavement. The boy squatted near his pet and wailed.

Ken drove past the scene without slowing. Mom saw that I was upset by the accident, and so was her new "daughter." "I want everybody to be happy," Mom ordered sternly in English. Then she refixed her gaze on the square-shouldered girl beside me and switched back to sweet Spanish.

A few miles before the U.S. border, Ken pulled off the highway, hid the Caddy behind a building, and popped the trunk. The mute young girl got out of the car and lay down in the trunk. Mom covered her with old clothes and dirty newspapers and slammed the lid shut.

The border crossing at San Diego is the busiest in the nation, and on that Sunday afternoon we idled in line for what seemed like hours before a guard waved us through. Ken didn't stop till we were a hundred miles north of Tijuana. Only then was our new family member released from the steamy confines of the trunk.

She was one of Mom's countless stream of maids, some of whom lasted only a few weeks. They did all the cooking and washing and vacuuming while my mother supervised. They were always young women whose sole language was Spanish.

They came from Mexico, El Salvador, or Peru. If they had a work permit or citizenship papers, Mom didn't want them. She'd say, "I don't think you're the one I'm looking for." She told the acceptable women that she'd pay good wages and help them to obtain legal status. When necessary she'd throw in a few guarantees about finding jobs and green cards for other family members. Then she'd put the girls to work seven days a week, compensating them only with room and board. Her promises were hollow, and her cruelty would escalate over time.

Procuring the maids was surprisingly hard labor. She and I sometimes trolled the Latino neighborhoods of L.A. and Orange County, but Mom preferred going straight to the source; she often traveled to Mexico. Sometimes I went along, as I had for many years before the Ken Kimes era. Mom knew that a cute little boy is good cover.

Attracting candidates wasn't a problem as soon as our huge shiny sedan, which cost more than any of the houses we passed, loomed into view. The Caddy seemed to be a magnet for desperate Mexican mothers, who shoved their daughters at us. Carrying the human cargo back north across the border rarely caused a hiccup.

But there were bumps in this long road. On one alien-smuggling trip, a female friend of Mom's rode shotgun, and the U.S. Customs official sensed something suspicious. Mom never betrayed a hint of nerves, and I didn't know any better, so the bad vibes must have been coming from Mom's pal. The Customs people found a teenage girl in the trunk and took us all into an office. I waited in a bright room for hours while Mom and her friend were elsewhere, being interrogated.

Then it was over. The contraband stayed in Mexico, and we proceeded north. No charges were filed, but Mom's friend was a friend no more. From then on, my mother got angry at the mere mention of her name.

Mom could have gotten her servants through a middleman, but she'd tried that in L.A. and for some reason it didn't work. I overheard a phone call from an agency that ended in an argument about Mom's nonpayment or ill treatment or both. Either accusation was wholly believable.

Besides, Mom liked the chase. She offered to find maids for other people, including some who didn't know they wanted or needed any. "You're too busy to worry about the housework," she'd proclaim. "I'll get you a maid. All you have to do is feed them. You're really doing them a favor. You should see the conditions you'd be saving them from!"

Strangely enough, the maids she saved were treated rather well in the early days, when we were in Palm Springs. She never paid them, but compared with the abuse that would develop later, Mom was downright angelic. She allowed the help to call their families every night and often gave them Sundays off. She didn't lock them in their rooms or make them wear uniforms. No one burst into tears or got hit.

Instead Mom would bring them gifts and make them feel like part of the family. I remember the string of happy young Latinas in their late teens and early twenties who baby-sat for me in Palm Springs and seemed like older sisters. Mom sometimes played matchmaker for the girls, invading construction sites, where she'd coax Mexican laborers to her car window and try to get them to date the help.

Once we moved in with Ken in Newport Beach, *happy* no longer described Mom's servants. Maybe she felt threatened, sexually competitive. Mom always had to be the prettiest woman in the room, or be treated as if she were. She chose unattractive women as friends and acolytes, favoring older, heavier, needier types. Mom was incapable of sharing the stage.

The maids had been immune, until Ken appeared. Whatever it was about being rich that wasn't enough for Mom, and whatever inspired her increasing mania for control, Mom took it out on the maids. She had finally realized that she could do anything she wanted to them.

The first time I saw one of the maids in a uniform was in Newport Beach. She was standing in the kitchen in a white dress that looked like it belonged on a nurse. I asked her, in Spanish, "What's with the uniform?"

"Your mother came home this afternoon with these new clothes," she answered. "She made me give her all my old clothes and said I was supposed to wear nothing but this. She also said I was to stay in my room after my work was done and not come out for any reason." That was a new rule.

The maid wanted to know if she'd done anything to upset *la señora*. I told her no, not to my knowledge. The maid seemed worried, so I reassured her. "I'll talk to *la señora* and see what's going on. Okay?"

As I turned to leave the kitchen, I saw Mom's raised hand

coming at me out of the corner of my eye. I lifted my arm just enough to keep the thick wire coat hanger she was swinging from connecting with my head. The pain in my forearm shot up to my shoulder. I looked up and saw the rage in her eyes.

"What are you doing?" I yelped.

Without a word, she whipped the coat hanger through the air again and hit my back. I could feel a welt rising. It was like being hit with a metal switch. Nothing compares with it. "Get your ass to your room, you son of a bitch," she screamed. I obeyed, at full gallop.

From my room I could hear Mom yelling, this time at the hapless maid, then smashing a glass on the floor. Finally she stomped off to her own room, slamming the door.

An hour later, Mom came to see me. She had collected herself, but I was afraid that anything could send her spiraling out of control. Her eyes still held fury. The pink welts on my forearm and back still burned.

"I'm going to let it go this time, Kent," she said, very solemn, sitting too close to me on my bed. "But . . . you are never to talk to the maids about *anything* personal. Let them do their jobs, and stay out of the way, okay? Okay? Don't make me tell you this again."

Later that week, I noticed that some clothes had been burned in the fireplace, along with what looked to be an identification card. I assumed they belonged to the maid, but I said nothing to anyone.

The poor girl lasted another week before Mom blew up at her again. This time Mom dragged the maid to the front door and shoved her out so hard that she fell. The maid bawled and begged for her belongings, which my mother had confiscated for "safekeeping" — having sent them up the chimney seven days before.

That, to my knowledge, was the first time Mom got violent with a maid. I don't know why Mom snapped. Maybe she lashed out because her target, unlike most of our legion of under-the-table employees, was pretty. Papa the millionaire might take a shine to her. Mom's anger was so palpable I never thought of interfering.

After I found the burned clothes and ID in the fireplace, the help stopped eating at the table or going to restaurants with us; Mom forbade it. Workdays lengthened from eight hours to twelve and sometimes fifteen. The turnover accelerated. In

Palm Springs their tenure could be years. In Newport it was months, sometimes weeks. The maids came to see me, the pre-pubescent son, when they needed something personal like a tampon. They were so scared of Mom that they wouldn't ask her for a toothpick. But I had withdrawn from them a little myself. It was hard to keep track of names and faces when they were out of my life so fast, and it got still harder a few years later when Mom began to "hire" them two at a time.

Mom's handling got rougher, and the maids started to dis-appear. If they vanished in the middle of the night, it meant they'd run away. If it happened while I was at school, Mom had fired them.

When Mom was about to fire one, she'd get bizarre. She'd mess the house up on purpose and yell at the maid for not hav-ing finished her tasks. She'd plant worthless curios from our shelves in the maid's belongings and accuse her of theft. She expected the worst and did her best to bring it about.

At first Ken tried to intervene. "Santee," he'd intone, with the "now dear" unspoken, "I've had hundreds of maids work for me in my motels, and you shouldn't treat them this way." His comments drove Mom crazy. They'd fight for days. "You don't know how to *handle* them!" Mom would blare.

Soon enough, worn down by the battles, Ken stopped pay-ing attention. Ten years later, when the feds came to investi-gate, ignorance would be Ken's defense.

8

THE HEIR AND
THE CREEPS

On my twelfth birthday, September 27, 1974, Mom was hit with a grand theft charge for something she pilfered from a shop in Newport Beach. I think she might have been stealing me a very expensive gift. It meant we had to have my party without her—the usual lavish affair, as planned with love by Mom. Once Ken bailed her out and hired an attorney, Mom got off with a $250 fine and two years' probation.

Something got Mom and Ken fighting in earnest that fall, and at the time I thought it was that bust. All of a sudden, Ken was often the instigator of the fights, and they came weekly instead of monthly. Whatever he was mad about, it was serious enough that Mom would back down occasionally. Part of me was glad that someone was standing up to Mom, but mostly I hated being kept awake at night by the noise. I'd pray for my parents to go on one of their frequent vacations, so the maid and I could live in peace.

Maybe Mom's poor physical condition was irritating Ken, or making her too weak to hold her own against him. Mom seemed to be feeling ill, and when I asked her what was wrong, she told me her stomach was giving her trouble. According to Sante, there had been complications surrounding my birth in 1962, and her stomach had never been the same. Her explanation made perfect sense to me because as long as I could remember she'd had days where she would swell up like a balloon.

In March 1975, to my relief, Mom and Ken went on one of their trips. But for the first time, Ken came home without Mom, and I was upset. No matter how much I'd wanted her to disappear, I felt bereft when Ken and his suitcases arrived alone after two weeks. I hadn't missed the combat, but I'd suffered from the lack of her smothering warmth, the hugs, the kisses, the pep talks, and all the spontaneous fun. The house was empty without her.

Ken told me not to worry, that Mom had checked into Cedars Sinai in L.A. for some minor surgery and there was nothing to worry about. She'd be home soon, and there was no need to visit. It seemed strange that after being far away— Europe? Hawaii?—for weeks, she wouldn't want me to come to a hospital a few miles away, but I didn't push. She called to reassure me that she was fine. What with her breast implants and her face-lift, I decided she'd gone in for more nips and tucks.

Ken and I lived in the Vista Entrada house without her for two weeks, the longest time we'd ever spent together. That's when I really started to think of him as my father. He'd seemed aloof before, but the distance evaporated in Mom's absence. He laughed and joked and appeared to be at peace. I asked questions, and he gave honest answers. Later I would revise my opinion, but at the time, without Mom to distract me, I came to see Ken as a kind, accomplished, confident, and dignified man. Mom had issued orders that I was to love Ken and make him love me, since that would help her hold her millionaire, but now the emotions were real.

During those pacific weeks, Ken took me to a fancy restaurant called Rubin's late on a school night. I was the only kid in the place. The waiter said something to me that Ken found condescending. "This young man is a customer," Ken snapped. "I expect you to treat him as such." His tone was commanding, and I was thrilled.

The waiter left. As Ken tore open a roll from the bread basket, he said, "Don't ever be afraid to stand up for yourself, Kent. People respect strength." As I got older I would understand that in Ken this strength was often nothing more than a brittle pride.

"I know your mother isn't always the easiest person to be around," Ken told me that night. "I want you to know that I'm here for you. You know what's right and what's wrong, and you have a good heart. I don't want to see you lose that. Just . . . don't take your mother too seriously when she gets angry."

"I get nervous when you and Mom fight so much," I admitted.

"Don't worry, Kent. I love your mom, but she . . . has a way of getting to me sometimes. Know what I mean?"

"Believe me, I know what you mean."

From that point on I trusted Ken, and he seemed to trust me too. He confided his frustrations with Mom. It was strange to have my mother's common-law husband, a near senior citizen, allied with my twelve-and-a-half-year-old self, but allies were what we were becoming. Ken needed a sympathetic witness, someone he could go to after a spat with Mom who would validate his sanity, who would say yes, the earth is round, Mom is the crazy one. I think he also needed my approval.

Two weeks into our idyll, I came home from school, put my schoolbooks down, and there was Mom. She was standing between me and the stairs that led down to my ground-floor bedroom. I hadn't been told that she'd be back from the hospital. After I recovered from the shock, I tried to hug her. She held me at arm's length. "Honey," she said, "I need to talk to you."

She led me into her bedroom. She wore the usual gauzy layers of white, but I could see that she'd lost weight. The swelling had gone down. She seemed to have recovered from her plastic surgery, though I wasn't sure what she'd had done. Her face looked the same.

Generally a trip to Mom's room meant a lecture, either the occasional high-volume angry kind or more often her unique version of motherly advice. Both were Sante-style marathons, spinning round and round in circles, the same points retold a hundred ways: money, power, family, keeping secrets, making Ken love me so he'd put me in his will, et cetera.

She sat me down on the bed and hugged me at last, and I decided she was going for the maternal approach. It would be boring rather than scary, but I didn't care. It was good to have Mom home again and be wrapped in her protective arms.

"What's up?" I asked.

"I have some news for you," she said with a grin. "Honey, it's really good news!"

"What?" I asked.

"Are you ready?" she said, grabbing my two hands in hers. "You're not going to believe it!"

We didn't always agree on what was good news. Good news could mean moving or changing schools. Military school flashed through my brain, and I got nervous. I said nothing, so Mom repeated herself. "You're not going to believe it!"

"Okay, already," I said, laughing, getting in the spirit of things. "What's the surprise?"

"You have a brother!" she said.

Many times I've been speechless when confronted with something Mom has said or done, speechless and dizzy, with a feeling of vertigo I never got used to. This shock was one of the worst. My first reaction was disbelief. Then I remembered it was Mom talking. Anything was possible.

"I have a brother?" I gulped.

"Come here," she insisted, and pulled me off the bed by my hands. The house on Vista Entrada had a large den outside my bedroom. Mom led me to the den, and I saw the crib.

Mom reached in, picked something up, and handed it to me. "Kent," she declared, like a giddy hostess, "I want you to meet your new brother, Kenny Kimes!"

It all made sense now, how she was gaining weight, the morning sickness, her trip to the hospital. Even a twelve-and-a-half-year-old should have realized what was happening. I was angry and embarrassed and thrilled all at once.

I took my little brother in my arms. I was petrified. He was the first baby I'd ever held, and I was worried that I would drop him. He seemed so tiny, smaller than any baby I'd seen before. As I discovered much later, he was premature; the forty-year-old mother and her secret, sickly, underweight infant had both had a rough time at the hospital.

The excitement remained as I held my new brother, but my embarrassment was giving way to anger about being deceived. I handed the baby to the current maid, who I assumed had become a nanny overnight.

"Why the hell didn't you tell me?" I growled at Mom.

"I wanted it to be a surprise!" she trilled. She was disappointed in my reaction. "I thought you'd be happy, honey."

"A surprise? We're not talking about a puppy!" Along with drinking, driving, and smoking, I was introduced to sarcasm at a young age.

"I can't believe the way you're acting," she said, pursing her lips. She looked like a petulant little girl. "Get hold of yourself!"

I crossed a line that day. I'd raised my voice to my mother, something I'd never done before. But I'd never been that mad before, and I knew I was on sound footing. By the standards of any family but this one, what she'd done to me was wrong. It was the last and best evidence I needed to convince me that I was like most people and she wasn't. I was rational, and she wasn't.

I shouted, "This is crap! People don't do this! You don't wait to tell your son that he's going to be a brother until a week after the baby is born. You don't *do* that!"

Then my supposed ally poked his head into Mom's room. Ken was home.

"Why didn't you tell me?" I demanded. "You knew!"

Ken had a sheepish look on his Gene Wilder face and a lame comment to offer: "Settle down, Kent." He didn't seem so strong to me now.

"What kind of a family is this?" I yelled. "This is beyond weird. This is freaky!"

Ken explained that the two of them hadn't wanted to "upset" me and that the secrecy was Mom's idea, which I'd already guessed. What I hadn't figured out was the answer to a question straight from the recently concluded Watergate scandal: What did Ken know, and when did he know it?

Maybe she'd sprung it on him too. Kenny was born on March 24, 1975. He was at least a month premature, which meant she'd gotten pregnant before the Newport Beach arrest in September and sometime after a vacation/maid-hunting trip to Mexico. Ken had been resisting Sante's pressure for a wedding in the wake of the Ambassador imbroglio. He didn't correct her when she dropped words like *wife* and *Mrs. Kimes* into conversation, but he wouldn't agree to a ceremony. A baby, Mom must have wagered, would bind them together. She could have been months gone before Ken found out, which would explain his anger in the fall and all that vicious, mysterious fighting. Ken had made no secret of the fact that, rounding sixty, he didn't want another child. Mom had allowed herself to get pregnant anyway and then hidden it from him.

However he'd felt earlier, Ken seemed happy about the baby now, and he'd willingly joined in the don't-tell-Kent strategy. But now I'd found out, and my buddy Ken couldn't handle it. The tension in the room was palpable. Mom told him she'd deal with me, and he fled.

I resisted being dealt with. "I'm excited about having a baby brother. It's having two crazy people as parents that scares me! I hope you're more honest with the baby than with me, or you're going to screw him up too!"

I ran into my bedroom, slamming the door. The infant woke up and began bawling. Mom didn't come after me. I'd stood up for myself. I'd told my mother that there was a fundamental difference between us: I was normal and she wasn't. And the world hadn't ended. Now she knew what I thought of her, if she hadn't before. I expected reprisals, but there were none. To my relief, Mom and Ken were too jazzed about the baby to bother with me. It was like they were on happy pills for a few days.

That's how it happened: I woke up an only child, went off to school, came back seven hours later, and we'd become a family of four. I don't remember feeling jealous. I did wonder why my mom liked the letter K so much, and whether Kenny would take attention away from me—but I saw the latter as a blessing. It was like having a blocker in football. And it was good to have someone in the world besides me, my father, and my stepdad to share the burden of being a man in Sante's life. I had a baby brother in arms, and I would come to love him dearly.

My hurt and shock passed quickly as the newly expanded family settled into a routine. Ken was home more than before. He was great with the kid, whose full name was Kenneth Kareem Kimes. Despite the lack of a marriage license binding his parents together, Kenny had the same first and last names as his father and the same unfortunate initials. Mom told people, variously, that the Eastern-sounding middle name was either a tribute to her long-lost East Indian natural brother or to my "godfather," C. V. Narasimhan, since Kenneth Kareem happened to be born during Mom's Indian period.

Mom embraced her new-mommy role happily and with gusto, except this time she wasn't middle-class mommy in Sacramento, as with me. Now she was millionaire mommy, Sante style. Meaning that she'd play with the baby for an hour and hand him off to the maid when something messy like a diaper change or feeding was necessary. But it was Mom who "shopped" for her baby. Every day she'd come home with a new toy. There was never a shopping bag or a receipt, and the toys always fit into her purse.

*   *   *

I CAN ONLY HOPE that my kids are as secure in my love for them as I was in the love my mother had for me. I never once questioned it, and that was a wonderful feeling. Whatever her methods, she had a passion for making me happy—she'd do anything to make me feel valued and important—and I knew it. When Kenny arrived, she enlarged this cocoon of love to include him too.

Kenny was a happy, cute, and fun-loving kid. There were hugs and games with me and Mom and Ken and the maids. Mom got down on the carpet and played with Kenny for hours, giving him constant attention and physical affection. It was a reprise of my early years, but with the refrigerator full and most of the strife offstage.

Kenny was different, though, because of the circumstances of his birth. My mother liked to make people reach for their hankies with a saga about Kenny dying in the delivery room and coming back to life. She called him her "miracle baby." Mom liked medical lingo, and she liked to invent tales of peril. She could read about a disease and then weave the symptoms into a gripping narrative starring Sante, and that's what I assumed she was doing with the story of my little brother's birth. I think she was telling the truth, though, when she said she'd had a difficult labor and that Kenny was premature.

Kenny was also different in that his father was always present and always attentive. After his son's birth, Ken Senior forgot that he'd ever objected to Sante's pregnancy. He pampered Kenny, who could do no wrong. I saw Kenny at age three fling the contents of a full tumbler of booze in my napping stepfather's face. Ken was ready to explode till he saw who'd thrown the drink. His eyes stinging from the alcohol, he tried to laugh along with his son's practical joke. In fact, Ken, for whom every relationship was a contest, was competing for Kenny's affection, but I couldn't see that at the time. I saw a doting father and a happy toddler, bombarded with love.

What I did understand from the very beginning was why Kenny was so important to my mother. "Kenny is the reason Ken is still with us," Mom told me. My brother may have been conceived without his father's approval, but once born he was Mom's guarantee of a share in his father's millions. She'd produced an heir, and by doing so she'd outmaneuvered her rivals for Ken's money. In her mind, she'd defeated her enemies, the worst enemies she'd ever had.

Mom's worldview is driven by enemies. No one is neutral. People are either friends or foes, and the foes want to take our money and destroy our family. Since the day she met Ken, she's considered his family her mortal enemies — the Creeps, she calls them. My mother believes that the Creeps have plotted her destruction since 1971, that they've been behind her every misfortune, and that even at this very second they're still plotting against her.

When my mother and stepfather first became a couple, we used to spend occasional holidays with members of Ken's extended family. I met his son, Andrew, and his daughter, Linda, both of them already over twenty-one, and they seemed harmless. Mom, however, put a stop to the shared holidays. They were too dangerous, she claimed, because long-haired college dropout Andrew, who lived in Central America, was a violent drug-dealing hippie, and the rest of the Creeps had their own evil plans.

Within a year of latching onto Ken, Mom started to report strange, frightening events. The Creeps were out to get her. They wanted Ken's money, and they wanted Mom to vanish.

Mom was the sole witness to most of these alleged acts of terror. Hyperventilating with panic, she rushed into the house one afternoon shrieking about a covey of rattlesnakes that some Creep had planted in her car. Perhaps they'd slithered away by the time help arrived. There wasn't a single rattler in there that anyone else could see.

Mom's "blood on the walls" story, however, was corroborated by her friend Sandy Spears, who testified under oath that she and Sante had entered the Vista Entrada town house to discover a scene worthy of Charles Manson. A Creep had smeared oaths and threats in blood on the white walls of our home. Could it have been Ken's brother, Chuck the dentist, popping over between fillings to vandalize our home? Or Ken's daughter, Linda, on her lunch break? Fortunately for me, every trace of the blood on the walls seemed to have been scrubbed off by the time I got home from school.

The only incident that might plausibly be blamed on a Creep transpired in the bar of an Orange County hotel not long after Kenny's birth. Mom was sitting in a quiet corner booth with Wayne Hendricks, a graphic designer who'd helped my parents with their flag posters.

Mom claimed that Linda Kimes, then twenty-nine, nearly six feet tall, and wearing a gray sweatsuit, barged through the door and ran toward her. "She's going to kill me!" Mom yelled as she jumped over the wooden bar and hid behind it. She hunkered there until hotel security wrestled her would-be killer off the property. Years later, Wayne would testify under oath to Linda's attack.

Though Linda did go to a bar to intercept my mother, she has a different take on what happened. Linda says she needed to talk to her dad's weird girlfriend, who had convinced Ken to fire his daughter from her job as his assistant. There had been no intent or act of violence on Linda's part; however, Linda adds, she did surprise Mom in the act of stroking Wayne's inner thigh.

Mom, declaring war on the Creeps, took out a restraining order in Ken's name. The Kimes clan sometimes fired back but never with violence. I doubt that any of the crimes Mom describes ever occurred. I certainly never witnessed one myself. The worst thing any Creep ever did to me was the time Andrew locked me outside my Lake Tahoe hotel room, barefoot in the snow. He did it for less than a minute, as a practical joke. He was not violent, he was not a drug dealer. To this day, though, Mom insists that Andrew's crimes were legion and that he once flung me against a wall. Try as she might, she can't implant that memory in my head.

I never liked them much, but Ken's relatives weren't Creeps. They just hated Mom. They'd identified her, correctly, as a brazen gold digger. She had snared Ken with sex, insinuated herself into his business dealings, and then methodically shut out every other living soul who might have a claim on his millions. From day one she wanted them out of Ken's will, and they knew it.

Ken also knew what Sante was doing. He realized she'd been pounding a wedge between him and his family since the dawn of their relationship. Her strategy worked anyway. I never heard him say a kind word about any relative, even his own kids, except for the occasional regret that Andrew had opted to kick back in Costa Rica instead of following him into the building trade. He called Linda a bitch and tossed her off the board of his construction company.

He was clearing the decks for the Heir, at Mom's behest. He accepted her designation of my little brother as the rightful inheritor of his empire. But Mom's victory over the Creeps didn't make her feel any more secure. The stakes had risen higher than ever before, by her reckoning—now that she'd won her millions, she worried about losing them. She spun a new fantasy in which the Creeps wanted to kill or steal their new-born rival for Ken Sr.'s fortune. When Kenny was two months old, Mom came home from a drive with him and claimed that the Creeps had tried to run her off the road. Mom decreed that the Heir had to be protected at all costs.

9

SURFBOARDS

Every kid develops a strategy for breaking bad news to the grown-ups. During the years alone with Mom, I hadn't had any options but duck and cover. With Ken around, I could finally confess my screwups to an elder who had a sense of proportion. He was easier to talk to about problems than Mom and, at least in those days, he never overreacted.

During the spring semester of seventh grade, maybe a month after Kenny was born and while we were still in Newport Beach, I went to Ken with some bad news. My pubescent friends and I had started sneaking out at night and goofing off. We raised hell, clambering onto the connected roofs of the houses and playing tag. One night I'd crashed through the tiles into a garage and barely escaped getting caught by the frightened homeowner. But that wasn't what I had to confess to Ken.

My little gang of three was out on a ramble on a warm evening, cruising down a circular street of town houses called Vista Huerta. Passing an open garage, we saw two battered old surfboards inside. We dared each other until a friend and I each grabbed a board and slunk away to his house, where my friend stashed them. A slick move, we told each other. We'd be cool on the beach come the weekend. We might even learn how to surf.

Then we forgot about our booty, until our stupidity came back to haunt us. We all knew the kid who owned the boards, and someone had recognized us while we were in the act of stealing them. A couple of weeks later, I got home from school and the maid told me in her limited English that a detective had left a message for me. I called the number. The detective told me I had twenty-four hours to show up at the station with my parents, or the Newport police would come to the house and arrest me. I agreed to appear and didn't deny what I'd done.

Mom and Ken got home soon after the call. Mom headed for the bathroom, and as soon as I heard the water running I rushed over to Ken.

"I've got a big problem," I whispered.

"What's wrong?" He glanced toward the bathroom door, then looked back at me and chuckled. He was amused by my fear.

"You guys are going to kill me," I said, cringing, thinking Ken would smack me but without the painful foreign objects Mom favored. If I told him what I'd done first and let *him* relay the bad news, maybe she'd dump some of her rage on him.

Something made Ken realize how scared I really was. "Sounds pretty serious," he murmured, without chuckling. When Mom returned, Ken told her that he and I were going to the store. Instead we drove to a little park near the school. I told him about the surfboards.

"Well," he said, "you should know better than to pull a stunt like that." I couldn't get over his weird calm. When you did something wrong, adults were supposed to flip out and start punching. "You'll have to tell your mother, of course," he reasoned, "and it sounds like she'll have to go down to the station with you."

It wasn't the cops I was afraid of. Maybe Ken wasn't going to kill me, but Mom was, or else we wouldn't be having our chat in a parked car a quarter mile out of her earshot. Ken sensed my panic. "Let me see if I can help you ease into it," he offered.

My stepdad toiled hard on my behalf. He took the three of us out to dinner at Mom's favorite restaurant, and on the way we stopped at the Fashion Island Mall, where Ken bought Mom her special brands of perfume and bath oil. By the time our food arrived, we were all in a good mood. Ken must have decided it was time.

"Santee, I think Kent has something he needs to tell you."

Ken's buttering-up seemed to have paid off. As I spoke, I kept waiting for the explosion, but it never came. She was only a little upset.

"Kids do things sometimes, Santee," crooned Ken. "I think he's learned his lesson."

Mom and I agreed that we'd go down to the station the next day. It was over just like that. I couldn't believe my good fortune; I felt like a prisoner who'd gotten a last-minute reprieve. I slept well.

But the minute I walked in the door from school the next afternoon, my mother lit into me. "You stupid son of a bitch!" she screamed. "What the fuck is wrong with you! I didn't think I had a moron for a son, but the way you're acting . . . I'm ashamed of you!"

Mom was Mom after all. "I'm sorry," I stuttered. "It was a stupid thing to do. I swear I'll never steal anything again."

At that, an expression of mockery spread over my mother's face. In her eyes, I was a sap. "I don't care if you *steal* anything," she spat. "Just don't be so stupid as to get caught, you fucking idiot!"

Mom went on to explain to her bumbling son how to do it right next time.

"I drove by the house where you guys stole those boards," she said impatiently, "and it was plain stupid of you. It was a busy street, and you went right up to the front of the house! You should have gone in the back way where no one could see you!" It was the poor execution of the act, not the act itself, that drove her nuts. She was truly disappointed in my lack of criminal talent. "What the fuck is *wrong* with you? I thought you were smarter than that."

After all, she'd been training me in the fine art of theft. For two years, I'd been popping through town-house windows in East Bluff at her behest. She'd give me an address and tell me what to look for, and I'd come back with a doctor's letterhead or a manila folder from some acquaintance's desk.

But I didn't want to do it anymore, and she knew it. The last time she'd sent me breaking and entering—to a neighbor's house six doors down—I hadn't brought her the document she ordered. Instead I raided the man's fridge and loped back to our patio with a six-pack. After sabotaging that mission and weathering Mom's abuse, I'd started ducking her requests. I made excuses. I was going through puberty, I told her, and getting a little too ungainly to slip through windows.

A mother getting pissed at a son for botching a burglary is perfectly natural, if the mother is mine. Maybe she was also mad at me for freelancing. But I knew that in the world of mothers at large, her attitude was very unusual. It was in that other world that I wanted to live. Fitting in with the normal people meant not climbing through windows.

Mom had never yelled so loud. Her tirade was as jarring as the punch in the mouth in Palm Springs. I wondered where the current maid was hiding, and if she could understand what Sante was bellowing about, and at what age Kenny would be old enough to hear and understand the lectures to come. I wondered if any other kids in my balmy suburb had ever heard a speech like that from their mothers. If not, they were getting one from my mother right now. The houses were attached, and Mom was so loud the neighbors could have transcribed her words verbatim.

Mom wasn't finished, either. "Why did you call the fucking cops?" she screeched. "*You know better! What have I told you! You practically confessed! Use your head!*

"Do you know what I have to do now, you fucking idiot?" she steamed. "I have to get this under control, or it could turn into a real problem."

She needed to wallow in anger. She enjoyed her own rages the way some people enjoy a warm bath. I half listened as she continued to vent. Finally she wound down, and said something that made me pay attention. "Go put on some fresh clothes. The detective is going to be here in an hour."

"I thought we had to go to the station," I said, confused.

"Shut up and get ready," she barked. "I'll handle it. You've already done enough!"

As she moved toward her bedroom to slap on some gardenia scent and mascara for the benefit of the Newport cops, she called out something she knew would hurt me. Over the next twenty years I would become immune to it, but the first time it stung a bit. "And don't get Ken involved in things like this. You know better—you're just a *step*son!" I wanted to be Ken's stepson, and I wanted him to acknowledge that after four years together and a half brother he *was* a father to me, but that first syllable sounded so ugly the way Mom said it. She made a *step*son sound like a lower form of life.

The detective rang the doorbell right on time. Mom went to the door in full-tilt Liz mode, and I could smell the gardenias ten feet away. Before she opened it, she hissed, "Let me do the talking. Don't say a fucking word unless I tell you to, understand?"

I nodded yes.

As the detective walked into our living room, the first thing I noticed was that he was wearing heavy-duty lifts. He was short; his bootheels added three inches. Mom noticed it too, and used it. Smiling seductively, she purred to the cop, "My, I had no idea you'd be so tall." She offered him a drink but he refused.

The three of us sat down. I had my hands folded and my lips zipped as the detective ran through the evidence: The person who'd seen us in the garage, another kid from school, had tipped off the cops. My accomplice had already confessed. "He told us everything," stated the detective. "Sounds like you guys don't know much about surfboards. They were only worth about thirty bucks apiece."

He said that I could be sent to juvenile hall for one year, sentenced to probation until I was eighteen, and forced to register at school as a juvenile offender, but since this was my first offense, he was offering a lighter penalty. If I went on probation for six months and stayed out of trouble for two years, my record would be expunged. My side of the deal was to make a full, formal confession.

Sounds good to me, I thought, but didn't utter a peep. Mom was in charge, not me, and she'd stopped sugaring the cop. "First of all," she claimed, "I've talked to my attorney, and you were dead wrong to contact my son without talking to me first. In fact, my attorney and I think that your department has violated the rights of a minor. We don't intend to press the issue as long as you understand that my son has done nothing wrong, and you drop this matter *now*."

I wanted to jump up and scream, "No! I'll take the probation! I'll stay out of trouble!"

The detective rallied fast. "Ma'am, I left messages for you to call me on several occasions over the past two weeks. In fact" — and now he was mocking her — "it's strange how much you and your secretary sound alike on the phone."

Con artists depend on the gullibility of others, the instinct that makes people extend the benefit of the doubt to strangers making unlikely claims. It's a cop's duty not to be one of those people. Cops have to develop a darker, more suspicious view of human nature. This one had guessed who the "secretary" was and probably had the right idea about the "attorney" too. I was getting nervous.

"I don't like your tone," parried my mother, "or what

you're insinuating. If you think I'm going to let you bully my son into confessing to something he had nothing to do with, you have another think coming." She was gaining confidence, despite the odds. "Kent would never do anything like this. He's a straight-A student."

I stifled a gasp. The only A on my report card was in my last name.

The detective stood up. "Ma'am," he stated, unimpressed, "this doesn't have to be a serious matter, but if you don't let your son cooperate with me, it may become one."

I felt like I was falling. The cop spoke to me. "Kent, did you steal those surfboards?"

I have never wanted to say yes so badly, but before I could open my mouth, my unappointed legal counsel had practically shoved me into juvy hall. "I'm afraid I'm going to have to ask you to leave now," snipped Mom, hands on her tightly sheathed hips. "I won't tolerate this treatment of my son. I'll have my attorney contact you."

"What's your attorney's name?" smirked the detective.

"You'll know when he calls," said Mom, glaring. "Now please leave."

Before the cop's unmarked car was out of the driveway, I was yelling at Mom, pleading with her to stop "handling" things. *"What are you doing?"* I roared. *"You're going to get me in jail."*

"Don't be such a jackass," Mom groused. "See what you've caused! Go to your room and do your homework." Things hadn't turned out as she'd planned, I could tell, but Sante would never admit that.

I lay on my bed and stared at the ceiling. Instead of doing my homework, I tortured myself with fantasies about juvenile hall. Would they have TV? Would I be the youngest prisoner? What would big kids from bad neighborhoods do to me?

Within a week or so a summons appeared. I had a date in court. Mom responded by coaching me for hours on how to proclaim my innocence. She ordered me never to admit doing anything wrong. I saw no way out. I was going to be in big trouble with Mom or the courts, or both. All for a couple of beat-up surfboards.

I tried logic on my mother. "They have a witness. I told the cops on the phone I did it. My friend already confessed and *said* I did it!" I pleaded with her to let me take the probation.

She was immovable and unrepentant. "Are you out of your fucking mind? Listen to your mother and stop being a baby! If you were so fucking smart, you wouldn't be in this situation in the first place." I don't remember why I thought I could get my mom to admit she'd made a boo-boo. She continued her barrage. "Smart-ass. Idiot. Fucking idiot."

My court date arrived too quickly. I watched the clock all day at school, and afterward I waited for my mother to pick me up, as she had insisted, instead of taking the school bus. I said good-bye to my friends, since I thought I might wake up the next morning in a juvy hall bunk bed. I didn't know if they had bunk beds, but that's what I imagined. I'd sure as hell been in court before, but never as a defendant. I didn't know what to expect.

When the Cadillac convertible pulled up, I was surprised and happy to see that Ken, neatly knotted tie and all, was at the wheel. "Where's Mom?" I asked.

"I'm taking you instead," he explained.

Ken and I were together again, two rational beings. I got him to swear he wouldn't rat me out to Mom, then told him every detail of the detective debacle, except Mom's "only a *stepson*" crack. I told him I was terrified of jail.

Ken kept doing his calm thing. He said, "I have a friend who might be able to help us out. We'll stop there on the way."

We pulled up to a fancy glass office building near the Santa Ana courthouse. The place looked like a palace. I felt intimidated just sitting in the waiting room.

The attorney gave Ken a backslapping bear hug. "It's been a long time, Ken."

"Thanks for seeing me on such short notice. This is Kent. I was hoping you could help him with a little problem he has."

"How do you do, Kent?" said the big man in the expensive suit as he shook my hand. His face was familiar. I thought I'd seen it on a TV commercial or the news. Everything about him said big shot.

We went into his office and I explained everything. The lawyer was kind and patient and a gentleman, but I was taken aback by his laughter. When I told him what Mom had said to the detective, he cracked up. He made me repeat the story twice and then again, and he found it hilarious every time. "She's really something else," he said to Ken, shaking his head. He acted like he knew Mom well.

Then the attorney returned his focus to me. "I think we can keep you out of jail for the time being, as long as you promise to stay out of trouble. Deal?" he asked

"You got a deal!" I gushed, elated. For the first time in weeks I wasn't a nervous wreck.

I was relaxed in the courtroom too. When we stood before the judge, he asked who Ken was. "I'm the boy's stepfather," answered Ken. That was the first time he'd ever acknowledged me as his stepson. It felt good, regardless of the context. *Step* didn't sound cut-rate and ugly when he said it, the way it did from Mom's pursed lips. From Ken, it just sounded like a prefix to *son*, the word I'd been longing to hear.

And when the judge had finished speaking, I was in orbit. Three months of probation—yes, sir, I promise to stay out of trouble—and one Saturday morning of picking up trash at the local park.

At that moment I was cured of any criminal desire, petty or otherwise. It wasn't the first time I realized that Mom's way of life was hazardous, but for me it was a turning point. I resolved to make my retirement as Mom's accomplice official. As painfully gradual as my retirement turned out to be, I date it from the moment I stepped out of that courthouse. I had barely escaped imprisonment, and that has a lot to do with why I'm not a prisoner twenty-five years later. Maybe Kenny would have turned out differently if something similar had happened to him when he was twelve years old.

With Ken and the lawyer, I walked out into the sunlight and crossed the parking lot, still floating. When we reached the attorney's car, I stopped and thanked him. "I was pretty scared," I admitted, with an embarrassed little laugh.

"If it happens again, you may not get so lucky," warned the lawyer, but he was smiling.

"I don't think we'll have to worry about anything like that again," said Ken. He asked me to keep walking to our nearby Eldorado and wait while he spoke privately with the attorney.

I moved away slowly, listening closely to see if they were talking about me. I heard the lawyer tell Ken that he thought everything was going to be all right, but something had to be done about "the situation" before it got "totally out of control." Ken agreed. So, I thought, the surfboard heist was an even bigger mess than I'd imagined, and my newly minted stepfather, no matter what he said to my face, seemed to think I was trouble.

But it wasn't me that Ken and the lawyer were talking about. Later I found out why Ken had picked me up at school that day instead of Mom. She had been arrested that very afternoon for shoplifting at the Fashion Island Mall. I'd guessed right. This lawyer did know Sante very well.

10

CASTING SPELLS

I n twenty-plus years of life with Mom and Ken, I learned a lot about lawyers. I met every decent criminal attorney in Las Vegas, because my parents plowed through all of them eventually, starting at the penthouse and working down to the fly-by-nighters with kitchen table offices. My parents would hire one, drive him crazy, refuse to pay him, then move on to the next number in the yellow pages.

When Mom and Kenny were arrested for Irene Silverman's murder in 1998, I received so many calls from New York cops and the FBI that I got nervous. I decided I needed a lawyer myself. I reached for the phone and dialed the best of the dozens my mother had auditioned. His name was Dominic Gentile.

I'd last seen him in the mid-eighties, when he represented my mother at her slavery trial. He'd been a *GQ* poster boy back then, partial to Armani suits and expensive shoes. When we met again almost fifteen years later, he'd gone biker. After we'd hugged and shaken hands, the first thing I said was, "What the hell happened to you?" Mr. *GQ* had stringy shoulder-length hair, leather pants, and a shirt unbuttoned to his sternum.

You can get away with the Hell's Angels look—and having an ex–porn actress as a live-in girlfriend—if you're among the top three criminal lawyers in the state of Nevada. Dominic had established a reputation as a peerless legal mind, a killer in the courtroom with a sweeping knowledge of the law.

He'd defended murderers and gangsters and was in no way the superstitious type. But before he agreed to represent me, he demanded an answer to a single startling question. "In all seriousness, Kent," this master of logic and law asked, "does your mother worship the devil?"

I laughed nervously, but Dominic wasn't kidding. He'd spent his career working for unsavory characters, but it was Sante who really spooked him. He thought she'd put a curse on him back in the eighties—after she hired and, inevitably, fired him, his practice went into a prolonged skid. A dozen years later his business was thriving, but he was still wary of doing anything that might infuriate her, like representing me. She scared him more than the Mob did. "At least those people have rules they live by," he explained. "You can predict their behavior."

Soon Dominic and I were looking for reinforcements. We met with a second, even better-known attorney, from Los Angeles, Howard Weitzman. He wasn't a stranger in Sante's circle either. The same man who'd briefly represented O. J. and then run Universal Studios had also kept Ken Kimes from going to prison with Mom in 1986.

By this time I understood what was expected of me in terms of small talk. "Have you ever had a client," I asked Weitzman, "as evil as my mother?"

He was silent for a few seconds, thinking back, and then he answered. "Charles Manson," he said.

Ultimately I couldn't afford either Weitzman or Gentile. I could only pay them in vacuum cleaners and publicity; I'd already given them the former, and neither wanted the latter. Dominic suggested I engage the services of Oscar Goodman, Nevada's legendary Mob lawyer. I knew him too, from the appeal in the maids case.

Dominic and I appeared in Goodman's office about two days before he announced his candidacy for mayor of Las Vegas. (He would win.) His walls were covered with pictures of himself grinning and grabbing the hands of celebrities. He'd done a cameo turn in the film *Casino*. To say that Oscar Goodman loves the limelight is an understatement.

The three of us had been yakking about old times and Mom when Dominic startled me again. He offered this assessment of his former client to his colleague: "She's the single most evil person I've ever met."

"I know," agreed Oscar. He was actually grinning. "That's what I admire most about her." After that, in private, I begged

Dominic to stick by me for a little while longer. I didn't appreciate Oscar's flippant attitude.

Great. Charles Manson, devil worshipper, most evil person ever. That was the verdict of three high-powered, thick-skinned lawyers who'd seen it all. My mother ranked up there with the very worst of the very worst. The national media had been exhaustively hyping the sins of Sante Kimes, and yet the people who actually knew her made the news stories sound like puff pieces. And in all honesty, I couldn't disagree.

Having read about my family life now, you may wonder why I didn't flee from it. If I could baby-sit myself while my mother and stepfather were away for weeks at a time, why did I stick around as I got older? My eyes were wide open by the time Kenny arrived, so why didn't I simply leave?

I was just a boy. It was all I knew. I loved her. I was scared to leave, scared she'd come after me. The money made her worse, but I stayed because I thought that if I behaved myself and made her happy, things would get better; *she'd* get better. These are the same reasons a battered wife gives for staying with her abuser, and they're all true. But they're not enough.

I was under a sort of spell. The spell wasn't really broken until 1999, after my mother had been in jail in New York for a year or so. That's when I changed my home number so she couldn't call and upset my kids. For a year she'd been phoning us at all hours with her speeches about family and loyalty and how much she needed and loved us, all the things she'd been telling me my whole life, and suddenly there was silence. She could no longer do her magic. Without her voice in my ear I realized that I could have broken away long before, that it really was possible to be free. I should never have let her near my children, ever, from the moment they were born. Yet I had, and now they loved and missed her, as I did. I missed her because this supposed sociopath was a ceaseless well of love and support. For all those appalling "oh, God" moments I've detailed, there were days and months in between when my mother was just my mother and loved me.

My mother's friends — her ex-friends — know what I'm talking about. Mom was the most charismatic and generous person most of her friends had ever met. She dispensed free meals and hundred-dollar bills at casinos, and people followed her like she was the Pied Piper. She gave away plane tickets to Hawaii and the Bahamas. Houseguests were treated like royalty. Mom was the excitement in everyone's lives and the fount of all good things.

Her friends responded with grateful loyalty. Kay Frigiano had been a lounge pianist and led sing-alongs at a now defunct Vegas joint called the Alpine Inn Rathskeller when Mom and Ken met her. They came night after night just so Ken, drink in hand, could sing "Embraceable You" to my mother as Kay accompanied. Kay became a devoted friend who adored my mother and would do anything for her. While Mom was in prison in the late eighties, Kay delivered home-cooked Italian meals to my house on a regular basis, simply because Mom had suggested it.

Mom was capable of friendship, though she would always demand repayment down the road. She would do for you, and you had better do for her. Most people obliged — some because it was a good deal, but all the rest because they loved her.

While living in Hawaii in the late seventies, my mother had a close friend named Beverly Bates. Ken and Jake, Beverly's husband, had been neighbors in a Southern California trailer park in the early fifties, when both men were married to their first wives and struggling to make it as developers. By chance they'd become neighbors again in Honolulu. Now they were both successful middle-aged men with big houses in a ritzy neighborhood, attractive second wives, and a thirst for alcohol. The two couples went out to dinner together quite often.

Jake started cheating on Beverly with a younger woman. Devastated, Beverly told Sante about the problems in her marriage, and my mother proved to be a loyal, supportive confidante. Beverly remains grateful to this day for the way Mom showed it.

Mom was at a restaurant in downtown Honolulu when she spied Jake at a table with his girlfriend. The illicit couple were leaning toward each other over a table and cooing; when they looked up, Sante Kimes loomed above them. Mom, who never shied from making a scene, delivered a lecture on morals loud enough for every diner to hear. "You are out with a married man! He has a wife and children at home! How dare you!" After a few minutes of high-volume abuse, Jake's girlfriend ran crying into the restroom. Mom then shifted her vitriol to Jake. I can imagine the fervent conviction with which she delivered her sermon, never seeing the irony. Sante herself had been the other woman far more than once.

Beverly heard about how Sante had shamed Jake and his bimbo in public, and the revenge by proxy gave her some satisfaction as her marriage crumbled. But now she owed my mother a favor, though Sante never said so. The time just came for my mother to call in the debt, and she got a sane, intelligent housewife to do something insane and stupid.

Mom had "neglected" to pay a contractor for repairing fire damage to her house, and the contractor had sued. The process server caught my mother at home and handed her a summons. In tears, she called Beverly and said that we were about to lose the house because an evil contractor had tried to rip her off, and when she fought back he'd slapped her with a lawsuit. Would Beverly save her?

Mom cajoled and pleaded until Beverly gave in. At our house, Mom gave her friend a makeover. She plastered eyeliner on Beverly's eyes and white pancake makeup on her face. With a black wig covering her head and a white organdy dress from Mom's closet on her body, the effect was eerily complete. Beverly had become Mom's doppelganger.

Dressed in identical outfits, the two women tottered on high heels down Alakea Street toward the sheriff's department. "I felt like I was going to a Halloween party," says Beverly, still amazed twenty years later by what she did.

Sante's attorney escorted them into the building, where the trio confronted the sheriff. "This," proclaimed the lawyer, pointing to Beverly, "is the lady who got served." He pointed to Beverly. Mom's ploy was to dupe the sheriff into believing that there were two Liz Taylors from outer space living in the same Honolulu neighborhood, and that the summons had been wrongfully delivered to Beverly. Sante Kimes had never received a summons at all. It wouldn't kill the lawsuit, but it would gum up the works and force a postponement, and simply wearing out her enemies was Mom's favorite legal tactic.

No one bought the charade. The sheriff spewed forth a string of cusswords and threats. "He called me a rotten liar," remembers Beverly. "He called me everything in the book. He said, 'You don't look anything like the woman I served. You're going to go to jail for perjuring yourself.'" Beverly fell apart, humiliated. She apologized abjectly to both the sheriff and my mother and started bawling. She was grateful when the sheriff didn't press charges.

Beverly went along with this scheme despite being well aware of Mom's track record. She'd had firsthand experience in Sante-land.

Beverly was an interior decorator, and when Mom wanted new wallpaper, Beverly sent her to a friend's shop. Though Kenny was already walking by then, Mom had kept his baby carriage — it came in handy for "shopping." She wheeled the empty pram into the wallpaper store, with a maid beside her. Later that day, Beverly got a call from her buddy the store-owner. "Your friend Sante was just here," said the merchant. "She didn't buy anything, but I noticed after she was gone that three rolls of wallpaper were missing." Mom and the maid had stuck them in the baby carriage and left the scene.

As Beverly tells that story now, she laughs. Yet back then she didn't. She knew what my mother was about, and still she did her bidding. "She was so warm, and so convincing, you'd do whatever she wanted to make her happy," Beverly recently explained to me. But that leaves out the importance of Beverly's own temperament. Mom picked her targets well.

The friends she made all had a few qualities in common. They tended to be Mom and Ken's social inferiors and were easily impressed by any hint of wealth. They were gullible and soft-hearted. Mom searched far and wide for the right mix of passivity and kindness. Nine out of ten people might turn her down, but the tenth would reveal some exploitable weakness.

In retelling the past you can layer on paragraphs of detail — the furniture in the room, what people were wearing, what words they stumbled over and how they sounded, but to understand the essence of Mom's magnetic force you had to be subject to it. She was relentless. She was powerful. She got people to do extraordinary things they could never have imagined doing. Anyone might have succumbed. Including you.

The closest way to approximate being in her presence is to play her audiotapes. For as long as I can remember, Mom has taped her phone calls — not as consistently as her favorite president, Nixon, but for many of the same paranoid reasons. She also had "enemies." There were times, though, when I wondered if she bugged her own conversations for the sheer joy of listening to herself work.

In 1997, after I fought with Mom and Kenny over their homeless "maids" and threw them out of my house, I found a couple of these cassette tapes and played one. What I heard was a snippet of a scam that had been sparked by a minor car accident.

Kenny wrecked a lot of cars. In the summer of 1996, someone ran into *him* for a change and dinged his Camaro at an intersection in Santa Barbara. Besides a fist-sized divot on the right front quarterpanel, the Camaro escaped unscathed. The damage was so slight that Kenny drove the six hours back to Las Vegas with no problem.

When Mom heard about it, she sensed an opportunity and charged into action. She tried to slip more than a thousand dollars of repairs, including a brand-new high-end stereo, past the Farmers Insurance company. Knowing that there was no possible link between a tiny dent and a broken stereo, Farmers balked.

On the tape, Mom is alternately badgering the insurance agent and charming the stereo repairman. She's already talked to both men a dozen times. I have abridged the long, numbing, circular conversations, and added some exposition and some stage business, as if this were a movie script. (It seemed appropriate, since Mom was often working off a loose script in a notebook when she pulled a scam.) By including the script here, I hope to convey a sense of the master plying her craft.

SANTE: Is Patrick Galloway in?

PATRICK: This is Patrick.

SANTE: (*Brightly*) Hi! This is the Kimes [*sic*], returning your call. How are you doing? How was your vacation?

PATRICK: (*Officious, wary*) Fine. This is in regards to the stereo. How do you guys relate this to the loss? I've talked with the body shop, and we have a hard time relating this to the accident.

SANTE: I'm just writing this down.

PATRICK: We've looked at a lot of damaged vehicles, and this is out of the ordinary.

SANTE: (*Now more officious than Patrick*) We've been with Farmers a long time. I would like to register a complaint with you against your employee Kermit Flowers, which I will also do with your district office. I don't know if I've ever been treated more rudely on the phone. He certainly doesn't have your professionalism. He was rude and degrading.

PATRICK: (*Cowed*) I will check that out.

SANTE: (*Referring to an imaginary person*) [My] secretary was listening on the other line, and I had her write things down. That's a topic we can go into another time. But I'm not going to let it go. Now that I have *you* on the phone, you said the body shop is in concurrence with you. Exactly the opposite is true. We will get you a sworn statement. If you see in front of you that the body shop and the stereo company refute what you say, will that be enough?

PATRICK: (*Confused*) If they can tell us *why*. Nobody ever gave us an opportunity to inspect the stereo. How do you attribute the damage to the accident?

SANTE: Let me answer that this way. If you were in surgery, and you asked me, "How can I reconnect this nerve?" I couldn't possibly answer, but I would assume that the people you selected to do the operation know what they are doing. But I can't tell you. We're not mechanics.

PATRICK: (*Exasperated*) That's the problem. *We are.*

SANTE: But your people don't agree with you. We have every intention of letting you see we've been treated improperly, and letting you see the facts. You need to see the facts.

PATRICK: I have no problem with that.

The insurance man hangs up, angry and suspicious. Sante dials another number.

FEMALE VOICE: Empire Audio.

SANTE: Hi, is Tim there?

FEMALE VOICE: Hold on.

TIM: This is Tim.

SANTE: (*Gushing*) Hi, Tim! We just got in. We had to run over to Europe.

TIM: (*Impressed, never having been east of Salt Lake*) My!

SANTE: Anyway, how are you?

TIM: Busy, busy, busy.

SANTE: (*Lying*) We had to go to a wedding, and now we're back. Anyway, honey, we got to the point where the bad guys are out of it [meaning Kermit Flowers]. Now we're just trying to get it resolved and paid. I need you to help me with some vocabulary. In your vocabulary, what happened?

T I M: (*Slowly, and after a pause, since he knows what's going on*) The actual tape transport mechanism . . .

S A N T E: (*Writing*) The . . . actual . . . tape transport mechanism . . .

T I M: Was damaged due to some kind of external impact.

S A N T E: (*Editing*) Was . . . damaged . . . due to external impact. Is that enough, do you think? In other words, would that disconnect the wires?

T I M: (*Embroidering the lie*) The mechanism that takes the tape inside to where the tape head is, that was bent out of shape.

S A N T E: The transport . . . was bent . . . so tapes would not insert correctly, thereby it had to be replaced. That should be sufficient, shouldn't it?

T I M: Yeah.

S A N T E: Thank you, honey. When are you coming to the Bahamas?

T I M: (*Excited*) That's up to you.

S A N T E: I'll get this typed up and fax it over to you. You can sign it and get it back to us and we're fine. Let's go out for a drink sometime.

T I M: Okay.

S A N T E: And if Mr. Galloway from Farmers calls, you just tell him the same thing. (*Yelling*) *It's the truth!*

They hang up. Tim will never come within a thousand miles of a free drink, much less the Bahamas. Sante places a final call.

S A N T E: Mr. Galloway, please.

P A T R I C K: This is Patrick.

S A N T E: Yes, this is the Kimes [*sic*] again. I wanted to tell you what's happening in the process. Empire . . . whatever the name of that company is, they believe that the stereo defect was caused by impact. The actual tape transport mechanism was bent, so tapes would not insert correctly, thereby it had to be replaced.

P A T R I C K: (*Suspicious*) I've never dealt with Empire Audio before.

S A N T E: I assume they're reputable. I could get an attorney to get an affidavit. They've already told you that it was caused by impact.

P A T R I C K: (*Desperate*) Do they still have the stereo?

S A N T E: I don't know. They probably do. The damage to the mechanism was due to abnormal external impact. Just talk to them. (*Like a mantra*) The actual tape transport mechanism was bent, so tapes would not insert correctly.

P A T R I C K: (*Admitting defeat*) I have to document what I pay. I have to document it. I want something in writing.

S A N T E: (*Cheerful*) We'll help. We've got some secretaries.

The check from Farmers didn't satisfy Mom. She didn't want to pony up the deductible either. Kenny sneaked onto the body shop lot and drove the car out without paying. Somehow he got the car past two security guards and through the lot's single entrance. Ultimately, because the body shop threatened action, but more because I was furious at her, Mom had to write a check. I knew the guy who'd done the body work, and I didn't want Mom and Kenny ripping off my friend. For all the lies, bad blood, hours of phone calls, and legal risk, including possible criminal charges against Kenny, Mom realized maybe $350 in profit. Somehow she thought it was worth it.

It was always worth it to her. She found it exciting. If you're always searching for an angle, you'll find it, and if you're always looking for a mark, you'll find one.

Even marks get smart eventually, though. It was one thing to con an insurance company and a sad-sack stereo repairman, and another to do it to friends. Mom couldn't help herself. That story about the scorpion and the frog applies perfectly to her. The scorpion talks the frog into giving her a ride across the river, promising not to sting him. But halfway across the river, she stings him anyway. As the frog is dying and the scorpion is drowning, the frog says, "But why?" The scorpion replies, "It's my nature."

She burned her friends, even sweet, giving women like Kay and Beverly. When she did, they retaliated, usually by disappearing from our lives. But sometimes they took more serious action.

Beverly Bates ran afoul of Mom in 1979, when she helped a maid escape from our house. The maid claimed that Mom had burned her with an iron and that Ken had raped her, so Beverly hid the terrified woman in her closet.

Mom and Ken sped over to Beverly's house and confronted her through the car window. "What did you do with our maid?" growled Sante. "You two are out of your heads," quavered Beverly. She denied everything, praying that her soon-to-be ex-friends would stay in the car. She stalled long enough for Mom and Ken to turn on each other. "I told you you were going to get in trouble!" bellowed Ken. Mom hissed at him. "You had *your* fun."

That was the end of Mom's relationship with Beverly Bates. Beverly said, "I never want to see you again." Mom replied, "I'll never forget this." Aware of what had happened to the maid, aware of Mom's fearlessness and volcanic temper, Beverly took the threat seriously. She went out of her way not to run into Mom, afraid at first even to drive past her house.

A few months later, Beverly noticed a big white Caddy parked at the bottom of her hill. It was there again the next day, and the next. Beverly walked down to it and saw Sante inside, just sitting and waiting. Beverly was rattled. Sante was the sort of person who'd sit for hours at the end of her street purely to scare her, or maybe she was about to pounce. Swallowing her fear, Beverly demanded, "What are you doing here?" Mom was nonchalant. "Oh, I'm looking for playmates for Kenny." Beverly walked back up the hill and locked her door. Mom's car didn't move.

The image of Mom, implacable, parked at the bottom of a hill, refusing to depart from an ex-friend's life, rings true. That was my life for as long as I can remember. My angry, fearsome mother, stretched taut as a trip wire, blocked the exits. It was so much safer for me to stay put, knowing that most days would be good days. When I was twelve and we were about to move to Hawaii, I was ready to escape but didn't believe I'd succeed. When I was thirteen, I tried anyway.

11

ESCAPE

oney, pack your clothes! We're going on a trip, and where we're going is a surprise!"

We traveled constantly after Mom hooked up with Ken, and she tried to make the constant upheaval fun by turning my questions into a guessing game: When are we leaving? Where are we headed? How long will we stay when we get there? The only clues I got were her packing instructions. A couple of changes of light clothes meant a short trip to some beach resort. Warm clothes meant a ski weekend in Tahoe.

I didn't mind the game, even though I rarely got more than an hour's notice and even though Mom was doing it as much for the control as the fun. We always wound up somewhere pleasant. But on a June morning in 1975, soon after I finished seventh grade and not long after my trip to court for surfboard larceny, Mom gave me orders I hadn't heard before. "Pack all your clothes," she said. "We're going to stay awhile."

The surprise never lasted beyond the airport gate, where I'd learned to look for the name of our destination. On that day, the sign at the L.A. airport read Honolulu. The game had ended well again. I'd already been to Hawaii with Mom and Ken and loved it, and apparently this time we were taking an extra-long vacation.

But when we touched down on Oahu we didn't take a cab to a hotel, as we had before. We drove to Kaneohe, on the windward side of the island, where Ken's nephew Don lived. The next morning Mom and Ken took three-month-old Kenny and disappeared. I'd been dumped, just like the old days in Palm

Springs, except this time I didn't see my parents for a full month. I took it in stride. Mom always came back.

When they returned, Mom revealed the last part of the surprise. I'd already figured it out. "We're going to live in Hawaii," she said. Our other moves had been gradual. We'd oozed from one city to the next, spending less and less time in Palm Springs and more days in Newport till the change was complete. Now, surprise, we were making a clean break. I hadn't had a chance to say good-bye to any of my friends.

I told Mom I was mad that we'd moved. "Well, honey," she sniffed, "it's *your* fault. We had to leave Newport Beach because you stole those surfboards." I half believed her, though I suspected there were other, more pressing reasons. In whatever order you prefer, we were in flight from Mom's growing rap sheet, the Bicentennial ambassador snafu, and the Creeps, starring Linda Kimes, who Mom said wanted to kidnap Kenny. When Mom made a mess, moving was the best way to clean it up.

For the first six months we rented a house near Don, on the water next to the Kaneohe Yacht Club, and I spent the fall semester of eighth grade in a Catholic school called St. Ann's. I missed my friends, but I adjusted fast. I discovered the ocean. I became obsessed with boats.

Mom and Ken seemed distracted by something on the mainland, and Mom kept flying to California for weeks at a stretch. I never knew why, but that fall of 1975 in Kaneohe was the first period where Mom and Ken spent any extended amount of time apart. I guessed the absences were due to a lawsuit or a criminal case—nothing serious.

We were all present in Kaneohe for Christmas, though, and presents covered the floor around our plastic tree. On Christmas Eve, Ken stared at the loot with a look of raw fear on his face. Whatever was preoccupying him, it had made him forget to go shopping. "Kent," he whispered, "there aren't any presents for your mother."

It was late, and every store was closed as we raced around the island in the Lincoln. Finally we chanced on a cheesy pharmacy about to lock its doors. Ken emptied the shelves of bath oils, toiletries, and tacky knickknacks. The next morning Mom had nothing that cost more than ten dollars, but Ken had saved the household from a holiday in hell.

After the New Year we packed up and moved again, and I changed schools. To me it was an ominous echo of the pre-Ken days, when I was as mobile as an army brat. But this move was meant to be permanent. Mom and Ken had settled, at last, on a neighborhood, Hawaii Kai, in the shadow of Diamondhead on the southeast side of Oahu. Hawaii Kai was among the most affluent and gorgeous areas on the island, and Portlock Road was its swankest street. My parents had rented a mini-mansion ringed by palm trees on Portlock, with a thousand-square-foot living room that opened onto a patio. The beach was steps away. I loved it.

At thirteen I was finally old enough to connect with my stepdad in the manner he understood best: I could make money. At the Portlock rental, Ken and I began a business partnership. He bought beat-up boats, and I fixed them. I scraped and painted the hulls of cabin cruisers and did minor repairs on the engines, and when Ken resold the boats he gave me a cut. My biggest paycheck was three hunded dollars, from a project that had netted him eight grand. He didn't get rich by being generous.

But if growing up made me more valuable to Ken, it made me a problem for my mother. At thirteen I looked eighteen. I'd shot up to six feet during the summer of 1975 and I was still growing. I had longish hair, like most of my peers, and a bad attitude, at least where Mom was concerned. Since the surfboard incident, I'd seen ever more clearly the gap between Sante and the real world, and I'd become sullen and uncooperative. I was an adolescent, and Mom couldn't stand it. She hated my hair, my size, and especially my attitude—everything that said I was getting older. Adolescence led to adulthood, and she could sense an adult on the way who wouldn't be like her.

"Kent, I need you to do me a little favor." When I heard those words in early 1976 on Portlock, I could predict what was coming next. If it were really a little favor, she would have named it. She wouldn't have wheedled either. It would have been a command, as in "Kent, go to the store and buy some milk." Sidling up meant the favor was big. I thought, *Oh shit*.

"There's this house down the road—"

"No way." I cut her off so fast that I startled myself. I knew right away that she needed a break-in for some documents. Her next sentence confirmed my hunch. I didn't budge. I wasn't going through any more windows. I had said no, finally, and because I was now far bigger than she was, she couldn't change that no with her fists. She was losing control.

My resistance drove Mom crazy. Since she could no longer order me around at will, she took some of her frustration out on Ken. She poured the rest into ramping up her battle with her enemies, the Creeps. Claiming that the Kimes relatives had attacked her on the beach and tried to steal Kenny, Mom began to Creep-proof the house. She stuck padlocks here and there, added extra interior locks on the doors, and began tape-recording phone calls. Fear of the Creeps became the spurious rationale for a host of alarming security measures that would be part of Kimes family life for the next twenty-five years. The locks kept the Creeps out, but equally important, though Sante would never admit it, they kept everybody else in, including me and Kenny and the maids.

While she decorated the house in dead bolts, Mom was also working on Ken. She lectured him daily on the sins of the Creeps, which after the "beach attack" grew more fantastic and deadly. But when we first arrived in Hawaii, Ken still wasn't convinced. He had a reservoir of love and trust for his family. In fact, as soon as we rented the house on Portlock, his ancient mother and aunt came to live with us. Though Mom had run far — three time zones and several thousand miles — her enemies were closer than ever. Mom was partly to blame, since she'd urged Ken to sell his mother's house in California out from under her.

Mom pasted on a smile and told me we were saving these two sweet old ladies from the machinations of Ken's Creepy brothers and sisters back on the mainland. She installed them in the little cottage that was attached to the rambling main house by a walkway. Both were in rapid, palsied decline. They spent their afternoons in lawn chairs on the patio, heads lolling in tandem. Meanwhile, Sante was fuming.

She couldn't stand Ken's mother, Neoma, who was pretty hard to like. She was a stern, cranky eighty-five-year-old who deeply resented being uprooted so late in life, and my mother disgusted her. Aunt Alice was slightly younger and exponentially warmer. She enjoyed Hawaii.

Soon the two old women were at serious odds. Grandma Neoma yearned for the mainland, Alice was all for the islands. Mom exploited the breach like a general.

My mission was reconnaissance. Mom told me to sneak into the cottage while Grandma and Alice were slumped semiconscious on the patio and steal their mail. Though I'd vowed not to help Mom anymore, I came out of retirement. I didn't steal any letters, but I did rummage through the old ladies' things.

The fight that Mom wanted erupted that afternoon. Grandma Kimes figured out that I'd been rooting through her belongings, and she confronted Mom in the den. I tried to slink away, but Mom and Ken barred the door. Then Grandma Kimes and Alice turned on each other, as Mom had hoped. Alice demanded to stay in Hawaii. Grandma demanded to go home. She wanted Ken to buy her a ticket back to Los Angeles. Mom chose that moment to unsheathe her secret weapon.

"Why don't you tell Ken the truth?" she shouted at Grandma Kimes, shaking her finger.

The old lady looked puzzled. "Pardon me?"

"You're not even his mother!" Sante announced, steely-eyed and triumphant. "Your sister is Ken's real mother!"

Mom's big revelation was completely false, though no one has ever explained to me how this melodramatic plot twist got stuck in her mind. According to Sante, Alice had been raped by Ken's father, and Ken was the fruit of their irregular union. The evil father and sister had then stolen the child, enslaved poor Alice for years afterward, and suppressed the real story of Ken's birth.

Instead of collapsing, Grandma shouted right back. I admired her. She was a rugged old bitch, a match for Sante. "How dare you!" she hissed.

Mom underlined her charge, screaming at the old woman again. "Alice is his real mother! Tell him the truth! Get the charade over with!"

I don't think Mom and Grandma Kimes ever spoke another civil word. The ladies retreated to their cottage, and for some weeks the tension in the compound grew so wearying that I thought about the airport myself. Ken must have sensed I was close to bolting. "Hang in there, buddy," he said. "Neoma and Alice are just old and cranky."

He'd taken Sante's side against his own mother. He'd balled his fists when Mom revealed her "truth," but all he did was demand that she explain herself. Sante never abandoned the Alice theory, and Ken stopped fighting it within months. She'd planted this particularly outlandish idea in his skull with so little resistance that I had to stop and wonder. Did he suspect it was true? What did he know? Or was he that afraid of disagreeing with her?

Soon afterward Ken's brother Chuck and sister Hannah flew to Hawaii and retrieved the two old ladies. Mom, shed of her houseguests at last, pretended to be outraged and threatened to call the police, but Ken considered us lucky to have avoided a visit from the cops ourselves. The Creeps were that angry.

In the wake of the "Who's Your Momma?" fight, my parents battled without pause and without mercy. Although booze fed the flames, Mom and Ken were coherent enough in those days to stick to their chosen themes. They tried to be logical and make points, subtleties that often escaped them in later years. On Portlock Road, their pet topics were loyalty and money. Mom: "You cheap bastard, why won't you give me a checking account?" Ken: "Because all you want is my money." Mom: "You don't care about us. You're a Creep-lover. You love the Creeps more than you love us." Ken: "We've got a good life here, Santee. What's your problem?"

The bummer about being thirteen was that I now looked and sounded old enough to referee the fights. I had a bedroom with a private bath and a huge picture window full of ocean, and I could put a Cat Stevens album on the stereo I'd bought with my boat profits and drown out the screaming at the opposite end of the house. (It doesn't take a shrink to guess why my musical tastes have always leaned toward the soothing and mellow.) But my room ceased to be a refuge. As the spring of 1976 wore on, Mom and Ken would drag me out of bed late at night so I could stand in the den and monitor their arguments. They started tattling on each other—to me. "This fucking millionaire won't give me a checkbook." "She steals, and she's cheating on me." They would ask me to render a decision. Once, exasperated, I blurted, "I'm thirteen fucking years old. What do I know?" It didn't register with them. They didn't care what they told me any more than they cared if I cussed or drank.

In mid-April, Mom and Ken pressed me into duty on a weekend night. They were especially drunk and had an especially stupid question. "Who are you loyal to?" Mom demanded. "Who do you love more?"

"You're both fucking nuts," I snapped. "You're both drinking too much."

I turned and started walking toward my room. It gave Mom a chance to try a new fighting technique that would counter my new size and strength. She picked up an electric razor, swung it around her head by its cord, bolo-style, and let it fly. It hit me hard between the shoulder blades, stinging like a pony-league beanball.

I spun back around and said, "I'm out of here. I'm going to live with Dad." I'd already mentioned the idea to Ed Walker in furtive phone calls.

Mom saw her opening. "He's not your real father!" she shouted, triumphant. "Your real father is Bob Prescott!"

Apparently the razor hadn't hurt me enough, so Mom had hurled a version of the verbal bomb that had wounded Ken a few months before. My first reaction was scorn. "Bullshit," I scoffed, with a bitter laugh. Mom had sent everyone's life into rewrite—she was a Hindu named Shawntay, Ken's aunt was his mother, and now it was my turn. I was suddenly the son of an airline magnate.

But then Mom provided the evidence. She rattled off the many lovers she'd had in the early years of her marriage to Ed Walker, and as I listened with growing alarm, I started to take her seriously. I hadn't known that the chain of men stretched back before my birth. "Let's call your so-called father," she insisted, "and I'll prove it!"

Mom dialed Carson City and made me pick up the other line. I knew that Dad still loved her. He'd be happy to hear from her and crushed by what she said. He answered after many rings. It was past midnight in Nevada.

"Ed," said Mom, with no preamble. "I told him about Earl Wagner and Bob Prescott."

What followed didn't reassure me. Dad didn't contradict anything Mom said about her boyfriends. I crumbled. Dad and I cried on the phone while Mom listened dry-eyed.

"Is it true, Dad?" I whimpered, a little boy again.

"No, Kent. I love you," he answered. "You'll always be my son." Which meant, even if you're not. Because of the way my mother had deceived him, he could never be entirely certain, and therefore neither could I. Mom had won our fight by knockout.

The end of the school year neared. The battles between Mom and Ken continued. I had no one to confide in but a teenage girl who lived next door. She could hear the screaming from her house, and we used to meet on the beach and talk about it. "I want to leave," I told her.

A week before the last day of school, I was awakened in the middle of the night by Ken's shouted pleas for help. "Kent! Come in here! Kent!"

I ran into the kitchen. Ken was in his jockeys, and there was Mom in her nightie, in some transcendent rage, pissing on the linoleum floor. She saw me and got embarrassed and took it out on Ken. She slapped at his bare back. Ken raised his forearm to ward off her blows and accidentally hit her in the face.

Just a week before, Mom had undergone plastic surgery on her eyelids; Ken's arm had brushed the stitches. Tiny beads of blood appeared above Mom's eye. The room went silent.

Mom ran into the bathroom, and Ken and I waited. We were scared. For my mother, who never shut up, silence was the lull before the storm.

When Mom emerged, however, she seemed to have collected herself. She hugged Ken. He sat on a stool by the kitchen counter and she climbed into his lap. Soon she was running her fingers through his hair.

"Those are nice implants, aren't they?" cooed Mom. "They really did a good job." Two months earlier a California surgeon had filled Ken's bald spot with hair plugs. They'd grown in nicely. You could hardly tell the difference between the new hair and the old.

"I'm not the only one who's had work done, am I?" said Mom, in the same saccharine tone. She kept stroking Ken's hair, and I could see him relax. When he did, Mom closed her fist in his hair and yanked as hard as she could. Ken screamed like a scalded child and bolted for the bathroom.

Mom, with two bloody hanks in her hand, wasn't done. She tried to run after Ken, but her feet went out from under her. She landed hard on her back. She'd slipped in a pool of her own urine.

I jumped on top of her and pinned her arms to the floor. "Calm down," I urged, and my mother reached up and bit my wrist so hard that I let go. I retreated to my room.

The next morning I walked into the breakfast nook, and there sat my parents, looking like sane, civilized people. My wrist was swollen, but Mom had no marks on her. Ken had combed his hair over the red hole in his head. "Good morning," he said, beaming. "Do you want to work on the boat today?"

It was time to go. I told Ken that I was planning to run away. He took me out to dinner and begged me to stay, but I told him I couldn't take it anymore. "I think I'm part of the reason you two fight so much," I said. "Maybe things will be easier when I'm gone."

I had kept a one-cylinder portable motor I'd found stashed in one of the boats I'd rehabbed, and I sold it for $165. With that and the other boat cash I'd saved, I had enough for a one-way ticket to the mainland. I called my dad in Carson City and told him when I was arriving.

On the evening of my departure, I pulled Ken aside as he and Mom were about to go out to a restaurant, and said, "I won't be here when you return." I could tell he was upset, but he kept my secret. As he and Mom drove away, he looked back at me and flashed a double victory sign, Nixon style. He was saying good-bye and good luck.

When the car was out of sight, I snatched a wig from my mother's closet. I built a dummy in my bed, like I'd seen in the movies, and then put a note under it for insurance. "Gone camping for three days." Within hours I was aboard the red-eye to San Francisco, with no intention of ever coming back.

12

YO-YO

t felt like déjà vu. It must have unnerved my father as well.
But for some reason, he'd agreed to meet my mother by the
side of the highway in Washoe Valley, Nevada, not far from the
lonely spot where she'd pulled a gun on him seven years
before.

Mom had come to Carson City a month after my escape
from Hawaii to lure me back. Dad glowed with excitement at
her visit, but he refused to let her set foot in his little weathered
green tract house. He'd insisted on a neutral meeting place, and
here we were, parked on the gravel shoulder, with Mom's big-
ticket Detroit rental ten yards in front of us. It was 1969 all over
again. Somebody had a perverse idea of neutral.

Well-dressed ladies with perfect makeup poured out all
four doors of Mom's car. The doors swung shut with a heavy
chunk, and the ladies trooped down the shoulder toward me in
formation, Mom in the lead. She'd pressed three of our Southern California friends into service, marching them to Carson
City to confront me. They looked like a SWAT team from Mary
Kay cosmetics. On the shoulder of the road, they each hugged
me in turn. Then Mom made her pitch.

It was a two-parter. I could tell by Mom's half smirk that
Dad's digs were as modest as she'd hoped. He'd never become
rich, just as she'd predicted. He was everything she'd left
behind when she stopped being Sandy, and now she'd returned
to her hometown, wealthy and triumphant, as Sante. She
wagered that after five years with Ken, I too had become
addicted to the soft life, and with the big shiny car she'd made

sure to remind me of the luxury I'd left. She didn't say it, but her question was, Do you really like the little green house in the little hick town?

Part two of her campaign was love and what she assumed was my loneliness. She'd brought her friends so I could see familiar faces, and she'd chosen women I liked: Sandy Spears, one of Mom's lieutenants in Newport; Maggie Miller, who lived in a Barbara Cartland cloud of pink pillows and white lap dogs in the Hollywood Hills; Memphis Cipolla, a warmhearted, fat Latina who'd cared for Ken's mom and aunt in Hawaii. She wasn't a nurse, but when Mom had asked for her help, she'd dropped everything and flown to Honolulu. Memphis was generous to a serious fault, like most of Mom's friends.

Mom was right, I did miss my other life, especially my baby brother, Kenny, but the memories of domestic warfare were still fresh. "We all want you with us so much, honey," begged Mom, but I told her I wasn't coming back. "I love you," I said, "but we can't live together. I think you and Ken fight so much because of me."

The posse went back south later that day, after more angry and abject pleading by Mom that made everybody uncomfortable. But she didn't give up. In September she flew me down to Newport so I could celebrate my fourteenth birthday with friends from junior high. She mailed me cards every other day that she said were from eighteen-month-old Kenny. She sent me her own fifteen-page, single-spaced obsessive letters. "Honey, I miss you," they said. "I'm holding your hand right now."

But I stayed put. Nevada was hot, dull, and beachless, but I'd done what Dad and I had whispered about in our secret calls for a year. I'd run away from Mom, and we were together. Dad wasn't a big developer anymore, but he was solvent and sane. I thanked God for the peace and quiet.

Not long after Mom's failed rescue mission, Dad hired a lawyer and applied for custody. I was about to turn fourteen and had some say in the matter, and I chose to stay in Carson City. Mom didn't show up for the hearing, and Dad won uncontested legal custody of me till I was eighteen. Mom tried to get her revenge by suing the man whose credit she'd ruined for $250,000 in back child support, but Dad shrugged it off.

But life in Nevada began to grate on me as soon as school started. Carson City High sucked. It was weird to live in a town where people had known your parents growing up. The old high school had been replaced by a new, bigger building that was already overcrowded, but some of the teachers were the same. They remembered Ed, the star athlete, and Sandy. They asked me about Sandy, and not one said a bad word. I couldn't believe it.

The worst of it was that I, not my mother, had the bad rep. I played football and basketball, but I never fit in. I was the beach geek, the tan, longhaired oddball from Hawaii with puka shells around his neck. I'd been teleported into a pickup-truck town, and the goat ropers with the Copenhagen tins in their jeans pockets liked to sucker-punch me in the halls. The local girls sort of liked me, which made the guys hate me even more.

I coped by tinkering with a vintage Chris-Craft boat, an outboard from the forties that lay idle in Dad's backyard. I worked with Dad, listened to music in my room, and ventured out sometimes to shoot pool. I had one friend, a fellow high school outcast.

Still, it might have been bearable if Dad's marriage to Vicky weren't slowly disintegrating. Vicky, the woman my mother had dragged around by her hair, didn't want me in Carson City. She and Dad drank too much and fought too much. Compared with the grand-opera standards of Mom and Ken their battles were tame, but that didn't make them any more fun to witness. I began to wonder whether Dad had a taste for tempestuous relationships. It would explain why he'd endured Sandy so long.

The situation in the little green house kept slipping, and Mom kept calling. Kenny had started to talk. She would put him on the phone and he'd jabber at me. I missed him badly.

In June 1977, with the school year finished, Mom talked me into a two-week visit to Honolulu. I left the elastic boredom of cowtown life and landed in the most beautiful property Mom and Ken had rented yet, a mansion on Hanapepe Point in Hawaii Kai, perched high on a cliff above the breakers. I opened my bedroom window to sunshine, with blue skies, a slight breeze, and ocean stretching out as far as I could see.

Mom arranged a welcome-home party and invited six beautiful teenage girls I'd never met. I was a horny fourteen going on eighteen, with facial hair. I'm sure she told the girls I was about to inherit a fortune in oil wells. That's what she always told the pretty ones, and it always worked. Later, one of these guests admitted that Mom had issued orders before the party: "We were supposed to beg you to stay."

Mom went all out. She bought me sailing lessons. A year shy of a learner's permit, I drove the Lincoln as often as I pleased. I lived like the young lord she'd advertised.

It was the same two-pronged pitch that Mom had tried in Carson City a full year before, the material and the emotional. My talkative little brother would crawl into bed with me at night, tugging at my heart. Mom never stopped entreating me to stay, but otherwise she was on her best behavior.

But the most affecting plea came from Ken. He told me, in private, how it had been while I was gone. Crushed and humiliated, Mom had taken it out on him. She blamed him for pushing me out of the house and for buying my getaway ticket to Reno. She had never been able to acknowledge her own role in anything bad. My absence had meant a year of hell for Ken. He begged me to stay and protect him.

I extended my trip for two weeks, then another two weeks, and then two months. There wasn't a raised voice in the house on Hanapepe Point all summer. I thought, or so I told myself, that something had changed for the better and that Mom and Ken needed me there to keep it that way. I liked the easy life in the big house as much as I loathed the goat ropers of Carson City. In Hawaii I was cool, and I was happy.

Ed Walker had extended himself for me, risking Mom's lawsuits and further damage to his second shaky marriage. In August I made a difficult phone call. I told him I wasn't coming back. He'd gone to court and obtained custody for nothing. I felt like I'd used him. It was easy to take advantage of his simple goodness—Mom had done it, and now I had too. Selfless and gracious as always, Dad didn't complain. He wished me the best.

We had to find a school for me, fast. Now that Mom and Ken realized they had to keep me happy or I'd run, I was too good for public school. The better private academies balked at adding an unknown sophomore right before classes started, so by default I landed at a boarding school called Mid-Pacific Institute. It had a good academic reputation and a student body of four hundred, and it was willing to take me.

Mom and Ken regretted the choice right away. Eighty percent of Mid-Pac's students were what Ken referred to as "Japs." Half the student body hailed from the home islands of Japan, and most of the rest of the students were Japanese-Americans, the dominant ethnic group in Hawaii. *Haoles,* the local word for whites, accounted for no more than 20 percent of the pupils. "You go to the Jap school," other *haole* kids would tell me on the beach at Hanapepe.

A month into the school year, the four of us moved into the house that became our permanent Hawaii address. We always referred to it as "the Portlock house," a run-down, rambling, L-shaped wooden ranch house hidden behind a screen of palms and an eight-foot brick wall. It was a beachfront property next door to our first Hawaii Kai rental.

It was a ratty house on an ultradesirable lot. Ken was getting bored with the slow pace of island life, and I wondered why he was buying any property, especially such a ramshackle one, till I heard the price. It was bargain basement, less than two hundred thousand dollars. Sante, meanwhile, had her own radical plans for bringing the shoddy digs up to her standards.

I loved it the way it was. I lived in a separate guest cottage. I hung out on the beach, drove the Lincoln downtown, and nobody knew where I'd been or even asked. I could pull a beer out of the fridge in the main house and take it back to my cottage. I brought girls there too.

The cottage represented an unspoken acknowledgment by Mom and Ken of something that had been true for years: I was raising myself. As long as they didn't need me—as witness, drinking buddy, chauffeur, referee, boat painter, partner in crime—they let me be. They imposed no curfew and no rules.

Another teenager might have run wild, but I didn't. It didn't occur to me to stay out all night. I needed to be able to get up early and hit the beach, or work on someone's boat for pocket money. I didn't become an alcoholic and, aside from the usual youthful experimentation, I didn't become a druggie. If I abused my freedom, it was sexually. I always had girls around. But then I had a mother who asked her teenage son, "Didja get any?" That was her crass, nonchalant approach to sex. Coming from Mom, the question made me cringe, but the answer was often yes. Luckily, when Mom got that answer, she didn't press for details.

Once I'd enrolled at Mid-Pac, settled into the Portlock house, and made some friends, the honeymoon was over. Mom and Ken stopped putting on a show. The truce ended and the arguments began. Soon the frequency and volume of Kimes versus Kimes were back to normal levels, circa 1976. Again I was the underage ref, though it was a longer walk to fetch me in this house, and I was often gone.

These days Ken's gripe was that Mom was cheating on him. He had been jealous since the first days in Palm Springs, and Mom had been adept at using it. He would get mad if men looked at Mom, and since she wore low-cut dresses and flirted outrageously to make sure they would, he got mad a lot. This time Ken had a good reason to gripe.

In the legend of Sante Kimes, she's always described as "a former Washington lobbyist." It makes superficial sense because a con artist is a persuader, and that's what lobbyists get paid for. But the con artist goes for the quick hit. The idea that Mom could hoodwink people for a sustained length of time in a sophisticated and very small city like political Washington is laughable. She and the Ambassador had already been run out of town once.

Mom collected doctors, especially those who could be persuaded to diagnose Ken or her with whatever illness she named. She became a lobbyist because one of her medical allies in California, Alfred Caruso, had launched an HMO and needed help getting federal certification for his company, HMO Concepts. Senator Sam Nunn of Georgia had advised the undersecretary of the Department of Health, Education and Welfare, Hale Champion, to deny certification because Caruso's company, though nonprofit, wrote checks to eight different for-profit firms that happened to be owned by Dr. and Mrs. Caruso. In short, HMO Concepts looked like a shell corporation.

Sante the lobbyist dropped in on William McLeod, director of HEW's compliance office, and threatened him with unspecified retribution if he didn't certify Caruso. She said she knew big people.

In reality, the biggest person she knew was dear old C. V. Narasimhan, the UN undersecretary, who for some reason had kept in touch with Mom and Ken even after the Ambassador fiasco. He had visited us in Hawaii and talked with my parents about starting some loopy boarding school on the Big Island to be called Freedom University. Kids from around the world would attend the school—run by my racist, anti-Semitic parents—in hopes of promoting international understanding. It was another empty scheme that came to nothing.

So Mom, masquerading as C. V.'s associate, called Hale

Champion's office to talk about the school. Once inside the door, she started spewing about Alfred Caruso instead. Champion passed her up the ladder to Joseph Califano, head of HEW.

For the second time, Mom made the papers for telling lies in Washington. She dropped names ranging from *Washington Post* owner Katharine Graham to Senator Alan Cranston of California. My little brother kept getting new godfathers. C. V. wasn't good enough for Kenny anymore; Califano and UN Secretary-General Kurt Waldheim took his place.

Before the lobbyist scam blew up, someone at HEW approved a $437,000 loan for Caruso. Mom might have been responsible. Caruso evidently thought so, because he bought his lobbyist a white Cadillac Eldorado and gave her $15,000 in expense money.

The money helped Mom spend weeks away from home in California and Washington, sometimes without Ken. He suspected that Mom and Caruso were having an affair. Since she cheated on Ken only when it was profitable for her, I think Ken was right. Cars and money would qualify as Sante-style aphrodisiacs.

In late 1977 and early 1978, cops began banging on our doors at regular intervals. It was just like old times. Mom and Ken would cruise by the house to make sure they had no unwanted company before they'd come inside. Among other things, the Honolulu Police Department was interested in a baby grand piano that had been delivered to the Portlock address. No one had paid for it. Ordering baby grands and "forgetting" payment was one of Mom's quirky habits. She couldn't play a note. She just thought they looked nice.

One day I came home from school with my friend Eric Price, and there were no cars in the driveway. Since Mom never drove, and neither car was hot, it made no sense. When Eric and I went inside, Mom was alone. "I need you boys to go to the airport," she said. "I think the cars might be there."

I don't know how she knew, but she was right: both cars were in the airport parking lot. Mom had been out of town till that morning, and before she returned, Ken had driven first one car and then the other to the airport. Then he boarded a plane to the mainland. He had run away.

Ken complained about the humid languor of island life. Every morning he got up and made his business calls to the mainland by seven because he wanted to keep his hand in. He still fancied himself a deal-maker and go-getter, and building a few houses on spec didn't cut it. To him, Hawaii wasn't the real world.

Mostly I think Ken had gotten tired. He'd weathered that awful year of abuse while I was in Nevada, clinging to the hope that if I came back Mom would cool down. Now he saw that she never would. And she was sleeping around.

Eric and I used spare keys to drive the cars back to the house. I told Mom she'd been right about Ken. She never flinched. There was work to do.

"Kent," she stated, "we need a new car." It was pure reflex. If she was a single mother again, she would have to grift. She asked me what kind of car I wanted, as if she were ordering take-out food.

As a fifteen-year-old gearhead, I suggested the hottest ride of the mid-seventies, a tricked-out Pontiac Trans Am with an eagle decal on the hood. She dialed the dealer and put in her order, and I got excited. I had my head next to hers as she talked, babbling into her ear about all the extras we needed. "Does it have a rear window defogger?" I blurted. I could hear the salesman on the other end snort. "This is Hawaii," he said. "Why do you need a rear window defogger?"

Then I reconsidered. "Since you're going to be driving it," I told Mom, "maybe we should get something bigger and more comfortable, like a Lincoln."

She glowed. "That is so considerate of you. And very mature."

Within an hour, a Bill Sachs Diamond Jubilee Lincoln Mark V appeared in our driveway, thanks to Mom's bullshit about the Ambassador and how she had to have the car ASAP, thank you. I put on a tie, and when the salesman arrived, I made him a drink. Ken had been gone less than a day, but our mother-and-son teamwork was as smooth as ever. The drinks and the chatter flowed, the salesman got wobbly, Mom promised to drop off the paperwork the next day, and before long we had the car keys without signing a thing.

In the morning, Mom issued instructions. "Drive the car to school," she said. "After school, hide it." Unsure of what would happen next, believing that Ken would never come back (ditching Mom seemed perfectly sensible to me, even overdue), worried that Mom and I would be penniless again, I obeyed. That afternoon I stashed the hot car in the Coco Marina shopping center parking lot, within walking distance of our house.

Mom flew to L.A. the next day. When the cops came to the house and asked me to produce the Lincoln, I said I didn't know where it was.

Meanwhile Mom had found Ken—within twenty-four hours of her arrival in California. Breaking his resolve was a breeze for her. He'd lasted three days without her, and within minutes of returning to Portlock Road they were locked in an embrace in the living room. His escape had failed, though he did convince Mom to return the Lincoln.

I think he came back because he adored Mom—and he had nowhere else to go. A half-dozen years with Sante had stripped his life clean of anyone else who might give a damn about him. He'd alienated his relatives, and his only friends were those Mom had chosen on the basis of usefulness. Ken's return symbolized his acceptance of the rules—Mom's rules. It was a capitulation as much as a reconciliation, and Mom knew it.

Two months after Ken's return, on April 17, Mom called me into her room after school. "Honey, we're going out of town," she said. *We* meant everybody but me, including three-year-old Kenny. "Why don't you stay at a friend's tonight?"

It seemed like an odd request. I lived alone anyway, tethered to the rest of the family only by a walkway and a few shared meals. But I arranged to bunk down at my friend Eric's house. Mom, Ken, Kenny, and the maid caught a prop plane to Maui.

At school the next morning, the headmaster intercepted me as soon as I arrived, and pulled me into his office. "Kent," he began, with concern in his face, "I'm sorry to tell you this, but your house caught on fire last night."

My reaction became the talk of the school that day: I said, "Oh wow." I was expected to freak out; I didn't. I was already doing the math in my head. To myself I thought, *Here we go again.*

I left school, went to the Portlock house, and got the story out of the firemen who were tromping around. As usual, the job was botched. The blaze had started in the bedroom in four separate hot spots. Accidental fires usually have a single point of origin. Hose companies had arrived soon after the first alarm at

1 A.M., and most of the house was unscathed. The firemen were still on site because they were investigating an obvious arson.

My cottage hadn't even gotten warm. I was there that morning, waiting, when my phone rang.

As soon as I heard Mom's hello, I said, "You did it again." Mom, standing at an airport pay phone, pretended not to understand me. She asked, "What are you doing there?" She was fresh off a return flight from Maui, blissfully ignorant. That was her story and she was sticking to it.

"You know exactly what I'm doing here."

"I don't know," she insisted.

"You do too," I said, disgusted, and then asked her a trick question. "Where are we staying tonight?"

"The Ilikai."

I had beaten her. If she didn't know her house had burned and she didn't know why I was home from school so early, why had she already picked out a hotel for the evening? I laughed, and she smacked down the receiver.

I picked them up at the airport. Ken sat next to me in the passenger seat, Mom and the maid with Kenny in the back. As we pulled away from the terminal, I gave them the "news." To my surprise, it really was news to Ken. He was stunned. Mom merely pretended to be stunned.

I looked at her in the rearview mirror and then glanced quickly over my shoulder. "Why are you acting all shocked?" I demanded, with full-on teen snottiness. She punched me in the back of the head again and again as I drove, till Ken stopped her.

Ken probably understood what had transpired as soon as he heard there'd been a fire. But when he got to the house and saw the sloppy evidence, he said it aloud. "We didn't need this," he muttered. Ken had lost irreplaceable boxes of photos and war mementos in the blaze.

But he bit his tongue and went along with everything. When Mom blamed the fire on the Creeps and their desire to kill Kenny, my stepdad didn't say, "Bullshit." When the insurance company paid for the damage despite the obvious arson, Ken convinced himself that the fire had been a blessing. The man loved money.

Mom got her rehab job, free of charge. The insurance windfall allowed the house to be rebuilt, bigger and better than ever, while we waited out the construction in a rental. When the insurers had chafed at meeting the full $125,000 claim—almost as much as Ken had originally paid for the house—Mom harangued company executives. She accosted one man in his Honolulu office upon his return from a funeral. She flew to New York, took a limo from the airport to New Jersey, and knocked on the front door of another executive's suburban home—on a Sunday night, no less. She got the claim paid, in full.

Construction on the Portlock house was completed before school started, and when we moved back in, I saw how hard Mom had been working. I stopped counting the fur coats when the number hit twenty-two. They filled the master bedroom closet, and Mom stuffed the rest in a coffin-sized space under the floor of the closet, concealed by a trap-door. All the linings had been ripped out. She must have stolen them from someplace cold, probably Washington in the winter, and brought them to this tropical city, where they were useless. She wasn't selling them, and she couldn't wear them. She was hoarding them. This wasn't crime; it was pathology.

I keep thinking of Ken and myself in the wake of the Portlock fire as frogs. If you put a frog in a pan of room-temperature water, he'll just sit there. Place the pot on the stove and turn on the burner and the frog still won't move. The water will slowly get hotter, but the frog won't feel the temperature rising. His body will keep adjusting to the heat till the poor dumb creature is thoroughly cooked.

But Ken and I, back in those days, were even stupider than frogs. We'd both jumped out of a simmering pot—me for a whole year—and then climbed right back in. And now we were staying put, and the water had started to boil.

13

THE SNITCH

The first time you eat out of a garbage can is the hardest. You're standing at the Dumpster looking down at a mound of slimy plastic bags and half-gnawed food, and you have to steel yourself to stick your hands right in it. It takes another act of will to put whatever you find into your mouth.

The second time is easier, which allows the shift from disgust to fear and shame. *Someone you know might see you.*

That's what I was thinking a few weeks before Christmas 1978, as I dug through the trash in the alley behind a seafood place on Waikiki called the Chart House. No one from school or the neighborhood had spied me the night before, and I hoped my good fortune would hold.

"Hey!" yelled a gruff male voice. Behind me a dark silhouette was outlined in a yellow square of light, the open back door of the Chart House. "What're you doing, buddy?" The voice came closer and I tensed, ready to run, but then I could see the man who was talking and he could see me. I was a well-dressed *haole* teen, and he was the middle-aged *haole* manager of the restaurant. "What are you doing?" he asked again, now softly, and with concern.

"I'm homeless," I said, and then I explained.

Forty-eight hours before, in the early evening, I had come home from an afternoon of working on the boats to a swirl of activity. Mom and Ken were rushing in and out of the house, dumping fur coats into the trunk of their gray Eldorado.

"Can you give us a hand here?" asked Ken, with a tight smile.

I followed him into the master bedroom and saw that he'd barely dented Mom's stash of purloined furs. There were dozens more, shoved into corners and hanging in the closet and crammed into the secret compartment. I grabbed an armload and took it to the car.

When the trunk was full, Mom and Ken piled the coats into the backseat. Next came boxes of legal documents. Once the closet had been emptied, Mom led Kenny out of the house and jumped into the passenger seat, plopping Kenny on her lap. Ken handed me five one-hundred-dollar bills.

"What's going on?" I demanded, without expecting a straight answer.

I didn't get one. "You're on your own," Ken said. "If I were you, I wouldn't be caught near here." With no further explanation, the Caddy peeled away from the Portlock house.

I ate a steak dinner at a fancy place called Chuck's. The waiter didn't hesitate to serve me when I ordered one cocktail after another. The drinking age was eighteen in Hawaii in those days and I looked it. I tipped 20 percent, about four times Ken's average.

I was toasting the fact that Mom and Ken were thirty thousand feet above the Pacific and farther from me with every second. I didn't think their exodus was anything serious. It was far too soon for another fire, so my parents were probably dodging the cops over some misdemeanor. When they returned in a week or two, Mom would blame their flight on some plot by the Creeps to kill her and her baby son, and things would return to normal. Meanwhile I welcomed the break from their bickering. I continued the celebration by going back to the house and crashing in the master bedroom.

Between 2 and 3 A.M., a noise woke me. I sat up in the huge bed. I heard the clanking of the heavy chain that my paranoid parents kept padlocked across the front gate. Hunched over, I crept to the front window. In the moonlight I could see cops with flashlights. One had his gun drawn, another had a German shepherd. They'd cut the padlock and were coming in.

I threw on shorts and flip-flops and ran from one window to the next. There were two more cops at the back of the house and two at the side. I could hear them jimmying the sliding glass door with a crowbar. I was trapped.

With the right training, in a crisis situation your instincts take over. Mom had prepped me well for this sort of crisis. I could hear the heavy breath of the dog and the jangling of his handler's belt; they were inside, headed in my direction. I scrambled to the trapdoor in the closet, pulled back the plush gray carpeting, said, "Please God," and yanked open the secret compartment. With the furs gone, it was empty. I grabbed a bottle of Mom's gardenia-scented perfume off her bureau and sprinkled it on the patch of carpet above the opening, thinking it might stymie the dog. Then I crept inside and pulled the door shut.

I don't know if the cops ever came near my hideout. Squeezed into the coffin with my knees bent, I couldn't hear or see anything. I fought the panic of claustrophobia as the minutes and hours dragged by, and the anxious waiting for the dog to bark and for the door to be yanked open. At some point I fell asleep.

When I woke up, I had a cramp in my thigh and knew I couldn't stand the hot black confines another second. I pushed up the lid and climbed out. Day had dawned, and I was alone in the house. As I padded from room to room, I saw that apart from the snipped lock and the busted door, very little was disturbed. The police hadn't been searching for evidence. They'd come to make an arrest, and had failed.

I got dressed and went to school as if nothing had happened. Hiding the facts of my life and my parents' behavior had become habit by then. My friends knew a little of the truth about my parents, but this was way too much to share.

Belatedly I took Ken's advice and stayed away from the Portlock house. But I had nowhere else to go, and after my smug steak dinner, the remainder of Ken's cash must have fallen out of my pocket. I was broke.

Most afternoons I went straight from Mid-Pac to the marinas in Waikiki. I picked up jobs working on the expensive cabin cruisers, some of them seventy feet long, that lined the wooden quays at the Hawaii and Waikiki Yacht Clubs. The day after the police raid I worked on the boats as usual and sneaked back into the Hawaii after dark; compared with the Waikiki, it had a feeble security system. I picked out a big sailboat that I knew never left the marina, crawled aboard, and made a bed in the sail compartment.

I lived like that for three weeks. It was easy to get back into the yacht club and easy to find a comfortable, rarely used sailboat, but it was hard to kill time. The sun set at six, and fear of discovery kept me from using the lights in the boats. If I felt really daring I might flick on a penlight and read a book, but the nights were long. Finding clean clothes and food was another problem. I slipped back into the Portlock house for about forty-five seconds to grab some fresh shirts and underwear. While the fall term lasted, I ate multiple lunches at school.

The man who nabbed me in the alley of the Chart House was the restaurant's manager, Jack. He took pity on me and gave me food. He paid me to work as a boathand on weekend and dinner cruises in Honolulu Harbor, and as my earnings from day jobs at the marina and on Jack's cruises accumulated, I had cash for meals and movies. I'd wait out the long nights in dark theaters. In a few weeks I had nearly a thousand dollars.

But sleeping on top of sails got old, and even in my unique life, it was a uniquely depressing experience to spend Christmas wandering downtown Honolulu alone and hunkering down for the night on an empty boat, afraid to make a sound.

During the week between Christmas and New Year's, I headed back toward Portlock, tired of my routine. I was also curious. No one had stopped me during my last hurried visit; I doubted there'd be any cops around. And I was badly in need of a shower and a real bed.

At the house, the lights were on and both cars were in the driveway. "Look who's here!" blared Ken, grinning, as I opened the sliding glass door. He and Mom acted as if we'd all been on a great adventure somewhere. "We've been back for four days," laughed Mom. "Where've you been?"

"None of your business," I snarled. I didn't think it was very funny. "What did you expect me to do for a month?"

"We thought you'd go live with your dad," pouted Mom defensively.

I got even angrier. "I'll tell you where I've been," I said. "I've been at the Honolulu Police Department. I gave them every address, every alias, and every phone number you've ever used. They'll be here in twenty minutes."

After half a second, they realized I was kidding. I continued yelling until they made a few guilty noises, but I knew they'd never apologize. I'm not sure they even understood what they'd be apologizing for. Resigned, I retreated to my cottage.

They did understand I was pissed, and the cop threat worried them. They tried to appease me. During the spring semester of 1979, I was once again Prince Kent, and the Queen

Mother became my pimp. She and I colluded on a sexual scam that makes me squirm a little as I remember it, though while it was going on I didn't mind one bit.

I had a girlfriend named Rhonda Blaine, a fellow Mid-Pac student from a straitlaced Christian family. Our relationship didn't survive high school, but at the time I was as serious about her as a horny, short-sighted sixteen-year-old could be. She lived clear across the island, and driving her home ate up lots of our makeout time.

Rhonda may have been a Christian, but she wasn't a virgin. I asked Mom to call her parents and suggest that Rhonda sleep over at our house after dates. Mom would chaperone, and Rhonda would stay in the guest cottage. Amazingly, Rhonda's parents agreed. It was all true, technically. The guest cottage, of course, just happened to be my room, and the "chaperone" was committed to her self-assigned role of getting me laid.

There were perks to life with Mom and Ken. But during that spring of 1979 I began to feel disgusted with them. They lived the way they thought rich people were supposed to live, but to me it looked empty. They drove big cars, ate heavy meals, and drank every day. They had plastic surgery and dyed their hair as alcohol rotted their guts. Between them they had one hobby—making money.

I'm a hypocrite to complain about it, since I enjoyed the good life as much as they did, but unlike them, I often felt remorse. I felt guilty for conning the Blaines. I was mad at myself for ditching Dad in Nevada and for helping Mom to grift a car. I was mad at Mom for setting the fire. Neighbors had rushed into the house while it burned, risking their lives to make sure we weren't inside. And I felt shame for the rush I got from the roller-coaster excitement of our chaotic lives.

I collaborated in it, but I began to try to compensate in small ways. When Mom and I went "shopping," I'd retrieve the stolen items she'd stuffed into her cavernous vinyl purse and slap them back on the shelves. I treated it like a game, to avoid triggering her rage, but soon I was no longer invited on many "shopping" expeditions.

Mom's treatment of the maids had also started to bother me. It had never been great, but now things were getting worse. In California we'd had one maid at a time; in Hawaii, it became two, and Mom somehow kept them both busy from dawn to midnight. She yelled at them constantly. She ordered them to stay in their rooms and not talk to each other. She wrote these and other rules on lists full of capital letters and exclamation points. The general drift was to prevent them from having contact with the outside world. There were locks on the phones and locks on the inside of the doors. It was getting ugly.

My response was, typically, milder than it should have been. On four different occasions during 1978 and 1979, I drove one or two servants to the Honolulu airport and put them on flights to L.A., stealing the plane fare from Ken's pocket. I told him that he and Mom were in danger of being sued, but he just shook his head. Mom, for her part, taunted me as a "goody-goody," "the Saint," and "the Saintly One" when I unstole the things she'd slipped into her purse. In her book, to be good was to be a sucker.

Mom and Ken couldn't last in Hawaii. They ruined the place for themselves the same way they'd ruined Newport. Contractors who rebuilt the Portlock house hadn't been paid, and summonses began to arrive. Mom and Ken were still dodging other criminal cases, including the piano heist. Needless to say, they'd stopped answering the door.

One afternoon Mom came into the living room and wailed, "Let's go!" She was certain her enemies were outside in the street poised to pounce. She didn't specify which enemies, or I don't remember—the cops, the Creeps, you name it.

Her fear infected Ken. He followed her outside, as I trailed behind to see what Mom planned to do. She scampered toward the eight-foot wall on the east end of the property, stepped on a planter, and tried to launch herself over the wall.

My mother has battled a weight problem her entire life. She used to "diet" in restaurants by sharing meals with Ken, but when she got home she'd eat a bowl of buttered mashed potatoes. She never understood why the diet never worked. She was a roly-poly five-foot-five with big fake tits and a rubber gut.

Ken and I watched as Mom got stuck. She was too fat to pull her legs over the wall and too scared to jump back down into our yard. She began to totter back and forth, squealing with distress, her feet pointed toward us, her boobs and her head hanging in the alley. She rocked to and fro like a beach ball with legs, whimpering, "Help me! Help me!"

We tried to smother giggles. "Well, Kent, help her!" Ken finally ordered, as sternly as he could manage. "Either push her over or pull her back down!" I let her seesaw for a few seconds more, squelching the urge to push her, then gripped her ankles and helped her return to earth.

In April 1979 they bolted at last, in flight from real or imagined pursuers, taking Kenny and the two maids with them. I stayed behind in the cottage, while Sheila and George, a cosmetics counter clerk and her son, came to house-sit at Mom's request. I recognized what was happening. Mom and Ken were closing up shop in Hawaii.

Soon I heard from Mom. She asked me to come visit them in their new base of operations, Las Vegas, and sent me a ticket. She'd wrangled a complimentary penthouse suite at the Las Vegas Hilton, and for a week I lived with my parents and my little brother in a plush air-conditioned womb. Ken handed me five hundred dollars in chips and invited me to gamble it away. They didn't want me to go back to Hawaii. They didn't live there anymore.

But *I* did. I'd made good friends there, Eric and my best buddy, John, and several others. I had a sweetheart, Rhonda. After years of bouncing from town to town on the mainland and developing into a wary, rootless loner, I'd spent two years in one place, at one school, and I'd come out of that shell. I raised my hand and talked in class, maybe too much. I was popular and I was happy. I wanted to return to Mid-Pac for my senior year.

Mom took my decision badly enough to retaliate. While I pleaded with her to stop, she called up my girlfriend Rhonda's parents from our Hilton suite and told them the truth about what had really been going on in the Portlock guest cottage for the past year. "I'm sorry, Mrs. Blaine," lied Mom, "I had no idea what Kent and Rhonda were doing. Kent has betrayed my trust. I don't think it would be a good idea for our children to see each other anymore."

Her ploy was obvious. She was trying to destroy my world so I'd have nothing to return to in Hawaii. But it backfired. A week later I was back in Honolulu, determined to stay away from Mom and Ken. I returned home to Sheila and George, who pestered me about why the cops kept ringing the doorbell. I told them to forget about it, and I warned them not to put any faith in Mom's assurances that their tenancy would last three years: they were liable to be out on the street long before that, without notice.

Right before the end of junior year, I ran for student body

president, mostly to annoy another kid who wanted the office. My crowd was more likely to be found at the beach than home studying or going out for school activities. I was a C student and a half-assed jock who'd quit the football team. Somehow, though, I won 80 percent of the vote in a three-person race. For a perpetual outsider, a kid who'd been banished from the homes of classmates in Palm Springs and Newport Beach, it was an awesome validation.

When Mom and Ken returned temporarily, soon after my victory, they were less than impressed. They collected their things and told Sheila and George to get lost. I still refused to join them in Las Vegas, so they threw me out as well. As the school year ended, I was once again homeless.

Though Rhonda and I had deceived them, Rhonda's parents took me in. When I returned from Vegas, I'd apologized to them for the sleepover scam, and they'd forgiven me. I'd started to confide in them about my parents, and between that and their own nascent suspicions about Mom, they got very worried. They learned so much about Mom, in fact, that they lobbied me to do something I'd been thinking about since before the fire. To protect myself—legally, from police charges, and physically, from my own parents, because I knew too much—the Blaines said I needed to walk into the Honolulu Police Department and start talking.

Snitching went against everything I'd ever been taught, which included a deep fear and mistrust of law enforcement. But keeping so many secrets had exhausted me, and Rhonda's parents argued convincingly. On a Saturday morning, I let Mrs. Blaine drive me to police headquarters on South Beretania.

She preferred to wait in her big yellow van in the parking lot while I went in; she admitted that she was afraid to accompany me. I walked up the worn concrete steps and entered the boxy beige police building alone.

Inside was a kind of receiving desk, a low circle of varnished wood. It looked like a place you'd stop to get a tourist brochure, not to report a crime spree. Sitting there was a civilian with her hair pulled back in a bun. She glanced at me quickly and returned to her work. I leaned forward. "Excuse me," I began, as calmly as I could. Bun-head swiveled toward me. "My name is Kent Walker. You might be interested in what I have to say."

She waved toward a row of plastic chairs and told me to

have a seat. There were a few other people in the room. None looked happy. I waited. A half hour went by and no one came to get me. I'm not sure what I'd expected, but indifference wasn't it. I sat and brooded and tortured myself with guilt and fantasies of what Mom would do if she saw me there. I became agitated and fearful. I got up and paced around the room. Sleeping on boats hadn't been so bad, I thought. I could walk out that door and go down to the marina. But Rhonda's mother was waiting in the parking lot. I couldn't just disappear.

While I fretted, the choice became moot. A cop marched over and said, "Come with me." As he led me down into the windowless basement with his hand placed firmly on my back, I realized he was the same man who'd punched me in the stomach three months before, when he caught me driving one of Mom's hot cars. She'd forged a promissory note from her quasi-employer, Dr. Caruso, and that plus a thousand bucks had separated a Southern California Cadillac dealer from a top-of-the-line eighteen-thousand-dollar Biarritz. Mom had shipped the sedan to Hawaii, and I'd had the misfortune to be behind the wheel when HPD, in the person of this same cop, had come after it. Before he pushed me over the hood and cuffed me, the guy had taken a cheap shot.

Now he deposited me in a cinderblock-walled interrogation room lit by long fluorescent bulbs. A detective was already there, smirking. "We've been looking for you, Kent," he said. His name was Earl Hoke. A typically Hawaiian mélange of genes had given him the thin face of a Japanese and the height and bulk of a Polynesian. I don't know who was to blame for his personality. As Sante Kimes's son, I quickly IDed him as a hard-on.

"What do you mean, you've been looking for me?" I countered, regaining my snotty sixteen-year-old attitude. "If you need to find me, I'm at Mid-Pac high school every day."

Hoke ignored me and plopped an enormous manila folder on the table between us. He didn't say anything. He took a stack of photos from the folder and arrayed them before me in a row: the front and back entrances of the Portlock house; Ken and Mom in a car, backing out of the driveway; me.

"We've been investigating this family," said Hoke. "We think you have some information." Hoke, it turned out, was an arson investigator.

He'd succeeded in intimidating me, as he'd planned, but

fear gave me the itch to run. "I don't want to be here," I said, with as much bravado as I could muster, and rose to leave. They shoved me back down in the chair, one cop at either arm.

"Are you questioning me?" I asked. "I'll walk out of here." I was sure I could leave because I'd come in voluntarily.

"You can't walk out," lied the cop who'd hit me. "You're a minor."

They did let me leave, but Hoke turned up at Rhonda's house that evening. He used his scare tactics on her parents, telling them that Mom might have a contract out on my life already, which confirmed their worst fears. It worked on me too. When Mrs. Blaine said I had to go with Hoke, I didn't protest.

Hoke told me I'd be unsafe at home, and he couldn't find me a hotel room, so I spent the night in the Mid-Pac dorms. It was an unofficial, illegal form of protective custody, no protection at all if Mom had really meant harm. All the Mid-Pac staff could provide on short notice was a cot in a converted broom closet with a tiny window that was sealed shut. Here I was on a thin bed in a locked room, not guilty yet in jail, so tense I didn't sleep all night, while Mom and Ken were playing craps and drinking complimentary cocktails at a casino in Vegas.

The next morning was Sunday. Hoke picked me up and took me to a restaurant in Kohala, across from the mall. "I want you to meet some of my friends," he said. He was acting nice, but it was too late.

I guess that after a couple of years on the job, cops associate only with other cops. Every guy at our big table was a cop: they met for breakfast on their days off. But while the other guys seemed sympathetic to a scared kid who was wrestling with the idea of snitching, Hoke was a jerk. He joked with his buddies about my dysfunctional family and my mom's rap sheet till I'd had enough. I mouthed off at him. He returned the favor.

"I've dealt with worse criminals than you," he sneered.

"I'm sick of this," I said. "This time I'm really leaving."

"Before you get up," he warned, "take a look under the table."

He had his revolver between his legs, pointed at my guts, here in this sedate suburban restaurant. As his fellow cops, no longer my cool compadres, snickered, I thought, *What an asshole. What a stupid stunt. It's something a teenager would do.*

But I *was* a stupid teenager. I jumped from my chair and ran out of the restaurant and down the sidewalk, heading toward a nearby drive-in theater to hide. The older, heavier cops couldn't run as fast as a boy whose lungs had been conditioned by wind sprints on the football field. *This is why cops shoot people in the back,* I thought. *They can't keep up.*

Then Hoke, in his car, cut in front of me, and a pair of wheezing cops appeared behind me. I stopped. They pushed me into the backseat of Hoke's cruiser.

"I was just showing off," said Hoke. That was all the explanation I ever got for the business with the gun.

Hoke and another officer drove me around all that day. He kept insisting that I had to stay in protective custody because Mom wanted me dead. Much as I hated Hoke, he wore me out. At 11 P.M. he booked me a room at a Waikiki hotel called the Pagoda. "Don't bolt," he said. "I trust you now."

At police headquarters, starting at 7 A.M. Monday morning, I talked for two and a half days straight. I told a room full of cops, including someone who said he was from the FBI, about every questionable act my mother and stepfather had ever committed. I'd go back to the Pagoda to sleep, and the next morning I'd pick up where I'd left off. It was exhausting and exhilarating. I'd had no idea how good it would feel to let it all go. It was like a marathon session with a squadron of shrinks.

I was shocked by how much they already knew. They were aware of the furs, the cars, the pianos, the "shopping" trips, the lobbying scandal. They listed arson jobs that Mom pulled off in L.A. when I was a baby, blazes I couldn't remember. Somehow they'd learned about one I thought was a secret. "Weren't you in close proximity to a certain fire?" hinted the FBI agent. He meant the explosion in Newport that sent me flying.

They seemed most interested in the Portlock arson of the year before. I got the impression that someone wanted to build a case against Mom for insurance fraud. They were fully versed in her outlandish claims and threatening visits to the offices of firms that didn't want to pay. "She took a shack and turned it into a fucking palace," said Hoke admiringly. It was true: insurance money had meant a serious upgrade of the Portlock property. We'd even added a pool.

I also told them things they didn't know. I described Mom's favorite travel game. Every time she passed through baggage claim at the Honolulu airport, she'd retrieve her own luggage from the carousel and then grab a few more bags for good measure. I also solved the mystery of a missing tapestry for which Mom expected an insurer to pay her a hundred thousand dollars. She'd stolen the gaudy rendering of an American eagle from a Nevada hotel and hung it on the Irvine office wall of Ambassador Kimes, the great patriot. Eventually she torched it in our Newport Beach fireplace and filed an insurance claim.

By Wednesday afternoon, the tag team of cops had squeezed me dry. They presented me with a typed statement an inch thick and made me read it twice. I signed. It was all true, and I was glad to be finished. "You know, Kent," said Hoke, "your mother and father will be going away for a long time because of what you did." He meant it as a compliment. He had a talent for saying the wrong thing.

And I wasn't finished. "We want you to wear a wire," Hoke said, and when I refused, he threatened me. He had seen how I reacted when he suggested we get in touch with Ed Walker in Carson City. I felt like I'd burned my father two years before, and I dreaded the idea of dragging him into this mess. In fact, I didn't want *anyone* to catch on to what I'd done till Mom and Ken had been arrested.

So Hoke, again, raised the issue of contacting Dad. He said it was an obligation, because I was a minor and Dad was my legal guardian. I agreed to the wire on two conditions: I'd be free as soon as the wire operation was concluded, and no one would bother Ed Walker.

Once Hoke signed the agreement, I let him drive me to Portlock. I got out of the car just down the street from the house. A black microphone was taped to my chest. There was little chance that Mom and Ken would be in town, but they'd suckered an acquaintance, Susan, into watching the property. Maybe she'd know where they were staying.

Susan, whom I'd met before, was there when I opened the sliding glass door. "Where've you been?" she said. "Everyone's worried." Either she didn't know or wouldn't divulge Mom and Ken's whereabouts, so I left.

The cops tried to get me to wear the wire again, and I refused. I had finished with them. I didn't go back to Rhonda's, since her parents were likely to deliver me to the police on demand. Instead I bunked with my friend Eric Price. His mother welcomed me as long as Sante didn't set foot on the property.

That first night at Eric's, I received a collect call from Ed

Walker. I promised Mrs. Price I'd reimburse her and accepted the charges.

"Hi, Dad," I gushed.

"Hi, honey," said my mother. She could always find me if she wanted. "We miss you. We need to get you out here."

"Well, where's here?" I demanded. I knew it wasn't Ed Walker's house in Carson City. Though in my mind I saw Mom huddled in a casino pay phone in Vegas, I kept after her to give me some clue to her whereabouts. She wouldn't bite. I got irritated and asked how I could join her if she wouldn't tell me where I was supposed to go.

"Get your ass back to your *dad* then," she spat. I hung up.

I did what she suggested. I caught the same red-eye from Honolulu to San Francisco to Reno as I had two years before. For a month I helped my dad with a construction job on an Indian reservation near Carson City. In July I flew back to Hawaii and moved in with my best friend, John Bower. His dad, a contractor with a goofy sense of humor, had just gotten divorced. It was an instant bachelor pad.

I lived there for the next sixteen months, paying my own two-thousand-dollar tuition by working three different after-school jobs. Mom and Ken might have been in Hawaii half of that time, for all I know. Mom did call Mr. Bower once—to complain about the low grades on my midterm senior-year report card. He replied, with admirable restraint, "If you don't like it, you can come back and take care of it yourself."

At no point did any law enforcement agency move to arrest or detain my parents for the crimes I had detailed in two and a half days of gut spilling. For months I thought their capture was imminent, but that wasn't my concern. I wondered what kind of relationship I'd have with them when they were in prison. I wondered if I'd be able to cope with the absolute and permanent absence of my mother's love. But when nothing happened, I got scared. I felt like a fool for trusting the police. Hoke and the others had persuaded me my life was in danger if I didn't talk, but now the opposite seemed to be true. I'd snitched, and I was unprotected. It was years before I could relax and believe Mom would never discover what I'd done. I don't think she ever did. If she's reading this now, it's probably news to her.

I wish I had a copy of the statement I signed or a video of my interrogation, some evidence that twenty-two years ago I handed the police every weapon I could think of to use against

Sante Kimes. I gave them everything and they . . . forgot? Took
a pass? Perhaps the questionable way the statement was
obtained made it useless, and it went into a file and never came
out again. Perhaps, even with my testimony, there still wasn't
enough evidence to proceed. Mom escaped prosecution more
than once for that reason. Regardless, I feel as if I'm saying I
overheard a room full of people plotting the Kennedy assassi-
nation. I can't prove I was ever in protective custody or uttered
a word to the Honolulu Police Department, much less an FBI
agent. If Detective Hoke were alive, maybe he'd confirm it, but
he died in 1990.

14

HIGH ROLLERS

F lying into Las Vegas at night you see an island of light in a sea of black. The island has sharp edges, because the city that was the nation's fastest growing in the nineties is spreading into the empty desert subdivision by instant subdivision. Stitched down the center of the pool of light is the famous Vegas Strip, an L-shaped seam of enormous multicolored landmarks. A giant black pyramid rises next to a replica of the Sphinx, down the street from a mock-up of Manhattan and a space needle and huge hotels glowing green and pink and blue.

None of it existed twenty years ago, when my parents moved there. Vegas then wasn't half the size it is now. It was still the town portrayed in the movie *Casino*, a mobbed-up resort with an old-fashioned Rat Pack sense of martini-glass glamour. It hadn't yet become a family playground of theme-park hotels where employees wander the casinos in togas and Star Trek outfits. But it was already a city of high-grade imitations, of celebrity impersonators. When my mother the Liz wannabe arrived in 1979, she'd found her spiritual home.

In those days Vegas attracted losers and high rollers, not the in-betweeners, the minivan jockeys, who dominate now. A high roller could flash a major wad in a casino and get a complimentary suite, free meals, limo service, the works. To be "comped" in Vegas was to be royalty. The casinos would treat you like a prince in the expectation that you'd lose a kingly sum on the tables.

The high rollers still come and still get comped. Before the age of computers, though, the casinos had a harder time keeping tabs on how much their supposed high rollers were really rolling. Now machines track the amount of money wagered by individual players. Someone who's not putting enough cash on the table will be booted out of the penthouse fast.

When Mom and Ken hit town, putting on a good show was enough to get comped. They'd create the impression that they were wagering many thousands of dollars, and the casinos would come through with the room, the steak and lobster, the tray of fresh drinks at the elbow. "Ambassador" Kimes and his entourage scored their free penthouse at the Las Vegas Hilton because Mrs. Kimes had called ahead to drop the names of dignitaries, and when Ken got there he had real money, opening an account worth a hundred thousand dollars. Down on the casino floor, however, he wouldn't bet more than twenty-five dollars on a hand of poker, and management soon realized he wasn't much of a high roller after all.

When the manager told my parents they'd have to leave, Mom fought back as if she were being evicted from the family farm, buying a few more days, until they finally got the boot. Within forty-five minutes, Mom had convinced somebody at the Landmark that the Ambassador had just landed in Vegas and would love to lose a fortune on the craps tables. Ken cashed out his Hilton account, and the show moved down the street.

In this manner Mom and Ken lived in Las Vegas for half a year without paying for food or lodging. They preyed on the second-tier casinos, bouncing from the Hilton to the Landmark to the Tropicana to the Frontier and a few others. Mom would call Hawaii sometimes from a pay phone, and I would hear the sound of a thousand ringing slot machines in the background.

Early in Mom and Ken's casino-hopping period, members of the Honolulu Police Department came to the Portlock house door and asked, "Where are your parents?"

I was truthful. "They're in Las Vegas."

"What's their address?"

"I have absolutely no idea." Again the truth.

Eventually high-stakes drifting got old for Mom and Ken. They decided to settle down in Vegas and went house hunting. For my parents, this didn't mean finding a good real estate agent and discussing school districts.

Being a con artist takes research and stamina. You need a plan, and you have to be willing to stick to the plan. Mom had a method for snagging expensive properties at far under market value, and she used it to get the house at 2121 Geronimo Way that became her principal residence for two decades.

First the romance. Mom met a strange old man with a crystal-topped walking stick named Dr. Zellhoefer. She wanted his four-thousand-square-foot house next to the Sahara golf course. She let Zellhoefer borrow the Portlock house free of charge and bought him dinners and drinks.

Then the seduction. Mom made a verbal commitment to Zellhoefer to buy the Geronimo house. She suggested that the Kimes family move in and pay rent while the details of the deal were finalized.

Finally the kill. Before and during her dance with Zellhoefer, Mom had cultivated various officials and building inspectors and done research on the house. She learned which property improvements had been legal and which were not. She found some minor discrepancies and flaws in the house and began to threaten Zellhoefer with lawsuits. Beaten down, unable to back out of the deal without launching eviction proceedings, he agreed to lower the price so that she'd leave him alone. Mom had her house at the price she wanted.

Mom lived at 2121 Geronimo Way far longer than any other place. I think it suited her because it was designed by a fellow paranoid. No car could sneak up on the two-story mega-ranch; it sat at the end of a cul-de-sac, backed by a chain-link fence and a golf course. The long tan brick-and-siding front had no windows, except for a narrow gun slit of an opening on the first floor above the kitchen counter. Inside, Mom had so much space she dubbed the two ends of the house the West and East Wings, à la the White House. She and Ken had a whole suite of red-carpeted rooms to themselves, with a walk-in closet big enough for a double bed.

In that house, behind the fortresslike wall, Mom created her own world. Kenny was about to turn five, and Mom began hiring naive young women straight out of college to be his tutors. She sold them with tales of travel and glamour and then did the usual—stole their passports and driver's licenses and never paid them. Until they ran away, which every one eventually did, they were hostages.

The maids, who had come in pairs since Hawaii, were given a new assignment: sewing. Though Mom was way ahead of her time in wearing lingerie outside her clothing, most of her signature garments—the white lace and organza and turbans and bustiers—had become hard to find in stores by 1980. They were out of style. Rather than update her look, Mom changed her means of achieving it. She began stealing fabric instead of clothes and turned the maids into seamstresses. In Vegas, where there was no such thing as tacky, her weird movie-star-from-the-sixties getup didn't seem so strange.

Life would have been good for her except for those pesky process servers and cops. She'd escaped the mounting scrutiny of the Honolulu Police Department, but for Sante any fixed address meant stress, and not because of danger from the Creeps, as she claimed. Mom bragged about her jet-setting lifestyle, yet she really didn't have a choice. Staying in any one place for more than a month at a time meant the risk of visits from the authorities. She scammed all of her first-class tickets, buying coach seats for her growing entourage months in advance and then sweet-talking some airline employee she'd discovered into giving her and Ken upgrades. Still, constant motion—permanent fugitive status, really—cost Ken Kimes twenty thousand dollars a month in American Express bills.

My parents' sojourns had a pattern. They flew from Hawaii to Las Vegas and back again, with many side trips to Orange County and Ken's flagship motel, the Mecca. But much of their time was spent in cross-country jaunts to a city that exerted some pull on my mother, Washington, D.C. The capital had been the scene of her greatest embarrassment, the party-crashing binge of 1974, but Mom shrugged it off. Ken was still the Ambassador, and Mom was still a lobbyist.

The only lobbying she did, however, was hanging around in hotel lobbies so she could steal fur coats. While I was living with John Bower and his dad in Hawaii, Mom and Ken prowled the tony gathering spots of D.C. and New York as charming, well-dressed, well-spoken fur thieves.

On February 4, 1980, the lobbyist and the Ambassador were holed up at the Mayflower Hotel with Kenny, a maid, a tutor, and a person my parents later told the *Washington Post* was their English butler. That night the outside temperature never got above twenty, so Mom had an excuse to wear an ankle-length white fox fur when she and Ken hit the Town and Country bar on the ground floor of the hotel.

Conventional wisdom would say that the successful criminal is an inconspicuous criminal. Mom, of course, preferred the brazen frontal assault in full regalia. She strode up to the hotel coat-check window and flashed a smile. "Could I have my coat, honey?" she asked. She was still wearing her own fur and hadn't checked anything, and when the hotel employees, and then the manager, couldn't find her imaginary garment, she staged a scene. She screamed and cried until heavy black mascara poured down her cheeks. "Did you see how I was treated?" she wailed, collaring passersby. "Did you see how I was just treated?" I'm sure she looked like one of those women in *Valley of the Dolls,* a nouveau riche Bel Air matron having some kind of pill-induced nervous breakdown. With everybody in the lobby staring at her, she then rejoined my stepdad in the bar.

A Connecticut couple entered the Town and Country and sat down. Robert and Katherine Ann Kenworthy put on industrial trade shows for a living. In Washington to produce a mass transit show at another hotel, they'd bought dinner for their employees and then brought them to the Mayflower bar for a round of drinks. They piled their coats on an extra chair at their table. Later estimates of the value of Mrs. Kenworthy's brown mink ranged up to ten thousand dollars.

My parents drifted from their stools at the bar to sit at a table near the Kenworthys. Ken traded chitchat with Robert. He apparently mentioned Nixon; I'm sure it was some kind of quick sideways segue from small talk to Ken's reminiscences of his close personal friend Dick. He had, after all, met Pat, and Mom had glommed onto both Nixon and Agnew on a Palm Springs golf course.

Everybody returned to their drinks. As the Kenworthys resumed talking to their guests, Mom slipped off her white fox wrap. She snaked a hand back toward the brown mink at the next table and tugged. She pulled the coat toward her and, without rising from her chair, donned first the brown mink and then the white fox to hide it. Theft complete, she and Ken made a beeline to the elevators and took the coat to their seventh-floor suite.

Maybe in Vegas people don't stare at women dressed all in white with big black wigs, painted faces, and fake rings the size of walnuts, but in a Washington bar, Mom couldn't escape notice. She invited it. Two patrons at a nearby table, Charles Crane and Rena Cusma, both in town on business from the West Coast, had been gaping at Mom's getup and snickering when they saw her swipe the fur.

But the pair were so taken aback by what they'd seen that they convinced themselves they were hallucinating. Then the Kenworthys got up to leave at closing time, and Mrs. Kenworthy couldn't locate her coat. She burst into tears, and two cops, already in the bar because of an earlier incident, came by to investigate. Cusma spoke up. "It was a large woman in a white coat that looked like a bad Elizabeth Taylor."

After the theft, Mom and Ken, cold and professional, had come back down to the bar and made a bit more small talk with the Kenworthys. Reassured that they were safe from suspicion, they'd retired to their room for good. At least three patrons had seen the theft, however, and Mom and Ken's curtain call gave them a second look.

At 2:00 A.M., Mom heard a knock and then "Police, open up." Mom would claim later that she was naked and that ten strange men burst into the room and manhandled her. In fact, she cracked the door, acting drunk and wearing a negligee, and pretended not to understand what the four men on the other side of the door chain wanted. Ken invited them inside, saying, "We have nothing to hide."

Three D.C. cops and a hotel detective searched the suite. Though they found Mom's white pelt and a short gray mink, both sans lining, and they turned up a man's wool herringbone topcoat, Katherine Kenworthy's fur was not in any of the rooms.

But on a freezing night, a window had been left ajar. Guessing what had happened, one of the cops peered out of the window and spied the crumpled lining of a fur coat on the lobby roof five stories below. When he retrieved it, he read the telltale monogram: KK, which did not stand for Ken Kimes.

My parents left the Mayflower in handcuffs and spent the rest of the morning and the next afternoon in the city lockup. Mom, forty-six, insisted she was a thirty-four-year-old who spelled her name Shanté. Ken tried to talk his way out of jail by protesting that he and the little woman were missing a meeting with President Carter. In fact, they *were* due at the White House—they had tickets for a generic tour.

Mom and Ken appeared before a judge so bail could be set. The Englishman who'd been staying with them at the Mayflower stepped forward to vouch for Ken, saying that Ken was worth twelve million dollars and wouldn't be a flight risk.

The judge set bail at four thousand dollars, and Mom and Ken were free.

Never did my parents have any employee who could be described as an English butler. In those days they preferred their help Spanish-speaking, brown-skinned, and terrified. The man who spoke on Ken's behalf was an old friend of my mother's, Jeff David, a kind, honest British transplant who'd never stolen a fur or lied to a judge in his life. That day, thanks to much arm-twisting from Sante and misplaced loyalty to my family, he compromised himself.

My parents faced two counts of theft. In addition to the Kenworthy mink, which by then had been found behind a hotel ice machine, they were charged with stealing the wool coat found in their room from a different hotel bar a night earlier. Lest anyone think that Ken Kimes merely winked at Mom's exploits or got a voyeuristic thrill from watching her work, it was my stepfather the millionaire who snatched the wool coat, worth at most a few hundred bucks.

Mom did an interview with the *Post* upon her release, hoping to get her version of the truth on the record. "It's an outrage," she fumed. "To *think* that *I* would need to steal someone's fur!" The reporters typed up Mom's remarks and then appended a rehashing of the Ambassador Kimes party-crashing binge of 1974. Mom had exposed herself to ridicule again, yet she remained oblivious.

While the reporters were laughing at my mother, they couldn't have guessed that Mom and Ken would have the last laugh. During the next five years, they waged a fairly successful campaign of attrition against the D.C. courts.

My parents picked up the pace of their already hectic travels, spending more and more time in Mexico. The D.C. prosecutor couldn't hit a moving target. Mom and Ken hired and fired twenty different defense lawyers. Every time they changed counsel, they earned a delay from the courts. After two years, they saw the first dividend of their stalling tactics. The charge against Ken for the topcoat theft was dropped when the owner of the jacket died.

Most of these attorneys, during their short tenures with my parents, forwarded to the court seemingly legitimate letters from doctors stating that Mom and Ken were too sick to endure a trial. As my parents, supposedly too sick to *travel* as well, ran from city to city, they always seemed to chance on doctors ready to certify their poor health. One swore that Ken suffered from high blood pressure, "peripheral vascular insufficiency, and cerebrovascular insufficiency with transient ischemic attacks." In other words, his brain didn't get enough blood, and he had weathered many tiny strokes.

My mother, in turn, was due to have a tumor removed any minute and, according to a letter from an M.D. in Mexico, was subject to "abdominal distention," pancreatitis, cysts, tumors, and "generalized edema." There was a grain of truth there. My mother had bad gas, and she used to swell up a lot.

One afternoon in the early eighties, my mother dropped by to see Ken's bookkeeper in her offices on Decatur Avenue in Las Vegas. Chirpy and upbeat as always, Mom soon busied herself at one of the office typewriters. When she stepped away for a minute, the bookkeeper stole a glance at the paper in the typewriter. On a doctor's letterhead, Sante was typing up an affadavit certifying that she was too sick to make it to court. The note was stuffed full of Latinate medical terms that the book-keeper didn't understand. As always, Mom had done her homework.

15

THREE STRIKES

I had rigged the back door of the Geronimo house so that I could sneak around and jimmy my way in when my parents were out of town. In the fall of 1980 they were often out of town, hiding from the authorities in Mexico and Hawaii.

Two weeks before Christmas, I'd become so used to their absence that I'd begun to act as if I lived at 2121 Geronimo, which I didn't. I had started coming in the front entrance.

Late one night I parked my battered Firebird in the driveway. As I unlocked the huge double doors on the nearly windowless front of the house, I heard a small explosion inside. I recognized the sound of gunfire. I'd heard it up close in Washoe Valley. I rushed into the living room to make sure everyone was okay.

Before I reached the living room I heard giggling, and when I got there I saw Mom on the couch, with her feet drawn up beside her, leaning against a wiry stranger who wore cowboy boots. She was in full regalia: wig, makeup, white lace top. She was laughing. There were drinks with wet napkins curled under them on the coffee table. Mom had her hand on the man's shoulder. Ken was three thousand miles away in Hawaii. If Mom hadn't already slept with the urban cowboy, she would soon.

The rail-thin man had a little gun in his hand. He was showing off. He'd had someone make him a big gaudy silver Western belt buckle with a built-in derringer. He could reach inside the epic buckle, pop the tiny pistol out of its slot, and fire it. The thin man had decent aim. He had just turned a vase atop our fireplace into a pile of ceramic shards.

I was taking all this in within seconds, and I hadn't stopped moving toward the sound of the bang since I came in the door. I was striding toward the thin man when he swung the deadly toy toward me, with that shit-eating grin on his face, and Mom snuggled against him, still laughing. I grabbed another piece of casino trash, a giant deep-dish glass ashtray that Mom had big-pursed out of Caesars, and swung it overhand at the man's grin. I think I hit him somewhere in the shoulder or in the arm that he raised to protect himself, and he slid off the sofa, scared but remarkably unhurt.

He'd knocked over the drinks on the coffee table, and he'd dropped the little gun. I checked the chamber and it was empty. The thin man was packing a one-shot peashooter.

"Who the fuck are you?" I shouted.

Mom sprang up and grabbed my arm. "This is Dick," she said. "He's a friend." She calmed me down. At that age there were occasions when I scared myself because I was so much like Mom. I could handle more stress than she could, but when I snapped I was too much like Sante. I got violent, like her. It didn't happen very often, and as the old mobster once said, "I never killed anybody that didn't deserve it." I never smacked anybody who wasn't begging for it. But I resolved right then to get my temper under control. The next asshole might have more than one bullet.

As Dick pulled himself up off the carpet and I sheathed my fist, I recognized him as a loudmouth pit boss I'd met at Ken's favorite casino. I'd written him off then as a jittery, annoying early-eighties-model cokehead.

Mom required a good reason before she would cheat on Ken. Not an excuse—a good reason. In her way she was faithful to my stepfather and she loved him. She cheated on Ken at least three times but never out of boredom or lust. It was always a means to an end.

Twice she slept with another man to enlist him as an accomplice in one of her projects. I could read in the body language between Mom and Dave Kazdin—the man she'd later be charged with murdering—that the two of them had a sexual history. In 1985 she had sex with her doctor because she needed his help. This time with Dick wasn't any different, no matter how it looked.

Was Mom screwing this stick insect so Ken could get comped? I didn't think she'd consider a couple of steaks and a rack of free chips a good enough reason. When Dick left, I badgered the truth out of her. She needed Dick, she said, to finish a job that I had failed to complete.

At the time, I was living in the same town as my parents because I had nothing better to do. I had been an indifferent high school student, a sort of motorhead/beach bum/keg-party jock, and hadn't given much thought to college. Since I had no real plans of my own, Mom had picked out a college for me and written up the application. The University of Nevada–Las Vegas was the only place "we" had applied.

I hated leaving mellow Hawaii for scorching Vegas, but in August 1980 I was sitting across the desk from a lady in the registrar's office. She was peering down at my high school records, and she looked confused.

"Why didn't you apply for an academic scholarship?" she asked.

I didn't understand. I'd dined on a heavy diet of Bs and Cs at Mid-Pac. Unless UNLV had lower standards than I thought, I was a profoundly average student.

I hadn't responded to the registrar, so she rephrased her statement. "With a three point seven GPA, you'd have a good shot at an academic scholarship."

I wavered between amusement and worry. Mom had indulged in some grade inflation on my behalf. She'd doctored the transcripts. If anybody ever called Hawaii, I'd be in trouble. Time to improvise.

"Well," I said, "my family's pretty well off. We didn't think it was fair for me to take money that someone else might need." The woman was impressed. And Sante would have been proud too.

To me, the lie was ironic. Ken could have paid Stanford's tuition, much less UNLV's, out of his sock drawer, yet I'd paid my own way at Mid-Pac. On graduation day, I'd worn a cap and gown and gone through the receiving line like the other students, but the principal had handed me a black folder without a diploma in it because I was short three hundred dollars.

I had to admit, though, that Ken was trying to make up for it. He'd given Mid-Pac the missing three hundred — out of a roll in his pocket — and he was footing the bills for college, including room and board. Despite the spare space at the four-bedroom Geronimo spread, Mom and Ken and I agreed that I should live in the dorms for the first semester so that, as a stranger in my new hometown, I could meet some people. By then I'd lived apart from them for more than a year anyway, and I enjoyed maintaining a little distance.

To earn pocket money I took a job as a salesman at a stereo store. I discovered that one of the benefits, or side effects, of being Sante's son was my training in seducing and convincing. Even as a twenty-year-old I recognized the irony of it, and appreciated the thin gray line between selling and conning. Con is short for confidence, and there's nothing wrong with being confident. I sold many stereos.

There was a bar near the stereo store, and when Mom and Ken passed through Vegas they'd arrange to meet me there. They'd tiptoe into town and book a room at a hotel, avoiding Geronimo Way. That fall the doctors' letters and affidavits in the furs case were flying, and Mom and Ken, both supposedly at death's door, didn't want to be found.

Right at the end of my first semester in college, Mom and Ken met me at the bar after work. We had a few drinks, and then Mom unleashed that phrase I feared.

"Honey," she said, "I need you to do me a little favor." Before I could protest, she added, "And we'll pay you five hundred dollars."

She'd never offered me cash before, so I listened. With Mom pitching and Ken clutching his cocktail beside her, she told me that (surprise) the favor wasn't really little. She wanted something bad to happen to her dear old friend Jeff David.

As a family we'd loved Jeff for a decade or more. During the California years, as early as 1965, he'd fallen into Mom's net. He ran a real estate escrow firm, which is why Mom had cultivated him. She hunted for people in real estate–related industries whom she could befriend and manipulate. Those who weren't instantly appalled by the wig and the makeup and the forest of gardenias were charmed. She waited till she clicked with someone, and then she went to work softening them up with gifts and compliments. By the time she needed them to undot an *i* or uncross a *t* on a document, they were goners. I'm not convinced that her stooges were always aware of what they were doing. They trusted her, even loved her: she was a friend. Once they did it, whatever it was, she'd push harder. Some would balk and drop out of our lives. Others could be wooed. At that point they were no longer sinning out of friendship, but acting in the name of mutual self-interest, greed.

With so much arm-twisting going on and so many spurious documents in so many files, repercussions were inevitable. At some point every friendship blew up because every scam blew up. People got mad or scared and stopped cooperating with Mom. Or they started cooperating with the authorities. Mom dealt with traitors harshly. While they were still our friends, these people were usually lovely. A little pliant, of course, but that was part of their trusting, open, generous nature. They were the kind of people I'd want to be my own parents.

Jeff David and his wife, Daphne, were two sunny, proper Brits transplanted to Southern California. They baby-sat me often, and I adored them. In the early seventies I'd watch prime-time TV with their three kids while Mom and Ken and Jeff and Daphne did the town. I threw up in their den and marveled when no one yelled at me. Jeff sometimes chauffeured me to school and the airport. After we moved to Hawaii in 1975, though, I had seen the Davids only once or twice.

Now Mom said she hated good old Jeff. She was talking about him in the terms she reserved for her legions of enemies. He had joined the other side. He was a fucking traitor, how dare he, she'd show him, and so on. Ken, in vice presidential mode, seconded all the insults that Mom spewed forth.

The five hundred dollars would be my fee for paying Jeff a visit at his new place of business in Northern California. They wouldn't tell me what offense he'd committed, though I was so versed in the twisted Kimes logic that I could make some educated guesses: Jeff had either refused to lie for Mom and Ken or told the truth about something that had happened. There might have been a document he wouldn't alter or an already altered document he wouldn't defend. I'd also gotten the idea from somewhere that Jeff might be a hostile witness in the D.C. fur caper. It didn't really matter.

Mom didn't tell me to kill Jeff David, not directly. She appealed to my loyalty. She said he'd done something unforgivable and needed to be taught a lesson; I got the hint that the lesson should be harsh and physical and final. I took the money, rented a car, and drove north alone.

There is a single two-lane state highway in the lee of the Sierra Nevadas from Vegas to Reno that runs through an outsize landscape devoid of people and trees. During the six-hour drive, I brooded. Mom hadn't said "kill," but there was no mistaking what she wanted. Or was there? She hadn't slipped me a gun.

I spent the night at my dad's in Carson City. I said I had to do an errand for Ken, making it sound like business. Dad didn't ask any questions.

Early the next morning I swung west and headed down the other side of the mountains toward the Napa Valley. Jeff's offices were in the bucolic vineyard town of Napa. I arrived during the lunch hour, and when no one answered my knock, I sat down on the curb beside my rental and waited. Vegas and Reno had been cold, but here it felt comfortable to be outside. For some reason I had carried my overnight bag out of the car with me when I went to Jeff's door, and now it rested beside me on the sidewalk. I used to bring a little backpack with me whenever I stayed at the Davids' as a little boy.

I had just lit my second cigarette when Jeff appeared. I hadn't heard him approach, but there he was, standing ten feet from me, with the same harmless, open face I remembered, ruddy and blond, a working-class British clerk made good.

"Kent?" It started as a question but he knew he was right before he finished. I stood up with my bag in my hand and watched Jeff's expression change from glad to worried. He remembered me as a quiet little kid, and here I was, grown up, shaggy, black-haired, and six-foot-three, cupping a cigarette. He looked at my car and blanched as if he'd seen someone inside it. I could tell he knew Sante was after him. He thought I was Mom's muscle and that she might be watching from the passenger seat. He moved quickly toward his office door.

"Jeff," I bleated, "what's going on? Mom wants to hurt you. I don't know why."

On the drive up north the night before I'd resolved to warn him, but Jeff had slipped through the door and locked it behind him almost before I finished speaking. I knocked on the door and tapped on the glass but he wouldn't come out. I had been the reserved little boy he'd once baby-sat. Now Jeff was sure I'd become a thug.

Mom had jetted to Hawaii by the time I got back to Vegas. Over the phone I told her how Jeff had run from me, terrified. Mom finally told me why. Jeff had been at the Town and Country bar the night of the fur theft, though he hadn't witnessed

anything. The next morning he'd wrangled a lawyer for Mom
and Ken and even swallowed his pride to play the "English butler" in court. But these acts of loyalty weren't enough for Mom.
She condemned him as a traitor because he was too much of a
solid citizen to keep on lying for her. He had testified against
Mom and Ken in front of the grand jury, and she wanted him
silenced before the criminal trial began.

I hoped that Mom would consider my little trip a success,
that Jeff's fear would satisfy her and make her feel safer, but it
didn't. The skinny pit boss shooting up our living room was the
proof. Back in those days, before Vegas became a family fun
center, there were guys around who knew guys, and you didn't
have to work too hard to find a jerk who claimed he was
mobbed up. Dick was just the sort of blowhard to advertise it.
Mom had put his connections to the test. To get into her bed, he
had to come up with a hitter for the job I didn't do.

A week or so later, Dick found his hit man. Mom referred to
him as the Black Guy or, occasionally, the Nigger. After she'd
met the Black Guy and given him orders, I reinserted myself in
the process. She really meant it — she wasn't going to stop or be
satisfied until something happened to Jeff. Pretending that I
wanted to participate, I offered to share the driving with the
Black Guy and direct him to his target. Mom agreed.

I estimated that the drive to Jeff's home in San Rafael,
across the Golden Gate Bridge from San Francisco in Marin
County, would take eight or nine hours. In that amount of time,
I figured I'd have a decent shot at talking the hitter out of the
hit. It depended on what kind of guy the Black Guy was. Whoever he was, he'd never met Jeff David.

I don't remember the man's name, but I learned very
quickly that murder wasn't his business. He was young, short,
and overweight, a light-skinned guy who worked in the kitchen
at Dick's casino. I assessed him pretty quickly as a wannabe, an
eager geek who wanted to get hooked up with the Mob and
thought Dick had the connections he needed. In exchange, this
young guy had come on like a hardass. Within an hour of meeting him, I doubted whether he'd ever committed a crime more
serious than slinging some dope.

I worked on him, telling him he'd never see payment, that
Mom couldn't be trusted, that he'd get caught, that the plan
was flawed, that we should wait. I said, "You don't want to do
this," a hundred different ways. By the time we reached the

green hills of the Bay Area he was ready to have a beer instead of bash Jeff's head in. We crashed at a cheap motel. "Let's talk about it in the morning" became "Fuck it." We returned to Vegas in the morning without taking the baseball bats that Mom had supplied for the head-bashing out of the trunk. The wannabe seemed relieved.

This time Mom and Ken were waiting at the Geronimo house, primed to hear that the mission had been accomplished. I blamed the "hit man" for chickening out, and hoped that time and more delays would quell Mom's obsession with Jeff. But I hadn't solved anything. Mom reacted by fuming about the Black Guy, who was now the Nigger forever.

A few days later, drunk, depressed, or maybe weary after another fight with my folks, I summoned the courage to call the Las Vegas Police Department. I would have done it sooner, but the merry-go-round with Hoke and his cronies in Honolulu had left me bitter. I had hand-delivered my mother once, and the cops had let me down. But I had no other ideas about how to stop her, so I dialed the Vegas department's Secret Witness program.

"I'd like to report an attempted murder," I told the cop who answered the tip line. I was nervous. I hadn't told anyone about Mom since protective custody in Hawaii, and I'd never accused her of anything this serious. "This lady is trying to get me to kill somebody. Her name is Sante Kimes."

"What's your name?" asked the cop.

"I don't want to give you my name. I want to be a secret witness. I want protection and I want to stay out of this."

"Okay," agreed the cop. "Give me five minutes." I held the receiver for less time than that and then heard the officer's voice again. "Okay," he said. He'd accepted my conditions. What I said must not have sounded as crazy as I thought. This person believed me. He was patient and concerned, pressing me for details about Jeff David and the two trips to California. "She wants him dead," I explained. "She's going to continue to try to do it."

By the time I got off the phone, I had a scenario laid out in my mind. Mom and Ken were going to jail, or they were going to beat the charges. Regardless, there'd be hell to pay. They'd never forgive me for betraying them. I had lost my family one way or another. Kenny would probably have to go live with

Andrew or Linda Kimes. I cringed thinking about Mom's reaction.

That evening I sneaked onto the Sahara golf course, beyond the fence next to the Geronimo house. I sat on a green hillock and smoked cigarettes and watched the driveway of my parents' house. Nothing seemed to be happening. It got dark, and there were no sirens or flashing reds and blues. I had a pair of binoculars with me, and I raised them to my eyes to see if there was an unmarked cruiser under the Geronimo streetlights or cops with drawn guns in the bushes.

I waited past midnight and no one came. I went back to my place, telling myself the police were investigating and I'd been stupid to think they'd pounce before they'd confirmed my story.

But just as in Honolulu, in the weeks that followed nothing happened. By then I was wondering what would happen to me. I had snitched, and no one believed me after all. Nobody was at risk besides me, for opening my mouth. I'd called the police and told them my mother was plotting murder and they treated me like a screenwriter trying out the convoluted plot of a B movie. It seemed as if Mom and Ken never suffered any consequences for their actions. They just grew bolder and bolder, and I grew more bitter and cynical.

Mom decided that to get the job done right, she'd have to do it herself. I decided that the only way to stop her from harming Jeff was to go with her to San Rafael.

Mom flew from Hawaii to San Francisco. I met her at the airport, where we rented a car. I was to be the wheelman and the muscle too. There was a tire iron in the trunk.

We made it all the way to Jeff's street in San Rafael. The driveway was empty. We waited in the car for hours up the hill from his house, but he didn't appear. Mom was in the backseat, chattering, cussing Jeff, filling the dead air. She couldn't stand silence.

Then she shrieked and pointed. Jeff's car was headed down the hill. We followed him until he turned onto the two-lane highway toward Napa. Soon we were the only two cars on the road, and Mom shouted commands. "Pull in front of him!" I did. "Now," Mom ordered, "slam on the brakes and he'll have to stop! We'll jump out, and you hit him over the head and throw him in the trunk!"

I didn't slam on the brakes. Jeff didn't run into us or stop. Instead, I slowed down enough so that Jeff would have to see Mom's angry head swiveling around in the backseat and run away. He must have recognized her because he gunned his motor and swerved past us on the left. I saw that he was clenching his teeth, though he didn't glance in my direction. After a few miles I gave up the "chase."

The usual fight ensued as we drove to the airport, but this time I won by scaring Sante. "He'll go to the cops," I insisted. "You can't touch him now. He saw you. If anything happens to him, the cops'll come get you."

That was the last I heard about killing Jeff. He didn't testify at the trial; Sante scared him more than the D.C. district attorney. He simply joined our legion of lost, burned, used, frightened, and otherwise alienated ex-friends.

16

MS. PACMAN

he Jeff David nonsense persuaded me not to move into the Geronimo house during my second semester at UNLV. I couldn't beat the rent, but I didn't like getting sucked into Mom and Ken's chaotic, criminal life. I kept selling stereos and leased an apartment with a college friend.

I attended classes, but from day one at UNLV I put about as much effort into my schoolwork as I'd put into my college application. I drifted from business administration to psychology to the theater department. All were easy subjects for the troubled son of a mogul and a drama queen, but I couldn't fake an interest in any of them.

I started dropping by Geronimo more often when my family was in town. I missed them, and they missed me. Mom welcomed me. She behaved toward me as she always had, which means that 95 percent of the time she was an enveloping cloud of maternal warmth, supportive, protective, generous, and fun. She could yank me straight out of a funk. Once again she became my refuge.

But she continued to dog me with a refrain of *step*son, *step*son, *step*son. Sweet, hyperactive Kenny, busy with his tutor eight hours a day, was the heir apparent. Ken had a fortune that sometimes sounded Rockefeller-sized when Mom described it, but she warned me I wouldn't get a cent unless I could make him love me. I had a whole menu of mixed emotions toward Ken. We understood each other, as the only two members of a special club, and we needed each other. I wanted a relationship with him, and I admit that I wanted a relationship with his money. During my two years of semi-exile I'd been all too aware of its absence.

In Ken's limited, money-obsessed way of forging personal ties, he'd bonded with me in Hawaii when we were in business together fixing boats. As I hung around the Geronimo house, I realized I'd rather be out in the world making money than making C's in college. Soon Ken and I began to bat around ideas for a new small business.

The project we settled on during that second semester of college was the Century Arcade. The idea and the name came from me. In 1981 video-game warrens had sprouted in every suburban mall. I'd found a neighborhood near the Strip that was begging for one, and told Ken about it. The venture seemed big enough to interest Ken but too unglamorous to interest Mom, who would otherwise meddle the project into disaster. I'd picked a site in a faded strip mall with a high school and a low-income apartment complex nearby. The customers would be black and brown and lower-middle-class white schoolkids, and they'd be spending quarters. I figured the arcade would hold about as much appeal for Mom as knocking over parking meters.

Ken laid out five thousand dollars up front. We rented the strip mall space and contracted with a local vendor for video-game machines. We agreed to split the drop fifty-fifty with the machine company — the standard deal.

Kids packed the Century Arcade from the day it opened. The location was perfect, and the machine company gave us the hottest games as soon as they were available. We had three Asteroids and two Ms. Pacmans before most venues in town had one. My drop the first week was $2,800, far above average for an established arcade, according to a stunned machine-company rep. Less the rent and the vendor's cut and wages for a tiny staff, I netted $2,200 a month, a healthy salary for an eighteen-year-old in the spring of 1981.

Mom smelled money, even if it was lunch money, and acted accordingly. About two months after the arcade was up and running, I got a pissed-off phone call from the machine company. "If your mother ever comes here again," vowed the rep, "we'll sue." Mom had paid him a threatening visit. She said she'd sic a lawyer on him if he didn't treat us right, unaware that he'd been supplying me with the best stuff all along.

Soon Mom was hanging out at the arcade, firing my staff,

hiring drifters to replace them, shooing away customers she didn't like. A friend of hers did the books and cooked up numbers that showed our healthy and profitable business to be losing eight grand. Ken began to grumble, despite the money I deposited in our joint account daily.

Soon after the fight with the machine-company rep, Mom and Ken asked me to go with them to Anaheim for some reason I can't recall. That very day, the only day I'd been off the arcade premises, someone robbed it. I kept my suspicions to myself, but I resigned myself to the fact that Mom wanted to destroy my business. She couldn't help herself.

My career as a video-game entrepreneur lasted till summer, my classes neglected and my grades sliding, but the silver still pouring into Pacman's maw. I began living at the Geronimo house. One July night I went out carousing with a few guys from school. We drank beer and shot pool at a bar called the Elbow Room. I had been drinking in front of my parents and with their encouragement since puberty. I was doing what I'd been trained to do, in one of their favorite watering holes. Long practice and a large frame meant that by eighteen I could soak up booze like a sponge and never wobble.

At four in the morning I drove back to the Geronimo house in my Firebird. I plopped down on the kitchen counter and lit a cigarette. It would be light out in a few hours, and I was due at the arcade at 6 A.M. to split the previous day's drop with the guy from the machine company. The money sat next to me on the counter in a zippered vinyl bag. Sleep seemed pointless. I flicked on the coffeemaker.

Ken shuffled down the stairs in a bathrobe and flashed me a weak smile. He needled me about the late hour. I could tell he hadn't slept either. From the weary sag of his features I guessed that he and Mom had been fighting all night. Mom's tactic was overwhelming force. She exhausted her husband till he backed down. It didn't work on me.

Ken and I were discussing the arcade when Sante swept into the room in one of her see-through nighties, pendulous breasts swaying. Her thin hair was covered by a cloth cap instead of the usual wig.

"You son of a bitch!" she snarled, proceeding to hurl curse after curse at me. The woman who'd mixed me drinks when I was in high school and who'd encouraged me to have girls sleep over had taken offense because I was smoking and had been out late at a bar. She threw something at me. I can't recall what.

I was a little drunk, and she was high on anger. At that moment I was just another target for her, an extension of Ken. She was mad because the arcade had given me a little independence and mad that Ken had helped me to achieve it. She wanted Ken to help me succeed, yet she didn't. She pushed us together, and when we got too close she pulled us apart. There was no way to satisfy her.

Car keys in one hand, money bag in the other, I slipped off the counter and headed for the door. Since I had to leave in an hour and a half anyway, I decided to skip the combat and make an early exit. I was in the front hall when something thin and hard came crashing down on my skull. My keys fell on the Spanish tile floor as I dropped to my knees. Blood filled my left ear and dripped on the tile. "What'd you hit?" I asked Mom calmly, as if we were at a target range. "My ear?"

Mom had broken a broomstick over my head. I looked at the splinters lying next to me, pawed at the wetness above my ear, and figured out that I'd been cut. While I knelt there, Mom grabbed my car keys, sprinted up the stairs, and locked herself in the bedroom.

I followed, walking straight through the flimsy bedroom door. Mom stood by the bed. She didn't look scared. I yanked the keys out of her hand and she fell backward onto her bed.

In the bathroom downstairs I inspected the gash above my ear and decided I might need stitches. "I should get out of here," I told Ken, the innocent bystander in the bathrobe. He didn't disagree.

On my second attempt to get out the front door, Mom delivered the knockout blow. There was an expensive foot-high crystal decanter in the den, designed to hold three different kinds of liqueur, with a chrome pump on each spout. It was as heavy as a bag of sand and took two hands to lift. I don't know how Mom threw it, but when it hit my lower back I crumpled. My legs went numb.

"Santee," pleaded Ken, "he's really hurt," but Mom kicked me while I was down anyway. Ken had to hold her back or she would have done it again. Then the two of them started arguing and wandered back into the kitchen. I was alone on the tiles. I felt as if a linebacker had plowed his helmet into my spine and trotted off downfield. My legs tingled, so I knew I could still walk. I got up and called the cops.

When they arrived, Mom pulled an officer aside. Within minutes, though I was the complainant, the cops had focused their attention on me. "Have you been drinking, son?" asked a cop. *Son* is such a cop word. I admitted I had. "You're not supposed to be here," he muttered. "I live here!" I protested. "Take a look. All my stuff is here." By then, though, he'd already slapped cuffs on my wrists and was steering me toward his cruiser.

Outrage is pointless in these situations. Sirens, lights, and badges were routine to me, though the bite of the cuffs on my wrists was a fairly fresh insult. I reasoned with the cops. "There aren't any marks on her," I said as patiently as I could. "Look at my ear. Look at my back."

It took the cops a little time to process the idea of a middle-aged woman beating the hell out of her large college-age son, but they finally got it. They gave me the keys to the Firebird, and I drove myself to the emergency room. A bleary-eyed doctor sewed up my scalp and told me he was pretty sure I hadn't suffered a concussion or any permanent spinal injury.

My first stop after the hospital was a hardware store. I bought a new bedroom door. When I delivered the door to the Geronimo house around noon, Ken accepted it, and my apology, without smiling. He was angry at me because I'd called the cops.

My belongings were waiting for me, piled in the driveway. It seems so melodramatic and final, but members of my family were always doing that, kicking each other out and stacking boxes in driveways, and it was only rarely final.

The resident adviser from my freshman hall, Fred Treadway, came to my rescue. He gave me a key to the dorm, and I spent the summer of 1981 in vacant housing, alone and lonely, hiding from my parents. My few friends had left town till fall. I never went back to the arcade. Ken hired his bookkeeper's daughter to run the place, but she couldn't stand Mom's constant interference and quit after a few months. The business died soon after that. Mom killed it. She couldn't leave success well enough alone.

17

PARTIES

My mother has always insinuated herself into my passions. If I have a dream, she'll move mountains to help me achieve it. If I desire something, she wants to be the one who gets it for me. Once that dream or desire is within my grasp, however, Mom gets nervous. She can't tolerate the idea that any person, job, or thing might come between us. She doesn't really want me to be happy unless she's the one making me happy. She's willing to destroy that dream or desire so that it's just me and her again.

I have my mother to thank for my wife and my career. She gave me both of them, and then she tried to take them both away.

At the start of my sophomore year in college in the fall of 1981, I was broke. When I ran out on Mom and Ken, I ran out on the source of my tuition. I became, I'm willing to bet, the only student in Nevada with a millionaire father who had to take out a loan.

I lived off the loan and rented a small, shabby apartment in a bad part of town. A fellow UNLV student named Claudia joined me in my rathole. Claudia had large breasts, she loved me, and she was there. Those were her main qualifications for the job of girlfriend—Rhonda from Mid-Pac was long forgotten.

I had a series of dead-end jobs. I delivered pizzas. I was a repo man, until someone took a shot at me and I quit. I suffered through a few months of late hours as the front-desk clerk at a skeevy Vegas motel. I didn't mind the hookers who conducted business there. I minded the stickup artist who karate-kicked me in the stomach and stole the night's receipts. The motel manager fired me for having a "bad attitude."

After one of these uninspiring days I opened the door of my apartment to find intruders. "Hi, honey!" beamed my mother. Ken sat on the couch. They'd brought a bottle of bourbon and a bag of groceries in lieu of an apology. Instead of hello, I said, "How'd you find me?" and "You've got your own house. What are you doing here?" Not having seen them in four months, though, after a few drinks I stopped being petty and made peace. We were friends again.

Claudia lasted into the spring, but my college career didn't. I never took another class after the fall of 1981. I treaded water for most of 1982.

For much of that year I was a security guard. The company that hired me had a contract with the Las Vegas Convention Authority. I worked the graveyard shift at the convention center. It was just me and the silent exhibits and kiosks for whatever trade show was in town. Most of the displays were deadly dull. I preferred to sit at my desk and read science fiction rather than examine the latest in dentist chairs and farm equipment.

But one of the displays wasn't dull. I pulled an assignment for the convention center during the week of the helicopter show. I was transfixed. The floor of the giant hall, several football fields long, was covered in choppers. I wandered from one corporate booth to the next, alone in this impromptu helicopter hangar, climbing in and out of the sleek, shiny machines, playing with the controls. I turned on audiovisual displays and watched tapes of the choppers in action. I broke all the security guard rules.

The next day I returned to the hall wearing my guard's uniform over my street clothes. Once inside, I pulled off the rent-a-cop outfit in the bathroom and stashed it in a bag. I walked the aisles of the show, now packed with people. For ten hours I peppered the pilots who manned the booths with questions about helicopters. I asked them how I could become a pilot. Every last one told me that the fastest, easiest route was to join the U.S. Army.

I had been at loose ends. I had dropped out of college and didn't expect to go back. The choppers gave me an idea and a purpose. I had a passion again, like I'd had for sailing in Hawaii. This time I thought I knew what I wanted to do with my life. I marched down to the recruiting office a few days later and signed up.

The ink had been dry for weeks when Mom and Ken called one night at about 11 P.M. They'd been out of town for a month or so and, as usual, had dropped back in without warning. They always called me when they touched down in Vegas because they wanted a ride from the airport. The millionaires were too cheap to spring for a nine-dollar cab ride. It cost me four dollars to park my car at McCarran International while I waited for them.

On the ride home, I told Mom and Ken that I'd joined the army. I expected them to share my excitement, especially since Mom liked to brag about her father the brigadier general. Instead her reaction was "Are you out of your fucking mind?"

She lectured me for a week about how she needed me close to her, working for the family, and there was no money in becoming a pilot. She promised me that as soon as our current spate of troubles had been dispatched, meaning the furs case and three different civil lawsuits, she and Ken intended to set me up in business. "You'll be rich!" she insisted, but it had no effect on me. I could be swayed by money, but I had to see it first.

The army's flight school is very selective. At that time, according to my recruiting officer, it was accepting one of every 150 applicants. I passed my physical, and my test scores were above average, but I got bad news about four months after I applied. I hadn't made the cut.

What my mother did after that would almost qualify as selfless. She decided she would try to get me my wings by other means. First she talked Ken into buying me flight lessons. At $250 an hour, they were the reason most aspiring pilots preferred to let the army pick up the tab. Ken paid, but he groused. "This shit costs a fortune," he'd grumble. "Let's go build something. That would be more productive."

Mom's plan B was more successful. In December 1982, she and Ken asked me to move back to Hawaii and watch the rebuilt Portlock house. It was the best, and only, offer I had, so I accepted. They were never in one place for long, so I didn't expect to see them much. Once I'd been rejected by the army, though, Mom came back to Honolulu and made the Portlock house her base of operations for getting me a second crack at flight school. She dug up the name of a local army muck-a-muck, Colonel Steve Phillips, a man I still admire and respect. Phillips was in charge of recruiting for the state of Hawaii. Mom pursued him like a lover.

Within weeks, she'd planned a party for him at the Portlock house and told him to invite his friends. Mom supplied the booze, a retired marine officer named John Mitchell, and me. All I had to do was cut my hair short, dress nice, and introduce myself to Phillips and his fifteen military pals. Mom would do the rest.

At the party, the crew cuts and chests full of medals got Ken going. He had a fresh audience for his boozy stories about killing a hundred Japs with his bare hands. Not a bad body count for a cook. Mom floated through the crowd in her uniform, a white Hawaiian muumuu, and made sure the brass knew they could stay at any of the Kimes properties at any time. She shared her own anecdotes about growing up military with her beloved brigadier general dad. She told the crowd that my family's military tradition went back generations. I noticed that the pictures of Ambassador Kimes and Pat Nixon and Gerald Ford had come out of their crypts and were on the walls again, for the first time since Newport Beach.

After the party the army was deluged with letters of recommendation from Mom's new friends. The former mayor of Honolulu, generals, majors, C. V. Narasimhan, all penned ringing praises of Kent Walker. While I'd never met half of my benefactors, I think most of the letters were real and not products of Mom's letterhead collection. All she had to do was cold-call a few officers, start spouting about her father the general, and she had the hook in their mouths.

While we waited to hear from the army, Mom made it clear that her networking on my behalf had not been selfless after all. I owed her a big one, and the payback she wanted involved several trips to D.C. with Mom and Ken to find witnesses for the furs case. At bars in Georgetown, Mom would aim me at young, attractive female strangers. My part was to look good and make them feel comfortable. I never had to say anything approaching "Will you take the stand and lie for my mother?" She'd taught me how to charm people, and that's all I had to do. "Look at my big handsome son!" Mom would say. "When you visit us in Hawaii, he'll show you around!"

Mom would help the newfound witnesses remember that they were at the bar that night three years ago and that they'd seen someone swipe Mom's coat. She'd tell the story of her victimization, and they'd be appalled that anyone could accuse this wealthy, generous, fun old matron of stealing. I'd finish the job by saying, "Thanks for helping the family."

During the last junket to Washington I got the call informing me that the army had realized its error. I tell myself to this day that I got in on my own merits, because my test scores were good enough. Mom simply made sure that I got noticed. Her PR campaign on my behalf didn't differ terribly from what another affluent parent might have done to get her kid into Harvard.

Before I left Hawaii, there were more parties. My best friend, John Bower, had stayed on the island after high school. On the evening of February 25, 1983, John came over to the Portlock house so we could celebrate his twenty-first birthday. It wasn't shaping up to be memorable. He'd broken up with his high school sweetheart Sheelin, who'd been part of our tight group at Mid-Pac, and it looked as if it would be just the two of us old friends kicking back on the couch, having a few drinks and watching a broadcast of *Star Trek: The Movie*.

I soon found out, though, that it wouldn't be just John and me reminiscing about Mid-Pac over cocktails. Sante was in town, and she had an idea. "Kent," she said, "my stomach's upset. I need some Alka-Seltzer." I drove Mom to the Foodland supermarket in the Coco Marina shopping center and waited outside in the Cadillac. My mom walked into the store, an apparition as usual in her flowing lace gown and bustier, her big black wig, her white sunglasses. She was immediately the axis around which everything in the store spun.

Later I would hear what happened in the aisles of Foodland. In the dairy section, a woman spied Mom and beckoned to her two blond teenage stepdaughters. They were visiting from San Diego and had just popped across the street from their dad's house to get some strawberry ice cream. "You have got to come see this woman," hissed their stepmom, and pulled them back toward my mother's section of the store. "She looks like some kind of weird movie star or something."

The two girls, whose names were Michele and Lynn, gaped at the white wonder. "Oh, hello, girls," chirped Mom. "You two are so lovely. Where are you from?" Mom was starting a seduction. She scattered hints about her wealth and mentioned that she was the wife of Ambassador Kimes.

Michele and Lynn thought the woman was strange and funny, but it was exciting to talk to her. Before long my mom sprang her real reason for chatting up the girls. "You know, my son's best friend is celebrating his twenty-first birthday, and we're having a big party. We're all wearing costumes, and it's going to be so much fun. The maids are dressing up like hookers!"

The girls didn't know many people who had one maid, let alone plural. They recognized the address as somewhere deep inside the rich neighborhood across the street — and a chasm of class and wealth — from their own modest home.

"Are you girls doing anything?" continued Mom. "John's really a handsome young man, he's a sweetheart, he's like my own son, and you're so attractive I know he'd love to meet you. You could get dressed up in costumes and come to the party and it would be fun!"

Michele and Lynn looked at each other. Why not? They were only in town for the summer, and their plans for the evening had stopped at watching *Star Trek,* like John and me. It was a big night in Honolulu. Sante kept selling, and then added the kicker: "And you know, I could pay each of you twenty dollars just to come by and say hi to John and kiss him and tell him happy birthday."

It's a measure of Sante's charisma, or her sure eye for the right marks, that Michele and Lynn's stepmom didn't hustle her girls home right that instant. Somehow when Sante talked about twenty dollars it sounded like good clean fun, not prostitution. After all, there was no mention of sleeping with anybody. And when Sante urged them to stop at home first and put on something really sexy, that seemed innocent too.

When the sisters got to our house, they looked like heavy metal groupies, in spandex tights and makeup. Maybe on some level they or their mother sensed an opportunity to mingle with the rich and they went for it, but when they got to Ambassador Kimes's house, all they found were three couch potatoes — me, stick-skinny John, and eight-year-old Kenny. There were no maids dressed as hookers, only the usual scared, silent Latinas in white uniforms.

Sante slapped drinks into the hands of the underage girls and cooed. As promised, the girls sat down on either side of John, kissed him, and wished him happy birthday.

As soon as I saw Lynn, the seventeen-year-old in the Bad

Girl T-shirt, I was smitten. She was my physical ideal of a woman, a cute blue-eyed blonde with feathered hair, strong cheekbones, and a great body. John never got anywhere with Michele, but Lynn and I started going out that night.

When I got to know Lynn, I realized we had a great deal in common. She understood about moving too much as a kid, having to start over in new schools and make friends, and having an unconventional family. Her dad was an itinerant piano tuner, born and bred in Czechoslovakia. For three months out of the year and sometimes much longer, he'd pack his wife and son and brood of blond daughters, four in all, into a mobile home and traverse the country. He was looking for pianos to tune, and it had taken him from Florida to Maine to San Diego and then, when his marriage split up, to Hawaii.

I didn't mind that Lynn sometimes slipped and called me Trent, the name of her ex-boyfriend — and not surprisingly, the front man for a heavy-metal band. Her upbringing, or her nature, had made her spontaneous and open to new things, and I figured it was that "Why not?" attitude that had brought her into my living room in her rock chick outfit. I felt lucky. Right away I was in love, far more seriously than I'd been with Claudia back in Vegas or Rhonda in high school.

Mom caught on quickly and started to maneuver. She liked me to have sex, which was why she'd let girls sleep over at the house while I was in high school, and probably why she'd "accidentally" bought a huge trove of porno tapes at a yard sale and left it where I would find it. Though I never followed through, she urged me to seduce the maids and the tutors, since she thought that would make me happy and the lonely girls less restive. "You're young," she'd say. "Have fun."

Sex was fine; what Mom feared was that I might get serious about someone. I was too young and it was too soon, she'd say, or she'd raise objections to whichever girl I was seeing. What it was really about, though, was that there was anyone at all. Mom didn't want to sleep with me, she wasn't sexually jealous, she just wanted to be the only woman in my life. Actually, she wanted to run my life, without interference.

Mom wasn't in Hawaii often, but when she was, she dogged me about Lynn. "She's not good enough for you," Mom would say. "She's trashy." Ironically, it was the way we'd met that raised Mom's suspicions. She'd paid this girl to hang out with us, and now the girl wouldn't leave. Since everything in

Mom's world was measured in money and power, Lynn had to be after those things; she had to be a gold-digging slut. Kind of like Mom.

Lynn's mother, Lyla, lived in San Diego. One day Lyla got a call from a stranger. Soon Mom had segued from pleasantries to the heart of the matter as she saw it. "You know, Lyla," stated Mom, dropping her happy mask, "these kids are getting too serious. That happened with his last girlfriend in college in Las Vegas, and" — Mom paused, feigning discomfort — "there was an abortion."

The lie didn't faze Lyla. "That's not a problem," she said. "Lynn wouldn't have an abortion. We don't believe in it."

Mom's voice grew colder. "Kent doesn't have any money." Usually my mother was a sort of public relations executive for me. She'd tell people grandiose lies that made me blush, like the time she said I'd been accepted at Oxford when I was still in junior high school. The stories always featured me as a hugely fortunate dauphin, destined to inherit a shower of wealth when my day came. She routinely told young women and their mothers that I had a trust fund and a hip pocket full of oil wells. She was telling Lyla the truth instead. It was a truth that my mother considered desperate and scary, but it only confused Lyla. "Huh?" she fumbled. My mother must have thought she'd scored a hit.

"Kent doesn't have any money," my mother repeated, as if speaking to a dunce. "It all belongs to Ken, and Ken's not Kent's real father. Kent is only a stepson. He's not going to inherit anything."

"Oh." Lyla recovered. "I see, Mrs. Kimes. That's not important either."

Mom's revelation was not having the desired effect, but she was relentless. "It's going to go to Kenny."

"Mrs. Kimes, I don't really care."

When Sante got off the phone, Lyla was shaken and disgusted and told her daughter what her boyfriend's mother seemed to think of her. Mom, on the other hand, remained convinced that everybody had a price. I sometimes wonder whether she can recognize love when she sees it. She kept plotting ways to split up my relationship with Lynn, and "plot" is not a figure of speech when you're talking about Sante Kimes.

At the end of June when Lynn went back to San Diego, I was head over heels. My mom pretended to be charmed. Lynn and I missed each other terribly, and Mom tried to "help." She bought Lynn a ticket to Honolulu. She bought me a ticket to San Diego for the same day. Lynn and I would cross in the air and get worried and angry waiting for each other in terminals three thousand miles apart.

Kenny's tutor filled me in on the scheme right before I left for the airport. I skipped my flight and met Lynn at the Ala Moana Hotel in Waikiki. An elevator opened and there she was, despite Mom's machinations.

That day I bought Lynn an engagement ring at a mall in downtown Honolulu. We had just finished the transaction and were walking out of the jewelry store, laughing and kissing, with our arms around each other's waists, when we ran into Mom. All three of us put on a bubbly, happy front. Meanwhile I was thinking, *Did she follow us? Does she know?*

If Mom did, she played dumb. Before Lynn returned to San Diego, she and I made plans to wed in November, but we never mentioned marriage in our daily transpacific phone calls. Mom enjoyed eavesdropping and bugging phone lines, so Lynn and I spoke in code. "Hold on till November," we'd whisper to each other. Finally Mom couldn't stand it anymore. "What's going on in November?" she asked.

In September Lynn was still in San Diego and I was lonely in Honolulu. I was turning twenty-one on the twenty-seventh. Mom decided I needed the birthday party to end all parties.

On the evening of the twenty-seventh Mom led me to the edge of our green lawn, fringed by palms, with its beautiful view of the Pacific. I heard a telltale thwop-thwop sound. The palms bent, the grass in the yard lay down flat, and a Bell helicopter descended right in front of me. My mother knew how to throw a party, and she knew how to pick a gift. The pilot slipped over into the passenger seat, and I grabbed the controls of the rented chopper. I felt the rush of embarrassed excitement that I often felt when my mother went over the top with her generosity, but the chopper was such an appropriate gesture. It was a good-bye present as well as a birthday present, since I'd be leaving Hawaii soon for the mainland and basic training.

I took a long ride up around Diamond Head and over to the big breakers on the North Shore. When I set the chopper down on the lawn at Portlock two hours later, the yard was full of people. Friends and neighbors crowded around the pool.

Then I saw my other present. Near the pool stood four

blond girls, near clones of Lynn. They were all undoubtedly stuffed full of notions of a horny young scion ripe for the taking, heir to untold riches in the not-too-distant future. Here and there in the crowd were a dozen other attractive young strangers.

I was furious. It ruined the fun of my ride. I protested to my mother: She was underestimating my commitment to Lynn. She thought any blond tail served up on a paper plate would do. "What's the difference?" she snapped. "They're all as pretty as she is! Look at them! Why do you want to settle down so young?"

I ignored her. The girls ran up and hugged me around the neck.

Mom had found one young woman with an extra-strong resemblance to Lynn. The girl stared at me as Mom bent her ear. "He's not that serious about her," I heard Mom say. "It's a fling. He falls so deep that he spoils his girls beyond belief."

I introduced myself to my chosen date, and soon, just as Mom wanted, I'd taken her back to my cottage. When we were inside, I showed her a picture of Lynn and told her what my mother was doing. Five minutes later the girl and I had rejoined the crowd at the party.

Many of Mom's young recruits, male and female, were underage, and she had plied all of them with alcohol. Now they were drunk, the way Mom liked her guests. She stood at the edge of the pool in her snow-white muumuu and held up a wad of greenbacks.

"Listen, everybody!" she shouted. "This is a hundred-dollar bill! Whoever gets to it first gets to keep it!" She flung a crumpled piece of paper into the pool, and water sloshed onto the patio and screams bounced off the sliding glass doors as a covey of drunken teens jumped into the deep end and fought for the money. With John Bower and Kenny I watched in amazement as my mother laughed and wadded up bill after bill and pitched them into the roiling water. Maybe she was trying to teach me something about the true nature of human beings, or, more likely, she simply enjoyed the spectacle. The "C-notes" were actually singles.

Afterward many of the drunken underage girls could be seen puking their guts out in the grass. Mom could really throw a party. The next day Sante called Lyla to tell her that I'd thrown a wild bacchanalian bash, complete with sex and drugs, and that I'd shacked up with the Lynn doppelganger for hours. Neither Lyla nor Lynn bought the story.

The failure of her mission drove Mom nuts. A week after the party, I came home from a night out and she and Ken had trashed the living room. Glass lay everywhere. I knew they'd been having a pitched, incoherent battle about nothing. They lolled drunk on the sofa in their usual late-night sparring outfits, negligee and jockey shorts. Mom saw me, a new target.

"You son of a bitch!" It never ceased to amuse me a little when Mom hurled that epithet my way. I couldn't argue with her description. She followed with a string of insults about my slut girlfriend, and I escaped to my room.

There was a knock on my door, and I thought, *Here we go again.* But when I opened the door, a maid collapsed into my chest, crying. She begged me to help her and her cousin leave. I told her I would, but she had to get out of my room. I expected Punch and Judy to be at my doorstep before long, and I didn't want them to find her with me.

I was too late. Mom was at the door now too, in her nightie, with her eyes on fire. She closed the maid's upper arm in her angry claw and started dragging the woman back toward the main house. First, though, she glared at me and issued a warning. "I'll take care of you later, you son of a bitch."

The war raged on inside the main house, Mom and Ken and the wailing maids. I couldn't come up with a reason to wait for Mom to yell at me too. *That's it,* I thought. *I'm leaving.* I had three months to kill before the army, and I decided to do it with Lynn.

That night I slept on the beach. In the morning I borrowed a thousand dollars from Ken, cleared out my own account, and bought a ticket for the red-eye to San Diego. It was a slightly edited rerun of my escape seven years before, but this time I vowed it would be permanent. My only regret was abandoning Ken. It's absurd for a twenty-one-year-old to wallow in guilt about "abandoning" a healthy, ambulatory, solvent sixty-six-year-old, but that's how I felt, because I could predict what lay in store for him.

Lynn and I were married in November. We'd held on, just like we'd promised each other throughout the summer. I didn't tell my family we were married or where we were living. Lynn and I enjoyed a two-month honeymoon, free of interference, before I had to report to basic training in New Jersey.

The great irony of my life is that it was Sante who delivered Lynn to me, and it was Lynn who delivered me from Sante. Had I not met and married my wife, I can't guarantee I would have had the strength to resist my mother. I might be sharing a cell with Kenny today.

18

THE GOOD
SOLDIER

I didn't speak to Sante or Ken for a year.

In the meantime I reported for duty. For a kid from Hawaii, basic training in Fort Dix, New Jersey, in January was a hardship posting. But it led to flight school in Fort Rucker, Alabama, and flying a helicopter was everything I'd hoped it would be.

Learning to control a chopper can be frustrating. Imagine standing upright on an air mattress that's floating in a swimming pool and trying to keep your balance. You have to be vigilant, or you'll topple over. But once you get the hang of it, a chopper is like a hummingbird. You aren't compelled to move forward, as in a plane. You can move in any direction, up, down, sideways, or backwards, or you can simply hover. For me, it was pure joy and freedom. In the chopper I was alone and in charge, setting my own course, like in my sailboat.

I was as happy as I'd ever been in my life. I'd found my vocation, I was in love with my wife, and on August 4, 1984, our first child was born. Kristina was our honeymoon baby, conceived within days of our November wedding. Though we had no money and had to move from one base to the next, Lynn and I were building a healthy, independent life without lawsuits, enemies, conspiracies, hidden agendas, or drunken slugfests. I was no longer beholden to Ken's money.

I knew that Mom had left us alone and unmolested for a year on purpose, because she could find anyone on earth in less than twenty-four hours if she really wanted to. When she finally got in touch with me, I felt it was time to make peace.

She and Ken flew to Alabama to visit us and see the baby. It was pleasant. They seemed happier and more relaxed than when I'd seen them last. They brought the booze, and Ken the mess sergeant cooked up a great meal. They cooed to Kristina. Mom tried to show her love for us the only way she knew how. "You have a baby now," she said. "You need help. Let me send you a maid. In fact, I should send you two maids!" Not wanting to be the only trainee on the base with a domestic staff, I declined.

They left, and I realized I missed them. I had seen Mom's loving, positive side again and had enjoyed Ken's company. I wished that Kenny, almost ten, could have made the trip too. Being a grandmother might be good for Sante, I thought. It would bring her down to earth. I was falling back into the trap.

At flight-school graduation I felt sorry for myself as I watched the other fledgling warrant officers hugging their parents and siblings. I was lucky to be part of this group of a few dozen new pilots and proud that I wasn't among the 40 percent that had washed out. But I wished I could hear my mother and stepfather say, "Congratulations!" and that Kenny could see the pair of wings pinned to my chest.

Just then an unfamiliar colonel approached me. His booming voice silenced the room. "Are you Warrant Officer Walker?" he asked.

"Yes, sir," I answered, unsure what was coming next.

"I have a message from your family," he said with a grin. "Tell the ambassador and your mother that a full-bird colonel came by to congratulate you on their behalf. They said to tell you that they love you very much and are proud of you." At the reception afterward, he took Lynn for a whirl on the dance floor.

Mom had outdone all the other parents without even entering the state of Alabama. At that moment I thought we'd reached a new, healthier place in our relationship. She loved me, she supported me in my dream, and she wasn't going to interfere. Calling the colonel had been a grand gesture, typical Sante, but there was nothing destructive about it.

Lynn, Kristina, and I wound up in Fort Campbell, Kentucky, a sprawling installation an hour north of Nashville, Tennessee. As 1984 turned into 1985 I was spending my waking hours wrestling big blundering Hueys through the air, because the more modern Blackhawk choppers were grounded.

I saw Mom and Ken once that spring, in Washington. They were on another witness-finding mission, but I didn't have to do my bar boy routine. I'd been engaged as Kenny's baby-sitter. He'd grown and changed remarkably in the year and a half since I'd seen him last. He was hyper but otherwise happy, and he'd started to look like a little hawk-nosed clone of his dad.

No one fought that weekend. Mom and Ken had run out of delays and were facing trial in the furs case; they were worried, but their focus on a common foe brought a kind of peace. It fed my own feeling of contentment. After a year and a half as an independent, productive family man launching a career, I thought I might be free and clear. I was ready to uncross my fingers.

My illusions lasted till August 3, 1985, the day before my daughter's first birthday. The phone rang early that morning in our town house in Clarksville, Tennessee. Lynn answered, listened for a few seconds, and blanched. "Kent," she said, "you'd better pick up the phone."

On the other end, my little brother, now ten, was hysterical. "Mom and Dad have been arrested!" Kenny shouted. "They told me to call you and tell you to come get me! I don't know what to do!"

Kenny had been sheltered from Mom's criminal side. He'd made it ten years without witnessing an arrest, something I'd gotten used to by the age of six. But you never really get used to, say, men coming into the restaurant where you're having a family dinner, cuffing your parents, and hauling them off to jail. Sometimes the men will tell you that you'll never see your parents again unless you cooperate. There are few scarier things a child can hear.

"Who is with you now, Kenny?" I hoped he wasn't alone with a maid. I learned that there was a tutor in the room, but she wanted to leave as soon as she could. She probably hadn't bargained on working for felons. I had to reassure Kenny, who was shocked and sobbing. Maybe Mom had told him the Creeps were after him. "Hold on," I soothed. "I'll be there soon."

"I'm really scared."

"I promise I won't let anything bad happen to you. I'll be there soon."

"I'm worried about Dad," sniffled Kenny. "His heart is bad."

"He'll be fine, tiger. He's a lot stronger than you think." Anger welled in me. As far as I knew, Ken's only health problems were recurrent hangovers. Mom and Ken's sob stories about sickness almost unto death, stitched together with the help of pliant doctors and reams of pilfered letterhead, were meant for the courts. But Kenny had heard them too and now he thought his father, in addition to being ripped from his arms, was about to die in jail. Infuriated, I started thinking, *How could Mom do that to Kenny?* Then I stopped myself. Of course she could.

"Do you know what they've been arrested for?" I asked.

"I don't know," mumbled Kenny. "Something about the maids." The maids? I didn't understand, but whatever it was, it seemed serious.

I had thirty-six hours before I was supposed to fly to New Brunswick, Canada, for a five-week National Guard training mission. The antsy and about-to-be-ex-tutor told me Ken and Mom had been arrested at a house they'd rented north of San Diego in the wealthy beachfront enclave of La Jolla. I arranged to meet the tutor at the Mecca, Ken's motel in Anaheim, where I would pick up my brother.

Mom was now deluging my apartment with phone messages, all identical: "Get your brother." She wouldn't tell me why she was in a San Diego jail. Things were no less confusing but more alarming when I reached California. I still didn't know what the charges were, but I did learn that Mom and Ken had been arrested by federal marshals and were about to be moved to Las Vegas. *Well,* I thought, *it ain't shoplifting.*

I had no time to do research. I had to get back to the base. Kenny and I caught the first plane in the morning. He seemed to be calmer. He was accustomed to travel, at least. He had packed a carry-on full of Transformers and other toys.

We got into Nashville late, and I left for Canada before dawn the next morning. I had dumped Kenny with my wife and her sister Michele, who was staying at our place in Clarksville. I told Lynn and Michele that my parents would probably be out on bail soon and that my little brother would only be their responsibility for a few days.

It took our squadron of helicopters two days of flying to reach the rendezvous point in the cool green forests outside Fredericton, New Brunswick. We were northeast of Maine in the Atlantic Provinces of Canada, fifteen hundred miles from

Tennessee, at the opposite corner of the continent from Mom and Ken. We had just set up camp and reviewed the flight plans for the next few days when I was summoned to the commanding officer's tent. "Oooh," snickered my fellow warrant officers. It wasn't often that any of us were called to the CO's tent. I was apprehensive.

I ducked my head and entered the tent and saluted the major.

"Walker," he said, "I'm afraid I have bad news. There's a family emergency. Fort Campbell has authorized you to go on emergency leave."

I must have grimaced. I knew what the emergency was, and I didn't want to go. "Sir," I stumbled, "this is going to be hard to explain. I would much rather stay here and continue the mission. I'm aware of the emergency" — I tried not to load the word with too much skepticism — "and frankly, there is nothing I can do there."

The major looked at me as if I were some kind of cold, unfeeling bug. What had he heard was going on in Las Vegas? Mom was capable of inventing anything to get me where she needed me. He finally spoke. "Well, I'm not going to order you to go, and we can use you here. I'll inform Campbell that you'll be continuing with us."

"Thank you, sir," I said with relief. Whatever he thought of me, he hadn't pried, and I was thankful.

I flew two missions that day and had a blast. We raced fast and low above the maples and evergreens, fifty feet from the ground. Like kids, we chased a herd of elk through a marsh. I went to bed happy to be an army pilot.

The next morning nobody ribbed me when the major sent for me again. They could tell something serious was afoot. This time, the major was issuing an order. "Walker, the situation at home has become worse. Your father has had a heart attack. Take your leave and go home now. Your transportation has been arranged."

His manner accused me of being a callous son. Mom had pulled one over on the U.S. Army. I couldn't tell my commanding officer that the gracious, charming woman to whom he or his superiors had been talking, who'd probably wailed into the phone about some deathbed scene involving my stepdad and begged for my presence, was calling via a three-way hookup from jail and had a rap sheet as long as his arm. He would think

I was crazy or a liar. I tried anyway, because I sensed the bottom dropping out of my military career.

"Sir, I do not believe my father has had a heart attack." I put it plainly, and the major made another of his alarmed, disapproving faces. "You have to understand the whole situation. My parents were arrested a few days ago. I'm not even sure what the charges are. I went to California right before this mission and picked up my kid brother and he's with my wife." It did sound crazy. "Sir," I begged, "I really believe that's all I can do at this point."

The major was not swayed. "We both know how competitive it is to get promoted, Walker. Only thirty percent of warrant officers get to stay in the army after their first hitch. Disobeying an order would not look good on your record. Do you understand?"

"Loud and clear, sir."

A military transport plane was waiting at a nearby airstrip like an expensive, taxpayer-funded cab to shuttle me to the Boston airport. From there I'd been given a free commercial ticket to Vegas.

The idea that Mom no longer controlled my life, I realized, had been wishful thinking, plain and simple. If I stayed in Fredericton, I was disobeying a military order. If I took this bogus "emergency leave," my career was ruined. I couldn't come back until Mom decided Ken's "heart problems" were better. I had been allowed to be a pilot as long as it suited Mom. Now it was over.

My closest friend in the service, a guy named Steve, was assigned to chopper me from our camp to the waiting transport. I had confided in him about my predicament. He tried to find a silver lining. "Maybe this'll work out. You're a good pilot. This might not be as bad as you think." I didn't respond.

We went through our preflight routine, checking gauges and instruments. "Steve," I said, "let me fly this one. I have a feeling it might be my last chance for a while."

He shrugged. "You're in command."

I stretched a fifteen-minute flight into a half hour. I pushed the aircraft to its limits, executing steep banks, buzzing targets, skimming the treetops again. Had I been seen by my commanding officer, I would have been severely reprimanded.

On the radio, the voice of the transport's pilot came crackling as we approached the Fredericton airstrip. He was angry that I was late. He had a schedule to keep. I hovered the old Huey next to the big green plane, my ride back to my unique brand of civilian life. I set it down gently, said good-bye to Steve, and ran up the steps into the belly of the waiting plane.

I was right. That was the last time I ever held the controls of a helicopter. After six months of emergency leave, the army got curious and then angry. They threatened me with a court martial. My mother interceded from behind bars. She sweet-talked the colonel who was reviewing my case into granting me a hardship discharge instead. My mother had talked me into the army, and then she'd talked me out. She'd even arranged the terms of my exit. I was her soldier again. I guess I always had been.

19

REVENGE OF
THE MAIDS

I reported to Las Vegas ASAP, as Mom had ordained, but it was days before I understood what I was doing there. My parents never did tell me why the FBI had led them away in handcuffs. I had to piece together the cause and effect myself. I learned that the chain of events had started three weeks before, with Mom bouncing off a car bumper two thousand miles away. It's a complicated story.

In July 1985, a month before the phone call that brought me west, the clock ran out on Mom and Ken in Washington. They'd delayed the furs case for more than five years with their bobbing and weaving, but they were finally ordered to appear for trial on July 12.

Mom and Ken tried to throw the D.C. Superior Court a final headfake on the morning of July 12. Sante reported to the courthouse, as commanded. Ken didn't, and no one could agree on his whereabouts. He was, variously, convalescing in Puerto Vallarta or Portlock. In reality he was a cab ride away, across the Potomac in the Virginia suburb of Arlington. My parents figured their semi-no-show routine would force the judge to reschedule the trial for the twenty-second time. They were wrong. Sick of the stalling, Judge Sylvia Bacon ordered Mom to stand trial alone.

With testimony and closing arguments complete, the jury got the case a little past 11 A.M. on July 18. At midday, Judge Bacon called a recess for lunch, and instructed the jury and the defendant to be back by 1:30 P.M. After lunch, the jury deliberated for a few more hours. At five to four they notified the bailiff that they'd reached a decision.

Mom was convicted of grand larceny, but she wasn't there to hear the verdict. She'd disappeared. Three days later, from a bogus address in Southern California, she sent her lawyer and the judge an explanation via telegram: "Thursday afternoon, July 18, 1985, while awaiting the jury verdict in Washington, D.C., I was injured in an accident, knocked unconscious and hospitalized. I was unable to return to court or advise the court of my dilemma."

According to Mom, she'd gone to Arlington during the lunch break to get money to pay her lawyer, Gary Kohlman. She stepped off the curb of North Fairfax Drive and into the path of a Fiat. Taken to Arlington Hospital by ambulance, she told the doctors she couldn't recall the accident, and then listed aches and pains in every part of her body from her feet to her head.

Doctors couldn't locate any physical trauma, any cuts or bruises, and X rays showed no broken bones, but they kept her under observation at the hospital. They weren't observing her very closely. At 8:30 P.M. Mom jumped off her gurney, collected Ken, Kenny, and her maid, and took Amtrak to New York. There the foursome caught a plane to Vegas. Mom had beaten the D.C. courts again.

A coyote caught in a steel trap will chew its own leg off to get free. Mom has the same feral desperation. Her injuries were clear fakes, and her amnesia came straight from a daytime soap. I think, however, that a car really did hit her. She would do any-thing to avoid prison, including jumping in front of a moving vehicle. I wouldn't put it past her to pay someone to knock her down. Two facts support this theory. First, the alleged crash was ultralow impact—the car had moved only a few feet from a dead stop. Second, the driver had the same name, job, and hometown as one of the friendly witnesses in the furs case.

What Mom told me much later, while she was in custody, was that she'd gone to Arlington to get cash for her attorney because he was shaking her down. He allegedly demanded ten thousand dollars to fix the verdict and told her that if she didn't get it right away she was going to jail. I don't recall who the attorney was supposedly paying off, because I knew Mom was lying. (She also asked me to give a deposition in which I described witnessing the accident, though I was in Kentucky the day it occurred. I refused.) Her telegram to Kohlman about the accident, with its cc to Judge Bacon, supported this blackmail scenario. "As you know," she wrote, "I was acting upon your instruction to leave the court in order to obtain money which you insisted you must have immediately in that exact hour if you were to protect my interests and well-being pending the outcome of the trial."

Mom floated her libelous theory in hopes of imploding the verdict. Meanwhile, Judge Bacon had issued a warrant for her arrest. Mom and Ken scurried from one Vegas hotel to another, fugitives from justice. They never went near 2121 Geronimo.

On the lam, they rented a condo in La Jolla under the aliases Ken and Sandra Louise Estrada. They were preparing to flee to Costa Rica and stay indefinitely. I found their plans ironic, because Costa Rica was where Ken's son, Andrew, lived, the same kid Mom derided as a drug-dealing dropout. Mom and Ken had been holed up in the condo about a week when the FBI crashed their door.

But it wasn't the Washington fugitive warrant that had landed Mom and Ken in federal custody. Though D.C. asked for them, my parents didn't get shipped back east. Instead they went north, to Las Vegas. They faced federal charges far more serious, and far stranger, than simple theft of a fur coat.

When I got to Vegas from Fredericton, visiting hours at the Clark County Detention Center were long over. I let myself in to the silent, empty hulk of the Geronimo house and tried to catch a few winks, but sleep was a long time coming. My mind kept whirring. What had Mom and Ken done?

Early the next morning, the television news told me. The local media had its teeth in a fantastic story. "Local woman arrested on slavery charges," said a talking head. "More after this." As my confused little brother had said nearly a week earlier, "It's something about the maids."

The U.S. Attorney's office in Las Vegas accused Mom and Ken of "involuntary servitude." I had told Ken in Hawaii seven years before that he and Mom were breaking some obscure law, and now I knew its name. The government said Mom and Ken were keeping their maids as slaves.

People had reported my mother to the authorities as early as 1978 for the way she treated her maids. The first was Beverly Bates, Mom's ex-friend and accomplice in the Honolulu sheriff's office masquerade. By then, Beverly had already found

Mom's attitude toward the maids unsettling. "She said," recalls Beverly, " 'They're my slaves. I'll show you how to get one.' That was supposed to be a joke."

Mom called Beverly up one day and asked her to fly to California and do an errand. Too busy to pop over to Los Angeles herself, Mom wondered whether Beverly couldn't swing by an employment agency and pick her up a maid. The woman would be waiting when she got there. Beverly says she resisted, but I doubt she put up much of a fight. Mom pulled Beverly's strings. For a hundred dollars, she agreed to perform a "little favor" that involved two six-hour plane flights. Mom gave her tickets for a flight the next day.

That night, Ken phoned Beverly. Stone drunk, he bellowed abuse. "Don't you dare bring those fucking maids to my house!" he screamed. Shaken, Beverly promised not to make the trip.

In the morning, Beverly fielded an early call from a hungover, contrite Ken. "I'm so sorry I yelled," cringed Ken. "Please bring Santee a maid. I'll make it up to you." My stepdad had the courage to oppose Mom only when shitfaced.

Beverly went to L.A. When she reached the employment agency, she learned that the maid had been hired under her name. Beverly Bates was now responsible for the woman's welfare.

On the flight back to the islands, Beverly disobeyed one of Mom's orders. She told the maid, a seventeen-year-old Mexican, where they were headed. They chatted in pidgin Spanish. Beverly had a terrible premonition she was delivering the young woman to her doom.

When she dropped the girl off at the Portlock house, Beverly told her where she could come if she ever needed anything. "I counted off the houses over to mine — *uno, dos, tres, quatro, cinco*. I don't know why, but I had a bad feeling."

The girl never came by. Beverly went to visit her instead, when Mom and Ken were out of town and the girl had been left to care for Kenny. Beverly went to the front gate and knocked, and the girl ran toward her sobbing. Through the locked fence, Beverly heard a story of endless work hours, threats, intimidation, and abuse that regularly turned physical. The girl held up her burned forearm and said that Mom had pressed a hot iron into her flesh. She claimed Ken had sexually assaulted her.

Sante had taken her identification and wouldn't let her call home.

The girl could have walked out of the house and Mom's clutches, but she wouldn't abandon the baby. In the days that followed, Beverly sent a Spanish-speaking employee from her husband's restaurant to talk to the maid through the gate, and got more details about Mom's behavior.

Finally Mom and Ken returned home. Near dawn, the girl crept out the back door onto the beach and ran. Beverly hid her in a closet. When Mom and Ken came to retrieve their hostage and acted out the scary scene I've already recounted, Beverly played dumb. She then paid the girl's way to the mainland and filed a police report.

That was the end of Mom and Beverly's friendship. Some time after this episode, Beverly took a beach walk and noticed that Mom and Ken had built a tall fence across the back of their property. That escape hatch had been sealed.

Mom liked illegal aliens because she wagered they'd never approach the authorities, a smart bet. It was only when Kenny got old enough to have tutors that things got risky; now there were eyewitnesses. Mom was clever enough to hire young women fresh out of school who'd forsake a paycheck for a jet-set lifestyle, but she forgot that the tutors were U.S. citizens and had no incentive to stay mum about the maids' mistreatment.

In November 1982, one of those tutors, a recent Indiana University grad named Teresa Richards, approached the FBI in California and started unspooling a fantastic tale about a woman named Sante. Teresa said that a rich lady in white with a drunken, silent husband and a spoiled seven-year-old had stolen her passport while Teresa was living with the family in a beachfront villa in Puerto Vallarta. Sante had tricked Richards into smuggling illegal aliens across the border, forcing her to wade neckdeep through the rough Pacific surf onto the sand at San Diego. Once in the States, the illegal aliens were put to work as maids. They were held hostage and physically abused by Sante. Richards had helped one of them escape before she ran off herself.

The FBI got a letter from the Indiana University employment office soon after they heard Richards's story. Mom had pulled a gun on a second student, Richards's replacement.

That December a fourteen-year-old girl named Dolores

Vasquez Salgado turned up at the U.S. consulate in Guadalajara. An ex-maid, she too had things to say about Sante Kimes. She told an FBI agent that Mom had pulled a gun on her. Mom had also tossed Dolores in the shower and opened the hot valve full blast to punish her for burning a hamburger. As the water turned scalding, Vasquez had backed away from it into a corner. Mom had a pan of boiling water ready in case the girl tried to escape her "punishment," and promptly threw it on her.

Two and a half years before the slavery case, then, four different people had told horrific stories about my mother to authorities in multiple jurisdictions. The FBI knew about my mother and did nothing. I'm assuming they considered the cases closed as soon as the maids ran away. Assault on an illegal alien didn't qualify as a federal offense.

But the complaints kept coming, and Mom handed the FBI a smoking gun. She has a bad habit of keeping notes on her illegal activities, like some kind of evil to-do list. She continues to do so to this day, though it proved to be her downfall in the maids case. A cold-blooded sociopathic con would stop writing things down once it had been used against her. Mom didn't. She's hot-blooded.

In 1984 a tutor named Cynthia Montana from the University of New Mexico squirreled away a list of rules that Mom had written for the maids, capital letters and all:

> If you don't have your papers, BE VERY CAREFUL. IT IS VERY DANGEROUS!! Many times in the past the family has had beautiful women working for them, but they DID NOT PAY ATTENTION, AND SOME BAD, ENVIOUS AMERICANS called the police and the immigration, and they told them that the girls were illegal. THE GIRLS WERE VERY STUPID AND TALKED WITH THESE PEOPLE AND THEY ANSWERED THE DOOR AND THE POLICE CAME AND THEY TOOK THEM TO JAIL. IT WAS VERY TERRIBLE, AND NO ONE COULD HELP THEM.
>
> IT IS VERY IMPORTANT THAT YOU DON'T SPEAK WITH ANYBODY WHO IS A STRANGER. IT DOES NOT MATTER IF THEY CAN SPEAK SPANISH. DO NOT SPEAK TO THEM! That is how it was with these girls, they talked to them only because the Americans knew Spanish, and they took them to prison for many years. STAY IN THE HOUSE, OR THEY CAN TAKE YOU AND PUT YOU IN PRISON,

where it is like hell, where they treat you very ugly, they hardly give you anything to eat, they beat you, they molest you and everything!

IF YOU PAY ATTENTION TO THE FAMILY AND YOU DON'T GO TO THE DOOR AND YOU DON'T ANSWER THE TELEPHONE FOR ANY REASON, DON'T DO THESE THINGS, then everything is going to be very beautiful and you are going to have a very happy life. IF YOU DON'T PAY ATTENTION, IT IS GOING TO BE A HELL, HELL FOR YOU.

List of rules is actually an inadequate term for what Mom wrote. She wrote novellas. She composed a set of sewing instructions more than forty pages long. "[Papa's] shirts should look perfect, or we will get furious. Mama likes starch on her ruffles. Kenny's shirts should be ironed just like Papa's, PER-FECTLY."

Mom wrote volumes for the tutors and house-sitters also. Much of the tutors' manual was devoted to the all-important enforcement of Mom's commandments for the maids. She warned that she and Ken could become "Dracula" if the maids acted up. Rule four on the tutors' list is like a window into my mother's skull, where one single shrill note resounds at deafening volume. "4. Maid: CONTROL! CONTROL! CONTROL! CONTROL! CONTROL! CONTROL! CONTROL! CONTROL!" She really did write it eight times. It might as well have been a million.

In late 1984 a maid named Maribel Ramirez Cruz finally took my mother up on her bet that no illegal alien would have the guts to snitch. The nineteen-year-old El Salvadoran ran to a Las Vegas police station and told them she'd been held hostage in California, Hawaii, and Nevada for two and a half months. The local cops referred her to the FBI. There, Ramirez showed an agent the fresh burn on her arm and gave him the name of a second woman, a Mexican teenager named Adela Sanchez Guzman, who was still being held captive. She had secreted the name and address of Sanchez's family in her bra.

Finally a full-scale investigation began. The feds swooped down on the Geronimo house on July 12, 1985, the same day Mom stood trial in D.C. on the furs case. They found a seventeen-year-old Mexican girl, too scared to leave despite Mom and Ken's absence.

When Mom found out that she was under investigation, she placed a call to the U.S. Attorney's office in Vegas. Pretending to be a paralegal, she peppered U.S. Attorney Susan King with questions about the case. King wasn't fooled, but before she could have the call traced, Mom had hung up. The feds did trace a call from Mom's condo in La Jolla, and when they arrested Mom and Ken there, they liberated one more young, scared woman, the last illegal alien my mother would ever hold in bondage.

That first morning in Vegas after I flew in from Canada, I heard the charges and some of the more sensational accusations on TV and then drove to the jail to see the slaveholders. I didn't feel outrage at what my parents had done to the maids, only at what my mother had done to me. She had pried me loose from the army and damaged or ended my career, just so I could help her fight some penny-ante charge that would end with a fine and probation. I still didn't get it.

Behind the Plexiglas in the reception area, Mom dissolved into the usual wailing and rending of garments, except that in jail she couldn't trowel on the mascara that turned her tears black. "Please," she howled, "you have to help us, honey. You have to protect us!"

The gravity of the situation sank in when I saw Ken. He'd stopped dying his hair. Bedraggled and ashen, he'd aged twenty years. Never had he emanated such fear. And he said something that had gotten lost in Mom's hysterics. "We could die in prison, Kent. They want to put your mother away for eighty-five years." She faced seventeen counts, ranging from involuntary servitude to transporting illegal aliens, and each carried a five-year term.

It may be hard to comprehend how I could see Mom and Ken as victims in this scenario, but beginning on that morning I did. It didn't require elaborate rationalization. I knew that Mom had never paid the maids; I knew that for years she'd stolen and burned their identification, isolated them from the world, lied to them, worked them from dawn to dark. I could grasp the idea that it wasn't right, but on some level I'd hardened myself to what Mom did and to whom she did it. It was a game, and they were the losers. If they didn't like it, they could run away. Like the son of anyone accused of a crime, I ignored the wrongs Mom had done, and focused instead on the wrongs done to her.

And I was selfish. Eighty-five years in prison for Mom,

seventy-five for Ken—if they ever got out alive, I would be supporting Mom, at least, for the rest of her life. I thought Ken
would do the rational thing, take a plea and then leave Mom for
good, since the maids were her sick hobby and not his. Even if
he did stay, I could see his money evaporating fast. A Honolulu
attorney named David Schutter had filed a multimillion-dollar
lawsuit against Mom and Ken on behalf of the maids. The asking price started at twenty-one million dollars and then climbed
to twenty-four million and thirty-one million as he dredged up
more and more angry—and, I thought, opportunistic—women.
The civil suit depended on convictions in the criminal trial, and
if both dominoes fell, Ken, meaning Mom and I, would be destitute.

Before long, I believed as strongly as Mom that she'd been
set up by a shady, greedy lawyer. If she was bad, I told myself,
her enemies were worse, and she had the family united against
a common foe. Mom had me so scared of David Schutter, who
she insisted was hooked up with the Hawaiian Mob, that I
checked my rearview mirror constantly. I heard footsteps in the
Geronimo house, so I kept a loaded rifle near my bed.

I hated Schutter and had an equally visceral loathing for the
feds. I only imagined that Schutter was tailing me, but I often
did find two men in a white car with a federal license plate in
my rearview, from the pool of white cars outside the U.S. courthouse downtown. There was no sport in spotting them.

The feds had listed me as an unindicted coconspirator. That
meant they thought I was as guilty as Mom but couldn't prove
it, or they were still chewing over their plans for me. On more
than one occasion, a junior prosecutor fell into step beside me
outside the courtroom. "We can add you as the third defendant
if we want," she said. Panic was supposed to send me running
to the U.S. Attorney's office, begging to spill in exchange for
immunity.

But I didn't. I was too angry and distrustful, and I didn't
have the information they wanted anyway. Of the seventeen
counts against my mother, all concerned events between 1978
and 1985. During that period I went months at a stretch without
seeing Mom or Ken. We rarely slept under the same roof.
Among the maids whose allegations inspired the federal case, I
recognized no names, and only one face sparked the faintest
glimmer of recognition.

I had stolen money from Ken's pockets to buy plane tickets

home for half a dozen of the most unhappy girls. Other than that, I'd failed to intervene, and on same subconscious level I acknowledged moral guilt. But I knew I wasn't legally culpable, because I hadn't been there. If the government considered me a co-conspirator, there must be flaws in their case. They didn't know where I'd been living. They were trying to coerce testimony. If the feds were exaggerating my sins, couldn't they also be inflating Mom's? An assault charge, a nice fat six-figure settlement, and a few I-told-you-sos from me should have been enough.

We had real enemies after our money now, just like Mom had always claimed, and they were as greedy and unscrupulous as she'd warned. Schutter lied for money, I told myself, the government lied for convictions; and they were in it together.

I wanted to believe Mom because the allegations against her were so awful. I sat down and read the indictment, thick as a book, and explained it away. I had seen my mother physically abuse her "slaves" on only two occasions. The first time, in Newport, she'd thrown a girl out of the house by force. In the second, a maid fed up with Mom's hectoring had shoved *her*. Mom had pushed back harder, sending the woman across the room. That young lady had disappeared fast.

Yet in the indictment, one of the maids claimed that Mom had branded her with a hot clothes iron on her forearm. I saw a photo of the burn and began to deconstruct it, like a defense lawyer. Why did the wound look so fresh? Why, if the woman had raised her arm to keep Mom from scorching her face, was the mark at such an odd angle? I told myself it was self-inflicted and that my mother the con artist was being squeezed by a con with a law degree. Instead of the woman's pain, I saw a scam.

If I'd been more honest with myself, I'd have realized that I didn't know what I was talking about. Mom's control mania escalated daily. Not having me around to command probably frustrated her, and she took it out on the nearest available victims. My absence also allowed her to indulge her worst impulses without a disapproving witness. Her rages were a form of possession; if she could hit me with a toolbox full of foreign objects — razors, broomsticks, decanters — what could she do to a stranger? I would never have had a clue. I read about Mom whipping a maid with a coat hanger and forgot that she'd used the exact same weapon on me. I scanned Mom's list of rules for the maids and missed the implications. I read it and thought, *The feds are going to win the case* instead of *That's how Mom controls these women. They really are slaves.*

Today my point of view is very different, but in 1985 I lined up with my family. I was Mom's soldier. I left the Clark County lockup that first morning with the words *involuntary servitude* grating on my brain and went to war for my parents.

First things first: they needed the best lawyers I could find and they could afford. At that time, superstar attorney Howard Weitzman had just helped John DeLorean beat a federal charge of cocaine trafficking. Mom wanted him. Weitzman and his associate Scott Furstman flew in from L.A., and I picked them up at the airport.

Weitzman had arrived within hours of Ken's arraignment. With Furstman, we stood near the elevators in the detention center, and via a guard I sent a message to Ken that his attorney had arrived. As we waited, there was a buzz in the room. Officers and inmates and bystanders recognized the man in the power suit as the era's most famous defense attorney.

The guard reappeared minutes later, chewing his lip, struggling to control himself. "He says he doesn't have time to talk to Mr. Weitzman now"—the guard paused for comic effect— "because he's due in court." Everyone in the room burst into astonished laughter, except me and Howard. My face flushed.

You could never tell Ken Kimes he was a fool. He was too insecure. He once handed a waiter in a restaurant an ATM card, bragging about this newfangled credit card that had come in the mail, a special perk for big spenders. We had to slip the waiter a real credit card on the sly to salvage Ken's pride. I had to be diplomatic with the fake diplomat.

I went upstairs and very gently informed Ken that he and Mom had engaged the services of the best attorney money could buy and that acting as his own legal counsel at his arraignment wasn't the smartest way to pinch pennies. Weitzman joined me, and Ken wrote him a retainer for seventy thousand dollars.

When we appeared in court, the prosecution maintained that the judge should not permit bail, since Ken had the money to skip the country and never come back. It was a damn sound point, since Mom and Ken had been days away from doing exactly that in La Jolla.

"Your honor," responded Weitzman, "I say this not with tongue in cheek. He did obtain counsel not at a very minimal expense; he wouldn't have . . . spent that kind of money if he didn't intend to return and respond to the charges." Knowing that Weitzman's hourly rate must be painful, the judge bought his argument. Ken was free on a hundred thousand dollars bail. He complained, of course.

Mom had no chance at bail, given her rap sheet and the Arlington escapade. She had the toughest case all around. Weitzman, who'd been her pick as attorney, dropped her. He cited a conflict of interest, since he was already representing Ken, but I think the decision had more to do with the name on the checkbook and Ken's chances of beating the charges. Ken Kimes would look better on Weitzman's won-lost record. For years afterward, Mom would snipe at Ken, "You stole my lawyer." I got her a new attorney, Dominic Gentile.

Within a month, Weitzman and Gentile had cut a deal for my parents. Ken was to plead out on one count of misprision of felony, meaning he'd been aware of Mom's crimes and hadn't interfered. He would be a felon, and on probation, but he'd be free. Mom would have to plead on several more counts. She would go to prison, but she wouldn't have to serve more than two years. Both pleas carefully skirted any guilty pleas on charges that would cinch the civil case for David Schutter.

The deal wasn't perfect, but it would save us millions, and it might cure Mom of her maid fixation. Once the pleas had been crafted, though, the hard part was getting Mom and Ken to sign them.

It took weeks of lobbying to soften Ken up enough to take the plea. The specter of losing his fortune in a lawsuit convinced him to swallow his pride and sign. Ken, Dominic, and I went to the Foley Federal Building to meet Mom and see if she would follow suit.

She was in an old-fashioned holding cell, a dark, window-less affair with bars and benches against the walls. It had been built to hold a mob, but there were only the four of us locked inside that morning. Mom was expected in court on a pretrial motion, and she'd been allowed to change from her prison overalls into civilian clothes — a sober dark-blue pants suit without lace or cleavage.

It took forty-five minutes of yelling, hugs, crying, and bargaining to get Mom to do something that went against her nature. "We have to win the criminal case," she whimpered, "or they'll take all of Ken's money in the civil case." I flourished a copy of the notes she'd written for the tutors about CONTROL! CONTROL! CONTROL! "Look at this," I shouted. "Even if you are acquitted, the criminal trial makes things worse. The civil attorneys *want* you to go to trial. All the maids will testify under oath, and what they say about you will be part of the official record!"

I told her that if she did win the criminal case, there wouldn't be enough cash left to hire a good lawyer for the civil case. Mom was terrified of a long prison term, but it was hammering on the issue of money, money, money that finally broke her. I was shocked when she agreed to sign.

In the courtroom, I felt the sense of doom lifting from the family. Ken went first. He nearly fumbled his freedom by trying to plead guilty while claiming innocence. The judge got mad, but after some quibbling, he let Ken sign the plea bargain. In exchange for a seventy-thousand-dollar fine, my stepdad was free.

Next the bailiff handed the judge and Dominic copies of Mom's deal. Pen in hand, she was ready to sign, and then we saw it. A typo. Instead of *concurrent,* the word in front of Mom's sentences read *consecutive.* Her prison time had tripled because of a paralegal's boner.

Mom flipped out in the courtroom, trembling and screaming and crying, and had to be restrained. Nothing would console her. The deal was unsalvageable. She went back to her cell, and I steeled myself for the full-scale federal trial to come.

20

LIFE BEHIND BARS

We established a daily routine, Ken and I, in the months after his release on bail. In fact, I was just riding shotgun on his obsessions, and he hired me to do it. I didn't have a job, since my mother had engineered my discharge from the army. I went from helicopter pilot to Ken's chauffeur/bodyguard/paralegal/shrink/bartender/rent-a-friend.

It was a taxing tour of duty. Nearly every weekday was the same.

Ken the ex-army cook would get up early and fix breakfast for Kenny. He might make some business calls to his motel in California, the Mecca. Then Ken or I would drive Kenny to school. It was the first time he'd ever attended all day, five days a week, like a normal kid. With Mom in jail, the tutor era seemed finished.

I would try to grab some time with Lynn and Kristina, who'd joined me in Vegas, before the phone started ringing. It was always Mom, and the phone calls, dozens a day, never varied in content. What made it so hard was that Mom took the cash that Ken put in her commissary account and used it to buy up the other ladies' phone time. She had far more money than the other inmates and consequently cornered the market on telephone minutes.

An outsider would have found our side of the phone marathons with Mom strange. We rarely said anything but "Okay" or "Uh-huh." We could have made a tape of those words and let that play into the receiver while we got on with our daily chores, except that sometimes she would ask, "Do you think it will be all right?" and we had to answer, "I hope so." And she always had a list of instructions for us, a daily menu of things she needed done. Her orders to me always included the following, predictable as boilerplate: "Tell Kristina I love her, and be there for your father and brother, honey. Keep an eye on the attorneys. This is our lives and they" — "they" could be the Creeps, David Schutter, the FBI, the Hawaiian Mob, our own legal representation — "are trying to kill us."

The rest of the list didn't vary much either. Contact potential character witnesses, get information from the lawyers, pick up documents and make copies. I couldn't tell one day from the next. And every day Mom would work on me by saying, "We couldn't make it if it weren't for you, Kent," right before the line went dead.

After the first few weeks, Ken and I began to protest, telling her we had to get off the phone because we had things to do. Ken had a disturbing revelation, however — if she wasn't talking to us, she'd be calling the lawyers, and they charged as much as three hundred dollars an hour to say "Okay" and "I hope so." It therefore became one of my duties to baby-sit Mom on the phone and save Ken hundreds of dollars a day.

By ten-thirty or eleven I was driving Ken around in the Lincoln. We had to check the rented post office box at the Pony Express on Tropicana. The next stop was Federal Express. Ken ran his empire over the phone with his early morning calls and overnighted the signed checks necessary to keep his businesses running.

Three times a week we had to visit Mom in lockup, so we could reenact the phone calls in person. We were speaking into a receiver again, except this time Mom was looking at us through the glass, and we could see her holding her own receiver up to her wigless head and knitting up her brow when she said, "Do you think it will be all right?"

Every other day after the FedEx office, it was time for lunch and the first drink of the afternoon. Coachman's, Chatters, and Cattleman's were the most frequent stops. Ken and I would have a hamburger, fries, and at least two Seven-and-Sevens apiece, and hash over the Case.

When lunch was done I would squire Ken to his other appointments. There was always at least one bank stop, then a few more copies to be made. Then we'd cool our heels in the lobby of a law office, usually Dominic's, before a brief, expensive consultation. If we were finished in time, we'd swing by to fetch Kenny after school. If we were running late, I'd call Lynn at the Geronimo house and she'd do the pickup.

Then it was almost happy hour, and that's when the true drudgery began.

People who've visited Vegas are familiar with one side of it. Beyond the tourist Vegas, though, there's a city where a million people live, and they don't hang out on the Strip. Along the four- and six-lane surface streets that carve the booming city up into huge blocks are countless strip malls, and in these malls you'll find the local drinking holes.

Typically, you walk in out of the desert heat and sunshine, and when your eyes adjust there's a square bar in the middle of the room. There might be beer lamps or sports posters on the wall, or wood paneling. Booths line the walls, and sometimes there's a pool table. The real action, though, is at the central, square bar. The bartender is in the middle, surrounded by bottles and glasses. The bar itself is the usual high brown wooden affair, lined with drinkers sitting on backless stools. The difference is that, because it's Vegas, there are video poker machines embedded in the bar every three feet or so, one for each customer.

You would think the locals would know better. So many of them work in casinos that they're well aware of the odds, and with video poker you can't even pretend to count cards. Yet at all hours of the day, because Vegas doesn't operate on a nine-to-five clock, people stream into these establishments, climb up on the stools, and ask the bartender for twenty dollars' worth — two rolls — of quarters. That's enough for two free drinks.

The shift workers, the retirees, all the locals, show up and while away the hours drinking and buying roll after roll. From the day they arrived in Vegas, these were my parents' hangouts. Since they never ate a meal at home, they'd gotten to be regulars very quickly at half a dozen interchangeable places with names like the Huddle Lounge, the Elbow Room, the Coachman, and Bootleggers.

The bartenders and waitresses remembered Mom right away because she'd overwhelm them with requests. She'd phone ahead when she and Ken were on their way and ask, in her breathy, imaginary upper-class accent, which I guess she thought was the sound of entitlement, for everything to be just so when she arrived. She wanted this dish or that in exactly this or that way. She'd burst through the doors waving and yammering, "Hi, honey!" with her silent, well-dressed husband at her side, and order french fries with a side of ranch dressing. The staff would smile at her and do her bidding while cursing her behind her back. They hated her guts. Ken, they didn't mind.

Mom and Ken hung out in these places because in a local bar they could be lords of the manor. These were blue-collar joints, most of the patrons working men and women rather than doctors and lawyers. Ken wasn't a member of the country club, and he didn't associate with people who had as much in the bank as he did. His self-worth was his wealth and, in a bar like Chatters or the Huddle Lounge, he could look around and be confident that he was the richest man in the place. He was the lucky dog version of the other proles arrayed around the bar, and they would acknowledge him as such. My mother wasn't the only one who dropped hints about her wealth.

With Mom in jail, Ken and I practically lived in these bars. It's incredible to me, at this remove, how much alcohol we consumed during those afternoons, especially the volume that Ken, at seventy years of age, poured down his gullet. Alcohol permeates every family memory I have, unfortunately, and it's hard to conjure up any event, happy or sad, without spotting a drink in someone's hand, but those miserable afternoons topped them all. Seven-and-Sevens from two to six.

We drank and we gambled, most often at a place called Chatters, on the corner of Eastern and Tropicana. Each booth had a telephone and a sign with a number, the idea being that singles could come in and start a conversation with a stranger by dialing the number.

I never saw one person use the phone system, but plenty used the dollar poker machines at the end of the bar. Ken and I would camp out there. He bought "racks" of coins instead of rolls—a hundred bucks in silver dollars. He'd buy me two racks of dollar coins. If I lost the two hundred he gave me, it was his problem. If I won, I split the winnings with him.

It was fun at first, as I sipped my complimentary beverage. There wasn't any risk for me. But I tired of it fast and began to resent it. After enduring the mornings of phone torture with Mom to save Ken a few hundred bucks, it was infuriating to see him piss twice as much away himself every afternoon.

He was a terrible gambler. I would gnash my teeth as he

tried to fill inside straights. He held the wrong cards, and I quickly gave up on dispensing advice. He'd forgo the sure thing for the long shot. He lost fast and hard, and it made me wonder whether he'd done his own math when he was a contractor. It defied logic. The worst part was when he'd stumble onto a royal flush, because he wouldn't stop talking about it for days. It made him believe in his luck and skill, and it made him buy more racks.

While we were staring down at the glass-enclosed screens and sipping our drinks, we'd be rerunning the same subjects we'd chewed over at lunch. Except that now the whole afternoon stretched before us. The drinking, the rattle of the coins in the payout tray, and the clicking of the hold and bet buttons went on for hours, and so did the talking.

Ken and I would argue for eons about the attorneys. He refused to trust anyone and would second-guess and even undermine his top-drawer counsel. Dominic Gentile was ranked among the top ten criminal lawyers in the country. In Gentile and Howard Weitzman, Ken had bought the best, and common sense dictated that we let them alone.

Yet Ken, the high school graduate and proud self-made man, who wouldn't leave the house without his necktie just so, thought he knew better. Part of it was the insecurity of a blue-collar guy fighting a battle he didn't understand. The rest of it was the influence of my mother. He was paranoid. He was sure Gentile and Weitzman were out to get us and would sell us out in a heartbeat. "I don't trust those bastards!" he'd growl at least once an afternoon in those dim bars, as the simulated cards spun between his elbows.

My next line was always as follows, give or take an adjective or an exclamation point: "Ken, these guys are on your side." One especially exasperating afternoon, I slipped and added some sarcasm: "You and Mom aren't exactly easy clients."

Ken could turn bright red in a second. He had a temper, and there was never any mistaking it. "What the hell is that supposed to mean! Whose side are you on?"

I tried to pacify him. "I'm on your side, of course, but you have to let them do their jobs. We're not attorneys, and you're giving these guys big bucks to defend you."

"What do you mean we're not easy clients?" My remark had stung Ken, and now he was suspicious of me.

"You know the way Mom is. And you've refused to listen to the lawyers' advice." I picked my hands up off the bar and held my palms out in front of me, a semisurrender. "Let them do their jobs," I pleaded.

"That's the stupidest thing you've said yet." Ken was betting five bucks a hand and losing. He punched at the buttons angrily and refused to look at me.

I tried a new tack. "When you were a contractor," I ventured, "you just did the job. You didn't want the customer to get in the way. It made the job harder. There is no difference here."

Ken was now thoroughly disgusted. "Kent, I thought you were sharper than that." He believed that as a successful businessman, he had learned one simple truth that was eluding me. They — everybody, the world — are all bastards, and they're all out to get you.

After "happy hour," Ken and I repaired to another restaurant for dinner. It was a further round of red meat, alcohol, cigarettes, and speculation. By the time I finally got home I was more tired than someone who'd worked all day. My final task was to wake up Ken, who invariably fell asleep on the living room couch with the television blaring, so that he'd go upstairs to his bedroom.

I hated my life during this period. I dreaded the afternoons at Chatters. And I began to feel guilty, because I always wanted Ken to lose. The more money he lost, and the faster, the quicker we could go home. Some afternoons that would mean five hundred dollars, others more than a grand. The most frustrating days were those when he was down to his last few credits, and he'd play stupid and win big. If he hit a royal flush I'd be trapped in the bar for another hour.

Looking back now, I recall a few days when he went home a winner, but overall he lost big. Really big. Add up the afternoons, which continued for years past Mom's trial, entire years, from 1985 through 1989, and you'll get an idea of how much money Ken pissed away. It was still, indirectly, Sante's fault that he was doing this, because she'd left him friendless, drunk, and dependent on her, with no real job except to clean up her messes, and he killed the time by gambling. If you estimate, conservatively, that he lost three thousand dollars a week, that's nearly a million dollars in half a decade. A huge chunk of his fortune slipped away a rack at a time. No wonder the owners of those boring bars loved us. A million bucks is a high price for free drinks.

In those early days before the maids trial, though, I knew these rambles from bar to restaurant to bar were Ken's only escape, his chance to be selfish. It was before the age of cell phones, and he was blissfully out of reach. When he went home, he had to contend with Mom's calls and play dad to Kenny.

On December 30, 1985, a Friday night, after a routine dull day of drinking and smacking open rolls of coins, Ken and I headed for home. I was driving, as per my unofficial job description. The sun was setting. I was so used to cops tailing us that I hardly bothered to study my rearview mirror anymore.

The Geronimo house is in a cul-de-sac. It's a dead end, really, next to the first hole of what was then the Sahara golf course. As I pulled into the wide concrete driveway, I finally checked my rearview, and I saw red lights flashing. The Las Vegas police had been waiting for us on a side street, and now they had us cornered. Within seconds I'd been yanked out of the sedan and handcuffed. I looked across the roof of the car, and there was my seventy-year-old stepdad, also in cuffs.

"What's this all about?" Ken asked. He was sobering up fast.

"We'd like to look in the trunk," said the cop who'd cuffed me. Ken shot me a fearful glance. I didn't understand why he was so scared. It was unnerving to be stopped and cuffed by a quartet of armed cops, but this was garden variety surveillance, trumped up into harassment for some reason or other we'd learn soon enough. There was nothing in the trunk that could get us in trouble, just some of the legal files for the case.

I was the reasonable one again. "Go ahead," I said, as politely as I could. "We haven't done anything wrong." The cuffs were loose and they didn't hurt, and because of Mom I'd been through this routine before, but I was still fighting my temper. I didn't want my wife and baby daughter to see me this way.

Guns drawn, the cops popped the trunk. They didn't see what they were looking for. They gave the car another once-over and then uncuffed us. But they didn't relax.

"Has Sante Kimes contacted you?" asked cop number one.

"No," I responded. "Why?"

"She has escaped custody."

I laughed, in spite of myself. It wasn't actually that funny. I wasn't proud of Mom's resourcefulness in escaping, because I could see the implications immediately. Nothing good would come of it. My laughter was involuntary, the product of nerves, and on hearing it, the cop almost cracked a smile too. I recognized him as one of our long-term tails and guessed he'd developed a little insight into Sante Kimes.

"This is incredible," I murmured. Ken, meanwhile, looked as if he'd lost his will to live. He said nothing.

The cops told us that Sante had bolted a few hours ago, and there was a citywide womanhunt under way. We told him we hadn't heard from her since that morning. The cop wasn't going to leave it alone.

"Where have you two been this afternoon?" he asked.

Where are we every afternoon? I wanted to say, but I didn't. I looked over my shoulder and saw the white car that had been following us since morning, parked against the curb not fifty feet away. "Maybe you should ask those guys." I nodded in the direction of the feds. "They know every move we made today."

The FBI was now our alibi. The cop shook his head and stifled a laugh. His partner walked over to the white car and talked to the occupants.

Meanwhile the first cop told us that we were obligated to call him as soon as we heard the barest hint of Mom's whereabouts. We'd be hauled into court if we so much as gave her a drink of water. "Don't even think about helping her," he warned us, wearing his serious face again. "That is a guaranteed trip to jail. We're taking this very seriously."

The rest of the night was a blur. I remember that Ken and I talked about where she might be and the fallout from her escape. We'd called Dominic as soon as the cops left, and he'd told us that Mom's dash could be construed as an admission of guilt. An already difficult case would now be nearly impossible to defend, and once it was lost, the civil case would follow. Mom's flight was probably going to cost Ken millions.

Ken started talking about hiding money offshore. I got the impression from what he said that he'd already begun. The lawsuits, the alcohol, the drumbeat of Mom's they're-out-to-get-us scenarios, were revving up his paranoia.

Then Ken's mind swerved off into even more dangerous territory. "Well," he mused, "if they don't catch Santee, what will happen then? Will I still have to pay for her defense?"

"What do you mean?" I asked.

"Well, they can't go on with the trial if she's not here. I was just thinking that if she didn't get caught, it might not hurt us that bad."

I couldn't believe what I was hearing.

"Ken" — and I spoke slow and loud, as if to a stubborn child — "absolutely nothing good can come of this." But the alcohol was burning holes in his brain, and I could tell he was fixating on two stupid ideas: One, that if Mom ran, it would save him the price of a lawyer. Two, that he could see her. For some reason, he loved her enough after everything that he was excited at the prospect.

"She won't call here, she's too smart for that," said Ken, and what he meant was, How is she going to get in touch?

I felt like I was not only Ken's father, but his lawyer. "Mom will be looking for money," I advised him. "She will try to contact you. If you don't stay clear of her, you're going to wind up back in jail, and nothing will get you out."

Ken sat on the couch in the living room and brooded with a fresh tall drink in his hand. I thought I'd made an impression on him. He'd held up okay under the pressure of the maids case. He just needed a reality check, oh, every two hours or so.

Then came the call from Sheila. She was a bartender at the Huddle Lounge and a "friend" of Mom and Ken's. "Friend" meant that Mom had schmoozed her blind.

"I have your mother," said Sheila with no preamble.

I had answered the phone, but Ken grabbed a receiver in another room. He broke into the line and said, "I've got it, Kent." As soon as he did, I had no doubts about what would happen next. I went into the room where Ken was talking on the phone and could tell that Ken was going to help Mom get away. As soon as he hung up the phone, we started arguing.

"What the hell are you thinking, Ken? You can't help her! I can't believe you'd even consider it!"

"I can't turn her in!" he protested.

"The hell you can't," I countered. I kept pounding away at the likelihood of prison and bankruptcy if she didn't go back in her cage right away, but in his mind he was already meeting

Mom. He told me that if he turned her in she might take revenge on him, and if he didn't go see her she might take revenge on him, and anyway, he wanted to see her. "Maybe this is my last chance," he said with a shrug.

"What the hell are you talking about!" I yelled. I pleaded with him to stay put. "You know as well as I do that the civil case isn't going to go away just because Mom's on the run. She's going to get caught eventually. Please, Ken, stay clear of this! Tell Sheila to turn her in, now!"

"You act like you want her to get caught." He was a petu-lant, pouting septuagenarian.

I said that the phones were probably tapped and the feds might already be on their way to the rendezvous. I repeated what Dominic had told us about the escape being an admission of guilt and the likely effect on the civil suit.

Ken dealt with facts he didn't like by ignoring them. Drink made it easier. "You think you're so fucking smart," Ken yelled. "You don't know all the answers here. You're not an attorney." I wasn't, but we had again argued ourselves into a place where I was thinking like one and he wasn't. It was a replay of our afternoons at those depressing bars, but with the stakes higher and the volume turned up.

I told him he would hear the same things if he bothered to listen to his real lawyers. "Call Dominic again. Call Howard Weitzman. See what they say."

Ken shook his head and walked away. I accepted the fact that he was going to meet up with Mom one way or another, and I began to formulate a plan. My goal was to restore the status quo, as much as possible, and keep anyone else from going to jail.

While I was thinking, Ken walked out the door and jumped in the Lincoln. I didn't try to stop him. My daughter was already in bed, but ten-year-old Kenny was still awake, watch-ing TV. I put him to bed before the eleven o'clock news came on.

Sure enough, there was Mom on every channel, the ugly mug shot with the closed eyes that she hated so much and some footage in her orange jail uniform too. The newscaster's voice betrayed his amusement. It *was* funny, if you didn't know the people involved. Women in their fifties weren't supposed to escape custody. The cops were frantic because they were so damn embarrassed.

I could make sense now of Mom's behavior. I should have

seen the escape coming. For weeks she'd been complaining about every ailment and pain she could spell the name of. Long afterward, Dominic would tell me how Mom had turned her alleged health problems into a get-out-of-jail pass.

Mom conned her way into the University Medical Center with the help of Dr. Nick Stavros. He was the family physician. In the old days, Mom used to get me to steal stationery and pre-scription pads from doctors or do it herself, but Stavros was a one-stop shop. A delicate way to put it would be to say that he was very attentive to my mother. He listened carefully to her complaints. His diagnoses of Mom's ills seemed to coincide with her own.

While Mom was in jail awaiting trial, Stavros produced a file showing that she'd been in poor health for years. I have it on very good authority that the fee for his services was a quickie in the broom closet. Thus compensated, the good doctor arranged for Mom to be shipped to University Medical Center in the cus-tody of a female guard. I don't know what suasion Mom used on the guard—there were rumors of a seven-grand bribe—but somehow she talked her into taking off the cuffs. Mom walked out of the huge mud brown hospital on Charleston Boulevard and started climbing over fences in a nearby neighborhood of shabby bungalows. Just like in the movies, she nabbed a new outfit from a clothesline and melted into Vegas. (And just like in the cartoons, a big dog took a hunk out of her butt.)

Mom appeared at Sheila's apartment cut up from the hedges and fences she'd tried to jump—I'd witnessed her lack of skill at fence-hopping in Hawaii—and the first thing she did was take a bubble bath and drink some booze. She really thought she'd escaped for good.

When Ken got home after midnight, I was awake, waiting for him. He wouldn't make eye contact with me. "She's okay," he said.

"Ken, you're on your own with this one," I said calmly. "I'm going to do everything I can to help her get caught."

Ken looked surprised but not angry. He headed for the kitchen to pour himself the inevitable drink. He had some catching up to do.

The next day, I refused to saddle up and hit the bars with Ken. I didn't want to take the chance that he might try to see Mom while I was chauffeuring him. I didn't understand why the feds or the Vegas cops hadn't caught him the first time, and I didn't think he'd be lucky twice.

Instead I waited till I knew Sheila was on duty, and I dropped by the Huddle Lounge. It was two in the afternoon and she looked like hell. You could tell she hadn't slept and that she wasn't happy to see me.

When my eyes adjusted to the Huddle's dim light, I was thankful to see that the bar was almost empty. I walked up to her and said, "Are you out of your fucking mind?"

It wasn't really a question. Sheila looked sheepish. "She just . . . appeared, and she was all bruised and cut up." She smiled. "You know how she is. You can't say no to her."

Sheila had stashed Mom in an apartment that her daughter had rented but not yet occupied. She offered to have Mom gone by that evening. That wasn't good enough. I tried to scare her. "If I have to go to the police myself and tell them that you have her, I will. If you make the call yourself, you might not get arrested for harboring a fugitive."

That did the trick. Sheila looked as if she was about to cry. Maybe she'd been too dumb to realize till that moment what a felony was.

"Call them. She'll get caught even if you don't. Hell, they might already know that you have her."

Sheila's eyes got wide. "What do you mean?"

"This is a federal case. There have been guys in white cars following Ken and me every day since he got out on bail. Don't you think they might be tapping our phones? And you called the house!"

Sheila was pensive. "She thinks she's going to get away with it, and she says she'd rather die than go back."

"I'm not bluffing," I concluded. Sheila was still hemming and hawing when I left, but I'd made an impact.

The next two days were stressful, to say the least. I was scared that Mom or Ken would get shot or that choppers would materialize above Geronimo Way. We had gotten used to the feds and the Vegas cops watching our house. Now they were joined by camera crews from the local TV stations. We peered back at them through the pillbox slit that was the kitchen window.

The only break in the tension came from my wife and my little brother. Lynn sashayed downstairs one afternoon wearing a big black Sante Kimes wig. She wanted to walk outside and whip the cops and media into a feeding frenzy. I thought it was hilarious, but grumpy Ken said no.

My half brother was in his spy phase, fully indulged by his soft-touch dad. After Mom went to jail, Ken had bought Kenny all kinds of expensive surveillance tools, including high-quality binoculars. So Kenny and Lynn would spy on the spies, who would be startled to see binoculars looking back at them from 2121 Geronimo.

On one occasion Kenny and Lynn went further. They raided Mom's closets for some dresses, her 50DD bra, and a wig. Stuffing the clothes with sheets and pillows and slapping a bewigged styrofoam head on top, they created a Sante doll. They carried the dummy outside and stashed it in the trunk of the Lincoln, but not one of our official voyeurs stirred from their posts.

Our half-giddy days of stress ended with Mom's recapture. I first heard about it on the local TV news. She was nabbed outside another of her favorite dark blue-collar strip mall Vegas bars called the Elbow Room. She was disguised as a bag lady, wearing ragged clothes and pushing a shopping cart. She'd been caught, the reporter said, with the help of a tip from an unnamed source. I hope it was Sheila.

Personally, I was wrestling with yet another weird emotion inspired by Sante Kimes. I was in the position of feeling glad that my mother was back in jail. I also suspected that this might have been the first time I ever tried to get my mother arrested when it had actually worked.

As for Ken, his addled optimism about the escape helping his finances was proved wrong. The extra offense added a few hundred thousand to Mom's mounting legal bills, all of them payable in full by Ken Kimes.

Mom's trial began February 10. I sat through the long slow process of jury selection, watching as Mom took notes and Dominic struck the jurors he didn't like. I wore my army uniform most days because I had little else with a collar or buttons. Ken had never bought me many clothes. I was also in denial about the end of my military career. As soon as my army greens came off, I'd have to admit they were never going back on.

I think it was after voir dire and before opening arguments that the judge asked for the courtroom to be cleared. For some reason I didn't file out in the hall with all the other extra bodies.

Mom beckoned me to come take one of the newly empty spaces closer to her. I obeyed, and a member of the prosecution team, a Mr. Clark, complained to Judge Howard McKibben. "Your Honor," he said, "Mr. Walker is not only a possible witness, [he's an] unindicted coconspirator in this case. And, further, even if he were permitted to be present, which we strenuously object to, I believe it would be unfair and prejudicial to have him appear in the flight suit. . . . [He's] trying to influence the jury."

"Your Honor," I protested, before I had a chance to wonder if it was permitted, "I don't have any other suits. And as an unindicted coconspirator, don't I have a right to be present?"

A legal huddle ensued, and I sensed that no one in it could recite the rights of an unindicted coconspirator off the top of his or her head. Ultimately the judge opted to banish me from the courtroom because I was on both the defense and prosecution witness lists.

I spent the eleven days of the trial on a bench in the hall outside the courtroom in the black-and-white Foley Building, still in my military uniform. I devoted most of that time to my unofficial job on the defense team. As Dominic had told Judge McKibben, "Kent Walker knows more about this case than I do. He has helped me; spoon-fed me throughout."

I was my mother's investigator. Twice I'd flown to Hawaii to interview potential defense witnesses, and I'd also made several trips to Southern California. When the witnesses had arrived in Vegas, with airline tickets paid for by Ken, I'd picked them up at the airport and ferried them to their hotel rooms, also on Ken's tab. We had so many witnesses that we'd gotten a group rate at La Quinta.

During the trial my life flashed before me. Friends from Newport Beach, Honolulu, and Las Vegas would appear in that hallway, tense up, walk with a bailiff through the double doors, and then reemerge when their testimony was over. Seventeen people took the witness stand on Mom's behalf. These men and women didn't necessarily know each other, but they knew me.

I was there to keep their morale up, but not to coach their testimony. They didn't have to be bought or persuaded. None of them had ever seen Mom hit, kick, burn, or otherwise physically abuse any maids. To that they could testify truthfully. They were, most of them, adamant that the federal government was committing an injustice. I thought, as I sat in the hall and laughed and joked and commiserated with them, that they were the living proof that my family really could keep friends. I didn't realize I would never see most of them again.

Most of what I knew about the goings-on behind the double doors I gleaned from conversations with friends or chats with Mom and Ken—or from the media. Every day the case was front-page fodder and the top of the nightly newscasts. It's hard for the media to resist the word *slave* or the nickname "Dragon Lady," which one of the feds had hung on Mom.

The only time Mom's trial wasn't the lead story was when the honor went to the trial in the next courtroom. Down the hall in the Foley Building, mafioso brothers Tony and Jimmy Spilotro faced federal racketeering charges. Their lawyer was Mom's future lawyer, famed Mob attorney Oscar Goodman, now mayor of Las Vegas.

Joe Pesci played Tony "the Ant" Spilotro in the film *Casino*. Pesci captured his essence—short, grim, and wound tight, with a scary charisma. Though I saw Tony in the hall day after day, I didn't dare approach him.

His brother, Jimmy, and I made small talk on a half dozen occasions. Jimmy was taller and better-looking than his more infamous older brother. He had played a few small roles in movies; later, another bit-part actor would portray him in *Casino*. Talking killed a few moments in the dull and anxious days for both of us. We had, temporarily, something in common.

"How's your trial going?" he'd ask.

"I can't tell," I'd say. "How about you?"

"Fuckin' feds. These fuckin' guys."

At first I made the mistake of trying to be all civilized and answered, "Well, they've got a job to do." He looked at me like I'd farted. After that, I'd merely shake my head in time with his and echo, "Fuckin' feds." I meant it.

Thanks to Oscar Goodman, the Spilotros defeated the feds and the RICO charges. A few months later, however, their Cosa Nostra associates lured the brothers to an Illinois cornfield, crushed their skulls with baseball bats, and buried them, still breathing, in shallow graves. The old Mob Vegas died with them.

Fortunately, Mom's Mob enemies were imaginary. But she had less luck with her federal enemies. Mom's friends could take the stand, swear up and down that they'd never seen her lift a finger against the maids, and describe Christmas presents and birthday parties for the young women, but the prosecution had fourteen ex-maids and tutors who testified about what went on when the friends were gone and the doors were closed. And they had those damning lists.

The defense never called me, and if they had, I'm not sure I would have been any help to my mother. I could testify that the maids hadn't been incarcerated and that I'd never seen anyone burned with a hot iron. If the prosecution asked, though, I would have had to admit that I'd seen Mom manhandle the maids on a few occasions and that I'd helped a number escape. The biggest contribution I made to Mom's defense was overhearing some of the plaintiff's attorneys in the upcoming civil lawsuit—David Schutter's people—trolling for witnesses in the hallway as they left after testifying. I brought their presence to Dominic's attention, and he got the judge to bounce them from the building.

Inside the courtroom, Gentile tried hard to explain away Mom's behavior. She kept the doors locked and wouldn't let the maids use the phone because of the Creeps, he said. "Sante Kimes has good reason to believe from the conduct of the Creeps over the years that they are out to harm her and her family and most particularly her ten-year-old boy, Kenny."

After Grandma and Aunt Alice's stormy stay with us, our relations with the Kimes clan had gone from bad to litigious. Within a year Alice had returned to Hawaii to die, as she wanted, but when Mom and Ken shipped her body home to L.A., Ken's relatives demanded an autopsy and then accused Mom of mutilating the body—sewing her vagina shut, to be specific. That seems beyond even Sante Kimes. Enraged, Mom retaliated. Several years later, when Ken's mother died, Mom screened Ken's calls and didn't tell him. He missed the funeral. In lieu of Ken, Mom sent flowers and signed his name to a "condolence" note. In so many words, it said, "I never want to speak to any of you again."

Finally Mom had just cut to the chase and sued the Creeps. She charged every relative she could think of with invasion of privacy, conspiracy, and emotional distress. The suit, which Ken okayed, cataloged her tales of snakes in the car, blood on the walls, and attempts to steal Kenny, and charged, in more highfalutin language, that the Creeps were talking trash about Mom and giving Ken ulcers. The suit collapsed in 1984, in part because no one had seen any rattlesnakes except Sante. Two years later in a criminal courtroom, Mom's Creep show wasn't any more convincing.

My mother never took the stand, but she testified from her seat at the defense table. She glared, she hissed at hostile witnesses as they passed her, and she cried. She wept buckets of tears. She yelped in pain when a maid accused her of burning her with an iron. "These are lies," Mom shouted. "It's all lies. They just want money." The judge sent the jury out and told Mom to control herself.

The brute weight of the evidence, and my mother's demeanor, suggested at the very least that she was an unbalanced, paranoid, deeply eccentric woman. Gentile had a very unsympathetic client. He did the best he could with what he had. His closing argument would be paralleled fifteen years later by Mom's defense lawyer in the Silverman case, Michael Hardy. Both Hardy and Gentile would argue, essentially, that Mom was one crazy, nasty, twisted harpy, but there were worse people in this world. In fact, Gentile used the word that rhymes with *rich:* "Even if you think Sante Kimes is a bitch, if you follow the law you can't do anything but acquit." He picked up the leg irons that Mom had somehow stepped out of at UMC Hospital when she escaped. He pointed out that none of the so-called slaves had worn shackles and that they'd all run away. If they weren't incarcerated, he insisted, they weren't slaves.

"Maybe it isn't easy to be rich, maybe there [are maids] who start out happy and satisfied, but when they see how well you're doing, they get unhappy and they want more. . . . If they're entitled to money, let them go to a civil court and let them get a civil judgment and we'll pay for it."

Like I said, he didn't have a lot to work with. On the last day of February 1986, the jury convicted Mom of fourteen counts, including slaveholding, escaping from prison, and transporting illegal aliens.

In all the years since, I've wrestled with whether or not this was a just verdict. At this remove, I can usually see that it was, and that Mom committed most, if not all, of the awful, unforgivable acts of which she stood accused. Yet I can also slide easily into old habits of thought and stop seeing the big picture. No, Schutter was not pulling the strings on a huge mafioid conspiracy against my family. He had nothing to do with any Mob, Hawaiian or otherwise, and he hadn't done any of the spooky things Mom claimed he'd done. But he did play a large role in supplying witnesses to the prosecution. He did have an ulterior motive. I also hear myself saying, sometimes, still, "If the defendant had been anyone but Sante Kimes, this would have been a simple assault charge." Her persona, her grand manner, and her pretensions invited censure. I'm probably wrong. The maids case hurt my family so badly, however, ate up so much of Ken's health and fortune, and pushed Mom so much further down the road toward criminal violence that I can't help being bitter. I can't help agreeing with Sante a little.

I was also left, in the wake of the maids case, with the sad certainty that no one would ever be able to offer more than an educated guess as to why. Why did my mother do the things she did? During the maids case, for the first and only time, my mother endured hours of questioning by psychiatrists. As far as I can determine, she conned them.

As far back as September 1985, six months before the trial, Mom's own counsel raised the issue of her mental health. "There is reasonable cause," wrote Gentile, "to believe the defendant may be presently insane." Both defense and prosecution shrinks examined Mom and confirmed that, yes, there was something seriously amiss with Sante Kimes. A psychologist hired by the defense attributed her delusional behavior to something called Ganser syndrome, and the prosecution talked more generally about personality disorders, but their descriptions of her coincided. Mom was an impulsive, moody, paranoid narcissist and hypochondriac, loosely tethered to reality.

But Mom studied medicine the way she studied law. She recognized that mental illness might be her only escape route from prison, and early in the process she swallowed her pride and began to pursue a diagnosis of crazy. Psychiatry was simply another angle to her. She could read the most damning, penetrating assessment of her psyche and skip straight to How can I use this for my benefit? She would not pause to wonder whether there was really something wrong with her. She was not capable of introspection, even when someone else had done it for her.

She knew what to tell the doctors. She lied to them in a conscious, premeditated fashion. A couple bought the story about the car accident on the day of the fur verdict. They attributed her confused behavior to a concussion. Others believed her when she insisted that at the age of forty-nine, two years before her arrest, she'd had a second child by Ken Kimes, a boy named Kenian, but had given Kenian up for adoption in Mexico because Ken had suffered a heart attack and couldn't raise another baby. Both Kenian and heart attack were inventions. There are documents in the maids case court file that seem to show a hysterectomy in 1975. She claimed that her stepfather, Ed Chambers, had sexually abused her without cease from the day of her adoption. My grandfather couldn't defend himself because he'd been dead four years when Mom first leveled that accusation.

My suspicion of all the official versions of Mom's past arises from this trial, because it was during this trial, for the purpose of engendering sympathy and saving her butt, that Mom "revealed" that her mother had been a prostitute. With the same "sincerity," she trashed her adoptive dad and accused Jeff David of being the real thief in the furs case. I couldn't credit anything she said about her personal history, and at the maids trial I gave up on learning anything true about my roots.

And I gave up untangling what was true and false about Mom's mental state. I would never really be able to gauge how much of her was evil and how much helplessly crazy. I would never learn whether she'd stamped me with some warped gene at birth and whether I'd passed the same poison on to my own kids. I still check myself for symptoms.

In the two and a half months between the verdict and sentencing, the new, psychiatrically savvy Mom engaged a company called Alternative Sentencing Resources to turn her story of a troubled past into a report that would make the judge take pity on her. It reiterated her stories of early abuse and argued that Sante was "not a spoiled rich woman, but a troubled, emotionally disturbed individual." Friends and family, including me, wrote letters of support. "Mom has no midpoint on anything," reads my contribution. "Everything is to the extreme. She is very extreme emotionally. I've always thought she needed more leveling. . . . Everything she does is with good intentions, though. It's just that her methods are questionable." In retrospect, the final word is laughable, but I'd still endorse the rest of it.

If it meant she could go to a mental hospital instead of prison, Mom would say she was crazy. It didn't work. Judge McKibben sentenced her to five years in a federal facility. Previ-

Sante Kimes when she was plain old Sandy Chambers,
Carson City High School, 1948. Her classmates thought the
new girl from Los Angeles was a little unusual.

Sante convinced my stepfather Ken Kimes to adopt the title of Honorary Bicentennial Ambassador and print two million of these posters. He sold no more than 5,000. Washington Post, *reprinted by permission of the Washington D.C. Public Library*

Mom and the fake ambassador crash a party in D.C. and meet Vice President and Mrs. Gerald Ford in early 1974. They crashed three other events the same night, and made the papers. *AP/Wide World Photos*

Mom and I in our Hawaii house right before she burned it down. I'm in my sullen adolescent phase—I'd already run away from home when this picture was taken.

At seventeen, I was president of my senior class and spent my spare time at the beach.

Running from the law in Hawaii, Mom fled to Las Vegas and scammed a free penthouse out of the Landmark Casino. I'm posing there with my four-year-old brother Kenny the night before I flew back to Hawaii to live with a friend and finish high school.

Getting my wings as an army helicopter pilot was the proudest moment of my life, but I wouldn't get to wear them long. My mother was on trial for keeping slaves, and she needed me by her side.

My best friend John Bower got married in the backyard of our Hawaii house in 1990. Everybody in my family, including fifteen-year-old Kenny (left), attended. A few months later, the house burned down—for the second time.

SPECIAL AWARD

Presented to

Kent Walker

for

Being someone to talk to when I was confused

This *26* day of *May*, 19 *89*

Kenny Kimes

Kenny handed me this certificate when he graduated from eighth grade. Mom was still in prison, but she wouldn't be there for long.

Mom took this picture of the Millionaire and the Heir at Christmas 1990 in Tahoe. She'd been out of prison a year and was making Kenny's life hell. Ken wasn't too happy either—Mom told him our suite at the Cal-Neva was complimentary, but it ended up costing him $16,000.

Christmas in Tahoe, 1990. My wife Lynn is pregnant with our son Carson. A few months later, I caught Kenny trying to poison Mom and Ken.

Mom never wore any color but white after she met Ken Kimes.

Mom held on to her millionaire by making him feel like the most important man in every room he entered. And by keeping him drunk.

Kenny at sixteen at the height of his teen rebellion. This, believe it or not, is very close to his special "I'm telling you the truth" look.

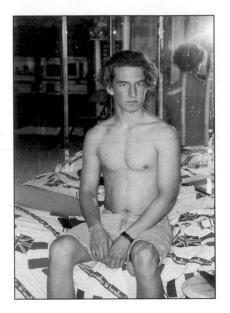

Kenny started working out religiously at age fifteen, which made it even harder for his father, who was in his seventies, to control him.

Mom and Kenny were at war from the day she got out of prison in 1989 until right before Ken's death. She severed his ties to the outside world, moving him from school to school and cutting him off from his friends.

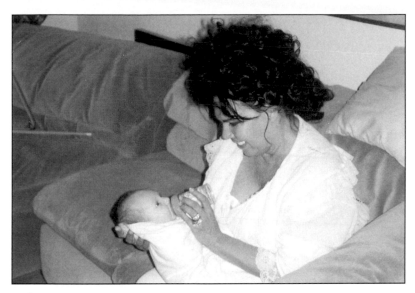

A proud grandmother feeds her youngest grandchild, Brandy, in 1996.

Mom convinced me that this was a picture of her. She even signed it. Once I realized it was Liz Taylor I felt foolish.

Kenny, with my wife Lynn at a Halloween party, never met a camera he didn't like, until he got arrested for the first time.

On our final trip to the Bahamas together. At age twenty-one, steroids and human growth hormone had helped Kenny fill out.

Kenny and I (with Brandy) were still on speaking terms in 1996.

Kenny made thousands of dollars smuggling Cuban cigars into the States and selling them on his website, cigarbiz.com.

When Ken died, Kenny and I began wearing his rings in remembrance. Kenny always wore his on the middle finger of his right hand.

This is the last shot of "Babish" with her three grandchildren. Not long afterward, I cut off all contact with Mom.

Can you tell that I'm growing uncomfortable in the presence of my little brother? By this time he'd signed on as Mom's partner in crime.

The woman my mother killed, Irene Silverman, was like the anti–Sante Kimes—equally flamboyant, from similar hard-scrabble roots, but benevolent, law-abiding, and respected.

David Kazdin was a friend of my family for twenty years. I have no doubt that Mom and Kenny killed him.

Corbis/Sygma

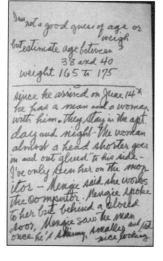

When Kenny moved into Irene Silverman's mansion, Irene realized something was afoot. She drew a sketch of my brother, and scrawled these notes about her strange new tenant and the older woman "'glued' to his side." Her notes helped send Kenny and Mom to prison.

Todd Maisel, Daily News

Irene Silverman's five-story mansion, which my mother and brother were trying to steal, has been valued at $7.5 million. *Ken Murray,* Daily News

The NYPD spent millions of dollars to solve the murder of Irene Silverman, covering the Upper East Side of Manhattan with these posters, but it still hasn't found her body.

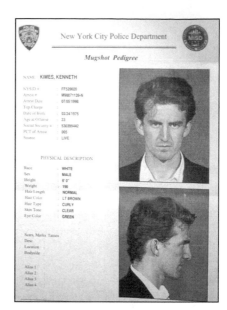

New York City Police Department

Mugshot Pedigree

NAME: KIMES, KENNETH

NYSID #   : FF529020
Arrest #   : M98071138-N
Arrest Date   : 07.05.1998
Top Charge   :
Date of Birth   : 03.24.1975
Age at Offense   : 23
Social Security # : 530399442
PCT of Arrest   : 065
Source   : LIVE

PHYSICAL DESCRIPTION

Race   : WHITE
Sex   : MALE
Height   : 6' 0"
Weight   : 190
Hair Length : NORMAL
Hair Color : LT BROWN
Hair Type : CURLY
Skin Tone : CLEAR
Eye Color : GREEN

Scars, Marks, Tattoos
Desc
Location
Bodyside

Alias 1
Alias 2
Alias 3
Alias 4

The NYPD took these pictures of Kenny after picking him up for car theft. They didn't realize until two days later what he'd really done. *Ken Murray,* Daily News

According to the police, Kenny stuffed Irene Silverman's body in a duffel bag, threw it in the trunk of his Lincoln, and then drove to New Jersey. Here the cops search the Meadowlands to no avail. *John Roca,* Daily News

Surprise! Having Sante Kimes for a mom was never dull. Sometimes it was terrifying, but more often it was fun, and I never doubted her love for me. I'll feel her absence every day of the rest of my life.

ously, she'd never been hit with more than probation or a fine, despite the length of her rap sheet.

In July, the District of Columbia finally got its chance to close the furs case, which had been opened more than six years earlier. When Mom appeared before Judge Sylvia Bacon for sentencing, she tried the crazy angle again and threw in some Scarlett O'Hara–style religion too, for good measure. "I'm not trying to excuse myself, your honor, but I'm telling you with God as my witness . . . I have changed. And, I'm dedicated and committed, trying everything I can do—what expert people are telling me I should do. I didn't know I needed any help."

Mom, of course, really *was* trying to excuse herself. She hadn't changed. She didn't believe in God, and she didn't think she needed help, but if acting sorry and telling sob stories to shrinks would keep her out of prison, she'd do it.

Judge Bacon, like McKibben in Nevada, paid more attention to Mom's record and her attempts to elude prosecution than to her newfound interest in mental health. She gave Mom three to nine years. Her sentence would begin as soon as she finished her five-year federal stretch. It meant that she faced as many as fourteen years behind bars.

Much as my mother hated the bleak prospect of all that time, it gave her something she needed as desperately as air and water: a cause. A war to wage. She started her tenure at Pleasanton Federal Prison, east of Oakland, with projects galore. She launched a campaign to discredit Judge Bacon as an alcoholic and get her D.C. sentence thrown out. She filed papers to win early release on the federal conviction. Mom was in prison, but she was busy, and busy was as close to satisfied as she could ever be.

Ken and I, meanwhile, free of Mom, he for the first time in fifteen years, went back to the bars. And that's where we stayed, drinking, gambling, talking about Mom, waiting for her to get out, for much of the next four years.

21

SILLY PUTTY

Silly Putty probably still comes in those little plastic eggs, blue and green and red and other bright colors. It did in 1982 in Las Vegas.

One afternoon Kenny was with me in my beat-up Firebird, a car I called the Ghost, when I stopped at a convenience store to pick up a few items. I decided to buy him some Silly Putty as a present. I didn't need a shopping cart for a couple of sodas, a pack of cigarettes, and a plastic egg, so I stuffed the egg in my pocket and carried the drinks and smokes to the checkout counter.

After I paid the clerk, my brother and I walked toward the glass double doors. I was already squinting in anticipation of the bright sunlight when I reached in my pocket for the car keys and found a plastic lump. I pulled out the Silly Putty and said, "Oh, shit."

Kenny's eyes got big. "I don't believe it!" he howled. "You stole the Silly Putty!" He wasn't impressed. He was prissy, scolding, and so alarmed I thought he might take off running.

I calmed him down. "No, Kenny, I made a mistake. I put it in my pocket and forgot about it when I started talking to the checkout lady. Now watch me. I'm going to give her the money I owe her." As I turned around, Kenny couldn't see the big smile on my face.

At seven years of age I'd seen everything, fires and fights and innumerable acts of shoplifting. There hadn't been one day in the pre-Ken Kimes era when Mom had entered a store and exited without stolen goods. At Kenny's age I'd been navigating the transition from bystander to accomplice. Mom had already shown me, for example, how to pay for one newspaper out of a sidewalk dispenser, then steal every copy inside and sell them for a profit.

That shoplifting could traumatize my little brother thrilled me. Kenny wasn't growing up like me. He'd been shielded from some of Mom's worst behavior, and as far as I could tell, he hadn't yet connected the dots on his own. He hadn't guessed the purpose of the cardboard boxes full of notary stamps in a hundred different names, or the origin of the dozens of tiny airline bottles of booze that Mom had snatched from liquor stores. He couldn't tell that our house had been furnished in chairs, ashtrays, and drinking glasses swiped from casinos. For a time he enjoyed something I'd never experienced — innocence.

There were plenty of parallels with my early years. Like me and Mom in the Palm Springs era, Kenny was in constant motion, albeit in the first-class cabin rather than grifted sedans. Like me he learned his *sirs* and *ma'ams* and *thank-yous*. Mom was obsessed with manners and grooming.

But his training, unlike mine, was fit for a little prince. I never even saw Mom hit him, though she must have. Instead she drove him to excel. I had studied three hours a day as a grade schooler; from the age of four he worked twice as long, and with a private tutor. Mom drew up a lesson plan and insisted that the tutors respond with a weekly written report on Kenny's progress.

Kenny missed much of Mom's bad behavior because he was home busily working while she stole. But to some degree Mom's decision to protect Kenny was intentional. In the early years, she spared him the trauma of the Creep stories she told everyone else; he was blissfully clueless that a hit squad was after him. And while I had to umpire Mom and Ken's fights, Kenny rarely heard them. My parents didn't want him near while they scrapped, so he was out of earshot or asleep.

Most important, I don't think he saw Mom get arrested once in the first ten years of his life. In 1980, the Las Vegas cops came to a mini-mansion that Mom and Ken were renting near the Tropicana golf course, a few doors down from Paul Anka. It was post–casino penthouse, pre-Geronimo. The police wanted to arrest Mom and Ken for stealing a piano, a crime they'd already committed at least once in Hawaii. I herded Kenny around the side of the house and into the Firebird before he saw the cruiser with the cherry on top. I told him that Mom and Ken had to go to Hawaii for a little while, and took him to a movie. Afterward I dropped him off at the house in the care of the maids. I got my parents bailed out the next day, and Kenny never knew the difference. The chaos that swirled around our lives in the era before the slavery trial stayed outside his bedroom door and beyond the high brick wall at Portlock and the windowless facade on Geronimo.

When Kenny was little I loved playing the role of big brother. Kenny had been a major reason for my return from Carson City. Mom and Ken would go out almost every night, and Kenny and I would eat dinner together. Often I'd take him for pizza or ice cream. We'd wrestle and fight with pillows, Kenny swinging wild and hard and laughing.

For the most part, Kenny was just another little boy who liked to watch cartoons and hated to be told to go to bed. But he did have his quirks. He was a little late in talking and a lot manic. Some of his tutors suggested that he should be sent to a doctor and tested for hyperactivity, but Mom never followed through. He had a talent for bratty pranks like pulling up dresses and bursting in on people when they showered.

He was also a little spoiled, because of Mom's constant reminders that he was special. It didn't matter that the Kimes fortune, at its peak, was minor league. To Mom, the millions gave Kenny a destiny and made him superior. Mom auditioned kids to be his playmates and rejected many as unworthy, something she'd never done with me — unless the kids were black or brown. She encouraged Kenny to think of the maids as less than fully human, and though as a toddler he played hide-and-seek with the maids and clung lovingly to their skirts, as he got older he realized he could be bratty and boss them around. Some of the maids claimed on the witness stand that he kicked their shins.

Later, this idea of superiority would fester into something lethal. As a child, though, he still had real regard for other people. He'd draw pictures and hand them to the maids simply to make them happy. He had compassion.

Back then, from what I could see, the worst side effects of Mom's disdain for mortal children were loneliness and a certain unnaturally adult cast to his behavior. I had grown up too fast on the inside, becoming jaded and suspicious before junior high; in a much more superficial way, Kenny was also too old too soon. He had few spontaneous, informal encounters with his peers, because the maids weren't supposed to let him play with unapproved kids, and the tutors were supposed to shield him from imminent kidnapping by the Creeps. As a result, most of the people with whom he spent time were adults.

As Kenny got to school age, I felt a little sorry for him. Eight hours a day, he went one-on-one with his tutor. There were no other students to distract the teacher and give Kenny a rest. His daily workload must have equaled that of a public-school week.

Every so often I'd rescue him. We went through many tutors, and I could pull the same trick on each newbie at least once. I'd get home from Mid-Pac in the afternoon and tell Kenny's private instructor that Mom had decreed he was due for a field trip. If the tutors tried to tag along, I'd say, "Take a break. You need it." Then I'd take Kenny to the beach or to the movies, and steel myself for the tongue-lashing Mom would give me on our return.

Mom ordered me to stay away from the tutors and not to interfere with Kenny's regimen. But I pestered her about his need for fun and friends, and eventually I got her to see my point. I convinced her to let Kenny attend a public school during the afternoons when he reached first grade.

Between my stint in the service and Mom and Ken's compulsive travel, I only saw my little brother in patches between 1980 and 1985. After an extra-long gap, I got a chance to catch up with him in 1985 when I baby-sat him for a weekend in D.C. Mom and Ken were prepping for the furs case, mere months before the FBI raid in La Jolla. I could see that Kenny had bikes and toys and — most important — playmates, with whom he seemed to interact well. I thought he'd emerged from his transient, sheltered childhood fairly normal, as playful and charming as ever and as prone to laughter.

Nothing in those early years gave any hint of what Kenny would do in his twenties. I think his problems started the day he saw his first arrest. Kenny began to go downhill when the FBI picked up my parents in La Jolla in August 1985 and left my ten-year-old brother keening and sniffling in the arms of a tutor. He lost his shot at anything approaching a normal life.

Since the Silverman murder, much has been written about my brother's childhood. Acquaintances have recalled the pre-teen Kenny as a strange, immature child, a mama's boy, isolated and socially awkward. Though my perspective may be skewed, I think they're exaggerating. I envy Kenny's early childhood. Similarly, I differ with Kenny's friends from Paradise Palms, the Geronimo neighborhood, about the period that followed. They call the years when Mom was locked up Kenny's "golden age."

It's a logical assumption. Her actions had attracted the authorities; to the uninitiated, Ken looked like a mere bystander. Mom was so manifestly unfit to be a mother that she had to be the source of every scar in Kenny's psyche. She looked like the fount of all evil in his life, and she'd been cut out like a tumor.

I'm proof that you can survive having Sante Kimes as a mother. I logged nine years, from 1962 to 1971, as the man in her life. Yet here I am, commuting to work, raising a family, a law-abiding husband/father/businessman. I'm free and Kenny isn't. The difference is Ken Kimes. I think people are wrong about Mom's influence. According to shrinks, you learn your moral code between the ages of ten and thirteen, on the cusp of puberty. Ken Kimes had a hammerlock on Kenny during the years when Kenny was internalizing the rules of right and wrong. Ken Kimes, raising his son alone, did grievous, irreversible damage.

People assume that in Mom's absence Kenny lived like a normal child. In some respects, his life did become more mainstream. When Mom left, so did the tutors, and Kenny went to school with other kids all day every day for the first time. My stepfather enrolled him in a Lutheran school called Good Shepherd within a month of the La Jolla arrest. Kenny transferred to a public school and then, at the start of seventh grade in fall 1987, to St. Viator's, an elite Catholic academy. Rich kids and celebrity scions attended St. Viator's, but Kenny's reason for loving it was simple: his friends went there.

With Mom gone, Kenny's social life had improved dramatically. He could follow the trends that other kids did. He dove into punk rock, moshing to loud music and wearing studded bracelets and collars and silver jewelry. He was still hyper, but he turned that to his advantage, becoming a class clown.

Kenny could also have more people over to the house, because his dad didn't have any strange feuds with the neighbors, like Mom, or any rules about which kids Kenny could see. The Geronimo house became a raucous magnet for neighborhood boys. Ken put out bowls full of empty calories, chips and dip and candy, and Kenny's new friends piled into the living room to stuff their faces and play video games. For Kenny's twelfth birthday, Ken took my brother and a half-dozen friends to Disneyland in Anaheim. For Kenny's thirteenth birthday, Ken put in a backyard pool. He paid the contractor extra to make sure it would be ready on time.

It sounds like heaven. A kid escapes from under his criminal mother's thumb, goes to school, makes friends, has fun. He stays in one place and sees the same people week in and week out. No more maids coming through the revolving door. No one forcing him to study eight hours a day.

Kenny thought it *was* heaven. He hated Mom for leaving him, but soon he hated the thought that she might come back. When she called from prison in California, he'd disappear so he didn't have to speak to her. She tried to reach through the earpiece and maintain her control over his life, and he couldn't stand it. He told his friends he thought Mom was crazy. He told Ken, with the eager bluntness of a child, the same words I'd needed liquid courage to form—"Divorce her."

A different man would've heeded our advice. But Sante Kimes had been Ken's life. Much as he complained about her ceaseless phone calls from Pleasanton, without them there was silence. The man without hobbies or friends had little else to do.

At twice his former pace, he drank. He'd been remitted to a halfway house for alcoholics as part of his plea bargain, which meant that for three months he had to report before curfew every night, but he drank Stoli on the 10 P.M. ride up and Seagram's on the 7 A.M. ride back. I know, because I drove him.

To keep busy, he rented an office in a strip mall. He didn't need it, however, for anything except boxes full of legal files. All the calls he made were about lawsuits. His business career was over.

So Ken embarked on a new career. His job became Kenny— not the raising of his son but the winning of his son. That's what was so abnormal and toxic about Kenny's "golden age." In a world narrowed by booze and paranoia, Ken campaigned for Kenny's affection because he thought he was engaged in a war and he wanted an ally. He thought he might be headed for a custody battle with Sante, and he began to mimic his behavior from the early sixties, when he'd been the heavy in the ugliest, most protracted divorce in Orange County history. Splitting from Charloette, he'd bribed his son and daughter with cars and money so they'd serve as witnesses against her. Love was another word for loyalty to Ken.

Kenny had been sheltered from the power struggle between his parents, but his innocence ended when Mom went to jail. Ken let him know what the fighting was about. Since Kenny could crawl, Mom and Ken had been arguing about which of them their son loved more. Ken wanted it to be him. Mom became the enemy.

My brother was vulnerable because at a crucial age he'd lost his mother. He wasn't that different from a little boy whose mom had died of cancer. She was there all the time, on the phone and in the visiting room, and he loved his new freedom and complained about her hectoring, but she wasn't in the house at night when he went to bed, and he felt it. He'd lost his bearings, and Ken took advantage of his weakness.

Ken began to sell Kenny on the idea that the two of them were blood and that most of the rest of humanity, including Mom, was suspect. It had to be confusing for Kenny to hear that his Kimes relatives weren't Creeps after all, as Mom and Ken had always preached, but were actually blood too. Ken did a 180-degree turn. He took Kenny to visit his long-lost cousins in California. The enemies had turned into friends.

To encourage the schism between mother and son, Ken introduced Kenny to a nasty habit that would stay with him all his life. It was something Ken Senior had picked up from Sante. When Mom called from jail, Ken Senior made Kenny listen in on another line. After she'd run out of time, Ken would sit with Kenny and decipher Mom's lies. He forced Kenny to sit through a sort of sick Sante code-breaking class.

My little brother didn't have to hear the feature-length lectures that I endured from Mom as a boy. Sante had snared her millionaire and didn't need to drill Kenny in the virtues of wealth. But Ken made up for it in the late eighties. Ken pounded his son's brain with the idea that no one was to be trusted, that you always had to keep up your guard. He told Kenny that people were after his money and were trying to drive him into the poorhouse. "Fuck everyone," he'd mutter. "They're all vultures."

Ken's paranoia became so perverse that he insisted that Kenny sleep in the same bed with him. Mom's obsession with control had never extended that far. There was nothing sexual in the sleeping arrangement, but Ken was scared to be alone and scared to let Kenny out of his sight. I'd walk by Kenny's room and see the unwrinkled covers on the bed and realize that the only nights he ever used it were when another kid slept over.

I watched Ken warping my little brother from close up. I'd quit my full-time job as Ken's rent-a-friend and had become a door-to-door vacuum-cleaner salesman, but I still worked for Ken. Our daily slogs from bar to bar had shrunk to more manageable proportions. We met for breakfast every morning at the Country Inn on the corner of Eastern and Desert Inn Avenues. We'd review the day's itinerary, and if Ken needed me to help with the lawsuits, I wouldn't sell vacuums that day. I worked on commission and had a flexible schedule.

My wife and daughter and I lived in the Geronimo house for a full year after the La Jolla raid, but even after we moved to a town house of our own, I'd check on Ken and Kenny every afternoon. Both of them called me whenever anything bad happened. I could see my stepdad's drinking accelerate. Twice I had to rush him to the emergency room when he coughed up blood and passed out. He had bleeding ulcers. Alcohol mixed with pain pills had burned holes in his stomach.

I stayed nearby because I loved my stepdad and I worried about him and, frankly, because he had the money. I also lingered in Vegas because my little brother needed a protector. The guardian role had been forced on me when Mom and Ken were arrested, and it deepened during Ken's stint at the halfway house.

I also tried to help Kenny have a good time. Ken Senior was rounding seventy, and I was in my twenties. My body could keep up with a twelve-year-old. My brother and I raced around the neighborhood in the go-cart Ken had bought him. Often I'd ferry him and his neighborhood posse to the pizza parlor or the mall multiplex, the way I had in Hawaii. When we went to Tahoe, I could sled down a snowy hill with my brother, while his father could only watch. I was also better equipped to help Kenny with advice about friends and school and emotions. Ken hadn't been Kenny's age since the 1920s. His stories about hard times in the Dust Bowl and stoop labor in the Central Valley meant nothing to his young son.

As the years of Mom's incarceration passed, Kenny began to confide in me. If he thought he was going to get in trouble, say, for scratching the car with his bike, he'd come to me for advice in dealing with Ken. He confessed that Mom's trial and imprisonment had humiliated him and that Ken's boozing worried him. Kenny and I would spend hours fantasizing about what life was like outside the scrutiny of law enforcement and the media.

And he retained his sweetness. I saw it, strangely enough, when we were out in the desert shooting at targets. After a few visits to his sister's ranch in Northern California Ken had procured some rifles. He couldn't throw a football with his son, so he'd settled on shooting as a manly sport the two could share. To the old farmboy and ex-soldier, guns were no big deal, and Kenny enjoyed it. They took their rifles to the desert several times a week.

I took Ken's place on one occasion. Kenny and I were shooting at targets. A small bird flew out from under a bush fifty feet in front of us, and without thinking I fired the .22 from my hip. The bird exploded in a puff of feathers. It was a freakish piece of marksmanship that I regretted before the feathers hit the ground.

"Shit," I said.

Kenny, meanwhile, burst into tears. "That poor bird," he sniffed. "Why'd you kill it?"

He stopped crying when I apologized and told him it was pure reflex, that I hadn't intended to shoot a living thing and wished I hadn't. I was surprised, though, at how upset he got. He still had his sense of compassion.

The night in June 1989 that Kenny graduated from eighth grade at St. Viator's, Ken and I watched from a church pew as he and the rest of his class sang, "Wind Beneath My Wings." Throughout the song, Kenny maintained eye contact with his dad. Afterward the students walked out into the audience and presented certificates to family members. Kenny handed his certificate to me instead of Ken. It read, "Thank you for being someone I could talk to when I was confused."

On that night I had high hopes for my brother. He had a chance at something I'd never had. He would live in one house and go on to the Catholic high school, Bishop Gorman, with his friends from St. Viator's and the neighborhood. He would have peace and stability. I knew that Kenny displayed more and more of the traits of a rich brat, but I thought he was a great kid.

I was overly optimistic. There were already signs that Ken's boot camp in paranoia had taken a toll.

Ken had, first of all, spoiled Kenny rotten. It was part of his seduction and indoctrination. He couldn't relate to anyone except through money. He believed that everyone was after his fortune, and when he bought affection with money, as he'd done his whole life, it only confirmed his lack of faith in humanity. He gave Kenny everything he could possibly want—a pool, thousands of dollars' worth of clothes, every video game, every cool new toy.

Before long, money was the only way Ken could influence Kenny's behavior. He had to bribe him to be good. He had to ask for my help in getting Kenny to curb his spending. If he'd been pampered and isolated as a child, Kenny was indulged without mercy as a teen. He liked to jump from our second-story balcony and bounce off a trampoline into the pool. No sober, responsible parent would have permitted it.

But the money and gifts and the whispering about enemies worked. People in hostage situations often succumb to feelings of admiration, or more, for their captors. They may even start to believe in their kidnappers' "cause," à la Patty Hearst. It happened to Kenny, who was held hostage by Ken's selfish fear. His father became his hero, and he embraced his hero's worldview.

When Ken said, "Us against the world," he meant it literally. And the world included me. I was the first person Ken redefined for his youngest son as an enemy. Though he quickly reconsidered, for a spell Ken saw me as Mom's surrogate and as a rival for Kenny's affection. It must have been confusing for my little brother to be told he should hate and distrust the person he considered his protector, the person he'd called to rescue him in La Jolla. But late in 1986, Kenny glared at me and parroted his father's words: "You and I aren't blood," he said. "You're not really my brother." The words wounded me, but because my little brother was soon confiding in me again, I thought that this part of Ken's training hadn't stuck. Later, with more perspective, I would look back on Kenny's statement and see it as a defining moment.

Eavesdropping on enemies like me and Mom was supposed to teach Kenny about the enemy's true nature, but it taught him much more. He learned Ken's true nature, and he learned that it was okay to eavesdrop. Mom had used Kenny as a spy on the maids. She would quiz him in a chirpy, upbeat voice about what he and the maids had done that day and then punish the maids for any infractions of the rules. Kenny knew the maids weren't supposed to use the phones, and he told them so. But he didn't know he was spying, and he didn't learn to do it on purpose until Ken Kimes the paranoid showed him how. He taught Kenny how to bug phones so he could play back conversations and deconstruct them at his leisure.

Kenny had developed an unhealthy interest in surveillance equipment. He used the credit card Ken had given him to buy wiretapping gizmos, hidden cameras—hundreds of dollars' worth of spy junk. The spy binge morphed into a taste for violent, potentially lethal gadgets like Ninja throwing stars. Where Mom would have said, "Hell no," Ken said, "How many?" When Kenny wanted bottle rockets, which were illegal in Vegas, Ken drove to the next county and bought boxfuls, not once but over and over again. He made the hour-and-a-half round trip weekly.

So by mid-1989 Ken had spoiled Kenny, given him a license to be destructive, and taught him that other people weren't to be trusted. Those were the lessons of Kenny's supposed "golden age." The worst thing Ken ever did to Kenny, however, was steal his compassion.

Mom had taught Kenny that he was superior to other children. But the day Mom and Ken were arrested in La Jolla, Kenny still had the ability to love. Not love Kimes style, where hugs and kisses are means to an end, but real unconditional love.

Mom had implanted Kenny's feelings of entitlement, but Ken's the one who turned entitlement into a rule for living. He brainwashed Kenny into believing that the money-grubbing strangers around them, all intent on stealing his wealth, were soulless scum. It didn't matter what you had to do to defeat them, because *they* didn't matter. Nobody was of any consequence except Kenny and Ken. It was Ken, not Mom, who during those crucial preadolescent years convinced my little brother that other people existed only as a means to an end.

I view what happened a few weeks after the St. Viator's graduation ceremony as the logical culmination of Ken's approach to child-rearing. It was also the symbolic end of an era.

On the night of July 4, 1989, Kenny and his neighborhood

cronies assembled on the Sahara golf course for what had become a yearly ritual. Thanks largely to Ken's willingness to truck a military volume of fireworks down from Pahrump, Nevada, Kenny's gang would fight a massive bottle rocket war every Fourth. They chased each other around the greens and through the streets of Paradise Palms.

Kenny called me for help that night. A bottle rocket had landed on the cedar-shake roof of a neighbor's house on Tioga Way, less than a hundred yards from our front yard and next door to the home of Dan Etter, one of Kenny's best friends. It ignited a fire so big that local TV news cameras appeared.

At the first sight of flames, Kenny had sprinted from Dan's house to 2121 Geronimo, but when the cops came to Dan's, someone ratted Kenny out. I helped Kenny tell a mercifully sober Ken what had happened. Kenny had to do some community service for his part in the fire, but I think what made Ken maddest was the lawsuit. It had been a super-sized, hyperexpensive act of teen vandalism. The owner of the house wanted $170,000 to cover damages.

The suit dragged on for four years, until Ken paid a settlement, and every time he thought about it he got angry at his son all over again. But he should have blamed himself. He had provided the means and the opportunity. He hadn't set any limits for Kenny's behavior. Instead he'd rebuilt Kenny in his own image. Ken had been training his son to be irresponsible, impulsive, secretive, and destructive since the day Mom went to prison. It was fitting that he should be the first one to pay the price.

22

FRENCH FRIES AND
RANCH DRESSING

I hate this," confided Ken as we lugged the two suitcases out to the car. "I hate taking Kenny into the D.C. jail."

Every two weeks in the late eighties, I drove my father and brother to the airport so they could fly off to see Mom. For much of the first three years, Mom was in California, and the round trip wasn't much of a strain.

In 1989, though, Mom moved to D.C. to begin serving her sentence for the fur theft. When D.C. extradited Mom, Ken cut his visits to once a month. He didn't like the expense or the cross-country flight, but mostly he loathed the dirty, frightening Washington lockup, where Mom was the lone white female. She had at least eighteen months to go, and Ken and Kenny dreaded those eighteen visits as much as they dreaded her eventual release.

I had accompanied Ken to D.C. several times in my little brother's stead, and I shared his uneasiness about the jail. In December 1989, though, it was Kenny's turn to go. I dropped them at McCarran and went back to work. I'd recently opened a vacuum-cleaner distributorship, bankrolled by Ken, and felt uneasy leaving the business for even a few days. Besides, I had a second job, helping Ken with the looming civil suit.

The next day I'd swung by the Geronimo house with a box of legal files for Ken when the phone rang. I picked up the receiver and heard his voice.

"Hi, Kent," he said. He seemed tense.

"What's up?" I answered.

"I have someone here who'd like to talk to you."

The next sound knocked me back into a chair. "Hi, honey," warbled Mom. I couldn't hear the clanging and shouting that had been the backdrop for our conversations since 1985, and I realized that Ken had simply handed her the receiver. She was free.

"How long have you been out?" I stammered. Instant panic, instant depression, made me say the wrong thing. You're supposed to be happy when your mother's released from prison. I forgot to pretend. She could tell.

"Aren't you glad, number one son?"

"Of course I'm glad," I fumbled. "It's a little shocking to find out this way, that's all. Are you out for good?" I still couldn't make the words come out right. "I mean, are you on furlough, or what?"

"I am out for good," she said, and it sounded like a threat.

"When did they let you loose?" I asked.

"Oh, about a week ago."

The drama had started again. Mom had been released six days before Ken and Kenny arrived, and hadn't said a word. She'd rented a twenty-four-hundred-dollar-a-month town house in the red brick colonial neighborhood of Georgetown and run up ten thousand dollars in credit card bills, ordering everything that popped into her head, everything she'd been denied for more than four years. She bought expensive clothes and gourmet food and took bubble baths drinking champagne.

The credit card spree had a hostile, punitive edge, directed at Ken. But the missing week was plain scary. Ken showed up at the jail, and Mom was gone. He'd found her by calling her lawyer. When had she been planning to call us? What had she been doing? Strategizing, I decided later, for the all-out war to come.

We shouldn't have been so surprised that Mom had wriggled out of prison early. She'd spent every waking hour since the cuffs hit her wrists trying to get free. Instead of studying medicine and real estate in school so she could become a doctor or a broker, Mom had taught herself the fine points of both disciplines so she could fool doctors and manipulate brokers and homeowners. Similarly, she studied the law so she could break it. She became a jailhouse lawyer. She worked as an assistant law librarian at Pleasanton so she could read law all day long.

Her first bid for freedom was an arcane proceeding called a 2255. Mom challenged the maids verdict because a member of the jury lived two houses from us in Paradise Palms. She claimed that the Arlington car accident had left her so woozy and disoriented during the trial that she hadn't recognized Rhonda Shonkwiler in the jury box.

It was as close to a legitimate appeal as Mom could get. I'd spotted the woman during the trial and pointed her out to our lawyer, Dominic. Mom tarted up the complaint by claiming she had a history with Shonkwiler. She alleged the woman had come to our door more than once to gripe about Kenny's dog running loose and had talked to the maids. She passed out photos of the woman and coerced a host of friends, including my wife, into revising their memories and filing affidavits. Kenny had to take the stand at the age of twelve to shore up this spurious story. He probably knew he was lying when he said he'd had seven separate run-ins with Shonkwiler over his errant terrier. The prosecutor's queries flustered him badly. "You just said, 'I don't remember,' " observed the prosecutor, "and I didn't ask a question." Kenny shrank into the witness box. "I was repeating myself because I blurred," he mumbled.

I testified as well, but told the truth. I didn't know of any particular feud with Shonkwiler, but on recognizing her in the jury box, I'd assumed the worst, since Mom *never* got along with the neighbors.

The 2255 motion failed. Mom had pursued another get-out-of-jail plan simultaneously, however. She'd filed a thirty-eight-page plea for an early release, in which she promised "never [to] break another law for as long as I live. . . . I hate myself for my stupidity and ignorance." Mom lamented that Kenny was being ridiculed in school and that she was "missing the cutest phases of Kenian's"—my other, nonexistent brother's—"toddler years."

Judge Howard McKibben had also received plaintive missives from friends and family, begging for Sante to be sent home. The one below, dated January 1988, bore my signature:

> I am writing this letter on behalf of my mother, Sante Kimes. For the past three years, an eternity to all of us, she has been incarcerated. We are all being punished. She was the heart of our family. Without her, it is a very unhappy and lonely atmosphere. The love and joy which she personified is gone from us and will not return until she returns. I realize she has to pay because of her convictions, your honor, but I feel the

government is failing us all by punishing us all too long. She is 54 years old, has serious medical ailments and is losing much of her vision as a result of an accident she suffered where she received severe head injuries. It would take too much of your valuable time to relate to you the unbelievable misfortune that has almost destroyed our family since that accident. We are being destroyed. My stepfather is in his seventies, himself very ill with history of stroke and liver problems, and I do not believe he can hold up much longer under these terrible problems we have. He suffers more and more each day without her help and love. Your honor, my mother is not a criminal type person. I just do not believe our government would want to totally destroy the family. It's [sic] aim would be to punish reasonably, but surely not to destroy completely.

I gave up my career in the United States Army and a cherished flying career to come and help in this nightmare, but no one can replace my mother. She is the hope of this family. Your honor, I know if you could see her and talk to her, if you could see the heartache and the grief . . . it is a pitiful sight to see how sorry she is, I believe you would see that she has been punished more than enough. She is desperately needed. Many times I have gone to my twelve year old brother's room, dried his tears and tried to ease the pain of her absence. But it doesn't seem to help that much. He needs her. Your honor, I am not exaggerating when I tell you the entire family is endangered. It has been three years! I am not asking as much for myself as for the others. I want my brothers to have what I did, the sweetest, most caring mother in the world. She raised me with good morals, with a strong sense of values and she gave me a love of life, instilling in me a desire to do my best. I was an "A" student eight times throughout elementary school because of my mother. I was valedictorian and class president and student body president my senior year in college because of my mother. I gave up everything [sic] my wife and young baby had to try and come and help when this tragedy hit three years ago, because of the love and loyalty my mother had instilled and taught as I was growing up. My mother raised me with a strong belief in God who I pray to now to give you the mercy and compassion to let her come home to us. Thank you.

It's a fascinating, appalling, laughable document. You probably guessed that it was a forgery by the third sentence, the one about "serious medical ailments." The first time I ever saw the letter, which was twelve years after it was written, I was sifting through the records of my mother's legal career in the library quiet of a federal records repository in Laguna Niguel, California. I literally jumped out of my chair and blurted, "You *bitch*," when I found it.

The letter is stuffed with lies. The health problems she invokes are imaginary, as is her faith in God, as are my achievements. You can't be valedictorian your senior year in college if you didn't last through your sophomore year. And you can't have plural "brothers" if one of them, Kenian, is a literary creation.

You can also see that she knew the end of my flying career had been devastating. She was sorry it had happened — the way she might be sorry if I came down with cancer. She couldn't make a connection between her actions and my loss. Sharklike, Mom moved ever forward, aggressive and watchful, never looking back, never looking inward.

But it's the obsessions and delusions that make the letter really interesting. My mother did consider herself sweet and caring and the heart and hope of our family. In the bunker of her mind, she thought her family was under siege. She feared we couldn't survive without her, or she feared that we could. She describes Kenny crying to be with her, when in fact he wept buckets at the mere suggestion that she might get out of prison someday.

I don't know whether Judge McKibben identified "my" letter as a fraud. If he did, the Kenny passage might have been the giveaway. During the 2255 hearing in October 1988, the prosecution proved that a similar note from Kay Frigiano, which depicted Kenny bawling and begging for his mother's release, was a fake. Kay had misspelled her own name.

The early-release con job didn't work any better than the 2255. Strange but true, what finally helped spring Mom from prison in 1989 was her own attempt to flee justice in 1985.

Incredibly, Mom got the D.C. court to overturn her furs conviction on Halloween 1989 on the grounds that she hadn't been present for the verdict. "A criminal defendant's right to be present at the return of a jury verdict," wrote the court, "implicates the right of due process under the Fifth Amendment."

Without any proof to the contrary, the court ruled that "her absence from the trial was involuntary" and threw out her three- to nine-year sentence. In other words, the car crash ruse had succeeded.

Rather than try Mom again, the prosecution let her plead to a misdemeanor. She was sentenced to a year in prison and fined ten, that's *t-e-n*, dollars. The court then nullified her sentence by giving her credit for time served. Her parole for the federal slaveholding conviction had already started. On December 11, 1989, Mom was free.

A veteran bartender at the Cattlemen's Lounge, one of Mom's favorite hangouts, remembers Sante's return to Vegas. She burst through the doors of Cattlemen's and ordered a half-dozen different entrees. She sat at a big table by herself grabbing hunks of six different dinners with her hands, prime rib and chicken and fish, till her face was greasy. Dessert was an order of french fries with a double side order of ranch dressing, her favorite. She used two drink stirrers like chopsticks to mop up the extra dressing. Mom came out of prison skinny. She was fat again fast.

She was making up for all the luxury she'd missed behind bars. When the prison gates opened, Mom forgot every tear-stained word of contrition she'd written to Judge McKibben. As soon as she and Ken and Kenny got off the plane from Washington, she began rebuilding the life she'd left behind. She even hired new maids.

Mom established a new pattern. The terms of her slave-holding conviction forbade her from having contact with illegal aliens. She found an acceptable English-speaking white substitute—no blacks, please—across town at the St. Vincent's and Shade Tree homeless shelters.

Much later, I walked in on my mother during a "recruiting" session. She'd summoned one of the directors of a local homeless shelter to the Geronimo house and fixed him a drink. The man was supposed to steer candidates from the shelter to Mom so that she could hire them as house servants. He sipped his cocktail, and she told him the rules.

"We want people over forty because they're more mature," said Mom, with the bland smile of a harmless housewife. "Also, they shouldn't have any family ties in the area, because we don't want them bringing their family problems into our house. We're going to be their new family."

"No problem, Mrs. Kimes," answered the patsy.

Mom continued to add specifications—no car because it would crowd the driveway. Nobody who looked like walking death. She went upstairs for a second, and I collared the guy from the shelter.

"Don't you think it's a little strange that she has all these specifications?" I asked.

He demurred, and I could tell he thought of Mom as a nice lady he'd met over the phone who just wanted to give down-and-outers a second chance. The very idea of telling him about Mom's slavery conviction fatigued me. He'd be confused, and then scared, and Mom would flip out. I shrugged and left.

Homeless people, especially those without friends, family, or transportation, were so desperate they did whatever Mom said. They never went to the authorities, and because of their white skin the authorities never looked twice at them either.

Before long Mom had settled back into her routine of browbeating, intimidation, and nonpayment. Rumors began to circulate at the local shelters about a crazy lady who locked people in their rooms and kept them as slaves. Despite that word, and her prison term, Mom couldn't control her need to have someone to control. The only lesson she'd learned from her stint as an inmate was to be more careful.

I raised the issue with Mom and Ken. It should have had more traction with my stepfather, who didn't have the same helpless compulsion to keep strangers in bondage. "Are you out of your fucking mind?" I said. That had become a stock phrase in my dealings with Mom and Ken. "Don't bring this slavery shit into your house!"

"Oh, well," hemmed and hawed Ken, "you know your mother."

"Stand up to her!" I demanded.

He didn't. As a bored, retired builder, with no projects to keep him busy, he liked acting the big boss man with the homeless guys, micromanaging their landscaping and painting. He tried to shield himself from lawsuits and prison time by cutting independent contractor deals with some of them, and he wrote them checks from his corporate account. It was a feeble, transparent dodge.

But it was easier than fighting Mom. Within forty-eight hours of her return from Washington, the rest of the Kimes-Walker clan was quaking in fear. We tiptoed around the Geronimo house like a bomb squad. Prison time had made Mom far harder, more desperate, and more dangerous. It had only confirmed her belief that she was blameless and victimized. Mom came out of prison angry, and bent on vengeance.

Mom and Ken were like two frontier knife fighters, tied to each other by a short rope so that neither duelist could flee. They circled each other for a bit, and then the blades came out. She snarled, "You took a plea and left me to rot in jail," and he spat back, "You wasted my money." But Ken was older, weaker, and drunker than he'd been five years before, and it was no contest. Despite all Ken's bluster during Mom's years in prison, the way he'd disavowed her and called her evil and reestablished contact with his relatives, when she returned he was in her thrall.

Ken had hung pictures of his relatives on the Geronimo bathroom wall; Mom ripped them off, and Ken let her. The Creeps were the Creeps again, and Ken was playing along. If he'd ever hoped to free himself of Sante, he'd lost the chance. I doubt, though, that he ever really wanted that. Sick of discussing the case and Mom, I'd taken Ken to a driving range in 1987 so we could hit golf balls and talk about something else. He lasted ninety minutes before he had to talk about Mom.

They resented and mistrusted each other, but they were mutually stuck. Mom needed Ken's money. Ken needed Mom. By 1986, before she set foot in Pleasanton, Mom had systematically gutted his portfolio. And still Ken didn't leave her, which proved he'd put up with anything.

One afternoon, during one of those grinding, boozy stretches in the late eighties when I worked for Ken, he asked me to add up the money he'd spent on lawyers. I sat in his office with a pocket calculator and turned pale. From the start of the fur case through the 2255, Ken had bled away $4.6 million in legal expenses. He'd sold the Mecca in Anaheim, the last of his motels, for $3.5 million to fuel the legal machine. I think he asked me to add the figures because he couldn't bear to do it himself.

A few years after Mom's slavery conviction, Ken had handed me forty certificates of deposit to sign. He was in the hospital with a bleeding ulcer and couldn't get to the bank, and he wanted me to forge his signature so he wouldn't miss a day's interest. I wrote his name on forty documents worth at least a hundred thousand dollars each. "Stay liquid," he'd always said, and that day I glimpsed the extent of his onshore liquid assets—at least four million dollars. He'd already stashed other money in offshore banks, and at that time he still owned the Mecca and an undeveloped twenty-nine-acre tract of 170 residential lots in Santa Maria, California, an hour up the coast from Santa Barbara.

But by Christmas 1989 he'd lost the Mecca and a million dollars to the lawyers and had dropped another million into the video poker machines. Ken retained his onshore and offshore cash, the houses in Honolulu and Vegas, the Santa Maria property, and some annuities from motels he'd sold long ago. He was still well-to-do, but he wasn't a mogul anymore.

And the lawsuits kept coming. In the biggie, the civil version of the slavery case, which still hadn't been settled, the plaintiffs wanted thirty-five million. A judgment a quarter that size would have wiped Ken out. Mom and Ken had the nerve to ask their insurance companies to pay for the civil judgment. The insurance companies refused, saying slavery wasn't in the policy, and they got in line behind the lawyers and plaintiffs asking Mom and Ken for money.

But Mom didn't get it. To her the Kimes trough was bottomless. She expected to return to the lifestyle she'd left, with constant travel from Hawaii to Nevada to Mexico and elsewhere. She could often scam first-class plane tickets and hotel upgrades—her favorite method was stashing a fish head behind a bureau in her room and then whining to management about a mysterious funk. But it still cost five figures a month in credit card bills alone to live the way she had in the eighties, and with the lawyers and Ken's gambling jones, my parents began to eat into their diminished capital.

Mom tried to pick up where she'd left off in my life too. During the prison years she'd been so desperate for news about me that she'd struck up a phone friendship with my mother-in-law. Mom could care less about Lyla, but she'd made nice and pumped her for information and then tried to get her to pass instructions to Lynn and me over the phone.

Mom also gave me her marching orders directly whenever she could; I ignored them. I took her phone calls, but I perfected the art of the autopilot conversation. "Uh-huh," "Sure," "Right"—I could mumble something every thirty seconds or so and do paperwork at the office while she rattled on about the Creeps and the 2255 and how I should help her find witnesses for the coming civil cases. I would agree to do everything she asked, and then hang up and do nothing. It drove Mom crazy that she couldn't run my life.

Early in Mom's absence from the scene, Ken's paranoia, as I've mentioned, had turned briefly on me. He'd ordered his new spy, little Kenny, to search the west wing of the Geronimo house, where I lived with Lynn and Kristina. Kenny found three bulging letters from Mom in a dresser drawer. I had tossed them there unread because I wasn't interested in book-length missives about what I should and shouldn't do.

Ken had read the letters, though, and in them Mom described a secret plan whereby I would wrench Kenny away from his drunken, incompetent, senile father and win legal custody. Ken believed that I was part of this conspiracy—a real conspiracy, for once. He began taping my phone calls, and then on Thanksgiving of 1986, in an alcoholic stupor, he'd set a small fire in our corner of the house. He wanted us out.

As soon as we left, however, he implored us to come back. He needed help raising Kenny, and he also needed company. Over time, he realized that I was his best friend, not his enemy. By the day Mom returned, he'd bankrolled my move from vacuum-cleaner salesman to distributor. He'd showed his affection with money, five figures of it, but the affection was real.

The bond that had grown in Mom's absence scared her. She wanted me close to my stepfather, but not too close. She began searching for a wedge that would push Ken and me apart. Mom thought that no one, not Ken or my wife or my daughter, should be more important to me than her.

My wife and I had lived in a modest town house on Pecos Way for three years before Sante's return. We'd established a household separate from Ken, a ten-minute drive away.

For opposite reasons, Mom and Ken both begged us to move back to Geronimo. Ken was scared of Mom. He wanted me to protect him from her. Mom, on the other hand, thought that if I were closer she could control me. I resigned myself to the move almost immediately because I could see I would have no peace no matter what I did. Both Mom and Ken were calling me at the office and at my house nonstop, insisting that I drive over and resolve their disputes. There were days when I drove across town to Geronimo and back half a dozen times. Moving into the house would save me gas money and time as well as rent.

My wife barely knew Sante. Mom had been the harpy who tried to break us up in Hawaii in 1983, the one we ran away to the mainland to escape. We'd seen her only a handful of times before the La Jolla arrest. Then Sante had been the tireless, wheedling voice on the phone, the inmate Lynn rarely visited.

About all Lynn knew about Sante Kimes firsthand was that the woman despised her. Back in late 1985, waiting for trial in the Clark County lockup, Mom had sent a few of her stalking horses to the Geronimo house to ruin our marriage.

For a short spell, I'd gone back to Fort Campbell, Kentucky, where I was living in a cheap motel while I tried to salvage my army career. Lynn, barely twenty, had moved to Vegas permanently with our one-year-old daughter because my parents had requested it. She was staying at 2121 Geronimo with Ken and Kenny, and she hadn't met anyone in Vegas.

Sante decided to find her some playmates. Through Mom, Lynn met a local bartender, an attractive twenty-something named Wayne. Lynn began to hang around with Wayne and his friend Diane, a high school senior who shared Lynn's love for heavy metal. Being a decent sort, Wayne soon confessed to Lynn that his motives in befriending her hadn't been pure. Mom had offered Wayne ten thousand dollars if he could get Lynn into bed and take pictures. The plan failed.

Mom didn't give up. Wayne's mother and stepfather, Roger and Jenny, lived in the Geronimo neighborhood. Via jailhouse phone calls, Mom pressed them to do what Wayne couldn't. I think Mom hinted about cutting them in on some seven-figure real estate deal. Smelling a big payday, they agreed to set Lynn up. Their lack of ethics might have had something to do with their day jobs—they ran an escort service. They were run-of-the-mill shady Vegas operators, strange pals for a millionaire's wife.

One night Lynn came back to Geronimo Way from seeing a movie with Diane, and Roger the drugged-out pimp was sprawled on the living room couch watching TV. Lynn found it a little strange that he was there by himself and hadn't gone home, but they chatted a bit, and then she went up to bed, leaving Roger downstairs.

The next day Lynn fielded a vicious phone call from Jenny. "You whore!" screamed the older woman. "I can't believe you slept with my husband. He didn't come home last night, and he's got scratches all over his back from your fingernails."

"Someone's been lying to you," countered Lynn.

"I'm going to kill you!" threatened Jenny. "I know people who are connected who'll do it for me!"

It wasn't hard to decipher what had happened. Mom had concocted a scenario that was meant to convince me my wife had been unfaithful. She and Ken had already hired a private detective to trail my wife around town. Ken had confronted Lynn with the "evidence" a week before. He waved a folder at her, hinting that it contained proof of her affairs and her drug use. She didn't fall for the bluff, because she knew the folder had to be empty. When Mom and Ken couldn't dig up any dirt on Lynn, they decided to manufacture some.

Close to a nervous breakdown from fear, my wife called me in Kentucky and gave me the details. I flew back to Vegas in the morning without alerting Mom or Ken. Soon after I walked into the Geronimo house, Ken called and Lynn answered. I picked up the other line, eavesdropping, a true member of the Kimes clan.

"I want you to move out," Ken muttered to Lynn. "I know what you did with Roger. If you don't leave, I'm going to take legal action."

I broke in on the line. "Who're you threatening with legal action?" I growled. "Suppose I tell the authorities that a convicted felon is hanging out with a pimp and a drug user?"

Still buzzing from the phone call, I decided to take Lynn out to dinner. I thought it would calm her down. As soon as I pulled out of the driveway, though, I saw Ken's car approaching. I turned the car around in the cul-de-sac and roared in behind him.

Ken pretended to be offended by my accusations that he'd tried to sting Lynn. "I can't believe you think I'd do anything like that," he protested.

I was shaking with rage. "If you say another word about legal action, I'm going to kick the shit out of you." I was threatening an old alcoholic, but I couldn't help it. I was so overwhelmed with righteous anger and frustration that I cried. "I'm going over to Roger and Jenny's right now," I declared. "I'm going to beat the truth out of them." I jumped back into the Firebird, gunned the motor, and Lynn and I made it to Roger and Jenny's house on the far side of the golf course in five minutes.

Roger and Jenny had forgotten to lock their door. I entered

without knocking or pausing. I followed my instinct and it took me down a hall to their bedroom.

They lay on the bed, fully dressed. If they had a gun, they were too stoned to pull it on an intruder. Lucky me. And I think I looked pretty intimidating in my army uniform, with my fists balled up and my eyes wide.

Jenny repeated her warnings about Mob hit men, but I was running on anger, too fired up to think straight. I was telling her to go ahead and try. "You're talking about my family," I howled. "I don't know what Mom and Ken have been telling you, but this isn't fair to my wife. The only reason she's living with them is because we're trying to help them."

Their phone rang. I snatched at the receiver before the druggies on the bed moved a muscle. Ken hadn't finished saying hello when I recognized his voice, cursed him, and hung up. I'd been expecting him to call.

Seconds later the phone rang again. This time it was Mom, calling from jail, linked through by Ken. She lied to me for a minute or two, professing innocence, before I slammed down the receiver.

I grabbed Roger and pulled him toward me. "Stay out of my way," I said, "and I'll stay out of yours."

Ken was gone when I got back to the Geronimo house. The next morning I found a note on the dining room table. It was almost an apology. "I know I've made some mistakes," it read, "but I've always had your best interests at heart. Love, Ken."

Later that day, Jenny called. "It was all a misunderstanding." She giggled nervously. "Roger got those scratches on his back from a swing set."

I forgave Ken, because I had no doubt he'd done it all at the behest of Sante. Five years later, when we moved into the Geronimo house with the newly freed Sante, she and Lynn were forced to coexist. Still trying to win my loyalty, Mom made nice with my wife. They did mother and daughter-in-law things together, like shopping. For Mom, of course, that meant shoplifting.

Mom and Lynn were in a store looking at some table runners when Mom slipped a few into her big black purse. "Why don't you take one?" she urged Lynn. "They're paid for anyway. They charge everyone extra to cover the cost of shoplifting."

Lynn approached the checkout counter petrified. I feel

guilty now; I should have warned her. She hadn't been through the routine a thousand times like me, and she was convinced Mom would get caught. Then she noticed that the corner of a skimpy white chain-mail dress, Mom's idea of middle-aged casual wear, was sticking out of Mom's purse.

When they got to the car, Sante began to emit a high-pitched whimper. "Help me, honey," she whined. "Hurry, hurry, hurry, it's stuck to me." She'd gotten a link of the chain mail snagged on her top and she was clawing at it. Lynn worked frantically to unhook the stolen dress from Mom's side and throw it in the car before security came. She hadn't yet learned that security was almost never coming, and how easy it was for an affluent woman in her late fifties to shoplift. No one suspects Liz Taylor.

Mom's toughest sell job, though, was Kenny. She'd been gone for a third of his life. In four and a half years, Kenny had become Ken Junior, Ken's acolyte. He'd also learned how to master his father and get anything he wanted. His life didn't resemble what Mom had crafted for him in the early eighties. Kenny wasn't the cute little kid she remembered. She'd returned home to a defiant adolescent.

It sickened my little brother, at first, to see his hero backpedaling before Sante. He heard Ken parroting all the nonsense he'd disavowed since 1985, like the lore about Creeps and rattlesnakes and blood on the walls. Kenny had met the Creeps, and he knew better. His father had brainwashed him into thinking of Mom as the enemy; now, browbeaten, Ken would chastise Kenny if he disobeyed her. My little brother watched as Ken and Sante downed five liters of booze a day. He became angry and cynical.

An independent, sarcastic adolescent didn't fit with Mom's plans. She decided to isolate Kenny and conquer him. She started by dismantling his support system. She ruled that Kenny was not to see his treasured friends because they were bad influences. They must be, proclaimed the serial arsonist, because they'd burned down a house with bottle rockets. Mom also used the house fire as an excuse to pull Kenny out of Bishop Gorman early in the second semester.

As a teenager, I'd been spared some of my mother's wrath by Kenny's very existence. He was Mom's special project, the blood heir to the fortune she'd always coveted. I could slip out of the Portlock house and build a bit of a life for myself, see other people, see how normal folks lived. Kenny was too important to Mom. She had to control him. In 1990 she turned him back into a prisoner, as if he were still ten years old.

But Mom discovered that her prisoner had inherited a temper as frightening as her own. It's the same scary impulsive flood of rage that I didn't learn to control until I was in my twenties. Mom had provoked it in Kenny by ruining his life. He began to join in Mom and Ken's battles and to bellow in protest every time Mom cut another of his links with the outside world.

I watched the temperature rise from my wing of the Geronimo house. Mere weeks into our tenancy, Lynn and Kristina and I fled from the tension to the first rental we could find. Living with Mom and Ken had been a stressful failure. But before we left, I saw how confused Mom got when her little mama's boy Kenny began to yell back. And I saw the stunned look on her face when his defiance became physical.

In his red-carpeted room upstairs, Mom was lecturing her prince about his disreputable pals and his loud rock music and the studded bracelets he liked to wear. "I'm going out to see my friends," huffed Kenny. "No, you're not!" yelled Mom. They went back and forth for a while, getting louder and louder, and I came into the room to make peace. That was my job. Before I could intervene, however, Kenny tried to squeeze past Mom. She wouldn't move. Deprived of his friends and everything he'd known for five years, he boiled over. He shoved her hard against the wall.

It didn't hurt that much. Kenny wasn't big yet—Mom still outweighed him. But she couldn't tolerate what he'd done. For the first time in his life, Mom treated Kenny the way she'd treated me. She slapped him hard across the face. The war between Kenny and his parents had begun.

23

ELMER

I was happy when my best buddy, John, got back together with his old girlfriend Sheelin, our mutual pal from Mid-Pac high school. In one whirlwind month in 1990 they reconnected and got married. Because they were such close friends of the family—my mother called John her "son"—we thought it was a great idea for them to get married in the backyard of the Portlock house, with the Pacific as a backdrop.

One of the reasons my mother liked John so much was that he was sort of her foot soldier in Hawaii, before, during, and after her stint in Pleasanton. She was away most of the time, even when she wasn't an inmate, but she had strict ideas about how the house had to be maintained. She had a yard guy and a pool man and they were on a weekly schedule, but she slipped John a few hundred bucks now and then to stop by and make sure the house was taken care of properly. He was supposed to put up an orange plastic barrier around the empty pool, for example, to keep neighborhood skateboarders from breaking their necks in the deep end and suing Ken.

His other job, which was more important, was collecting the mail and forwarding it to Las Vegas. Instead of putting a forwarding address on the mail, he threw out the catalogs and stuffed the rest into big manila envelopes, which he shipped to the Pony Express mailbox center in Las Vegas. That made it harder for those people in Hawaii who wanted to sue my mother, and there were many, to find her.

John was my closest friend, and it was hard for me to imagine the guilt I would feel if he somehow became entangled in one of my mother's legal problems. Still, despite the fact that we were so close, all I could bring myself to tell John about Sante was, "Be careful. Just stay away from her."

He knew. By 1990 he'd been acquainted with Sante for a dozen years and had glimpsed the dark side of her eccentricities. He and Sheelin and Eric Price were all aware of how the Portlock house had burned back in the seventies. John had testified for my mother in the Hawaii piano theft case and flown to Vegas for the maids trial but never taken the stand.

Mostly he and his new wife laughed and shrugged and endured Sante because they were very fond of Ken and Kenny. After Mom got out of prison in 1989, they let her take them out to expensive dinners as payment for their duties. Sheelin tried not to be alone with Mom because Mom was just too overpowering. It made her nervous.

They were so close to the family that when Kenny shoved my mother in early 1990, John and Sheelin acted as surrogate parents. Kenny moved back to Honolulu briefly to diffuse the tensions with my mother, and wound up living alone in the Portlock house with an elderly caretaker couple and a ditzy homeless guy named Willie Wump Wump, one of my mother's new-edition Shade Tree servants. Kenny ate dinner every week with John and Sheelin and confided in them. "I love my mother, but I hate her," he said. He told them how Sante had wrenched him out of his old neighborhood and his old school and shooed away all his friends. She was trying to regiment his life, just the way she had in the old days before Pleasanton. Kenny broke down crying.

Searching for something that would make Kenny happy, John and Sheelin took him to the gym one day and showed him how to lift weights. From then on he went four times a week with them. It was a form of therapy, I guess. His spirits improved.

Sante turned up, as was inevitable, and hired a tutor. She also hired a girl named Kara to be Kenny's friend—a platonic pal, though Kenny tried to make it more. And Sante took charge of life in the Portlock house. She and Ken continued to see John and Sheelin socially. Given my mother's burn rate with friends, John and Sheelin were probably the only intimates they had left in Hawaii.

John and Sheelin were married in July 1990. The day of the

ceremony, my mother gave Sheelin a present. "This is for the daughter I never had," she said, a line she used with lots of young women. It was a half-full bottle of Fracas bath oil, gardenia-scented like everything Sante owned, a decent product available in many stores. "It was specially formulated for me," Sante lied, wet-eyed. "I want you to have it." Sheelin nodded. When she used it one night on her honeymoon, John wouldn't touch her. "What is that?" he blurted with real horror. "You smell like Mrs. Kimes!"

A few months later, on the morning of Friday, September 16, Sante called Sheelin and said she needed a favor. "Honey, can you come over and let us borrow your car? Kenny needs to take his driving test, and our Lincoln is too big. It'll be easier for him to pass in your car."

Within minutes, Sheelin had pulled her Geo Storm into the driveway of the Portlock house. Sante opened the door and shoved a drink in her hand. Before Sheelin knew what was happening, Ken and Kenny had her keys and were rushing out to the Geo. Ken was wearing a suit and tie and carrying a nice tall cocktail in a plastic to-go cup. Sheelin was too flustered to protest.

Mom told Sheelin that the caretaker couple was leaving and that she and Kenny and Ken were headed back to the mainland the next day, Saturday. The driver's license was one task on a long list the Kimes entourage had to complete first. Mom ordered Willie Wump Wump to iron Ken's shirts. Then she sat down on the living room sofa and chatted with Sheelin for a bit, plying her with drinks. "Would you like to know how I met Papa?" Sante giggled, suddenly conspiratorial. They were just girls, talking. Sheelin already knew the story, that Sante had read about Ken in a magazine and made nabbing him her goal. But Sante added a twist. She said that she'd stolen Ken's credit card and then taken it to Mexico with a group of girlfriends from Palm Springs. "He tracked me down, and I said, 'If you want it, come and get it!' " Once she'd lured Ken to Mexico, she'd seduced him and he was hooked.

Sante switched gears. "Honey, we're going out to lunch with my insurance agent. You're driving, okay?"

Sheelin, a little tipsy, steered the Lincoln toward Honolulu. As she drove, Mom informed her that they needed to stop and "pick up a few things." Sheelin had become a chauffeur for a string of errands. They pulled over to the curb next to a Long's pharmacy. Sheelin was instructed to keep the motor running. Mom created a scene in the store, ordering employees to get her this and that. They obeyed. People always obeyed. Mom bought three hundred dollars' worth of the kinds of toiletries and cosmetics she usually stole, and threw the groaning bag into the backseat of the idling Lincoln. "We're going to lunch right here," Sante indicated. The restaurant was next door.

Waiting for them in the restaurant was a little man whose name Sheelin doesn't remember, in casual dress, not a business suit. There was yet another round of drinks. The "insurance man" tossed his down. He and Sante launched into a conversation that sounded scripted.

"Oh, you know, we have so many treasures in that house," said Sante, underlining the word *treasures.* "We have so many things worth so much money, valuable artwork. . . ." My mother warbled on and on, cataloging things Sheelin had never seen in her many trips to the Portlock property. To her recollection, there was little of exceptional worth in the home. It was solid middle-class furniture, boring couches, nothing more.

Then Sante sent Sheelin on another errand. "Here's a quarter, dear. Can you call Willie and see if he's finished ironing Papa's shirts?" Sheelin didn't know why it was important, but she complied. A few minutes after the first call, Sante gave her another idiotic message for Willie, and she was back in the phone booth. Sheelin realized that Sante needed her to miss parts of the conversation with her weaselly little tablemate.

Sheelin drove Sante back to the house. When they arrived, Ken and Kenny were in conference. Sante kissed them both and started her high-pitched yammering about whatever—empty happy small talk. When Sante wasn't listening, Kenny gave Sheelin the bad news. "I failed my driver's test!" He gulped. He and Ken looked like dogs who were about to be hit with a newspaper.

Ken and Kenny and Sante disappeared behind a closed door, and Sante's girlish chirping stopped dead. There was silence in the house, and Sheelin began to fret. Ken had her car keys and she couldn't leave. She'd have to sit and listen while Sante raged. She knew Sante was mad, because my mother had been softening up the staff of the local department of motor vehicles office with gifts of chocolates and liquor for a full week to make sure Kenny would pass. It was just the written part of the test, so Kenny could get his learner's permit—there had been no need to switch to the Geo.

Finally Kenny slipped out for a second, flipped the keys to Sheelin and she made a break for it. She felt sorry for Kenny, since failing the test was obviously a great sin in Sante's eyes, but she was relieved to be gone. It had been another bizarre, exhausting, and claustrophobic day in Kimesworld.

That Sunday John and Sheelin were sitting in bed watching the TV news. There was some footage of a house fire, and they had a simultaneous flash of recognition. It was our house on Portlock Road. "I can't believe she burned the place a second time," blurted John, amazed. He and Sheelin knew immediately that my mother had torched the house, and Sheelin had an explanation for the car switch and the staged lunch on Friday, as well as Mom's flight to Vegas and her suggestion that the caretakers get lost. Mom wanted some kind of witness for her talk about the valuables in the house, something to make it credible that items of value had been lost, in the event that an insurance company asked questions.

John knew that in the earlier fire only the master bedroom had burned because that's where the flames had been lit. The unique, elongated design of the house had given the firefighters plenty of time to arrive. This time the arsonist had made a different mistake. The blazes were set in so many places that the house was reduced to ashes quickly, but investigators recognized right away that it was an intentional act.

I knew what had happened too, as soon as John called me. I was in Vegas, with the newly arrived Mom and Ken, and I let them have it. I didn't know the specifics, but there was no doubt in my mind.

Eventually a lapsed lawyer named Elmer Holmgren admitted to the Bureau of Alcohol, Tobacco and Firearms (ATF) that he had set the fire. Sheelin doesn't remember the name of Sante's insurance guy, and Elmer says he wasn't in Hawaii until Saturday, the day before the fire and the day Mom returned to Vegas, but the coincidences are too obvious to ignore. He might have been the little man with the big drink whom Sheelin met at lunch.

Holmgren told the feds that he let himself into the empty house with a key and spread accelerant in room after room. Using a cigarette lighter, he set blazes in numerous places, starting with some curtains in the master bedroom, before getting back in his rented car and speeding away. Mom paid him in cash when he returned to Las Vegas.

John and Sheelin weren't so pliant. As often happens with decent people, they stopped finding anything funny in my mother's eccentricities. John finally heeded my advice and kept Sante at arm's length. It was hard, because she had more chores for him to do.

She called a week after the fire. "John," she pleaded, "could you go over to the house and go into the carport and get this box of papers out for me? They're very important." John and Sheelin drove over to the house out of sheer curiosity. They wanted to see what was left of the place where they'd been married. There was nothing there except the guest cottage, the carport, and the carport's concrete pads. The carport contained a little shed, and inside it were the papers Mom wanted.

John went home and called her. "Um, it's locked," he said.

Sante was insistent. "Kick the door down then. I need those papers."

John dissembled for a bit and told her he might, then never did. She kept calling and asking for things, but when he continued to ignore her calls or refuse her requests, she finally got the message and stopped.

Elmer Holmgren had no such compunctions. He was a meager, skinny, malleable little man with a nasal voice, a night-school attorney who'd failed his way down the employment ladder till he met my parents. In typical Vegas style, he'd left his home state, Illinois, shamed by charges of consumer fraud in a real estate venture. He answered an ad in the Vegas paper and became Mom and Ken's five-hundred-dollar-a-week in-house lawyer. His alcoholism made him easy prey for the free-pouring Sante. Mom got him to torch the house for three thousand dollars.

She wanted it burned because when she and Ken had tried to sell it, they discovered a lien on the property. A would-be buyer had agreed to a price near two million dollars, an astronomical 900 percent profit on their purchase price of fifteen years before, but the lien would take nine hundred thousand dollars. When they backed out of the sale, the buyer, a Hollywood producer, sued. Turning the house to ash would mean an insurance settlement and would destroy the necessary documents in sundry civil suits. There were enough ex parte motions stuffed in boxes in the Portlock house to wallpaper

Oahu. Without the papers, Mom and Ken could delay their court dates. Stalling had worked like a charm before.

The maids trial era of my parents' life took six-plus years. In addition to the criminal case and Mom's federal stretch there were numerous other related cases that lasted through 1992. There were civil suits by several of the maids. There was an attempt by my mother to void the criminal sentence, and the 2255 motion aimed at our former neighbor Rhonda Shonkwiler. There was a crossfire of suits and countersuits between my parents and their insurance companies when it came time to pay off the civil settlement, and there was the battle with the television mogul over the Portlock house.

Elmer Holmgren tried to help my mother convince her attorney for the civil cases, Doug Crawford, that the maids trial and Portlock fire number two and numerous other mysterious, ominous occurrences — everything that had gone wrong in my mother's life — were in fact the result of a malign conspiracy by that evil mobbed-up Hawaiian lawyer David Schutter. He was the neighbor who'd launched the civil case against my mother and landed her in jail.

One day Elmer came into Doug's office black-and-blue and bandaged. Someone had beaten up the little man, and in his grating, quavering voice, he told Crawford who. "It was Schutter!" said Elmer. "Look what his goons did to me!" Elmer said the goons had told him he was getting too close to the truth and the next time he'd be a corpse in the desert.

Crawford was amazed. Sometimes, when Sante had been warbling in his ear for hours at a stretch about the forces arrayed against her, he got sucked into her mind-set too. Five minutes after she'd left the office, however, his mind cleared and he felt like a fool. Looking at Elmer's battered mug, he was in awe of the lengths to which my mother would go, and Elmer's willingness to endure pain for her. But he didn't speak his thoughts out loud.

Five weeks after the Portlock fire, on October 24, 1990, my mother and Ken took Crawford out to dinner at Lillie Langtry's, the restaurant at the Golden Nugget casino. Crawford turned on the security system at his office at 6:25 P.M. and then drove over to the restaurant with my parents. The dinner dragged on for more than two hours because Sante wouldn't let him leave. She yammered at him about the usual things — Schutter, the Creeps, all her enemies. When Crawford got back to his car and restarted his cell phone, he found that his sister had been trying to reach him for an hour. "Your office burned down," she told him.

When Crawford got back to his little stucco bungalow on Seventh Street, he saw that someone had thrown a Molotov cocktail through the rear window. His uninsured office, full of papers relating to my mother's case, was a wreck. The first alarm had been tripped mere minutes after he left the office with my parents, and he knew in a heartbeat what had happened. "That bitch," he said, and the fireman at his elbow gave him a look. Crawford told the fire department who he thought had done it and why. All the warnings he'd received from Sante that someone from the Schutter camp was going to "get him" because he was too close to the truth were a clumsy con job by Sante. She'd been prepping him for the day when she decided to get him. He also guessed that Elmer had held the match. He's almost certainly right on both counts, but neither Elmer nor my mother has ever spent a second in jail or anted up a penny in compensation.

I know he's right about my mother, because she offered me a few grand to burn Crawford's office, and I declined. We'd been drinking in a bar when Mom had a sudden jolt of inspiration, as in, "Hey, honey, why don't you torch Doug's office?" I had argued with her while Ken pumped dollars into a poker machine, afraid to meet my gaze. I'd listed all the reasons not to do it (number one, it's crazy) and I thought I'd talked her out of it. I didn't learn that I'd been unsuccessful until after the Silverman murder eight years later.

Holmgren, the drunk, soon confessed his role in the Portlock job to a friend at a bar. The friend fetched the ATF, and the next time Elmer told the story, his pal was wearing a wire. Elmer ratted my mother out to the feds, and they launched an investigation. He agreed to hide a mike in his shirt and get Mom to blab about the arson. The last the ATF ever heard from Elmer, he was in a hotel room in Santa Barbara on February 8, phoning them with a hurried, breathless message that there would be a delay in the wire plan. He said Mom and Ken were in the next hotel room, and then he hung up. After that he disappeared off the face of the earth.

You will hear people in law enforcement say that a con artist, a grifter, doesn't kill. A grifter by definition isn't a violent criminal, and there's a line between fraud and murder that's hard to cross. Les Levine, the private investigator who worked for my mother's lawyers in the Silverman case, floated the same theory. His defense was, "Hey, she's a dirtbag, but she's not a murderer."

I told myself something similar ten years ago. Maybe it's hard to understand, but until you're presented with the proof, you don't want to believe that your mother could kill someone. You find a way to tell yourself that it didn't happen the way you think it happened. There are so many terrifying consequences to accepting the truth.

In mid-1992, Mom and Ken were having yet another of their booze-stoked fights. It was as familiar to me as the sound of traffic would be to someone who lives by a highway. On this road, however, the cars were always headed straight at you.

They sought me out and pulled me in. Wherever I was hiding in the house they'd find me. Then the fight would become a tug-of-war. Mom and Ken always wanted to test my loyalty. Who did I love more? Whose side would I take? To win, each tried to make the other look bad. They'd tell me terrible things. In the heat of an argument, they'd forget to censor themselves. That's how I learned what had happened to the guy who took the firebug gig I refused.

Mom and Ken were on either side of me, yelling at each other through me. It was Ken, I think, who veered off into the murder confession. To him it was an accusation.

"She killed that guy!" he proclaimed. He assumed I knew which guy he meant. "She was sitting in the backseat and she hit him with a hammer!"

Mom was dumbfounded for a second and then sneered. "You fucking son of a bitch! *You* killed him. *You* held him."

Each one blamed the other so completely that they didn't register my horror. I didn't know what they were talking about at first, but the details fell into place. They were roaring back and forth and tugging at my arm so they could pull me aside and breathe alcohol in my face and hiss their version of the tale into my ear. I felt sick. It was her idea, it was his idea, but the stories were so close together it didn't matter. Both ended with the firebug who'd torched the Portlock house dead in the front passenger seat of a rental car somewhere in Greater Los Angeles. I didn't get his name, but I heard how they'd cracked his skull and that there'd been more blood than they expected. I looked at my seventy-five-year-old stepfather, who always drove no matter what, and at my seething, superhuman, fifty-seven-year-old virago of a mom and got the picture. Ken had known what was coming, but he'd been hanging on to the steering wheel, drunk and scared, and Mom in the backseat had swung the hammer and bludgeoned this stranger to death.

The next morning I called the Los Angeles Police Department.

"I've got a suspicious situation," I said. "I think someone's been murdered."

"What name?" sighed a blasé male voice.

"I don't know," I admitted. That irritated the cop. I gave him Mom's name and said she had a rap sheet a mile long. I said that the night before, during a liquor-soaked argument, my parents had yelled enough accusations at each other that I was pretty sure someone was missing.

The cop on the other end of the line treated me like a crank. He was different from the cop in Las Vegas ten years before, the polite, interested, and disbelieving cop who'd done zero with my Jeff David tip. This one was openly skeptical. He didn't seem any more interested when I gave him the date and address of the Portlock arson and told him that Mom and Ken had decided their firebug was a snitch. I handed him the motive with a ribbon neatly tied on top.

No one did anything. Nobody came to question Mom and Ken. I called back twice over the next three days. The last representative of the nation's second largest municipal police department with whom I spoke said, "Why don't you get back in touch when you have *more information*?"

I filed the mysterious firebug murder in the back of my mind. I went to work on it and twisted it around until there was room for doubt. If anybody had gone missing, I unreasoned, the police would be all over it. They took murder seriously. Before long, in my head, Mom and Ken hadn't killed anybody. I decided the dead man was a character in one of their paranoid fantasies, an invented detail in their long, slow brutalization of each other.

When Mom was arrested in 1998 and I saw the name Elmer Holmgren in the paper, the long-ago murder mystery floated to the surface. I had a name for the man in the car, and he was real.

What I read made me angry. Holmgren, a federal witness *against my parents,* had vanished, yet to my knowledge the feds had never hauled them in for questioning—despite the fact that Mom had already done prison time for a felony.

I should have grabbed a pen and paper before I called the cops all those years ago. I should've written down the time and date and the name of every cop I talked to in Hawaii, in Vegas in the David case, and in Los Angeles in 1992. With that and the phone records, I could prove to you that I have ample reason for my low opinion of law enforcement. I respect the fact that they risk their lives in the line of duty, but maybe if the paychecks were bigger the cops would be smarter. Maybe they get too many bogus, loony tips to bother following up on any that come without a road map. Anyway, in 1992 they did nothing once again, and the third time was the charm. I became convinced that no one was ever going to believe me unless I delivered a videotape of my mother engaged in a criminal act, wrapped in her signed confession, with directions to her house and five bucks for gas. I gave up.

I GAVE UP. YOU'VE heard me say that before. This is where you give up on me instead. By now you probably don't like me too much, and you sure don't understand me.

Let me guess what questions you'd like to ask. Couldn't I have tried a little harder to get the police to listen? Why didn't I grab Kenny and run? Why didn't I dump my mother for good after she tried to get me to hurt Jeff David? After the nonsense with Roger the pimp? When I saw the picture of the maid's burned flesh? When Sante was in prison? After the second Portlock fire? After I heard her confess to a murder?

I don't have an answer. I don't know if I have a defense, in retrospect. Mom is behind bars now, and I'm alone here without her whispering in my ear, and my mind is uncluttered. Without her charismatic presence, right and wrong is obvious. I can't quite recapture the feeling of helplessness, the certainty that things were the way they had to be, that gripped me most of my days on this earth.

At thirty I was still living my mother's life. I've listed the reasons before, but let me list them again.

1. Habit. It was what I knew. The water did get hotter and hotter, but it's true—when you're in the pot, you don't really feel it.

2. Loyalty. It was Mom's fault that we were always in hot water, but when you weather adversity together, you bond.

3. Apathy. Also known as resignation. I didn't think anything would ever change. I thought that if Lynn and I and the kids did run off, to San Diego or San Antonio or wherever, she'd be on our doorstep within days.

4. Optimism. I thought things would change, and always for the better. They couldn't get worse.

5. Rationalization. Closely related to optimism, also known as denial. I convinced myself that the worst things Mom did—burning maids, killing Elmer—never happened at all. I convinced myself that there was a difference between my mother and me, when maybe there wasn't.

6. Fear of our enemies. Some of the things Mom said about them were true. Not many, but enough to keep the fiction alive.

7. Fear of Mom. Awe, really. She had such tenacity and sheer gall. You may be shocked to learn that Ken's insurance companies finally cried uncle after many years and many changes of counsel and paid the costs of the maids civil suit. That's right—homeowner's insurance covers you in the event of slaveholding. Mom had lost the case, but she won in the end because Ken didn't have to fork over a penny. Equally startling was the amount of the settlement. In 1992 the maids agreed to accept less than a million dollars from Ken's insurers. Mom had outlasted David Schutter. Before she did, her lawyers made him so angry with outlandish, irrelevant allegations, scripted by Mom, about him having sex with the maids and drugs and porno

that Schutter threatened to toss one lawyer out an eleventh-floor window.

8. Concern. I wanted to protect my stepdad and my half brother. One was too drunk to know better, the other was too young.

9. Greed. Which should really be reason number two. Mea culpa.

10. Love. Which should really be reason number one, the main reason. The horror show I've detailed in the pages of this book was really only one day out of every month with her. I'm not kidding. She made life fun, and not just because adrenaline and narrow escapes are fun. What can I tell you? I loved my mother. I adored her. We were happy together, when we weren't miserable. Beyond that, I can't offer an explanation.

24

ANARCHY

Fraud is such a Vegas crime. For a spell there in the nineties my hometown was the national capital of wire and mail fraud. Every other strip mall held a boiler room, those offices full of phone banks where aggressive guys jacked up on coffee or cocaine dial suckers and sell them things that don't exist. Before the feds cracked down, Con was a full-fledged industry in Nevada.

Wire fraud got Mom and Ken a house in early 1992. They hadn't committed the crime itself, but Ken, always in search of a deal, had heard about a boiler-room king who was headed to prison for wire fraud and needed money fast. He was missing his mortgage payments on a beautiful rambling ranch home on Almart Circle in the Vegas suburb of Henderson. Ken leased the house by paying a year's rent in advance, twenty-four thousand dollars. My stepdad thought his mark would be so desperate for cash and so loath to sweat the hassle of eviction that Ken could name a purchase price when the lease ended.

On a cold desert night in February 1992, I sat in a metal chair on the Almart patio by the pool smoking a cigarette. It had been a run-of-the-mill fight night at the Kimeses, which in the new improved early-nineties version meant a tag-team event. There was still plenty of Ken versus Sante, but now it was often Ken and Sante versus Ken Junior. My role remained the same. I thought I would be referee for life.

A frantic call from Mom had brought me across town from my home on Diamondback Drive, and when I arrived I found that Kenny had trashed the place. Broken glass crunched under my feet on the Spanish tile floor. I sent all the combatants to their respective corners and restored order.

By 2 A.M., Mom and Ken had retreated to the master bedroom, which was a multiroom suite with a garage-sized bath. Kenny had gone to bed, pouting and sniffling. I'd hung around, wrung out by the squabbling and too many drinks, stretched on the living-room couch. At 2:30, I woke with a start, realizing I'd nodded off in the blue glow of the TV. Now I was out on the chilly patio, shoulders hunched, smoking, and trying to decide whether to sink back down on the trusty sofa or start the car.

I snuffed my cigarette and slid open the noiseless sliding glass door of the house. There to my right, in the wide galley-style kitchen, was my little brother. Startled, he spun around and stared at me. He thought I'd gone home.

"What are you up to, Kenny?" I asked.

Mom and Ken were such inveterate drinkers, and Ken such a raging alcoholic, that they drank their liquor out of those jumbo-sized plastic Silo cups. The disposable containers were big enough for draft beers. It was their nightly routine to leave the cups on the kitchen counter, full of ice, napkins stuck to the bottom, and then come back out at three in the morning and pour another. Some people get up at night for a drink of water; to my parents, water was a mixer.

The Big Gulp cups were on the counter, and when I came through the sliding glass door I'd caught my little brother Kenny pouring a clear liquid into them from a tiny bottle. His favorite text, *The Anarchist Cookbook,* lay open at his elbow, stuffed with recipes for bombs and poisons.

When Kenny saw me he emptied the rest of his vial in the sink and upended the Silo cups, and threw the vial down the garbage disposal. Before he could dash out of the kitchen I had him in a bear hug. "What were you doing, Kenny?" I demanded as I dragged him down the hall to his bedroom and threw him onto his bed. "What was in the bottle?"

"Something to make them sleep," he whimpered. "I just wanted them to sleep."

I had reason to believe he never wanted them to wake up. I knew what was in *The Anarchist Cookbook*. I'd leafed through some of the black-covered volume's how-tos about homemade poisons. It disgusted me; Kenny said, "Isn't it cool, Kent?" The book was part of his unhealthy interest in spying and violence, an artifact of the Ken-Kimes-as-twisted-single-father era. I'd already told my parents about the book and thrown away Kenny's first copy. He'd gone out the next week and bought another.

I went into Mom and Ken's bedroom and told them what had happened, then hustled to my car and fled Almart Circle before the shit could start again. I drove home with a new fear of, and for, my sixteen-year-old brother. By then, though, I'd already had ample proof of his murderous intent.

After Mom jerked Kenny out of Bishop Gorman in early 1990 on the heels of her unexpected release from prison, she'd made his life hell. As a teenager, Kenny had the kind of existence I'd weathered before age eleven. He went to four different schools between his freshman and senior years.

Post-Gorman, Mom and Ken had shipped him off to Hawaii and the clutches of a tutor. For his sophomore year, he returned to the mainland, but not to Las Vegas. As soon as Mom got out of prison, the Geronimo house had become a magnet for lawsuits, so my parents started bouncing from one new address to another.

Their first stop was a castle by the sea in Santa Barbara, California. Ken the much-diminished mogul couldn't or wouldn't swing the cost of a full-on manse, so they rented the guest cottage of a property that was famous as the site of a murder. Kenny spent his sophomore year of high school in Santa Barbara, living in close quarters with his squabbling parents. Mom and Ken spent their days hatching schemes for stealing the main house from its owners, but they were thwarted.

In the summer of 1991 the trio sneaked back into Nevada, but not Vegas proper. Instead they rented a ramshackle, jerry-built white stucco house in Henderson on a street called Happy Lane. It had bad plumbing and a host of code violations, but they liked it that way. They could move in and start the scam, schmoozing the building inspectors and finding flaws in the house till the owners agreed to sell for nothing. But these owners fought back. Mr. and Mrs. Richards hired lawyers and, at a loss of seven grand, evicted Mom and Ken and Kenny after seven months. The scam had failed.

From Happy Lane, my parents moved to Almart Circle. By then, however, Kenny had gone nuts. Mom and Ken had guaranteed adolescent rebellion. The constant moves, the isolation, the fighting, the drinking, and the rules had rubbed Kenny's nerves raw.

In the first month that the three of them lived on Almart Circle, Mom had dragged me into the fray almost daily. She wanted me to control Kenny. He was too big, Ken was too old, and Mom seemed almost scared.

Kenny was a terror. He broke into Ken's safe and stole jewelry and thousands in cash. The spoiled brat thought it was his due. He wrecked cars.

But the violence was what unnerved me. Two weeks into their Almart tenancy, I had to keep my brother from strangling Mom. She sat in a chair facing away from him, and he crept up behind her with a rope stretched in his two hands. I tackled him. It was a draw. He couldn't reach Mom, and I couldn't keep his shoulders on the carpet. The mama's boy had become a butch weight lifter. I saw the fury in his eyes and the red that had rushed to his ears, and began to speculate. Steroids? Speed? Or just Sante's genes?

Kenny had made new friends at Green Valley, the nearest public high school in Henderson. He had his first real girlfriend. They had a lot in common. I picked up the phone during that first month at Almart and heard the two of them plotting to kill Mom and Ken and run away.

The girl could've been kidding, but because of Kenny's past behavior, I couldn't dismiss the plot as fantasy. I pulled Kenny aside and frightened him out of doing the deed, warning him about the consequences. Lynn tried to help as well. Despite Mom's unalloyed, irrational hatred of her, Lynn intervened on her behalf. Lynn and Kenny had been close, more like sister and brother, during the first year of Mom's incarceration, when my family lived on Geronimo. "Your mother loves you," Lynn told Kenny. "She only wants what's best for you. She can't help it. It's in her blood." As Lynn spoke, Mom was listening, secretly, via the intercom.

Lynn succeeded in quieting Kenny temporarily. But no truce lasted longer than a day or two. Soon Mom and Ken were begging us to move back in with them and help. They tried everything to get us to move to Almart Circle, but what finally worked on me was greed. Ken had already paid a year's rent, and because of the process servers stalking him he'd put the lease in my name. He and Mom promised to move out once things settled down, and then Lynn and I could have the house to ourselves. Ken was cutting me in on his score. When the lease ran out, we could use the money we'd saved to buy the property at two-thirds of book value from the wire-fraud sleaze. I would own my first house, and I'd get it in time-honored, cut-rate, underhanded Kimes fashion.

The doped drink incident happened mere days before Lynn and Kristina and I made the transition to Almart Circle. Our full-time presence did nothing to increase the peace. Kenny could only be managed, not controlled. He crawled out the window in the middle of the night to meet his friends and tryst with his girlfriend.

The girlfriend worried my parents. Mom opposed all but the most utilitarian, i.e., sexual, relationships with females on principle—they took attention away from her. She hated Kenny's girlfriend because she was a girl. She also hated her because she was half Jewish—or Mom suspected she was. Mom the money-grubber couldn't see the irony in her firmly held prejudice that Jews were cheap.

But she did have reason to fear this young lady, because Kenny and his girlfriend were making plans. I'd scotched their embryonic murder plot, but the scheming continued. Kenny wanted to get free of my parents without losing his inheritance. Aided by his girlfriend, he began to do a little of the legal research that had consumed Mom's days in Pleasanton. He and his friend spent hours investigating how he could peel off a few million without going to prison.

It was borderline criminal, but then again it wasn't. The girl's mother was a guidance counselor in the public school system. She didn't know about murder plots and poisons, but she did recognize a dysfunctional family when she saw one. She wanted to help my little brother, and her idea of help was the same as Kenny's: get him out of the Almart house and free of Sante.

Finally my little brother had an outside party interested in his life, someone willing to intervene on his behalf, as people like Evelyn, the Bowers, and the Prices had done for me in Palm Springs and Hawaii. There was an exact parallel, in fact, between my situation in Hawaii and Kenny's on Almart Circle. My girlfriend Rhonda's parents, when I was Kenny's age, knew that something was wrong with my family. They wanted to help. They wanted to free me from Sante and Ken. Now my little brother had a girlfriend with concerned parents who could sense disaster in our home. They were trying to figure out how to spring him. The similarities extended to the sleeping arrangements. Mom had permitted my friend to spend the night on Portlock Road in my bed; Kenny's girlfriend's folks allowed him the same privilege at their house.

I couldn't recognize the parallels. As I look back, I wonder whether there was any ulterior motive in the guidance counselor's desire to help Kenny flee. She probably knew about Kenny's designs on the money, but I doubt she wanted it for herself. At the time, though, these people seemed like meddlers. Blind instinct told me they might bring cops and ruin to our family. When Mom sicced me on them, I took the job without reservations.

On a spring night in 1992 Kenny had slithered out his bedroom window on Almart Circle and we all knew where he'd gone. I drove to his girlfriend's house and knocked on the door. When her mother answered, I didn't mince words. "My parents don't want Kenny sleeping here. You're not his parents. Let me take him home now."

And then, in my role as muscle, I delivered the threat: "If you promote this relationship, I'm going to call the school where you work and tell them what you're doing. You're letting two minors sleep together under your roof."

After that and another confrontation in a parking lot, Kenny's would-be saviors left the stage. Thwarted, resentful, and immature, Kenny vented his Sante-strength temper.

In June 1992, we tried to celebrate Father's Day in the Almart Circle house. Kenny wanted to go see some friends, and Mom and Ken wouldn't permit it. They stood in the front hall and stopped him from leaving. He bolted for the back door, and I blocked his exit. Kenny began to spray his ancient father with profanities and insults. I got mad. "Stick up for yourself!" I urged Ken. I regretted the results. Ken slapped Kenny across the face and yelled, "Grow up!"

A few years before, Kenny would have dissolved into Jell-O at the touch of his father's hand. I'd seen it happen. Back in 1988 Kenny had disobeyed his dad and gone skateboarding, and a bad spill had left a gash on the back of his head. I thought he might have a concussion. Too drunk and angry to gauge the extent of Kenny's injuries, Ken had hit his son, and Kenny's sobs had turned into shrieks as I rushed him to the emergency room.

Now Kenny didn't pout or cry. He sneered. At five-foot-eleven and 160 pounds, he knew Ken was no longer any match for him, and he lifted his hand, ready to strike. As he swung I shoved him backward and then pinned his arms to his sides. Like a bouncer, I dragged him down the hall to his bedroom, just as I'd done the night of the poison drinks. I deposited him on his bed and shut the door. Within a minute he'd jumped out the window and scaled the yard's side wall.

An hour later he hadn't reappeared. The doorbell rang. Two members of the Henderson Police Department were in the shady arbor on the front steps, ready to arrest me. Kenny stood behind them. He'd told the cops that I'd beaten him up.

Past experience with Sante Kimes had taught me what to say. "Look at my hands," I urged the cops. "Look at him." I pointed at Kenny. "There's not a mark on my hands or on him."

I gave the cops my version of what had happened. It had been an argument between a seventy-five-year-old man and his robust, agitated seventeen-year-old son. The officers didn't need much convincing. "If we have to come back here," they told Kenny, "*you'll* go to jail."

Kenny went to his room and slammed the door. I was relieved that the situation had been defused, but I was also depressed. Kenny had pulled a Sante-style hysterical stunt. I could see too much of my mother in him.

In the summer, with Kenny out of school, Mom and Ken hit on a solution for their problems with him. The year before, they'd "discovered" the Bahamas, thanks to my vacation. I'd won a free trip to the islands in a company contest, and Lynn and I had returned to Vegas raving about the beaches, shoving Polaroids under Mom's and Ken's noses. Mom was always interested in the Next Great Place, where Things Would Be Different, and that became the Bahamas. Ken didn't like the islands—too many blacks. But he liked the casinos, and the don't ask, don't tell offshore banks, and after some selling from Mom he got with the program. They were moving to Nassau.

Kenny didn't want to go. He didn't knuckle under as easily as his dad. Mom and Ken were going to have to put him on the plane forcibly, which meant I was going to have to put him on the plane. They tapped me to be the muscle again, and I did it. I thought Kenny should do what his parents said, even if his parents were Ken and Sante. But my motives were also selfish. I couldn't wait for the three of them to disappear. They would be in a different country, more than two thousand miles east.

What followed was a form of kidnapping. On the day of the flight I tried to keep Kenny from calling for help. When I saw him near the phone, I said, "Don't touch that." With the threat of physical force, Mom and Ken and I steered my brother into the van I used to deliver vacuum cleaners, and I drove the three of them to the airport. I guarded Kenny as if he were an inmate in a prison bus being shipped from one correctional facility to another.

At every stoplight I was afraid our hostage would bolt. As I eased into the passenger drop-off zone at McCarran Airport, I saw two of Kenny's friends in a car a few yards behind us. He had managed to make a phone call after all. He planned to leap out of our vehicle and into theirs, and then they'd peel away into Vegas traffic.

I walked back to the passenger window of our tail. Mom had told me that Kenny was hanging out with the wrong crowd, but neither of these college-bound seventeen-year-old rescuers in baggy skater pants were thugs. The thug was me. I leaned toward the driver and acted scary. "Get the fuck out of here," I growled. "Leave now, and nothing will happen to you." I was a burly thirty-year-old intimidating a fuzzy-faced kid.

Kenny got on the plane and went into exile. Mom and Ken had rented a multistory white and green house on Cable Beach in Nassau, not far from a casino. Within a week, my unhappy little brother had broken every window in the place. But he adjusted to his new home, as he'd adjusted five times since junior high. He completed his senior year and earned his diploma at a private school on Nassau. Lynn and I saw him off and on during the next year, but he didn't return to the States for good until he enrolled at the University of California–Santa Barbara in August 1993.

When Mom and Ken and Kenny's plane took off and headed east in July 1992 I exhaled. It was like when an armistice is signed and the shelling stops and you can hear the birds sing. The house was ours, the way Ken had promised in January.

Life at Almart Circle had been hell for us too. The last time we'd lived with my parents, on Geronimo in 1990, we'd lasted only a month. I'd moved back in with them two years later despite what I knew. I was thinking like a battered wife who convinces herself that her partner can change. I did it partly out of resignation—if I didn't move in with them, they'd only come to my office or home and act out their psychodramas. They already did.

But when Ken and Sante weren't battling their troubled adolescent, they were tearing at each other. They hadn't stopped bickering since Mom left prison. On Almart Circle Lynn and I had no escape from it. That's where I heard them talk about killing the guy I later learned was Elmer Holmgren. If I tried to hide behind the locked door of my bedroom, they'd bang and holler till I emerged. Mom once chased Ken in and out of our bedroom with a butcher knife.

I worried about my eight-year-old daughter and my wife. Lynn was three months pregnant when we brought our belongings to Almart. She was due in August. She carried the child while Mom and Ken and Kenny filled the air with violence. My parents belittled her in conversation. Once, cowering in the kitchen, hiding from a knife-wielding Sante, Ken had told my wife the truth. "Santee hates you with a passion. She wants you dead." Lynn protected herself by playing dumb and saying as little as possible.

After my parents took Kenny to the Bahamas, I shouldn't have been surprised when Mom and Ken, sans Kenny, were right back in Vegas and in our hair within weeks. Together we took a Kimesian stab at a Fourth of July cookout. Since she'd met Ken twenty years before, Mom hadn't lifted a finger in the kitchen. Ken the ex–mess sergeant shared cooking duties with me, and I specialized in barbecue. That afternoon I built a fire in the grill on the patio and then went inside to the stove to make my special sauce.

I was mixing honey, Tabasco, Worcestershire, and a few other secret ingredients in a saucepan. While the mixture bubbled, Mom and Ken argued. The heavy liquid got thicker and hotter, and so did the fight.

The spat moved into the kitchen. I could see Mom's eyes searching for a weapon. I assumed she'd pick up a knife, and Ken would sprint away. She grabbed the handle of the saucepan instead.

Only my blue jeans saved me from third-degree burns. Mom flung the boiling contents of the pan at Ken, but hit me. Sizzling red goo covered my thighs. Mom saw what she'd done and the house went silent.

I'm sure I'm the only person my mother's ever run from. In

a panic, she darted out of the kitchen and into her bedroom, trying to lock the door behind her. I crashed through the flimsy
hollow-core barrier like a linebacker, 220 pounds of anger.
Mom kept running, straight out the back door and into the
quiet tract-home streets of Henderson.

She stayed gone. I smeared lotion on my pink, stinging legs
and waited for her. When she sneaked back into her bedroom
later that night, I dragged her into the kitchen. I pulled her by
her upper arm, digging my fingers into her flesh, trying to hurt
her. In front of Ken and Lynn, I told my mother, "We're done."
The bodyguard/peacemaker gig was exhausting me. I couldn't
take it anymore. I didn't want my new baby living in a house
with broken glass on the patio and scalding liquids flying
through the air.

Ken and Sante begged me to stay, and I said no. Ken
reached for his wallet, which had always worked before. He
mentioned a six-thousand-dollar loan. It was reflex for me to
say yes to money, but this time I surprised Ken by saying no.
For once I couldn't be bought.

"Forget it," I said, fuming.

"Look at him," Mom told Ken. "We've lost him." She began
to bawl.

"Have we?" Ken asked.

"Yes," I answered. "We're done." I loved saying it. I wanted
Mom to cry some more.

But it didn't turn out to be true. With Mom out of earshot,
Ken made a private appeal. It was his "protect me" line again.
"I'm afraid for you to leave," he pleaded.

Weeks before, after Kenny's Father's Day outburst, my
stepdad had taken a big step. He hated seeming vulnerable or
sentimental, but that day the confrontation with his teenage son
had unnerved him. "Kent," he said, "you're the only one who's
never forgotten my birthday or Father's Day." It was a sad fact.
He'd created the situation himself, alienating his other kids and
spoiling Kenny. The heir apparent had taken a swing at him. By
default, that left me, the stepson who'd never called him Dad,
and who treated him more like a peer than a father.

I didn't follow through on my threat, which was not so
much to leave the house as to leave their lives. I cared about my
stepdad, and I wanted to help my troubled little brother.
Behind all of it, though, stood self-interest—real estate lust, of
the sort my mother could understand. It was too good a deal.

They'd be flying to the Bahamas any day, and if I could just hang on by my fingernails, the Almart house would be mine.

They left town, again, and we stayed. I don't think their plane was airborne before we started lugging our clothes and furniture into their master bedroom. On August 4, Lynn gave birth to a baby boy, whom we named Carson. We brought him home to a house where you could hear yourself think. For four months, my nuclear family, now four strong, enjoyed nearly unbroken tranquillity.

For Thanksgiving of 1992, Lynn's parents planned to drive up from San Diego to Vegas. I had to fly to Cleveland for a company sales meeting, but I'd be back Wednesday night, in time to cook the turkey. I looked forward to a different kind of holiday, one in which no one committed felony assault.

At 11 P.M. on Wednesday night, the taxi dropped me off at the Almart Circle house. I walked through the front door and took a left toward the master bedroom, lugging a heavy leather suit bag. There on the couch next to the bed were my mother and stepfather.

"What are you doing here?" I demanded.

Something had coarsened in me during the months of anarchy at Almart. Fatigue and disgust had transformed me from referee to combatant. Before my parents left for the Bahamas I had started initiating fights with them, anything for a chance to insult and degrade them and push them toward the street. I liked hurting their feelings. When I saw them sacked out in what I considered my room, having parachuted in from Nassau without warning, I didn't bother making nice.

"Get out of my room," I said.

We had to tell Lyla and Lynn's stepdad to sleep in a cheap casino motel in Stateline, Nevada, in the lonely clump of neon right on the California border. Mom and Ken retreated to the guest room, but they wouldn't leave entirely.

Mom had planned the visit because she knew Lynn's parents were coming. She couldn't stand for me to spend a holiday with someone besides her. She'd left Kenny in Nassau in her haste to disrupt our Thanksgiving dinner. She expected me to cave and add two chairs to the table. Instead I told her to make her own dinner arrangements. She and Ken went to the casinos, and I had a sane, happy dinner with my in-laws. I cooked the turkey.

That night, while I was washing dishes, my parents returned. Ken filled his Silo cup and went straight to the guest room. Mom lingered in the kitchen. "Your father lost thirty thousand dollars gambling tonight because of you," she hissed. My rejection, she claimed, had caused Ken to lose big.

I'm sure Sante had made the two of them the center of attention all night long on the casino floor, but it's still a lonely place to spend a family holiday. And it was no more than they deserved. When Mom told me about Ken's losses, I shrugged and kept scrubbing pots. I ignored them till they left a few days later.

But, of course, I couldn't keep ignoring them. I reasoned that even if I didn't want to see my mother, I shouldn't deprive her of her eight-year-old granddaughter. She loved Kristina and enjoyed pampering her with gifts and clothes and vacations. Right before Christmas break, Mom rang me from the Bahamas and asked if Kristina could come see her. "I promise I'll have her back by Christmas." We'd all heard so much about the wonders of the Cable Beach property that Kristina would have been inconsolable if I'd said no.

A few days before Christmas, my daughter called me. "Daddy," she quavered, "I'm afraid to fly back by myself. Please come and get me." Kristina had never betrayed a fear of flying before. She hadn't had a problem with the eastbound leg of the trip. It sounded fishy, but since Mom was paying for the tickets I thought, *What the hell*. It was a free trip to the beach.

When I arrived, Mom and Ken's house, for once, lived up to the hype. It was yards from a private white sand beach. That tempered my anger when I learned I'd been lured to the islands under false pretenses. Mom admitted that she'd scripted my daughter's plaintive phone call. "I told her to say she was scared so you'd have to come see me," she said, grinning. "And it worked, honey! Why don't you tell Lynn to bring Carson and we'll have Christmas together!"

As scams go, it was painless. Lynn and Carson made the trip. We swam in the eighty-degree water and lay out on the beach, and far from the battleground at Almart we all got along.

We got along too well. You know now that I hardly blinked at behavior most tax-paying family men would consider unforgivable. I look back on that Christmas holiday and begin to smile with the memory of good times and then have to catch myself. Yes, there was uncomplicated fun, but there were also incidents that only a grifter's son would consider happy memories.

I remember my mother following a drunk around in a Nassau casino. He had a fat roll of hundreds teetering out of his pocket, and Mom was trying to bump it loose.

I remember my daughter stealing a Walkman from a tourist, and me laughing about it, before I sobered up. It happened like this:

A heavy, unattractive European tourist spread out a towel on the beach behind Mom's house. The woman lay down with her crotch facing us, her untrimmed pubic hair spilling out the sides of her bathing suit. We were leaning over the railing of our balcony laughing at her and griping about how she'd staked out a spot on our beach, when Mom noticed she had on earphones.

"Look," said Mom, "that bitch is recording our conversations!"

We were deep into rum cocktails. Before long Mom had us convinced that the woman had a directional mike pointed at the house and was some kind of spy for the feds or the Creeps. Mom decided that we needed to seize the evidence. She tapped Kristina for the job. "Get out there and take that tape recorder. I'll pay you twenty dollars."

I watched from the balcony as my daughter, an innocent-looking blond child, sauntered out to the oblivious woman. Like a third-generation pro, she snatched the tape recorder from the woman's blanket, pulling the headphones with it, and sprinted for our house. I was cheering her on. In retrospect, it wasn't my proudest moment as a parent.

Within minutes the angry tourist had knocked on our door and demanded the return of her Walkman. Mom feigned outrage, her favorite emotion. "How dare you accuse my granddaughter of being a thief!" She lambasted the woman for a minute or two, mentioning important personages she knew and how much money she had, and then shut the door.

The woman returned with her husband to try again. Before long, Mom had them arguing with each other. They gave up and walked back toward their hotel, the husband sniping at his wife about getting him involved in a potential lawsuit over a cheap tape player. My wife and Ken and Kristina and I all hid on the roof deck, peering over the railing and stifling laughter.

The tape in the Walkman turned out to be Lionel Richie. I can't remember how we explained that to ourselves. I do remember that as soon as the alcohol wore off, I told my daughter that stealing was wrong.

We left the Bahamas after Christmas and returned to what we thought was our house on Almart Circle. We'd actually enjoyed ourselves in Mom and Ken's presence, and it made up, in part, for months of torture. But in January, Mom and Ken were back, and within days they were testing our patience.

Rather than blaming herself for what had happened at Thanksgiving, Mom decided that my hard line and bad attitude had to be Lynn's doing. She also told Kristina that only maids cleaned rooms, and that Lynn was treating her like a maid by making her clean up after herself. It was as if Christmas hadn't happened. "Santee wants your ass," Ken warned Lynn.

I had endured a lot for the sake of real estate, but when Mom and Ken turned on Lynn, I lost my last shred of patience. If you've ever seen the movie *The War of the Roses*, you'll recall the scene where the divorcing couple, neither of whom wants to lose claim to their dream house, divide the property down the middle and sit down to wait. That's what I did at Almart Circle in the first few weeks of 1993.

I didn't get out a paintbrush, but according to my rules, Ken and Sante had to stay on their side of an imaginary dotted line. They got the living room and the right side of the house. We got the den and the left side of the house, including the master bedroom. I'd broken the lock on the bedroom door when I'd barged through in pursuit of Mom on the Fourth, so each night I'd push a dresser in front of the door to block it. For years I'd locked my Social Security card and my driver's license in my glove compartment so Mom couldn't steal them; now I was locking my family in the bedroom so Mom couldn't talk to them.

"You're not involved with them anymore," I told Mom and Ken. "If you want to see Lynn or Kristina or Carson, you have to go through me."

It seems pathetic to me now, but at the time it was a great release to be the bully. I ran the house, not Sante. I told her and Ken that if they breached the invisible line down the center of the property I'd push them right back across. I don't think they believed me till I'd put them on their asses a few times. Often when I had to pass them in a hallway, or in the kitchen, which we shared, I'd shove them out of pure spite. I was enjoying the fights, and winning. Once, when my mother nagged me while I was feeding Carson, I squeezed the bottle and sprayed milk in her face.

Since my teenage years I'd known how to fence with Sante verbally. I didn't back down. During the end of the Almart era, when I was saying and doing things for the sole purpose of causing her pain, I thought of the perfect insult. It was something I knew would hurt her badly. I saved it up till a night when we fought past two in the morning, and Kenny was in town, awake and listening.

Maybe we were fighting about my refrigerator. Ken and Sante thought there was something "wrong" with it. Why couldn't the big GE with the built-in icemaker crank out enough cubes to keep their Silo cups filled?

I might have pointed out that the problem wasn't with the icemaker, although I don't remember what we were arguing about. It could just as easily have been a speck of dirt on the floor or the state capital of Idaho. What I recall is that the argument ended, and I won, when I said, "You're going to die a lonely old woman." It was the worst thing you could say to Sante. For her, silence equaled death, and not having an audience was worse than death. I'd reached into her chest and squeezed her heart, and it felt so good I nearly got goose bumps.

I finally convinced Mom and Ken to take their things and go back to the islands by threatening to call the cops. Since my name was on the lease and their names were all over the police blotter, they complied. But they came back again and again, flying back and forth from Nassau every few weeks. I realized that no matter how much of a bastard I might be to them, they'd never give up. I'd never own the Almart house free and clear.

In secret, Lynn and I lined up a rental property, hired a moving van, packed, and left. The whole stealthy process took no more than three days. We moved the way Mom and I had back in L.A. and Palm Springs in the sixties, except that we weren't running from cops or creditors. We were fleeing my mother, and when she found out what we'd done, she was furious. Five months later I bought my own house. I got my starter home the old-fashioned American way, without any scams — and with a nice, legal, massive, hernia-inducing, middle-class mortgage.

25

BODY DOUBLE

On March 28, 1994, I returned to my house on Joy Glen after a long day at work and found myself alone. The silence was welcome. I knew that my wife and two kids would be home soon and I looked forward to seeing them, but I was relieved that I'd have a chance to unwind first. I plopped down on the sofa and lit a cigarette.

When the phone rang, I didn't move. I decided to let the answering machine take the call. Whoever was calling hung up without leaving a message. It was only a minute or two before the phone rang again. I sighed and pushed myself up off the couch.

"Hello," I mumbled.

"Kent! Papa's gone, and they won't help him!" My mother was always hyper on the phone, whether she was up and bubbly, which was most of the time, or angry and paranoid. This time she was terrified, and beyond hysterical. I could hardly make out what she was saying.

"He's in the emergency room and they won't help him! They won't help him." My ear rang, she was shouting so loud.

"Mom, slow down, get hold of yourself." She didn't answer, but I could hear her crying and whimpering. I waited a beat and said, "What's going on?"

"He's in the emergency room, and they won't do anything for him! Kent, what am I going to do!? We had just dropped Kenny off, and he—why won't they help him?"

"Mom, listen to me. Where are you?"

"I'm at the hotel. Papa's in the emergency room, and the doctors won't do anything to help him!" Her voice rose at the end of every sentence. She was losing what little control she had left.

"Mom, tell me the number that you're at right now."

"I can't believe it!" she yelled, and the line went dead.

Sante was a consummate actress, and she could invest a broken fingernail with drama, but this sounded different. My heart raced. I didn't know if this was a ploy to get me to rescue her from a predicament, or if my stepdad, whom I loved, was in trouble for real. On so many occasions she'd tricked me into dropping everything by telling me Ken was on his deathbed. This time, though, the panic in her voice was far beyond her usual dramatic range.

I didn't know where she was. I prayed for her to call back. I stood near the phone waiting for it to ring. Was Ken okay? I thought back to the last time I'd seen him.

It was a week earlier. Mom, Ken, and Kenny, days from turning nineteen, had stopped by my house. You could tell that Kenny had been arguing with his parents. Mom was at high boil, and Ken's face sagged with exhaustion. Kenny seemed agitated too, but appeared to be calming down.

Mom marched straight to the bar. She chose the biggest glasses in my cabinet, filled them halfway with ice, and then to the brim with Seagram's. A thimbleful of 7Up on top allowed her to claim she was mixing Ken a "light" drink.

Kenny and Mom slipped into the other room to play with my kids, nine-year-old Kristina and nineteen-month-old Carson. As soon as they were gone, Ken materialized at my side. Up close he looked even worse, and I got concerned. Ken was seventy-seven years old. He didn't usually show it.

"I really need to talk to you," he said softly.

"Everything all right?" I asked.

He ignored my question. "We need to talk about something." His face was bright red, as if he had a bad sunburn. In his bloodshot eyes I could see fear and pain. He turned his head, checking quickly to see if Mom and Kenny were within earshot. We heard them laughing with the kids, and when Ken felt safe he sat down and unburdened himself.

"Kent, how's the business going?"

"I wish it were better," I answered, "but we're heading in

the right direction." I could tell that Ken wasn't going to come straight out with whatever was bothering him. He was sidling up to it, using his favorite subject, money.

"I need to find an investment right away." Ken proposed becoming the finance company for my dealership, meaning he would carry the loans for the customers. "What kind of turnaround would that have?"

"It depends on the terms," I explained. "A year to three years. It's profitable, but it does take a good-size investment."

"How much?" Ken pressed.

"Well, we could put in a hundred thousand to start. That should give you a good gauge of how the contracts will perform." So far he was with me. He hadn't balked at the amount, so I continued. "It isn't fast money, but the return on the investment could double your money in three years."

He gave a sad smirk. "When you get to be my age," he said, "you're not so interested in long-term investments."

That was the real subject, and it wasn't one I'd ever heard Ken raise before. He didn't talk about aging and death. He could seem quiet and reserved, especially around strangers, but underneath that placid exterior he was always full of energy, sharp, smart, brimming with pride and ideas. He was always on the go, always looking for something to accomplish. It was easy to forget that Ken was in his late seventies, especially since he was rather vain. He couldn't pass for fifty, but he tried to act fifty. He worked hard to look young. Mom gave him nightly facials and kept his gray and thinning hair and mustache dyed their original youthful brown.

So he was finally feeling old. "You'll be around a good while longer," I said, thinking he wanted to be reassured. "You still have a lot to teach me."

He didn't respond. During those painful years in the late eighties when we spent day after day hunched over video poker machines in dark bars, pissing money down the slot and rehashing the legal history of Sante Kimes, Ken would tell me anything. Now there was something he wanted to divulge, and I got the feeling he simply couldn't. "There's a lot of pressure, Kent," he hedged. "There's too much pressure. I just wish there could be a little peace once in a while."

"You and Mom fighting?" I asked. Was Las Vegas hot?

"Not really," he lied. "Kenny's been a handful, and those

two have been at it quite a bit. I try to calm her down . . . and . . . you know."

"I know," I said. He wasn't going to tell me anything new without some encouragement. "How about we go to dinner, my treat, just the two of us? Mom can play with the kids, and we'll kick back a little."

"Sounds good, but I still have to talk to you about something." We were going around in circles.

"Ken?" I implored. "What's wrong?"

He lifted his hand and put it on my shoulder. I saw the brown age spots and felt a tremor in the fingers resting on my body. When he was under stress, his hands shook. "Kent, you've always been there for me." He was forgetting about all the times I'd let him down, but I was touched, and alarmed. "I really need you to be there for me now."

"Whatever you need," I replied, "say the word." If he needed me to be his rock and confidant again, I would.

Ken still had his trembling palm on my shoulder when Mom rushed back into the room. "What are my boys up to?" Her voice was up and festive, and very fake. She didn't want her boys to bond too closely.

I suggested we go to dinner. Ken got up to use the bathroom. When he was out of sight, it was Mom's turn to pull me aside.

"I need to talk to you," she said.

I was afraid I was being pulled into their ancient war again, where I was referee and punching bag simultaneously. But Ken's appearance and behavior had spooked me, and I decided to be up-front. "Ken looks like hell," I blurted to Sante. "What's wrong with him?"

Sante had an answer. "We're both exhausted. The lawsuits, Kenny—it's everything hitting us all at once. I've got to get him back to the Bahamas. That's the only place we can relax." Then she blamed Kenny for his father's red face and shaking hands. "He's out of control. He's always demanding more money, and he forgets how old Ken is. He won't listen to me. Ken created this monster, and now we all have to pay for it. Maybe Kenny will listen to you."

In Mom's mind, Ken had spoiled her son while she was in Pleasanton. I could second her opinion—up to a point. Mom shared the responsibility for Kenny's rages, his petulance, his selfishness, but she wouldn't accept it.

Mom wanted me to talk Kenny off the ledge, as I'd done a dozen times before, but baby brother and I hadn't exchanged more than a hello since he'd arrived. When he came back from playing with the kids, he was businesslike. "I have some people to see," he told Mom and Ken. "We really need to get going." It was almost an order.

I put his behavior down to adolescent arrogance, and I cut him some slack because his upbringing would have warped any kid. He was a college boy now, trying on a new self, and he'd shed his alternative rock outfits for expensive suits. He stood before me dressed like a New York executive. His body was pumped up by the weight regimen John and Sheelin had shown him, with the help of the occasional steroid. He was far beyond the control of his elderly father, and I could tell he knew it.

My stepfather and I weren't going to get to talk at all, much less alone. I made a last-ditch effort. "Kenny, maybe you can get with your buddies later. I wanted to take you guys out for some dinner so we could visit. This might be the last time we can get together for a while."

"No, Kent, I've already made plans." His impatience mounted. He turned to Mom and said, "Come on. It's time to get out of here. I want to go now."

Ken came out of the bathroom and saw Mom and Kenny waiting to leave. He looked at me with an expression of pure fright. He was ill and scared, and he didn't want to leave me, but he did, and I let him. It's another of those moments I can't have back, and another time I felt helpless. Again and again I would have a sense of foreboding, and I nearly always failed to act.

I stood in the doorway of my house and watched them leave. It was March, and there was still some light in the evening sky. I could see their faces in the car. Mom waved good-bye to the kids from the back. Kenny was in the passenger seat. He had walked out of the house without making eye contact, and once settled in the car he never turned around. I saw Ken's dyed brown hair on the driver's side. Then he flashed a painful smile and waved a wan victory sign. He looked at me again, and it was the same expression I'd seen when I'd run away from Oahu to Carson eighteen years before, when we'd shared a secret and a storm was about to break. This time, though, I didn't know what the secret was. Then the car was gone. I turned to my wife and said, "Something's wrong."

A week later I was sitting by the phone, chain-smoking, drumming on the kitchen table, waiting for my mother to call me back. Before the line went dead, or she'd dropped the receiver, I'd learned that something was amiss with Ken and he was in the emergency room, nothing more. Twice in the past five years I'd taken Ken to the ER myself. Mixing alcohol with sleeping pills had eaten away the lining of his stomach. He'd been nearly unconscious both times before I got him to the hospital, where the doctors diagnosed bleeding ulcers and told him to lay off the booze. They were serious events, briefly life-threatening, but he'd pulled through.

Lynn and the kids breezed into the house with some friends. I was a mess. A half hour before I'd been eager to see them, and now I couldn't handle it. Lynn saw the expression on my face. Before she could finish asking "What's wrong?" I'd barked, "Just get everyone out of here!" It was so unlike me that the room was clear in an instant.

I was close to a panic attack, and still Mom wouldn't call. I couldn't stand it anymore and dialed the operator in Santa Barbara. I knew Mom had to be in the vicinity, because she and Ken had been with Kenny earlier in the day. I started calling every hospital in the Santa Barbara area, in no particular order. The third one was a hit.

"Can I help you, sir?" said a nurse. She was at the front desk in the ER at Goleta Valley Hospital. It was 8 P.M.

Trying not to sound too manic, I took a breath and said, "I'm calling from Las Vegas, and I just got a frantic call from my mother. I'm trying to find out if my father has been admitted to your hospital."

"What's your father's name?" she asked.

"Ken Kimes."

"Oh, can you hold on for a minute, sir?" said the woman. She put down the receiver. I knew she'd recognized the name. Her voice had changed from professionally cheery to worried. I waited an agonizing five minutes before a new, more authoritative female voice came on the line.

"Mr. Kimes?"

"Yes," I lied. I didn't feel like explaining that he was my stepdad. "Is my father there?"

"Yes, we still have him here," she said. She seemed to want me to ask the right question.

"What's his condition?"

"Sir, your father died this afternoon." She seemed surprised that I didn't know.

I don't remember what happened for a few seconds after that. I became cold. The nurse realized that she'd been the one to give me the news, and that she hadn't done it right. "I'm sorry you had to find out this way. I assumed your mother had already told you." She was more and more uneasy. "Mr. Kimes"—she paused—"do you know where your mother is? We're very concerned about her."

"I'm not sure," I said.

"Well, I hope you can get down here and find her. She was so hysterical that we had to ask her to leave the hospital."

Apparently my mother had tried to run alongside the gurney, hanging on to the aluminum bar, from the waiting room back through the swinging doors into the operating theater. The doctor had taken a quick look at Ken and realized that he had died before he reached the hospital.

Out in the waiting room, my mother was inconsolable. The doctor told Sante that Ken was dead, and she responded the way she always did when something didn't go her way. She turned up the pressure. But her usual approach to employees wasn't working on the hospital staff. "Fix him!" she demanded. "Fix him! Take him into surgery!" Her yelling and arm waving disrupted the whole ward and upset other patients. The doctors and nurses tried to reason with her and tell her there was nothing they could do, but she only responded with more volume.

Finally all the staff could think of was to take Sante back to see the body. The sight of Ken on the gurney just made Mom more agitated. He had a tube shoved down his throat, his clothes were missing, and his eyes were staring into space. Still she demanded action. "We do not operate on corpses," said one exasperated doctor, his patience exhausted by the flailing, irrational widow.

On the phone, the nurse told me, "I still don't think it's really sunk in." The last time she or anyone at the hospital had seen Mom, she'd hailed a cab, the makeup on her face a teary mess.

"How did my father die?" I asked the nurse.

"I'm not sure, but it looks like he had an aneurysm in his torso." The nurse, who gave similar speeches day in and out, had regained control of the situation. She was professionally compassionate. "We did everything we could, but I think he was already gone by the time he got to us. There was nothing anyone could do."

I said thanks and left my number in case Sante turned up. As soon as I cradled the receiver the phone rang. It was Mom. Our conversation was brief. I wrote down her address on a scrap of paper and caught the first flight to LAX. Two hours after talking to the nurse, at 10 P.M., I was picking up a rental car for the drive to Santa Barbara.

It was a torturous two-hour drive through thick fog up 101. I was hunched forward in the driver's seat, trying to see the taillights of the cars ahead of me, tense with worry about what I would find. I was grieving over Ken's death, but at the same time, after more than thirty years living by the altered rules of my mother's world, my mind constructed fantastic schemes to explain the obvious. There was no such thing as face value—there was always another reality, powered by Mom's agenda. I was the kind of paranoid who was often proved right. On the drive up to Santa Barbara, I was questioning whether Ken was really dead. With Sante, you couldn't take anything for granted.

But if Ken *was* dead, what would happen to my mother and brother? I wondered where Kenny was and how he was doing. Losing your father at nineteen was bad enough, but to be left in the care of Sante Kimes made it all the worse. And I wondered too, right away, about the money. To my knowledge Ken had plenty, and planned to leave it to Mom and Kenny, but he'd also played a bitter chess game with my mother throughout their relationship. "She'll never find my money," he'd say with grim pleasure. Part of him knew that Sante saw him as a big score, and he fought back by hiding his assets. Much of it was in offshore accounts. What would become of Ken's riches now?

Mom was staying in the Miramar Hotel. As I knocked and let myself in to her room, she was sitting at a makeup table, restoring order to the world by fixing her face. Ken's pants still hung over the back of a chair. He and Mom had spent so many nights in hotels that they'd established many rituals. They always made themselves at home with bottles of their favorite booze and bags of snacks, and they always cleared a space for their legal files. Mom and Ken's "work" traveled with them. The only thing missing from this familiar tableau was Ken. It was an eerie feeling.

When Mom saw me, she got upset all over again. She wasn't out of control, as she'd been earlier, but she was manic. She needed to tell me every event of the day in detail. Neither of us slept that night.

Mom told me she and Ken had dropped Kenny off at his dorm that morning in Goleta, the beach-town address of the University of California–Santa Barbara. They wanted to drive up and look at the Santa Maria property, but first they made a pit stop at the Goleta branch of the Wells Fargo Bank.

Once inside, Mom went to the restroom while Ken waited in line. She told me that she and Ken and Kenny had been having a great day. No arguing or tension, just a happy family. Later I'd learn that they'd been fighting since they left my house in Vegas. They fought in Palm Springs, where they'd paused for a night along the way, and they fought in Santa Barbara. They argued about money and a stereo Kenny wanted, stupid stuff, but Ken had yelled right back at Kenny. It wouldn't surprise me if the fight had continued that morning in Goleta. Kimes family bouts were grueling, multiday epics.

Mom came out of the bank restroom to find Ken no longer in line. Figuring he'd finished his business and returned to the car, Sante went outside. In the car she found Ken with his head lying back on the seat, taking a last labored breath. She said it sounded like a snore, only deeper. Mom told me she shook him, and when she did he raised his head and looked at her and gasped, "Don't tell Kenny!"

Passersby had tried to help. Paramedics arrived. According to Mom, they laid Ken out on the pavement and attempted CPR, ignoring her warnings about his ulcers and heart disease. Mom claimed it took them thirty minutes to get Ken to the hospital.

The coroner performed a limited autopsy. Then Ken's body was moved to a local mortuary.

Mom was so angry about what had happened that she had me drive her to an attorney's office that afternoon. She wanted to file a malpractice suit. The way she told the story, she was due a huge settlement, because her husband had lingered in agony for hours while lazy paramedics and insensitive doctors failed to provide the proper care. The attorney was suitably mortified and vowed to take a chunk out of the negligent hospital. I let my mother vent, then pulled the attorney aside and explained how upset my mother was. I urged him to contact the coroner's office as soon as he could and review the results of the tests that had been performed on Ken earlier that day.

Mom and I left the lawyer's office for an hour. When we returned, his opinion of the case had changed 180 degrees. He had reviewed the report, discussed it with the coroner, and talked to several doctors for their opinions. All agreed that nothing could have saved Ken. No one had been negligent.

Ken had died from a huge aneurysm in his aorta. The biggest blood vessel in his body had literally exploded, and 60 percent of his blood had drained into his abdominal cavity within thirty seconds. He died fast and without much pain. The loud breath that my mother described was a reflex, the dead body expelling air when disturbed. And it was physically impossible for him to have said "Don't tell Kenny," as my mother claimed, or anything else. His mind was gone before she left the bank.

As gently as I could, I summarized what the doctors had told me, leaving out the bit about Ken's last words. I told my mother that Ken was dead before the paramedics ever arrived.

Her eyes narrowed. "You had something to do with this, didn't you?" She didn't mean Ken's death. She meant that I'd scuttled her lawsuit, and deprived her of vengeance.

"Mom, I know you want to blame someone, but there's no one to blame. It was Ken's time. Nothing could've changed that."

The anger drained out of her face. She began to weep. All she could say was "Thank God I still have you." She was almost, at that moment, vulnerable. Then the moment passed, and a more familiar, steelier Sante reasserted herself. Everything began to snap back into place. It was spin-control time.

But the scheming had started before we got to the lawyer, while my mother was still, supposedly, hysterical. To my mind, seeing a lawyer was an honest expression of her paranoia. Talk of a lawsuit was more about her denial that Ken was gone than making a buck. The cold-blooded scheme that horrified me involved Kenny.

Kenny had still not been told that his dad was dead. The night before in the hotel room, while we were surrounded by the dailiness of Ken's life, I'd raised the issue.

"Mom, how are we going to tell Kenny?" I asked.

"We're not," she said.

My mother could still amaze me. "What do you mean we're not! Kenny has to be told. Let's go find him right now."

"It was Ken's last wish that Kenny finish college," my mother explained, with prim sanctimony. "His last words were 'Don't tell Kenny.' We're not going to defy Papa's final wish."

That afternoon I would learn that Sante couldn't possibly have heard any such thing. But she'd used the "last words" ploy on me because she had a plan, and by then her plan was in full effect. After the visit to the attorney's office, my mother worked the phones, calling her friends and proxies in the area to make sure Kenny didn't learn of the death. She told them that Papa was very sick and that if Kenny found out, he'd worry and his grades would suffer. She swore them to secrecy.

I began to chew over just how calm and collected Mom had been in that second phone conversation on the day of Ken's death. She'd called me in total meltdown, incoherent, inconsolable, and then disappeared. She'd contacted me hours later so I could make travel arrangements, and by then she'd been completely composed—too composed. Where was she during those missing hours? I decided she'd been scheming, and that "Don't tell Kenny" was part of the scheme.

That night was unbearable. Mom and I ate dinner, and I said very little. I was brooding about Kenny. When I couldn't stand it anymore, the words rushed out. "Mom, we have to tell Kenny. We don't have a choice."

She was stone-cold now. "I'm going through enough already. You need to listen to me on this. We can't tell Kenny."

"Why the hell not? His father is dead, and he has to be told!"

Mom dropped the pretense of Ken's last words with a thud. "If we tell Kenny," she said slowly and patiently, like a schoolteacher, "we won't have a penny. I don't know if Ken had a will. If we tell Kenny now, he might go to the Creeps." The Creeps again, that whole other Kimes clan. Not telling Kenny was about the money, like everything else.

"Kenny's going to hate us. We can't do this," I pleaded.

"Kent, can't you see—we're going to save his life. If we tell him, all three of us will lose everything. That won't do Kenny any good. We have to protect Kenny now, and I need your help." In my heart, I recognized that by keeping quiet I was protecting my mother and myself, not Kenny, but Mom kept cajoling and wrapping her self-interest in this gauzy familial all-for-one, one-for-all wrapping that never failed to get me. Part of me accepted the idea that Kenny was a young kid who might call his estranged relatives and tell them the truth and thereby lose out on millions that were rightfully his. And though I didn't believe a tenth of the monster stories that Sante told me about Andrew and Linda Kimes, through endless repetition some of her crazy suspicions had lodged in my brain. Maybe there was a shred of truth to what she said, and the Creeps would take Ken's money and leave us penniless. I hung on to that shred. I realized that I wasn't going to change her mind, and after a few hours of her tireless lobbying I gave up. I agreed not to tell my brother that his dad was dead.

The next morning we went to the morgue. The people there were kind. Mom was back to looking like a late-period Liz Taylor, which meant she was in full control of her faculties.

Her recovery was clear when she filled out the forms for Ken's death certificate. She larded the paperwork with false information. A few numbers and names altered here and there, and the Social Security Administration was unaware of Ken's death. It was part of her plan. In addition, there would be no death notice, no obituary, no mail from the coroner's office. Nobody knew Ken was dead except the coroner, the doctors, the funeral home, Mom, and me.

Her need for secrecy also dictated that there be no funeral. It sickened me, but I acquiesced. There would be a quick cremation, no tombstone, no evidence that Ken had lived or died.

I was torn between loyalty to my mother, to what appeared to be the best way to protect her, and the feeling that what was going on wasn't right. With all of the paperwork finished, I wrote the funeral home director a check for the cremation. My hand trembled as I reached over the desk to give him the check, just the way Ken's hand had trembled the last time I saw him alive. The mortician probably interpreted my shakes as grief, if he noticed them at all, but the cause was trepidation and guilt. Some kind of crime was being committed.

The body would be burned without any delay. Suddenly I had to see my stepdad before it was too late. "Can that be arranged?" I asked.

"What are you doing!" Mom hissed.

"I want to say good-bye."

"I'm not sure that's such a good idea," she fumed. "I don't think I like that."

I had understood that Mom was keeping Ken's death a secret for the sake of the money. Her machinations, illegal or unethical or cruel, made sense once you accepted her premise. But I had still wilder suspicions of my own, which had been festering in my brain all the way up 101 through the fog.

As soon as Mom told me she didn't want me to see Ken's dead body, I was convinced that my craziest suspicions were right on target. I brushed past her and burst into the cold, sterile room of steel tables and caskets where the body lay.

In the dim light, an old man rested on a metal table with wheels. It wasn't Ken. My head spun with feelings of vindication, elation, and fear. My theory had been that Mom and Ken had faked his death, and he was lolling on a beach somewhere, laughing, with a drink in his hand. Sante would call him and say, "It's done," and they'd be free of creditors and lawsuits and liens. Maybe it was Kenny he wanted to escape, since little brother was driving Ken's blood pressure sky-high, and I'd heard the word *disown* more than once. When I saw the body, I was stunned that Mom and Ken had actually found somebody else to do the dying, some poor loser from Shade Tree. Or they'd killed someone.

All these thoughts charged through my skull within seconds. Then my eyes adjusted to the light, and I saw it was Ken in front of me after all. It hadn't looked like him because death had slackened the muscles in his face. His skin was suddenly smooth, and his eyes and mouth were glued shut. It was as if all the features of the face I'd known for twenty-three years had become disconnected and unrelated to each other.

Ken looked younger, but he didn't look at peace. I saw pain and conflict, the two decades of sorrow he'd endured at the hands of my mother. The man who lay before me had been a decent person at one time, and had lived the American dream. He was an up-from-poverty Okie, a field hand turned millionaire by the sweat of his own brow. If he'd been struck dead the day before he met my mother, there would have been a funeral, with friends and family and tributes paid to his accomplishments. But since he'd known her he'd lost everything, and his world had grown smaller. He had outlived his ambition and had died old, querulous, alcoholic, nearly friendless, and on the run.

I put my hands on his body and prayed to God that he'd be forgiven for the biggest mistake of his life, letting himself be consumed by my mother. I prayed that God would overlook the last two decades and judge him only on his good qualities. I begged for mercy, since so many of Ken's evil deeds would never have happened without my mother. I was asking God to let Ken into heaven, though the expression on Ken's lifeless face told me he was already in hell.

Then Mom rushed through the doors behind me and started to cry again. Even in death she couldn't let Ken and me have a private moment together. "Papa, oh Papa!" she wailed. She pulled out a brush and combed his hair the way he wore it in life. We stayed there for a few minutes, each saying good-bye in our own way. Before we left the room, I leaned over and kissed his forehead. To this day I haven't forgotten the chill it left on my lips.

"Are you glad you did that now?" asked Mom.

"Yes," I said. Finally I was crying. There had been no body-switching scheme. My stepfather was dead.

"This is really hard on you!" My mother felt genuine surprise. It was another of those moments when I glimpsed the uncanny difference between Sante and the rest of the human race. Something was missing inside her. She couldn't recognize the signs of love. It was news to her that after twenty-odd years together I cared about my stepdad.

But she saw the tears, so she put her hand on my arm in a consoling gesture. She had no way of knowing that not all my crying was for Ken. The tears were because I wished it were her on that metal table instead.

26

KONA

Mom's friend Kay Frigiano almost never came to the Geronimo house without bringing food. A Brooklyn-born Italian, she'd cooked multicourse meals of meat and pasta for me and Ken and Kenny during Mom's Club Fed years, all because Mom had called and asked.

On Easter 1994, true to form, Kay rang the doorbell at 2121 Geronimo, and when I answered she had a glass dish of lasagna covered in tinfoil in her hands. I gave her a kiss on the cheek, took the dish from her, and let her in.

"Sweetheart, aren't you wonderful," Kay cooed, as she hobbled past on her bad knees. She was by nature warm and maternal, and she was an oddity in the culture of the Kimes family. Mom and Ken had met her during the days when she performed as a lounge pianist under the name Kay Astarita. Fifteen years later, Kay worked on the casino floor at Caesars, but she remained close to the family. Nearly all of Mom's relationships blew up long before their fifteenth anniversary, but not her friendship with Kay.

I was glad that she'd be sharing Easter dinner with us and helping me prepare a turkey. I thought Kay's presence might help fill the void. It was our first Easter without Ken, and Kenny would also be absent. He'd opted to stay at school in Santa Barbara, which made it easier for Mom to keep her secret. Three weeks after Ken's death, she still hadn't told Kenny or, for that matter, anyone besides me.

When it came time for dinner, I took my place next to my wife and my daughter. My baby son was in a high chair. In all, there were six of us for dinner. We sat around a long table crowned with a massive floral arrangement and heaped with food, including a generous bowl of Mom's favorite, mashed potatoes.

Mom brought in the turkey with a flourish and then sat at the head of the table. She was going to lead us in grace. Before she started, she placed a framed photo of Ken atop the flowers.

I had been waiting for Kay to ask why Ken wasn't with us. Mom had been telling people that a serious illness was keeping Ken in the hospital. I reasoned that Kay had probably heard that story. Whatever she believed, I braced myself to go along with it.

But now Mom had created what looked like a funeral bouquet. And then she began a long, maudlin speech about Ken's achievements and their life together that sounded like a eulogy. I can't recall what she said, except she started crying halfway through. I remember the ending: "Papa is watching over us now."

My wife burst into tears. With my head bowed and my hands still clasped together in prayer, I cried too. I also tried to shrink into my seat.

Kay was gasping. "Nobody tells me anything," she sputtered. Our guest hadn't missed the implication of Mom's speech. She was what passed for Mom's intimate, and the first outside the family to hear about Ken's death, yet Mom had been lying to her for weeks. She'd hidden his passing with cover stories, and she still couldn't bring herself to say, "Ken is dead."

I felt ashamed about aiding Mom with her cover-up. I had helped deceive Kay and many others. What made it worse, though, was that I would have to go on deceiving my little brother. Kay now knew that Ken Kimes was dead, but his own son didn't.

Mom continued to retail her stories about Ken's ill health after Easter and into May. She told a few people, gradually, that Ken was dead, but whenever she did she always emphasized that Kenny was not to know, because of Ken's last words and Ken's dream of a college degree for his son. She'd dropped that ruse with me. She appealed to my greed. She used my own weakness against me to make me do things I'd never dreamed of doing. I spent my days among people who thought Ken was alive, because I kept my promise and said not a word. But I never lied to anyone either. I prayed that someone would just ask me, "Is Ken dead?" but no one did.

To myself, I had to keep listing the reasons not to tell my little brother. In my mind, I was protecting him, but I was also protecting myself. The months after Ken's death represented the first cease-fire between me and my mother in fifteen years. She and Ken weren't fighting over me anymore, and my mom and I were fixated on a common goal — finding Ken's money.

I reveled in this short-lived peace. Before I knew it I was doing my mother's bidding again, living by her rules. But I thought that if I didn't, and Mom failed to find the money, Kenny might abandon both of us. That would leave only me to take care of her. If I couldn't keep Mom's secret and help her round up Ken's holdings, things might end just the way they began, with me and Mom against the world. I told myself that I was working for my own freedom.

Yet there would be days when I felt that I was betraying my late stepfather, and endangering any future relationship with my brother. At those times Mom kept me in line. "Don't let your holier-than-thou attitude destroy things for Kenny," she'd spit. "We need you to be the protector, not the enemy."

"I'm not trying be holier-than-thou, I just can't do this," I'd protest.

In response, Mom would always raise the stakes: "If Kenny or anyone else finds out, it could be the end of us!"

"What do you mean? I can help you. We're far from destitute. And Kenny can get a job." It was my turn to be caustic.

"Kenny isn't the type to go out and get a job, and you" — she stuck the knife in — "you've always struggled with your business. This is the only way we can survive, and you know it."

By June it had been three months since Ken's death and Kenny still knew nothing. Mom told him that she and Ken were in the Bahamas, when she was actually in Vegas most of the time, searching for Ken's assets.

During this Stalinoid era of secrecy my little brother had better things to do than call me. Classes and the busy social life of college kept him occupied. But he did contact me once.

"Kent, have you heard from Dad?" Kenny's voice was breezy. He didn't sound too worried.

"I haven't talked to him since the last time you guys were

over here." I wasn't lying. I hoped that Kenny would remember that his last visit was three months ago and ask some obvious questions. He didn't. "I talk to Mom a lot," he said, "but I haven't talked to Dad for a while. I wanted to make sure everything was all right."

I knew about Mom's Bahamas story. "I don't know what to tell you," I said. That was the truth.

"If you hear from Dad, tell him to call me, okay?"

"I will." I was a coward. "Kenny, how are you doing?" I asked.

"Okay. Studying and partying!"

"In that order?" I joked lamely.

"Don't worry about it, bro," he barked. "I have everything under control."

He spoke with the arrogance of a nineteen-year-old college boy with expensive clothes and a hot car who really thinks he does have everything under control. He didn't know that the ground had opened up under his feet. I couldn't stand it anymore. I never truly understood the emotion of guilt until that moment. I decided to tell him. "Kenny, we need to talk about something," I said.

"Sure, bro, but I have to go now. Call you later." He hung up. He wasn't interested in talking to me. I held the dead receiver in my hand and cried.

FLIGHTS TO HAWAII ARE usually fun, because the passengers are happy. Locals, headed home, have a habit of bringing Hawaiian food along and breaking it out in the cabin. The tourists radiate expectation. They're looking forward to vacations that many have planned for years. It's not like flying from LAX to O'Hare.

It helps too if you enjoy flying, like me, and if your mother has a knack for cadging first-class upgrades out of the airlines. But in mid-June 1994, I was riding coach to Kona on the Big Island, and it was the most unhappy trip I'd ever taken. Mom had failed to score first-class tickets, and now my six-foot-three frame was crammed into a seat next to her. We were embarked on a very unpleasant errand. We were going to meet my little brother in Kona and tell him the truth.

The flight seemed to last for days. Sante was droning in my ear about why things had to be the way they were. Her huge bust and stomach were pudging over the divider between our seats as she rattled on and on. I was trapped, and would have to endure her manipulation for hours on end. I felt resentment at everyone around me for being so happy.

I had learned at an early age how to let my thoughts wander during Mom's orations. In that uncomfortable 747 seat, I nodded and ate airline snacks while Sante talked, and I followed my own ruminations down a very dark hole. I admitted to myself that I suspected the woman beside me of murder.

It doesn't sound so unreasonable now, with four other people dead or missing from the Bahamas to Los Angeles. In the past two years, since Irene Silverman, several of my parents' ex-friends have hedged and hemmed and finally blurted out their suspicions that my stepfather was killed. Six years ago, though, trapped in the plane with Mom, I didn't let a flicker of emotion cross my face as I weighed the evidence. There was the sudden change in Ken's health, the fearful look on his face, his bright-red complexion. They might have been the symptoms of pure fright as an isolated old man felt a natural death approaching. But I had also received a strange phone call from Ken in the Bahamas back in January. "Kent!" he'd whispered to me, "I think I'm being poisoned." I'd dismissed it as alcoholic paranoia or perhaps the first disheartening signs of senility. Now I took it seriously.

Mom had been too much in control, too fast, too soon after Ken's unexpected death. I envied her composure, and I hated her for it. I could confront her with any hard truth about her behavior, and she was such an accomplished actress that she'd never stumble. I wasn't going to accuse her of murder on a packed flight to Hawaii.

"I'll never forget what you've done for me," she was saying when I started listening again. We were suspended above the Pacific, halfway to the islands. "I'd forgotten just how special you are. I don't deserve a son like you."

I ignored the flattery, looking past her at the happy tourists. "Are you sure that Kenny doesn't know?" I asked.

"He would have said something if he had any clue," she said. "I really think we pulled it off." A wave of shame hit me, then hatred. We had "pulled it off," and "it" was a scam. I was a con artist, the true son of a con-artist mother. We looked alike, we thought alike, and here we sat together, practically joined at the hip.

"What was the longest Kenny went without talking to Ken?" I asked, gritting my teeth. I still couldn't look at Mom.

"Oh, maybe a week or so, but that's all right. Ken was starting to distance himself from Kenny." That sounded plausible. "I talked to Kenny several times, and believe me, Kent, he doesn't know. Just remember"—she grabbed my upper arm and squeezed—"you saved your brother's life by not telling him." She sighed. "It's been hard on me too, Kent. But this was the only way to save the future and everything I've been working so hard on."

"He's going to hate us," I concluded.

Then Mom tried another strategy, though it wasn't a new one. She always went for the same buttons—greed, ego, fear, power, excitement, greed, and greed. She told me she had a dream that my brother and I would head a business "empire"— she loved that preposterous word. She liked any word that sounded like property and power. She started spinning a plan whereby the brothers would make a fortune on the twenty-nine acres in Santa Maria. "Remember, Kent," she purred, "I've loved you the longest."

I was ecstatic when the video screens lowered from the cabin ceiling. *In-flight movie, deliver me from Sante.* It wouldn't matter if it was *Ishtar.* If it was *Star Trek,* that would really shut Mom up.

Instead it was *Intersection,* a bomb that starred Richard Gere. Mom watched in relative silence for an hour. Then an ambulance rushed Gere's character to an emergency room, and as he lay dying on the gurney, Mom let out a banshee wail. I ripped off my headphones and tried to comfort her. She was making an enormous, caterwauling racket.

She was so loud that the flight attendant came by to see what was wrong. "Turn off the movie!" Mom demanded. "My husband died in an emergency room three months ago! I lived that scene! Turn it off!"

It was the first time I'd actually heard her admit to anyone but me that Papa was gone. The flight attendant brought us free drinks and apologized. She couldn't stop the film. She bent over and spoke softly to me. "You need to get your mother under control," she said. "We don't want to disturb the other passengers."

It seemed like sincere grief, and I couldn't handle it. I had to console her, while blaming her for the death she was mourning and the months-long soap opera she'd concocted. I was relieved when we touched down in Kona.

My mother and I walked in silence into the terminal. I had Ken's ashes in an urn under my arm. They'd been in the overhead compartment, above Mom's head, while she bawled at the movie screen. *What do you think of this, Ken?* I wondered. Would he laugh or curse if he could see me carting his remains through the airport?

The plan was to cast Ken's remains into the waves from a chartered boat. Lynn and the kids would arrive in the morning. They were already on Oahu. Kenny would touch down in Kona tomorrow afternoon. He was coming straight from final exams at college and he thought he was meeting his dad in Hawaii. Mom and I would intercept him at the airport, break the news to him, maybe back at the hotel, give him the night to recover, and we'd all convene at the boat the next morning. No one else would be there, because there was no one else. Besides Kay and a few Vegas pals, John and Sheelin were the closest thing to family, and they'd declined the invitation to Kona. As much as they loved Ken and Kenny, they wanted nothing more to do with Sante.

Mom and I checked into the Royal Waikoloan Hotel. She took a nap. I went to the hotel bar and got drunk on mai tais. It didn't work. I couldn't sleep, and I cringed every time I thought of Kenny's impending arrival.

The road from the hotel to the Kona airport is desolate. It's the other, volcanic Hawaii, not the lush, palmy paradise most mainlanders imagine. As we drove to get Kenny the next morning, the lava flow stretched to the horizon. White boulders by the roadside had been arranged to spell messages, but the black lava was otherwise bare of vegetation or ornament. Heat rose in waves from the naked rock.

We reached the airport parking lot. The time had come. A month before, when we scripted this scene, Mom had delegated me to speak the words. I wondered if Kenny would hit me. I wondered if he would hit Mom. This was the same troubled adolescent who a few years before had tried to kill his parents.

Kenny's plane pulled up close to the hangar, and I saw him walk down the steps onto the hot tarmac. He stood out. Everyone else was dressed in casual sportswear; he was in Armani. He looked as if he were walking out of a board meeting instead of a six-hour flight. As he walked through the gate, with a wide, big-toothed grin on his jug-eared face, Mom let me off the hook. "I've changed my mind," she whispered. "I'll tell him. I'll take him into the coffee shop by the parking lot—you wait for us by the car."

Kenny was getting closer. "What do you mean?" I blared. "This is crazy enough as it is. I need to be there too."

But she'd made up her mind, and Kenny was standing in front of us. We each gave him a hug. I thought it was strange that he didn't ask where Ken was. We walked out to the parking lot, and Mom turned and said, "Wait here, Kent. I need to talk to Kenny." I obeyed. Kenny gave me a quick, quizzical glance over his shoulder as he followed Mom into the coffee shop.

I leaned against the car and watched them through the restaurant window as they plopped down in a booth. Mom's back was turned to me, but I had a full view of Kenny's face. I watched him crumple when the news hit him. He was just like his mother. When he felt an emotion, it was never subtle. It took over his body. I saw heads swiveling in the restaurant as Kenny and Mom talked, and I knew they were being loud. Before I knew what I was doing, I'd crept across the asphalt and put my face close to the window.

Kenny kept nodding his head as Mom spoke, and the conversation dragged on. It lasted so long that I became angry about the wait. Then Mom turned and saw me standing a yard from the glass. I saw her face for the first time, and she'd been crying again. Her mascara had run. Her eyes popped when she spotted me, and she seemed almost angry that I'd left my post. She pointed at me and said something to Kenny. His eyes were strangely dry.

The two of them came outside. Every muscle in my body tightened as Kenny drew closer. The time had arrived for me to take my medicine.

"Hey, tiger," I said lamely, out of a combination of habit and nervous fear.

Kenny rushed over to me and, instead of hitting me, threw his arms around me in a bear hug and wept. I held him as he sobbed. I don't know who I was trying to comfort, him or me. We stood there like that for a long time.

Then he pulled away from me and stared into my eyes and said something very confusing. "Thank you, big brother. You did the right thing by not telling me. That's the way Papa would've wanted it."

I stood there in shock. I didn't want his compassion, I wanted his anger. He should be asking me to pay for the wrong I'd done him. Instead he was mouthing words from a script by Sante Kimes. Had he really bought her take on events in that five-minute coffee shop revelation? Or was there something else going on? To my suspicions about my mother, I now added questions about my baby brother's possible role in the demise of Ken Kimes. That was the first time I admitted to myself that my spoiled, sheltered, fun-loving little brother had become someone else.

The next morning we held a funeral. Mom had picked a church out of the phone book, an Episcopal chapel thirty minutes from the hotel. Ken was Catholic.

Although it was a small church, it still felt empty with just the six of us, Mom and Kenny, me and Lynn and our two kids. You could almost hear an echo. At the front of the sanctuary stood a single candle, and around it six urns, one for each surviving member of the family.

The priest said a few words. I could tell he felt awkward delivering a eulogy for a man he hadn't heard of until Mom's phone call the day before. What he had to work with were the "facts" my mother provided. She told him that Ken was important, a multimillionaire and a former ambassador. The priest probably wondered why such an important man was receiving such a meager send-off.

As the priest spoke, I looked at the huge bed of flowers to his left. A picture of Ambassador Ken, from the days of the Bicentennial fiasco, perched atop the blossoms. Mom had taken his greatest humiliation, a Sante-engineered farce that had ruined his reputation, and recast it as his crowning achievement.

Then Mom rose to say her good-byes to my stepfather, who'd been dead for three months. Her words are now a blur. I remember the name Papa repeated over and over, and something to the effect that he was still watching over us and we would never be apart. I also recall the thought that a stranger listening to her talk might have come away with the impression that Ken had simply moved out of state. Mom wouldn't say that he was dead.

After the service, we had a few hours to kill before the burial at sea. We spent it drinking wine back at the Waikoloan. By the time we reached the beach where our rented forty-foot catamaran waited, all four adults were sloshed.

Luckily, the weather was good. The day was a Hawaiian postcard. The wind was strong enough to push us along at several knots, but light enough not to blow a chop from the six-foot swells on deck. We each repaired to a separate corner of the big double-hulled boat. No one spoke. We listened to the wind in the shrouds and the water slapping against the boat.

Mom hadn't bothered to tell the rent-a-captain the purpose of her trip, and he hadn't blinked at the six urns we'd carried aboard. As we cleared the harbor he launched into a canned tourist spiel about the history of the Big Island. He thought we were just one big unhappy family out for a cruise.

"Be quiet," Mom barked. "We paid for the boat, not the chitchat." The captain clenched his jaw, but he obeyed. I felt that the captain and his crew of one deserved an explanation, so I told them what we planned. I asked him to position the boat so that we'd be able to throw the ashes into the sea and not have them blown back in our faces.

By the time we were ready to scatter the ashes, we'd finished two more bottles of wine. I don't know why nobody got seasick. We were drunk, but it wasn't the alcohol that made scattering the ashes such a nightmare. Mom was scrambling to open her gray ceramic urn, scratching at the lid, and nothing was happening. She started to panic. The seal was too strong. I tried to help, but Mom was becoming more unhinged by the second. The captain and the mate looked alarmed.

I talked Mom into letting me break the urn open, and when she agreed I closed my fist and slammed it into the side of the container. The only thing that came close to breaking was my knuckles. Mom was making a high-pitched whimpering sound and saying "Papa! Papa!" again. Desperate, I grabbed two of the urns and cracked them together. The contents spilled into the ocean and drifted away on the wind. I was surprised to see chunks of bone. I always thought that when a body was cremated only pure ash remained. For some reason I fixated on the bone fragments. They made Ken's death and the burial very real to me.

I helped everyone break open their urns, and as the last of Ken's ashes disappeared in the Pacific I cried. My mask had slipped, and I wasn't the Rock for a moment.

I later learned that the truth about that day wasn't dramatic enough for Mom. She told very few people about the burial, but the ones who heard the tale got the Sante-ized version. In her story we were off Oahu, hundreds of miles north, behind the old Portlock house. We hadn't consumed gallons of wine. The most interesting part of Mom's rewrite, however, was what Kenny had done after the last of his father's ashes had melted into the waves. He'd burst into tears, shouting "Papa! Papa!" and jumped overboard.

If this had been true, we might have needed a double funeral. With the wind at sixteen knots and the catamaran pointing into the wind in six-foot seas, a drunk in an Armani suit probably would have drowned.

27

SHOW ME
THE MONEY

Mom played the role of grieving widow better than anyone since Jackie Kennedy. Two weeks after Ken's death, as we walked into the Wells Fargo Bank on West Sahara, Mom took off her black sunglasses and put on her game face. She had a forged, home-notarized power-of-attorney form in her purse. Pretending to be a secretary, she'd called ahead to see what documents she'd need, and with the stamped piece of paper and her air of dignified suffering, she planned to gain access to my late stepdad's safety-deposit box. This was the first of four scattered around town, and she hoped that when she conned her way inside them she'd find the key to Ken's elusive riches.

"It's all going to charity when I die," Ken had told me more than once, and always in front of my mother, so there'd be no mistake. He was bluffing, but he was putting Sante on notice—keep me alive and you're a millionaire, but if I die you're broke. He'd hidden his money from Mom so he could have some leverage in the relationship and so she couldn't steal it. When he dropped dead, Mom and I had to go on a treasure hunt. I was happy to help because I believe, as I still do, that Mom and Kenny and I were the legitimate heirs. I was excited about the money, had been expecting it, and felt entitled to it.

Mom was sure there were millions somewhere. On the plane back to Vegas from Santa Barbara, days after cremating Ken, she unveiled her plan for splitting those millions up. "I have decided to give you and Kenny each a third," she intoned, "and I can live off a third. But you need to help me set up a trust for your brother. I don't want him to have the money till he's in his thirties." I took a sip of the drink on my plastic tray and nodded. I did some quick, guilty math and guessed I'd be worth at least two million. Then Mom stuck the knife in. "I do hope you use the money to get out of the damn vacuum business and do something with your life."

Sure enough, when Mom and I got back to Vegas we uncovered a trove of checkbooks in Ken's desk drawer. Most of them, however, were for defunct accounts. We dug up one live account worth sixty thousand dollars and another worth forty thousand. I thought I'd hit the jackpot when I tried on one of Ken's blazers and found a passbook in the pocket from a Bahamas bank. It listed assets in excess of half a million bucks, but Mom told me those assets had been drained before Ken's death. "Where," asked Chuck Stohl, Ken's longtime California accountant, "did all that wonderful cash go?"

We couldn't even locate a will. We were running out of options by the time we raided the safe-deposit boxes. They seemed like the logical place for someone as fearful and secretive as Ken to hide a fortune from his wife.

The bank clerk led us back into the vault. Hundreds of gray doors with tiny silver keyholes lined the walls. Inside were the boxes. Mom sat down at a little carrel and put on bifocals, the librarian-style horn-rims that made her look matronly and law-abiding. I'd brought a black gym bag with me to hold whatever goodies we found. The clerk set Ken's box in front of her and turned the lock.

Mom expected to reach in and pull out CDs and stock certificates and information on Caribbean bank accounts. Instead she found a stack of worthless papers, records of investments long since dead. She started emitting the high-pitched wail of pure panic. "Oh, Kent," she whined, "where is it?"

At the second bank, we thought we'd stumbled on the mother lode. The clerk dropped the case on the table with a heavy clank. Ken had filled the metal cube to the brim with old gold and silver coins. We assumed that Ken had stashed them in a vault because they were so valuable, but later we discovered that our grand haul was worth little more than its face value, two thousand dollars. Boxes three and four were busts also — Ken had used one of them as a hiding place for pictures of the so-called Creeps. I wasn't there, but I can imagine the look on Mom's face when she opened the box and found a photo of Linda Kimes.

Mom's last hope was the Bahamas, where she knew Ken had concealed some assets. She flew down to search the Cable Beach house for clues, and she wouldn't let me accompany her. She stayed on Nassau for a week, and returned to Vegas in tears. Rambling, barely coherent, she seemed to be on the verge of a nervous breakdown.

She seemed to be crying for *me*. "You're not in the will, honey," she said, sighing. She said she'd found Ken's missing testament at the beach house. I couldn't get her to show me the document, but a quick rummage through her luggage revealed it. The alleged will left 50 percent to Mom and 25 percent to Kenny, and split the remaining quarter between my kids and Andrew Kimes's daughter. Though Ken had told me I *was* in his will, the piece of paper in my hand looked plausible. Given that Sante the forger had gone to the Bahamas alone, however, and brought back this mystery document, I'd never swear to it. Something about it was too much like Moses coming down from Mount Sinai with the Ten Commandments, or Joseph Smith walking out of the woods with the Book of Mormon.

It left us so much and the Creeps so little that it was too good to be true. I decided the Bahamas will was real, however, when my mother suddenly "found" a better one in Vegas. The new will left every penny to her.

Mom wasn't really worried about my absence from Ken's will. In fact, only one thing could make Mom behave the way she had on her return from the Caribbean—poverty, actual or imagined. On some level she'd accepted what I'd realized in the Wells Fargo bank vault. Nearly all of Ken's money was gone.

It made sense. During the final years of his life, Ken had continued to jet-set with Mom. They spent their time in Nassau, Santa Barbara, Las Vegas, and Palm Springs. But I'd noticed a few chinks in their aura of wealth. Once nothing less than a luxury sedan was good enough for Ken Kimes when he rented a car. By 1992, though, he'd begun to slide down-market. I saw him looking sheepish in a Geo more than once.

It was no mystery where the money had gone. Mom had wasted millions in legal fees and settlements, and Ken had pissed away untold amounts during his long afternoons of video poker. He hadn't been such a great businessman either, as his Vegas accountant, Gloria Roberts, revealed to me. A good businessman had to keep up with the times, and Ken didn't.

The Mecca was a good example. As it turned out, Ken had

built many motels on the fringes of Disneyland. If he'd kept them, he might have been able to add a zero to the end of his fortune. But he only retained ownership of the Mecca, and the sole reason he'd kept that motel, which would become the centerpiece of his empire, was that he'd had to repossess it from a buyer. As more and more people flocked to Disneyland, the motels around the Mecca grew upward, adding multiple stories and new wings. The Mecca never did. Ken was set in his ways. He kicked back and counted his money as the world changed around him.

By the time Mom met him, Ken was already at the end of his winning streak. And together, the two of them were hopeless. In 1990 Mom had reeled in a rich Texan as a buyer for the twenty-nine-acre Santa Maria tract. The man from Dallas came to visit her and Ken in Vegas. I think my folks had been expecting some cowboy rube with a trophy wife, but when the airport limo arrived on Geronimo, out stepped an urbane, polished couple, a young man in a European suit and his beautiful blond mate. As soon as I saw them, I knew the coming night on the town would be hell. Mom would hate the woman for her youth and beauty, and she and Ken would scotch the deal with dropped names, lies, and boasts about their wealth. My parents were more comfortable with people who were easily impressed. Sure enough, the Texans left the next morning and we never heard from them again.

Ken tried to keep making money till the day he died. Any time he tried to invest in anything that paid more than 6 percent interest, though, he'd lose big. He was as bad at picking stocks as he was at playing cards. While the rest of America reaped profits from the booming stock market, he dropped more than four hundred thousand dollars with foolish gambles on penny stocks.

Mom wasn't really poor, at least by normal human standards. She owned the Geronimo house free and clear. She had a hundred thousand dollars in cash. A buyer still owed Ken nine monthly payments of six thousand dollars each for a motel he'd sold years ago. As I learned later, Ken also had a Bahamian bank account in the high six figures, if Mom could only hatch a plan for prying the money loose. Most important, in the sixties Ken had bought the tract in Santa Maria. That alone would bring two or three million dollars if sold.

But Mom, with her horror of poverty, felt poor, and that's

what mattered. She hadn't felt that way since 1971, and it added
to her vulnerability. For a few months after Ken's death, Mom
rarely had the energy to be Sante Kimes. She dropped the bluster and bravado and didn't lie as much or as often. I got my
work done at the office in the morning and spent the afternoons
with her, and I sensed a human side of her emerging, something that had been dormant since Palm Springs, hidden by the
regal air she'd affected since she'd landed her millionaire. I
thought that the reality of death had changed her. It was the
only time in our life that I ever thought she might behave herself. You could almost see what she might have been if she
hadn't become a con artist. She even began to look inward,
something she'd never done before. Ken's death had reminded
her of her own mortality, and it looked as if she might be in
danger of developing a spiritual side. She even used the word
God in a sentence without cursing.

My mother had always been a hardheaded materialist.
When my mother-in-law, Lyla, would talk to Sante about God,
Sante would usually cut her off by saying, "I don't believe in
that stuff." Ken, who'd been raised Catholic and had sent
Kenny to a Catholic school, didn't really believe in it either.
"When you die, that's it," he concluded.

Now, however, Mom began to contact people from different religious backgrounds to ask them questions about life after
death. Fittingly, given her alleged bloodlines, she got the
answers she wanted to hear from an East Indian mystic. He told
her that Ken was on the other side, watching over us and waiting for Mom to join him. After that, every time a breeze moved
the curtains, Mom would beam. "See, it's Ken! He's watching
over us!" What I really think Mom wanted was for Ken to send
us, via Ouija board, the numbers of his secret bank accounts.

Soon, though, Mom shook off her fog and went to work. I
realized that what I'd mistaken for introspection was mostly a
brief lack of confidence. Mom had been rattled by her partner's
death and felt real grief at his absence, but it wasn't long before
she was back in charge. She proved she hadn't lost her con met-
tle by arm-twisting the insurance company into replacing the
twenty-five-year-old air conditioner at the Geronimo house for
free.

Mom had to earn money herself for the first time since we'd
moved in with Ken. First she rented out rooms in the Geronimo

house. It was a sure sign of cash-flow problems. Sante Kimes didn't like strangers violating her privacy unless they were scrubbing her floors.

Next she announced plans for a new business. I looked at her idea from every angle and couldn't believe that it belonged to Sante Kimes. She planned to offer a legitimate product at a reasonable price. People would get what they paid for. There wasn't any con in it.

Mom got some of the homeless guys from St. Vincent's to build her a brown shed with the white outlines of gingerbread men on the sides and a faux frosting roof, and she called it the Kookie Hut. It was the prototype for a chain of cookie shops that would sit in the middle of mall parking lots, sort of like Fotomat booths. She'd even hired somebody to write a jingle— all I remember is the stuttering chorus, "K-k-k-k-kookies!" I've never understood Mom's obsession with the letter *K*.

The Kookie Hut never happened, which didn't surprise me—Sante had always said she wasn't the cookie-baking type of mom. Business licenses and health codes made her eyes glaze over, and what with the hard work and the tiny dollops of cash each customer would drop, the Kookie Hut was no more suited to Sante than the late Century Arcade had been. Last time I looked, the original was still sitting there at 2121 Geronimo, on the parking pad to the right of the house, full of garden tools and looking like something from Grimm's fairy tales.

When the Kookie Hut crumbled, I remembered how Mom had reacted in Hawaii in 1975 when for a few days it looked like Ken had come to his senses and left her. Raw instinct had made her pick up the phone and start grifting again, ordering up a free Lincoln from the dealership. Now, decades later, Ken was never returning, and Mom was old and more desperate than ever. I had my fingers crossed, because I was afraid she would morph back into a full-time grifter. It was what she did best. First, however, she reinvented herself as an expert on longevity.

My mother and stepfather had always been obsessed with looking young. Ken had suffered through hair transplants, face peels, and plastic surgery on the wrinkles around his eyes. He tinted his hair, and part of his morning ritual was daubing color into his mustache. His pillow, like Mom's, was always stained with hair dye. Mom had been a plastic surgery junkie as far back as I can remember. She was an early convert to the silicone breast implant. She refused to part with them even when the doctors suggested that double-Ds were too much for her frame and should be removed.

The two of them fussed over their outward appearance and ignored their insides. Hair dye won't keep you young if you're drinking liters of liquor daily. When Mom got out of prison in 1989, though, she and Ken both decided they needed to do something to extend their life spans.

This did not mean that they locked their liquor cabinet and joined a gym. Instead they opted for miracle cures. Mom had discovered a diet supplement named Geveral, and she made Ken drink it every night. If she did poison Ken, she probably mixed the poison in with the Geveral, since it had a strong, nasty taste that could mask anything.

After they moved to the Bahamas, which has laxer rules about what drugs you can buy over the counter and what doctors can prescribe, Mom and Ken became devotees of human growth hormone. It was something for the whole family — Kenny tried HGH too. My stepdad, at seventy-five years old, began injecting himself with a drug that professional wrestlers use to bulk up. Massive doses made him sick.

Widowed, Mom decided to turn her longevity research into a business. She printed up cards that said simply "Sante," and began hunting for clients as a "longevity consultant." The drinker and french fry fan became an expert on health. Kenny even got her walking on a treadmill an hour a day. I thought her shaky knees would give out. "Sante" soon became the much grander "Princess Sante," with a new box of business cards. She traveled around the world attending longevity conferences. She somehow met Lee Iacocca, the former head of Chrysler, and bothered him on the phone and in person at his Southern California home till his secretary got wise and started shielding him from the calls. I thought she was millionaire hunting again. I encouraged it as a relatively harmless pastime — relatively — but I should have seen it as a sign that Mom was backsliding.

Mom kept up her interest in longevity, but meanwhile, as I'd feared, she went back to what she thought she did best, which was falsifying documents. It wasn't as if she'd never forged Ken's signature before, but in the years after his death, Mom really developed her penmanship. Ken Kimes would be alive and well as long as she needed him to be. She was easing back into con artistry.

But in her eagerness, Mom made things harder for herself, the way she always did. Had she gone through legal channels, she could have won control of Ken's estate. Andrew and Linda Kimes, her only rivals for the estate, feared her. Whether or not Mom's marriage certificate was a phony, Ken had been referring to her as his wife in public since the seventies. I think he called her his wife in more than one deposition, under oath. Still, Mom was afraid that she'd lose any court battle with the Creeps. "With my record," she said again and again, "I wouldn't stand a chance."

Once she gained control of the Santa Maria property, she could have sold it and lived off the proceeds. Interest alone would have run into six figures, and she didn't owe a cent on the Geronimo house. Most sixty-year-olds would have found that more than enough to retire on.

That wouldn't work for Mom. It wasn't complicated or illegal enough. First she got the title to the Santa Maria acreage in her name by backdating a "love and affection" transfer to six months prior to Ken's death. She had cultivated a big-breasted Valley Girl named Carolene Davis who worked in a Santa Barbara title office, and she used Carolene as her gofer in all her real estate trickery. Mom had met Carolene a few days before Ken died and had started smothering her with affection—"You're the daughter I never had," and so on.

She got away with the title transfer. I lined up a deal to sell the property for $2.7 million. I was helping her because I knew that if she didn't get some money fast I'd be supporting her, and no one wants Sante Kimes as a dependent. She was a few signatures away from having a comfy annuity for the rest of her unnatural life when she backed out. Mom had convinced herself that the property was worth three times that, and she directed me to find a better deal.

Before long, Mom was transferring the property from one dummy corporation to another, all to hide it in case the Creeps learned that Ken was dead. The mound of junk paper and the pumped-up asking price scared buyers away. When she realized she couldn't sell it for nine million, she came up with a scam.

She hired a down-and-outer named Billy Lovekamp, an

alcoholic clone of Elmer, to be her in-house attorney. Billy's job was to sue the city of Santa Maria and force the government to pay Mom nine million bucks for the twenty-nine-acre parcel. Mom's research had revealed a concept called "inverse condemnation," wherein the owner can ask that her property be condemned if the city has damaged it. According to Mom, the city had directed drainage from surrounding tracts onto our parcel and was obligated to buy it. Billy would attend City Council meetings and tell the mayor that Mom's dummy firm, Aga Khan International or Atlantis Corporation or whatever, was prepared to sue but would settle "amicably" for nine million dollars.

My mother's motor was revving. She set Billy to work on the inverse condemnation and then, over dinner at my house, unveiled plans for a second, simultaneous con. She said the magic words, "Honey, I need a little favor," and chuckled when I clenched my jaw. "It'll be good for you too!

"I want you to have Kristina walk on the property," she said matter-of-factly, as if describing a new sales promotion, "and get hurt. We can make a lot of money."

Having lived in Vegas for years, I knew what "trippers" were. They'd go to a casino and pretend to slip and wrench their backs and then squeeze management for a payoff. There were people at one of Mom and Ken's favorite bars who'd flung that word at my folks as an insult. Now Mom wanted my teenage daughter to be a tripper, an apprentice con artist. Dinner was cut short, and Mom was asked to leave, but she considered me the bad guy for saying no.

When I said no, Mom turned to my little brother. She and Kenny convinced each other that if they couldn't get the inverse condemnation, they should develop the Santa Maria parcel themselves. It didn't matter that neither of them had ever built a house. Mom believed that her late husband's talent for real estate had been passed down in his chromosomes.

Santa Maria gave the two of them something to focus on. Together they ditched the idea of simply selling the land for a respectable profit of a few million, and wandered off into hare-brained, impossible schemes that would land them five times as much. Kenny was helping Mom with her "projects." I realized I was now up against a team, Mom and Kenny, both of them greedy and desperate and delusional. That's when things started to go terribly wrong.

28

CUBA

Your little brother's not like you," Mom told me the summer after Ken's death. "He's not a hard worker."

I'd been offering to hire Kenny as a salesman trainee at my vacuum-cleaner business. He'd never had a real job, and I thought that knocking on doors and learning to swallow rejection might be good for him. People tell jokes about sleazy door-to-door salesmen, but I was secure in the knowledge that I sold an excellent product, rated as the best on the market by *Consumer Reports*. I'd worked my way up to a distributorship with a tough, honest, rewarding expenditure of shoe leather. I was one of the tops in my division.

When I mentioned vacuums to Mom, though, she scrunched up her nose as if there were a bad smell in the room. Then she recovered with her line about Kenny being different. She was right. Kenny was so spoiled that she had to pay him to do his homework. But what she really meant was, He's too good for vacuum-cleaner sales. It was bad enough that her dirty-fingernailed, blue-collar eldest son sold vacuums. For Ken Junior it was out of the question. She intended Kenny to inherit his dad's empire. To prepare him for his career as a real estate mogul, she arranged her own training program.

When we got back from scattering the ashes at Kona, Kenny went to work for Carolene Davis's husband, Tim. Plastering walls became the first physical effort Kenny had ever expended outside a gym. But construction was slow in Santa Barbara that summer, and there weren't enough clients to keep Kenny busy. Mom tried to make a secret arrangement with Tim's boss whereby she would save his job by paying Kenny's salary. Tim's boss was put off by Mom's pushiness and refused.

The next summer Mom gave Kenny a promotion. He'd done his two-week stint as a manual laborer, so he was ready to move up the ladder and learn about the business of development. Because the owner of the Towbes Group had known my stepdad, the real estate firm hired Kenny as an intern. All he had to do was make copies and run errands, but he either couldn't or wouldn't do it. The company eased him out the door before the end of August. He had failed as a Xerox jockey.

It was never meant to be. There was no empire to inherit — it had shrunk to twenty-nine acres in Santa Maria and a few off-shore accounts — and Kenny couldn't have run it if one had existed. Not only had he never worked, he'd never actually seen anyone work except maids and tutors. He'd spent his whole life in my parents' never-never land.

His experiences at the Towbes Group and elsewhere in the real world made no impression on him. Pampered, raised as if he were an only child, he had always been told he was right. His sheltered upbringing heightened the natural arrogance of youth.

Kenny, though unemployable, was an expert by inclination. He would burrow into a new enthusiasm, read a couple of books, and come up for air knowing just enough to annoy you. The subjects in which he thought himself expert reflected both the trendy affluence of the mid-nineties and the unique culture of the Kimes household.

Raised in a paranoid home, he became a security buff, which is another way of saying he liked to spy on people. He was once present when an alarm salesman came by my house to demonstrate a security system. Kenny irritated me and the salesman so much with his barrage of questions that I had to order him out of the room. Some of the queries were meant to show off his half-baked expertise. The rest arose from a singularly Kimesian fixation: he thought the surveillance system might be used, not to keep prowlers out, but to spy on our family.

A second area in which Kenny had appointed himself family expert was the stock market. As a child of the nineties, he thought a rising index was his birthright, and from the time he hit college he'd been peppering me with stock tips. Mom was slipping him money to invest, and Kenny bragged that his portfolio had doubled in value every time he checked it. He and Mom claimed that he'd had an internship—brief, as usual—at a stock brokerage in Manhattan, secured by some of Mom's persistent string-pulling. I checked out a few of Kenny's tips. They were, how shall I say, contrary to conventional market wisdom. I kept my money in the bank.

Surprisingly, however, one of Kenny's obsessions ultimately did earn him a pile of money, and it was an obsession that married a nineties fad with a Kimes family tradition. My stepfather and I both enjoyed cigars. We would sit together on the patio of the Geronimo house and smoke, and as he got older Kenny would sometimes join us. Mom loved to see the three of us bonding, and she liked the fact that while I was puffing cigars, I had to take a break from chaining Benson & Hedges menthol 100s. She thought cigars were a slower road to the cancer ward.

In 1995 Kenny began to fool around with the internet, and he got an idea. He decided that he could sell Cuban cigars over the web without getting arrested, as long as he put a Bahamas address on his web page.

Kenny immersed himself in cigars. He memorized the most expensive and desirable brands from Cuba. He designed a web page that featured a photo, pirated from *Penthouse*, of a buxom blonde with a cigar nestled between her bikini-bound breasts. At the bottom was a list of the brands he had on offer and the prices, and the phone number of the Nassau house. He was charging as much as $750 a box.

By spring of 1996, Kenny had dropped out of college. He was with Mom full time now, and they'd moved their headquarters to the Cable Beach house in the Bahamas. They kept fiddling with the Santa Maria property, but now they talked about Cuba constantly. Direct travel from the States to Cuba was restricted, but Mom and Kenny were a short flight away from Havana in Nassau. They smelled money there, the offshore, unregulated kind they loved. They'd become so fearful of U.S. authorities that they felt freer in a Communist country. "America has gone to the dogs!" they'd tell me. "The real opportunities are in Cuba!"

I wasn't clear on the legalities, but what I figured Kenny was doing in his weekly puddle jumps to Havana was buying cigars at Cuban prices, bringing them back to Nassau, and then sneaking them into Florida a few boxes at a time. I was pretty sure it was smuggling, but I never checked the law. He mailed the boxes to his customers from Florida.

Late in the spring of 1996, Mom and Kenny breezed through Vegas for a visit. They came over to the house to see my kids, and I threw some steaks on the backyard grill. We were getting along. As I turned the meat over the flame, Kenny brought me a Cuban drink called a *mojito* and began braying in my ear about his new favorite country.

"You have to come with us next time!" he insisted. "That's where the real money is going."

Mom joined in, and they started spinning an idea whereby we'd all move to Havana and I would become a helicopter pilot at last. We'd start a helicopter business for rich European tourists, and get in on the gold rush before it was too late. Screw the U.S. laws against investing in Cuba. Mom had us building hotel towers on the beach.

It gave me pause. I did wonder sometimes if my humdrum life as a salesman hadn't gotten a little too predictable. I admit I envied all their rootless travel. I missed the adrenaline and the all-around cushiness. I pushed the thought out of my head.

"How's Kenny's cigar business going?" I asked.

"He's going to make a fortune!" Mom crowed. That was her ultimate compliment.

"Yeah, bro," grinned Kenny. "We got this one figured out! It's easy. Forget the vacuums!"

That smarted. I shook my head. "I'll leave the cigars to you beautiful people."

"Kent, you don't understand!" Kenny was emphatic. "We get the cigars for free!"

I stood there with a spatula in my hand next to the open flame as Kenny explained the stupidest inspiration he'd ever had in his life. On their trips to Havana, he and Mom had been taking a cab to a certain cigar factory. There they had a deal with a security guard, arranged by my Spanish-speaking mother. They'd slip the guard an American twenty, and he'd let them walk into the factory and help themselves.

"Last time the guard even helped us load them into the cab!" boasted Kenny.

"Do you have any idea what would happen to you if you got caught stealing in Cuba?" I tried to keep my voice down so the kids wouldn't hear.

Mom jumped in. "Kent, the locals are on our side! Twenty bucks is more than some of them see in a month!"

I snarled at her. "What do you think they'd do to an American woman who'd been convicted of involuntary servitude? What do you think they'd do to *you* if they caught you stealing?"

Mom and Kenny thought my attitude was funny. "Have a cigar!" one or both of them joked, but I was lost in a reverie in which Fidel Castro paraded my mother down the main drag of Havana in a cage. What a prize she would be—a capitalist thief, black marketeer, and authentic, certified slaveholder!

They were caught eventually. Luckily, it was closer to Little Havana than Havana. A few months after the barbecue, Kenny got popped by U.S. Customs at the Miami airport with a dozen boxes of Cubans in his luggage. They didn't arrest him, but they confiscated his contraband and put his name on a computerized list. Now, every time he came back into the States and flashed his passport, he'd be pulled aside and searched. Kenny, however, was really out nothing but his free cigars, a missed connecting flight, and a web page.

I was thankful the business had died before Kenny could see the inside of a Cuban prison. In the meantime, he'd earned tens of thousands of dollars. By Mom's lights, he'd been a success.

There was other fallout from Kenny's cigar caper. I think the interrogation by customs in Miami spooked him. That would explain what happened later that year when the Vegas airport police found the stun gun in Mom and Kenny's bags. It doesn't justify what they did, or make up for leaving Kristina in the hands of the airport cops, but at least it provides a reason.

It also explains what happened to me at the Miami airport that same summer, during the last gasps of cigarbiz.com. Kenny and I were flying back to the States from Nassau together. We approached the customs line and Kenny grabbed my arm.

"Go on without me," he said, smirking. "They're going to search me, and it's going to take a little while." Sure enough, while I was being waved through, agents were pulling Kenny out of line and taking him behind closed doors. We almost missed our flight to Vegas.

When I got home that night and opened my suitcase, I

found a box of Cubans inside. Kenny knew that customs would hassle him because his name was on the list, but he guessed that my odds of getting through without a search were excellent. It worked, perhaps because it's easy to tell a customs agent, without sweating, that you have nothing to declare when you really believe you have nothing to declare.

29

LIKE MOTHER,
LIKE SON

Mom was right. Kenny wasn't like me. He never really had been, but after the ashes went into the water in Kona, the bond between brothers grew weaker and weaker, while the bond between younger son and mother got stronger.

At first, though, it was us against them. Us was all three of us—me, Mom, and Kenny—and them was anyone who stood in our way. We wanted to find Ken's money, wherever it might be, and we needed to earn every cent possible from the Santa Maria property. In pursuit of that goal, there were times when Kenny and I teamed up to keep Mom from going overboard.

When Mom and I fought, Kenny would even support me on occasion. "Listen to Kent," he'd say. "He knows what he's talking about." But mostly Kenny hated to see Mom and me at odds. If we raised our voices, the six-foot bodybuilder who could bench-press more than two hundred pounds would crumble into a wimpy, wet-eyed mess. "I can't handle it when you guys fight!" he'd shriek, and it would give Mom the opportunity to lash out at me anew. "Now look what you've done!" she'd steam. "Are you proud of yourself, you big bully?"

Kenny had been angry with Mom ever since the maids case, and he'd been a terror in the home after she returned from prison. In the Bahamas, though, his rebellion seemed to sputter, and with Ken's death, Kenny's anger at Mom died completely. Before long, he was taking her side against me, and it was no longer us against them, it was me against Mom and Kenny. "She's trying to *protect* us, Kent," he'd insist.

Mom was ecstatic, because Kenny's loyalty was her insurance policy. No court in the land could deny Kenny's claim to his father's holdings, and what was Kenny's was hers, as long as she could keep him wary of the Creeps.

It was hard to understand how two huge egos got along so well. Between them they'd use up all the oxygen in a room. As a teen Kenny had been a class clown, eager for attention, and he'd grown into a flashy, loud-mouthed, conceited college boy. He grew more cocky with each passing day. He favored big cigars and Cosmopolitans, drove a vintage Caddy and then a Camaro, and dressed like a corporate executive. Even his jeans had creases.

What they had in common was a thirst for the big score, an easy fix of money, the source of all happiness. Kenny had been raised on Mom's lies about the boundlessness of Ken's wealth. He never thought he'd have to live on a budget. Santa Maria was supposed to put Mom and Kenny back in the lap of luxury.

But eventually they couldn't scrounge up a decent lawyer willing to work on the Santa Maria property. They couldn't afford the retainer.

I had, by then, accepted the fact that there wouldn't be any more money from the Kimes cash cow. I'd stuck by my family for many dubious reasons. In retrospect, some are understandable—like helpless love, and the fact that I was long used to an altered state of being that most people would find unbearable. High on my list of excuses for hanging around, though, was greed, and now that greed wouldn't be satisfied, I had only one reason to stick with Sante. That was a desire to save my brother.

But in the battle for Kenny, I soon found myself overmatched. All I had to show for my way of life was a house payment. The future I offered was monotonous and ordinary. Kenny the heir, Kenny the jet-setter, didn't want to hear that you had to work an honest day to make an honest buck. In contrast, Mom's worldview had a romance that appealed to an immature twenty-year-old. Kenny bought her illusions of grandeur and embraced her methods. She told him it was either easy street her way or poverty my way, and there was never a chance that he would choose poverty.

I tried. I told Kenny about the facts of life outside Kimesworld, that not everyone was an enemy or a mark, not every throat had to be cut. I tried to point out to my little brother that he and Mom were in over their heads. But Kenny chastised me for questioning Mom's business skills. He seemed to think that the very fact that Mom was underhanded proved she was brilliant. He made the same mistake as the reporters and outsiders who've described her as a cold-blooded, calculating, sociopathic con artist. He didn't notice that she was bad at her job.

As intent as she was on earning money, her inner demons destroyed every project she undertook. The master con showed a net loss for her career as high as eight figures. I tried to explain to Kenny that Mom did have a history of multimillion-dollar deals, and it wasn't a good one — the Bicentennial, the furs case, the Portlock fires, the slavery trial, the insurance frauds, and so on.

I made the obvious point to my brother ad nauseam. "You know how Mom is, Kenny. She's unreasonable. You have to see that. Have you ever thought about where your father's money went? Don't you think that if Mom were right all the time, you probably wouldn't have to steal to get what you want?"

Kenny didn't know how much money Mom had lost, and he didn't want to. He got furious when I accused him of being Mom's puppet. The more I tried to convince him that he was heading into dangerous territory, the more stubborn he became. "I thought you were smarter than that, Kent!" he'd retort. "Mom's right." Or, if we were talking about lawyers who were warning Mom and Kenny about some scheme they were hatching, he'd say, "We can't trust the fucking attorneys. Look what happened in the maids case. They sent Mom up the river!" That was history according to Sante Kimes, from the mouth of Kenny, rendered with an eerie echo of his late, irrational dad. "Why can't you just get with the program?" Kenny would pout. "Mom's trying to get us set up so we'll never have to worry about anything again."

Just going out in public with the two of them became an issue. Kenny shared Mom's gift for being over the top. Mr. Intelligent Man had to know everything, and prove it to the world at hyperspeed.

The three of us went to Morton's Steakhouse for dinner. He and Mom were buying, and they had to complain about the cost. Mom berated the helpless waiters. "I can't believe you feel good about charging these kinds of prices," she sniffed.

"I mean, with prices like these," interjected Kenny, "I

should get a blow job with my steak." He followed up with a staccato cackle. Mom didn't blink at her son's vulgarity. It had to shock the waiter. It humiliated me.

For half an hour, the two of them belittled any member of the staff foolish enough to approach the table, perhaps angling for a free entree or a discount. I couldn't listen anymore. "You've both been here before," I observed. "You knew the prices. Why the hell come back if you think it's too expensive?"

"I don't need to be lectured by you," groused Kenny. "We wanted to treat you to dinner, and you like it here."

"I can't enjoy it with you two acting like assholes. You make yourself look cheap." That was the worst thing you could say to an ex-millionaire.

"Kent," said Mom, sighing, "stop being such a pussy." The elegant Widow Kimes was a pottymouth.

"Maybe we should go someplace we can afford," I shot back.

"We're staying right here."

Kenny jumped in. "These are just *waiters,* Kent!" He sounded as if a waiter were something you wiped your feet on. "Mom's trying to stand up for us."

"Abusing people and standing up for yourself are two different things," I said. Too late in Kenny's life, I'd been forced into the role of pious, finger-wagging parent, teaching him lessons he should have learned in childhood.

He responded with contempt. "Why are you always against Mom?"

"Why are you always on her side?"

"Unlike you, I respect her. Who cares what these people think?"

Mom loved it. "Kenny's right. You shouldn't argue with me so much. I'm your mother, and I'm older. If you listened, you might learn something."

"I've learned enough," I muttered. I let it die. If I kept fighting, the volume would go up, Mom would flip, and another restaurant would be off-limits. We had a name for it in my family—*burning*. To Mom and Kenny, burning a place meant they'd scammed it and couldn't return. To me, it meant that because of something they'd done it would be too embarrassing to return.

I clenched my jaw through the rest of the meal. They never stopped complaining. They never got a discount. As we walked out, I apologized to the manager for their behavior. He told me to relax and forget about it. I turned around just in time to see Mom and Kenny, grinning, steal half a dozen big potatoes from a basket next to the kitchen. Not five, not seven, six. Why? There is no why. I'm glad I never looked at the name on the credit card they used to pay the check.

I was getting nowhere with Kenny, so I attempted something even more futile: I appealed to Sante's quirky maternal instinct. "Kenny's not as smart as you," I would plead, "and he's twice as cocky. You're going to destroy him if you don't watch out. Haven't you learned anything? Haven't we been through enough bullshit?"

Mom would then enlist a ghost in her defense. She'd pull Ken out of a hat whenever we argued. Somehow she knew exactly what he wanted us to do, and it was never what I wanted to do. "How dare you come between us!" she'd bellow. "You're not all that smart yourself! You're not his father, and Papa would turn over in his grave if he knew what you were doing. He was a fighter and a winner, and he'd never go along with your line of thinking."

I had my own guess about my late stepfather's opinion. "Ken confided in me more than anyone," I'd retort, "and I can guarantee you, he'd be afraid of both of you!"

Kenny, though, was a sucker for the voice from beyond. With that and the smell of money, and my humdrum, good-citizen life as contrast, my brother had gone from my ally to my very vocal adversary within six months of Ken's death. Mom had a look of sick triumph in her eyes every time Kenny tore into me. As Kenny yelled at me about how I was betraying my own mother, et cetera, et cetera, I thought about what lay ahead for my little brother, and I got scared.

There were signs that things were going wrong before Kona. During the week of final exams at Santa Barbara in June 1994, Kenny played his stereo at wall-shaking volume while the other students on his dorm hall were grinding away at their books. His next-door neighbor took exception, and he and Kenny got into a fistfight.

I'd been in scrapes when I was Kenny's age, plenty of them, before I learned to control my temper. Kenny had inherited the same combustible nature from Mom as I had, so I understood. But Kenny, in this case, was clearly in the wrong, and he'd sent the other kid to the infirmary. I wondered if steroids, with their side effect of angry outbursts, might be to blame. The incident got Kenny barred from the dorms at UCSB.

Kenny started living Sante style in 1995, when he launched the cigar web site, a full-fledged criminal enterprise. It wasn't strong-arm robbery or arson or murder, but it was illegal. Mom's protégé had hatched his first scam.

Then the same kid who'd been furious at me for "stealing" Silly Putty a dozen years earlier became an accomplished shoplifter. His room filled up with expensive electronics and his closet with designer labels. Mom, who long ago had shielded him from her stealing, had obviously been teaching him, because when I asked him where the stuff came from, he parroted her rationale. "It's a game. I'm just getting my share. The prices are inflated to make up for the losses."

One day he and I returned to the Geronimo house from the store and he emptied his pockets of cologne and electronic gadgets. He'd gotten so good at stealing, smoother than his coach, that I hadn't caught him in the act. "You don't even need this crap." I scowled. "I told you before, never do that around me. I want nothing to do with this shit." He gave me a haughty look. "Mom's right," he said with a smirk. "Your holier-than-thou attitude wears on the nerves after a while." I made it a practical issue—if he got caught, I warned, no one had the cash anymore to pay a decent lawyer. "Oh well"—he shrugged and gave me a smart-ass grin—"that's the risk I have to take."

I can see why Kenny found my lectures boring. None of my predictions had come true. He was stealing and scamming and there were no repercussions. Instead, as Mom had promised, crime paid, both in fun and profit. People were things, marks, targets, like she said, and separating them from their cash was easy.

There are friends from his college years who tell stories of resistance, of Kenny saying his mom was nuts, and of Kenny screaming at her behind closed doors in Santa Barbara. I didn't see or hear much friction, perhaps because around me Mom and Kenny presented a united front.

They only disagreed about girls. Kenny had a girlfriend who attended college in L.A., and he'd drive from Santa Barbara or Vegas to see her whenever he could. Mom had to interfere. When Kenny's Camaro broke down, she paid a pal of mine to fix it, then convinced him to wait a week before telling Kenny it was ready, to keep Kenny stranded in Vegas. Mom was all for Kenny having sex—she hosted alcohol-soaked bashes in Santa Barbara and the Bahamas, complete with kissing contests and skimpy clothes, for Kenny and a bevy of hot coeds. She just didn't want any serious relationship getting between her and her son. It was a rerun of my young love life, complete with the parties, except Kenny didn't fight back as hard.

Eventually Mom had to separate Kenny from college and his friends altogether. It wasn't a hard sell, since my brother had never mustered much of an effort academically. He did well in the subjects that came easily, logging A's in fitness and acting. He never picked a major. He fancied himself a developer, then a stockbroker, and he picked up enough HTML to impersonate a web designer. "Web designer" would become Kenny's cyber-era version of my mom's nebulous résumé—"welcomer"/public relations consultant/lobbyist—meaning that it was a cover for criminal activities.

Kenny's college career unraveled during the 1995–96 school year. After the dorm fight in 1994, Mom had hired a lawyer to get him readmitted to campus housing, but it hadn't worked. Kenny had boarded with the campus security dispatcher and his wife for a year. He didn't seem to get into spats with people older than himself, probably as a result of those early years spent among adults. In the fall of 1995 he tried to live with people his own age again, and it went bad within months.

He and four housemates had rented a duplex not far from campus at 6795-A Trigo Drive. Here's the abridged request for a restraining order sworn out by Carrie Louise Grammer, the girlfriend of one of those housemates, on October 25, 1995:

> I had considered [Ken Kimes] to be a friend. My boyfriend, Pat Lieneweg, has known Ken for over two years, and is one of Ken's housemates this school year. Pat also had considered Ken to be a friend.
>
> I had thought Ken to be a decent person. He is very charismatic, but over the past few months, I have realized that his charming behavior is an intentional cover to hide his true abusive personality. As of this past weekend, I am afraid of Ken.
>
> A few weeks ago, Ken brought his cat to my apartment to be watched for a few hours. The cat soiled my roommate

[Lauren Schmalbach]'s bed, which cost her seventy dollars to replace the soiled bedding, to which Ken agreed to reimburse the entire amount. When my roommate and I arrived at Ken's apartment to collect the money, Evan Dienstag, one of the housemates, answered the door and gave me thirty-five dollars, saying Ken had instructed him to give the money to us. Lauren and I told Evan that we wanted to speak to Ken, so Evan let us in. Ken's door was shut. But when Ken heard me ask Evan if [Ken] had locked himself in his room, Ken flung his door open. I walked in to see Ken sitting at his desk counting money. I could see that he had well over $100 in large bills. Ken was putting on a show for me. Ken is financially very well off and he was flaunting the money in an attempt to anger me.

He said he was not going to pay and told me that if our friendship was worth only thirty-five dollars then I can [sic] "fuck off." I said to Ken that he was being an "asshole." Ken . . . jumped out of his chair. He came at me in a threatening manner with an infuriated expression on his face. His eyes were squinted, his jaw stuck out, his lips were pinched, and his face was red. Ken is very large, he lifts weights every day. Ken is 6'2" and weighs about 200 pounds. I am five-foot tall and weigh 115 pounds. . . . Ken stood over me and with his finger pointed at my face, he proceeded to angrily curse at me. From this point on, everything Ken said contained excessive profanity. Ken's eyes looked crazy. . . . I thought he was going to hit me. I knew that he had hit his ex-girlfriend. . . . He called me a "classless bitch," a "slut," a "little whore who turns tricks," and many other degrading things. Ken told me that he "had more class than I ever would."

Ken continued to scream profanities at me for what seemed like forever. I was in shock. I couldn't move.

I am not an emotionally weak person. However, Ken's yelling, name-calling, lies and irrational behavior upset me so much that I started crying uncontrollably. I couldn't catch my breath. All the while Ken continued to curse at me. He told me that if I need [sic] an inhaler that they sell inhalers for "fucking asthmatics."

The next afternoon, [my boyfriend] Pat and I went to the apartment where Ken and Pat are housemates. Pat confronted Ken . . . Ken's lies got worse. He claimed that . . . I had pounded my way into his room and struck him. This is not true. I know that Ken did not directly threaten me, but he is very cunning. Ken only does things when he thinks he won't get caught. He is very good at not getting caught.

It sounds as if Carrie knew Kenny well. I believe every word of it, especially her description of his red face and slit eyes, so like his father when he got angry, and the torrent of *fucks* and *shits*, à la his mother. It was a mini-Sante tantrum with a little of Kenny's princely high-handedness thrown in. And he had started using his dad's name so he could be grown-up Ken instead of little Kenny. The only thing Carrie got wrong was the money part. She had no way of knowing that the riches were more show than reality, like one of those bankrolls of singles wrapped in a C-note.

My brother, by now a committed disciple of Mom's way of doing things, responded in Sante fashion. Together Mom and Kenny killed an ant with a hammer. The court received four letters from witnesses who supported Kenny's version of the truth, in which five-foot Carrie was the aggressor. All the affidavits were notarized by my mother's in-house bookkeeper, Nan Wetkowski, in Las Vegas on the same day, meaning that four students must have skipped class and driven twelve hours round-trip to sign the papers in front of her. Maybe they carpooled. All the statements were printed on the same printer and contained similar phrases. One student had misspelled her own name, just like Kay Frigiano in the maids case.

Before the matter was decided, Kenny violated a temporary restraining order by calling Carrie's house and leaving a message urging her to be "neutral" in court. Ultimately the judge issued mutual restraining orders, and then the matter seems to have died. I wish someone had filed criminal charges against Kenny instead. Coaching witnesses, forging documents— Kenny had used every illegal method Mom had employed with resounding failure in her past court appearances, but there wasn't any fallout. He was still Getting Away with It.

It was all over thirty-five dollars and a cat pissing on a bed. I tried to get Mom and Kenny to shut up and pay the girl, but they preferred a courtroom drama. During it, Kenny realized he could stand in front of a judge and lie and wave fake affidavits without sweating. I think it encouraged him to apprentice with

Mom in another of her favorite pastimes, insurance fraud. I've already related the saga of how in May 1996 Kenny got into a minor car accident in Santa Barbara and Mom grifted the insurance company out of a new, improved car stereo. I didn't mention that Mom and Kenny also tried to sue the driver of the other car for whiplash. Kenny scheduled visits with a chiropractor to shore up his tale of suffering.

The case was dismissed. The defendant could have called MTV's Jenny McCarthy as a witness. Years later, when my brother had become notorious, media outlets reran his appearance on the show *Singled Out*. On May 24, 1996, my brother, sans neck brace or any trace of discomfort, jumped higher than two other male contestants and won the right to ask a woman for a date. "Hey, Kandace," my brother said, grinning into the camera. "My name is Ken. I want to be the big guy in your life." She picked someone else.

Mom had dreamed of her two sons running an "empire," with Kenny the flashy front man and me the muscle behind the curtain. Soon after the car accident, Kenny ditched school for good and began hanging around Mom full time. The empire became Mom and Kenny. He had chosen a career at last: accomplice. He and Mom dreamed aloud about trading the house on Geronimo for a yacht in the Bahamas, making their empire offshore, immune and mobile.

They were in Vegas on a regular basis, but I grew apart from them. Kenny would get frustrated with my "negative" attitude, and I'd hear about it from the boarders at the Geronimo house. I would catch Mom and Kenny in lies, and they responded by keeping more and more of their activities secret from me, the moralistic spoilsport. I was no longer to be trusted.

Mom and Kenny never entirely gave up on me as coconspirator, just as I never abandoned hope that Kenny would change. Maybe he'd get popped for shoplifting and spend a gritty night or three in jail, rethinking his vocation. My mother and brother rationalized my preference for the straight life by blaming it on my wife. Kenny, who'd loved Lynn and considered her a sister and confidante, adopted my mother's attitude of withering contempt. Like Mom, he hated Lynn because he thought that without her, I'd be both on his side and at his side. Like Mom, he wouldn't accept the fact that I loved my safe, honest, middle-class existence.

By 1996 every phone conversation or meeting with Mom and Kenny had turned into a chess game, and it made me nervous. I'm not exactly sure when, but eventually I became afraid of my little brother. I figured that he and Mom together were capable of anything, as I would later tell the press. With their thought patterns, they'd be able to justify hurting me by saying they were trying to help me. It would be for the good of the "family," meaning Mom and Kenny, with the person known as Kent an obstacle to that greater good.

Mom hadn't gotten the good soldier in me after all. I'd chafed at the role and finally quit altogether. I was the kind of person she would have liked if she'd met me on the street. Whatever my faults, I was compassionate, honest, and a devoted husband and father. That's not what she expected from a son, though, and she was disappointed.

Kenny did not disappoint her. He displayed none of my reluctance. The same things that made my mother happy made Kenny happy. He enjoyed the money and he became addicted, hard and fast, to the rush of Getting Away with It.

But Kenny also brought two things to the mother-and-son crime team that made him especially dangerous. He was more than a gofer. He had ideas, like the cigar site and some kind of longevity scam in Cuba, and worse, he didn't shrink from violence.

Kenny became what my mother wanted because he'd lost his empathy for other people. He'd had it once, and knowing that had given me hope that I could somehow pull him back across the line. But when I consider the crimes my mother and brother committed between September 5, 1996, and July 5, 1998, I have to wonder whether Mom got even more than she bargained for when Kenny became her partner.

Today the cops and the media—everybody—see Sante as the brains and Kenny as the muscle. I have my doubts. I hate to admit it, but sometimes I picture Kenny as the muscle *and* the brains behind Irene Silverman's disappearance. Before Mom hooked up with Kenny, there was only one missing person, Elmer Holmgren. Afterward, at least three people disappeared. Maybe it's not coincidence. At the absolute minimum, Kenny Kimes made Sante Kimes more dangerous. By 1996, my evil mother had a sidekick with no moral code and a need to make his mark on the world.

At the time, I put it very simply in a phone call to John Bower, my old friend in Hawaii, who'd been a mentor and confidant of my little brother. John remembers what I told him very clearly: "Kenny's not Kenny anymore."

30

HOMELESS

Something pulled me away from my desk one spring afternoon in 1997. I was in my private office at my business headquarters on Decatur Avenue. I got up and hung a left down the hall toward the service department. Maybe I was trying to get one of the guys to clean the fifty-gallon aquarium at my end of the L-shaped building. The tank had turned into an opaque tub of purple crud. Maybe a customer had returned a vacuum, or I simply felt the need to smoke and gab. For whatever reason, my door was open and my desk was unattended.

When I came back around the corner five minutes later, the door was shut. I didn't think anything of it till I stepped into the room and saw Mom and Kenny. Mom was sitting behind my desk, talking on the phone. She waved. Kenny smirked.

I'd been playing a game of hide-and-seek with my mother my entire adult life. Since I'd been old enough to accrue the stuff that makes you a real person in America—driver's license, Social Security card, credit cards—I'd been hiding it, and she'd been seeking. While I was living at the Geronimo and Almart houses, every time I parked in the driveway, I'd stash my wallet in the glove compartment and lock it before I went inside. I'd learned fast that if I didn't, something with my name on it was bound to wind up in my mother's chest of drawers, which was crammed with hundreds of IDs and driver's licenses.

For that reason, I wouldn't let Mom in my office unless I was present. I'd hidden, in locked drawers and file cabinets, anything that could be turned into quick cash or an alias. But Mom had a habit of dropping by unannounced, and I'd forgotten to lock my door. Now she was sitting behind my desk, with her protégé in his creased jeans hovering over me, and they were giving me bookend blank smiles. I knew they'd been riffling through my papers. The game, however, required that I say nothing. I observed the rules. What bothered me most about the game was that now it was two against one.

When my brother began parroting Mom's put-downs about how I was a "saint" and a "goody-goody," and sneering at my attempts to scare him straight, I should have called it quits with both of them. The money was gone, and Kenny was a lost cause. What kept me in their lives was love. I loved them, and my kids loved them. They were blood.

Mom and Kenny weren't in town half the time anyway. They had their schemes, about which I tried to know very little, which took them around the Caribbean, from Cuba to the Bahamas to the Caymans. Sometimes I could learn about their hobbies by looking at my office phone bill. Before the total hit four figures a month and I put a stop to it, Mom had scammed my secretary into placing all her long-distance calls for her.

Around the time I caught them in my office, though, Mom had come to see me, completely distraught. "We don't have any money," she whined, in that high voice she used when the world was collapsing on her.

"Never con a con," my mother would often say. She'd been saying it in a light, bantering tone since the seventies, whenever she thought a friend or family member was bullshitting her. For a second she would drop her guard and give us a proud glimpse of her true self. Then the guard would go back up, and she'd be telling you that black was white, just like always.

I could read her con better than anyone. She wasn't lying about the money. I could see the fear in her eyes.

Mom asked me for a favor. She was planning to hang around Vegas for a bit and she needed a place to stay. She wanted to move in with me and Lynn and the kids at the house I owned on Joy Glen. It was a temporary thing, she insisted, till she found Ken's offshore fortune and sold the Santa Maria property and got these other surefire deals going, and so on. She said she needed to stay with me because of poverty, but I knew she was also avoiding the Geronimo house for another, more familiar reason—a flare-up in the number of visits from process servers and cops.

After fleeing Almart Circle in early 1993 for a rental, my

wife and I had bought a house. At age thirty-one I finally had a place of my own. The way I'd been raised, I had to overreach and buy a little too much house, but I was selling a lot of vacuum cleaners and I could afford it. My wife was in charge of the household, without competition from my mother. We had three children underfoot—our youngest daughter, Brandy, having arrived in 1995, a year almost to the hour after Ken's death.

I thought, what with me being the homeowner and all and my mother needing a place to stay, that I could set some guidelines. If the six of us were going to be under one roof, Lynn and I would make the rules, and Mom would abide by them. Number one, she was only living with us temporarily, for three days or so, and Kenny wouldn't be part of the package. He was in L.A. doing something or other. Number two, no "maids." Mom's habit of hiring from the local homeless shelter had given the whole family a case of head lice back on Almart. Number three, no telling Lynn what to do with her house and her kids.

In hindsight, I must have been smoking crack. Three days became a week and then longer, and Kenny materialized in Mom's bedroom at the top of the stairs. They whispered behind locked doors. It was an uneasy reprise of Almart, except that now my brother was the other half of the couple holed up in a suite across the DMZ.

Almost from the minute Mom moved her makeup and wigs and legal files into "her" bedroom, she violated the rules. The homeless people appeared. Lynn's house wasn't clean enough for Mom's standards, so she speed-dialed herself some domestic help. Despite what Lynn and I had promised ourselves, and though I had visions of meeting the FBI, we didn't complain. It was easier to pay the homeless people than to argue with Mom. So we paid. "Don't pay!" hissed Mom. "You don't have to!"

Lynn came home one day and found a guy from the Shade Tree shelter named Jack squatting motionless in the dark in an upstairs room. "What's going on?" she inquired, bemused. "Mrs. Kimes is angry," he whispered. "She ordered me to sit here without moving." He'd been making like a statue for hours. I almost laughed when Jack got his revenge by stealing Mom's car.

It was like the last days of the Mexican maids again, but this time we could understand what the victims were saying. "You're not like her," the poor mooks from St. Vincent's and Shade Tree would marvel whenever we canceled one of Mom's

abusive commands. The most abject of the maids, none of
whom lasted more than a few days, was a tall, heavyset woman
with an artificial leg. I can't remember her name, but Mom
reduced her to a puddle. "I'm nobody's nigger," she blubbered
to Lynn one day. "I don't know why I can't stick up for myself.
She had me feeling like I was worth *nothing*."

It had to stop, because the potential fallout was more
painful than a stolen Lincoln. Lucky for Mom that Vegas was
such a transient town, and that none of the staffers at the shelters or the vagrants themselves had ever heard of the Dragon
Lady. Nobody's memory went back to 1986. Still, there was a
danger that one of these doormats would stand up for himself
and land Mom in prison.

In 1996 it had almost happened. Mom had conned a German drifter named Dieter into taking care of her house in the
Bahamas. Then she "disappeared" his travel documents so he
couldn't leave the islands. After thirteen months trapped on
Nassau, without a dime of the money she'd promised, he
rebelled. Alone among Mom's drifter slaves, he seemed to be
aware of her past conviction. He threatened to go to the cops
unless Mom bought him a ticket home to Frankfurt and signed
a document promising twenty-six thousand dollars in wages.
Billy Lovekamp, Mom's in-house lawyer, the guy she had riding herd on the Santa Maria City Council, drafted the letter.

Dieter's mistake, besides falling into Mom's web in the first
place, was flying to Germany before he got his back pay. As for
what happened next, at the time I could only listen to (and
translate) Mom's version of events. I got the truth a year later,
when I found a few audiocassettes of Mom's phone calls, and it
was as bad as I feared.

Mom sicced Billy Lovekamp on Dieter. Of course, she
didn't trust Billy to know what to say. On the tape, you hear
Billy and Dieter talking, and in the background, hissing in
Billy's ear nonstop, there's Mom, feeding him his lines. Here's a
transcript, with Mom's comments included whenever they're
loud enough to unscramble:

> **BILLY**: Hello, is Dieter there?
> **MOM**: You didn't say "It's Billy."
> **DIETER**: *Ja.*
> **BILLY**: Dieter, this is Billy. How are you?
> **DIETER**: I was arrested yesterday.

BILLY: I was sick and I didn't have a chance to call you back and set anything up.

DIETER: I was yesterday *arrested*.

BILLY: You were? Why?

DIETER: The police were here. Somebody sent them. I think you.

BILLY: No, I didn't.

DIETER: They showed me a letter we wrote. In this letter were written some wrong things, some bad things, that if I don't get money, I will kill your daughter. All these wrong things. I didn't know you had a daughter. I thought it was you or Mrs. Kimes who gave them the letter.

BILLY: I haven't done anything like that.

DIETER: This was real criminal police, not for little small thing. Somebody accuses me of blackmail, telling somebody I kill them if I don't get money. They talked to me for *seven hours*. They told me Billy Lovekamp did this. Remember we wrote something down that said I don't do anything bad against Mrs. Kimes? It is manipulated so it looks like blackmail. I showed the police what I wrote. You can come and help me and prove I didn't write [the other letter].

MOM: Ask him how they got the letter!

BILLY: How did they get that?

DIETER: They told me you did it.

BILLY: They said I did it?

DIETER: They showed me the letter. I was so shocked. It was changed here a little and there a little. I was lucky we had two. It was like a bad movie.

BILLY: I'm speechless.

DIETER: Somebody make a fake letter. I think it is Mrs. Kimes.

Somehow, Dieter had been smart enough when he drafted the letter with Billy to keep a copy for himself. The police released him from custody when they saw the original, which was only an agreement not to sue Mom for slavery in return for the money she owed him. As the conversation droned on, Billy steered Dieter away from the obvious truth, which was that Mom and Billy had framed him for blackmail. German cops had burst into Dieter's sister's apartment, guns drawn, and shown Dieter the doctored note, and still Dieter was gullible enough to buy Billy's denial. Billy and Mom maneuvered Dieter into a stalemate, in which Dieter was free but had charges pending. The only person who could absolve Dieter was Billy, and Billy made excuses when Dieter tried to get him to contact the German police and clear things up. He said, "I don't want to get involved," and, "This is giving me a stomachache. I have to hang up."

Negotiations continued, which meant that Billy would call Dieter in Germany with the tape recorder running and try to get him to make noises that sounded like blackmail. "You want money, right?" Billy would say, and Dieter would answer, "I want my wages." Mom was perched on Billy's shoulder the whole time. At one point, she muttered, regarding Dieter's whereabouts, "He's got to be there, mooching off someone else." It was like a jailer calling a prisoner a leech because he'd consumed too much bread and water.

Finally Dieter gave up and disappeared without ever seeing a cent. I knew about the Dieter situation when Mom moved into my house, and it's part of what made me so nervous about the maids.

But Mom's brain couldn't process the idea that I might oppose her of my own free will. If I complained about the maids, it must be that bitch Lynn speaking through me. *Plot* is probably too strong a word, but Mom began to harass my wife. She canceled a limo that was supposed to pick up Lynn and some other women for a bachelorette party, leaving them standing on a Vegas curb for hours in their gowns and heels and ruining the party. Most often, though, she tried to get at Lynn through the kids.

She had an obsession with "her" babies. It was selective. She considered Kristina, my oldest, a sort of protégé. She wanted Kristina with her all the time, and spoiled her the way only Sante Kimes could spoil a child. She took her on trips to New York and the Bahamas and bought her everything. She adored Carson, since he was a man-child. My youngest, cute and sweet little Brandy, she didn't give a damn about. I never figured out why.

Her love, overwhelming and controlling, was more about her than about the kids. When she learned that the kids called their other grandmother Maminke or Minke, a Czech word for "mother," she decided she needed a nickname too. From some crack in her skull she produced the name Babish. Just as she'd forgotten about past selves named Sandy and Santee, Grandma became Babish overnight, without explanation. I have never seen the term elsewhere, though sometimes I wonder if it holds the key to my ethnic origins. It might be a nonsense word; it might be a lonely relic from Mom's real past.

Anyway, Mom had her own ideas about how her "babies" should be raised. Lynn didn't meet her standards. One day Child Protective Services came to the house. They had a report of a child who was dirty and improperly clothed. The CPS workers saw our clean house and healthy kids and left, shrugging, after five minutes. Mom had called the authorities because Brandy, not yet two, had a diaper rash.

We should have evicted Mom then, but despite our suspicions we couldn't prove she was the one who'd contacted CPS. Lynn didn't bite back till Kristina refused to clean her room. "Babish says you're making me a slave," reported Kristina. "She says the only reason I have to clean my room is because you're too cheap to get a maid."

Lynn erupted at Sante. "You fat fucking wig-lady bitch," she yelled. "Don't tell me how to raise my daughter!"

Lynn was losing it. Searching for some way to keep the peace, she hired a maid of her own. Mom was always going to insist on a spotless, nearly germ-free environment, but if we had to have a maid, Lynn wanted to pick her, pay her, and tell her what to do. So Lynn hired someone, and when Mom criticized her choice, Lynn threw a full teapot against the wall.

I had to defend my wife against my mother. Kenny knew that Mom was blowing it, and that I was close to pitching the two of them into the street. "Mom, you're screwing up," he lamented, as Mom ranted about Lynn's shortcomings without pause. Mom and Kenny and I ended up on the patio, arguing for hours. Kristina poked a camera through the window and took photos. I still have them. At Kenny's urging, Mom agreed, again, not to get any more slaves from Shade Tree.

But within days, the maids were back, and Mom was lying about their origins. We had that run-in I've already recounted, where Mom instructed her maid to say she was from an agency, and then after a few hours of Mom's terror, the maid collapsed, forgot her cover story, and demanded to be taken back to the shelter. Kenny, frightened, had called up the stairs, "Mom! Kent knows about Shade Tree!"

Within minutes, we were having our own, homegrown version of the maids case, with me as prosecutor and Kenny and Mom as the accused. Lynn stayed upstairs, leaning over the railing on the landing and listening to the fireworks. She was cheering me on silently, because she was too scared to do it out loud.

Mom was giving me her usual bullshit about checking the maids' references, and I was responding with my usual contempt. Then Kenny joined in. It drove me nuts whenever he spoke up for her.

"How can you treat Mom like that?" demanded Kenny.

"Why do you listen to this bitch?" I countered. "I wish I'd beaten the shit out of you when you were younger!"

As the volume increased, and Mom saw that her two sons were close to blows, she blanched. "Stop fighting!" she brayed.

"Hit me!" I screamed at Kenny. "Hit me!" I wanted an excuse to knock him cold. He had the cut physique of a vain gym rat, and I had a beer gut and a two-pack habit, but we both knew who the winner would be. I was angrier, and when I looked at Kenny I saw a coward. He'd never been hit hard. I had.

He wouldn't make a move, so I did. I slammed my right hand into a cabinet door next to his head. It splintered, and blood ran down my fingers. I swung around and faced Mom, jabbing my bloody finger in her face. "You're next! You're next!" Mom and her henchman scampered out of the house.

The fun continued. I wanted them gone, though there was no such thing as gone. No matter where they were, if they were broke I didn't see how I'd escape supporting them somehow.

It was Lynn, surprisingly, who talked me into letting Mom and Kenny stay at the Joy Glen house a little longer. She might have been afraid of the consequences, or like me, she might have harbored a few shreds of family feeling.

Then, finally, she cracked. She didn't do it in hysterical, violent Kimes fashion like me or Kenny or Mom. She chose flight over fight. "Kids," she said one afternoon, all false and bright, "we're going to see Minke. Everybody get your suitcases."

Mom saw the activity and Lynn's bag open on the bed and acted concerned. "Where are you going?" asked Sante. "Nowhere," lied Lynn, as she stacked underwear and slacks inside the suitcase. "Are you sure?" said Mom. "I'm not going anywhere," replied Lynn, packing as fast as she could.

"Honey, you seem upset," breathed Mom. "Let me get you some tea. It'll soothe your nerves."

Lynn didn't say yes or no, but Mom came back up the stairs within minutes with a full cup. Schooled since her late teens in paranoid logic, Lynn eyed the cup and saucer warily. When Sante was your waitress, tea wasn't necessarily tea. To refuse it would be suspicious, though, so Lynn decided she should take a few sips, then grab the kids and flee to her mother's in San Diego. She wasn't even going to tell me where she was going till she got there. She was giving me an ultimatum—your mother or your wife.

Fifteen minutes later my wife called me at the office. She hadn't made it out of our bedroom. "Kent," she whimpered, groggy and frightened, "your mother slipped me something in my drink." I raced home from the office and asked my mother what she'd done.

"Lynn was hysterical," Mom protested. "I put a little mela-tonin in her tea to quiet her down, that's all." Lynn didn't buy the story, but I did. Mom always had some of the mild, natural tranquilizer on hand for jet lag.

Lynn saved the tea in a plastic bag and brought it to the police station the next day for testing, but they didn't take her seriously. There's still a bag full of dried powder that used to be tea in a box in my garage. Knowing what I do now, I'm sure Lynn was right and I was wrong. I'm sure the stuff in the bag isn't melatonin. It's probably Rohypnol, the date-rape drug. Mom and Kenny had plenty of Rohypnol with them when they were arrested in New York.

It was then, in September 1997, with my hand still healing and my wife threatening to vote with her feet and leave town, that I scheduled the meeting with my mother and brother at the Macaroni Grill. First I called Shade Tree and St. Vincent's and demanded they stop shoveling warm bodies at the lady with the black wigs and the Lincoln. Without mentioning Mom's rap sheet, I told them they'd strayed into the land of prison and lawsuits.

Then Mom and Kenny and I met at the Macaroni Grill. Lynn came along, pulling Carson by the hand, with Brandy on her hip. I think Lynn showed up to make sure I didn't wimp out, and that I confronted my mother and brother with the way things would have to be.

I waited till we'd had a decent, happy family meal. Then,

after the plates had been cleared, I decreed that there wouldn't be any more vagrants at our home on Joy Glen. I told Mom and Kenny there were rumors floating around town about an evil old lady who makes you cut her lawn, then drops you back at the shelter and presses an envelope in your hand. By the time you open the envelope and find there's no money inside, she's already peeled off in her big fancy car, grinning.

Mom had been paying a staffer at Shade Tree to find her maids. "I think you should know," I told her, "I talked to your guy. If you call there again you'll get in trouble."

"You don't know who you're fucking with," sputtered Kenny.

It was ending suddenly and badly. Mom and Kenny and I argued in the restaurant foyer, getting louder and angrier, while Lynn herded the kids into the Mazda. That's when Mom said, "I can't believe that you put that cunt in front of me," and my hands squeezed her neck. His eyes wide, Kenny the badass didn't lift a finger.

As simple as that, after bending and bending, I snapped. From the driver's seat of the Mazda, I issued an edict. It felt as good as the days at Almart, when I would hurt Mom for the hell of it, except this time it was final. I finally had a use for a few of the lines I'd rehearsed in my head since my first attempt to escape in Hawaii, twenty years before.

"You crossed the line," I said. "Remember this moment. I no longer care about you. I don't know you. You're not my blood."

As I backed out, there was a final moment of suspense, Mom playing chicken with my rear bumper and losing. I drove home, cleared out their things, and we were done. This time, done meant done.

After that I entered a period of blissful ignorance. I didn't know where Mom and Kenny were or what they were doing. Mom kept calling me at work and trying to reach the kids, asking my secretary to forward some Christmas gifts to Kristina, Carson, and Brandy. "That tramp of a wife won't let Kent contact me," Mom groused. She couldn't process the idea that I was shunning her of my own free will. I met Mom and Kenny for a quick drink on New Year's, but I didn't falter. I left the two of them crying in the bar parking lot. The relationship had changed.

As mementos of the good times we'd had together I left

their pictures on my office wall. We'd always taken hundreds of snapshots, and I still had a few that Mom hadn't stolen or burned or stashed in one of her storage units. Ken looked down on me from the deck of a sailboat in the Bahamas. Kenny gave me one of his goofy, hammy grins. He was wearing a gorilla suit at a Halloween party out by the Geronimo pool, holding the gorilla's head in his hands. And for years I'd had a framed 8-by-10- inch glossy of my mother on the wall. She loved it, because it showed her young and beautiful circa 1972, posed and airbrushed in a white feathered hat and a white outfit, looking more like Liz Taylor than the diva herself. In fact, it's almost certainly a photo of Liz that my mother has passed off as her own, and that makes it all the more appropriate.

I thought that five or ten years down the road when my kids had gotten older, we'd fix things. Otherwise I resigned myself to the inevitable collect phone call from Mom or Kenny saying they were in jail somewhere on a fraud or theft charge. They'd been loosed upon the world, and I hoped they'd do their damage far from me and my family. Soon, I rationalized, Kenny would grow out of it, or be wrenched out of it by doing a little time, someplace where his roommates weren't as easily intimidated as the ones on Trigo Drive.

I wasn't prepared for what happened instead. It devastated me, even though I'd been training for it my whole life. I just thank God that Mom and Kenny and I had our falling-out when we did.

I have also been looking for Billy Lovekamp for two years, without any luck. To ease my mind, I've tracked down a lot of people recently, but I haven't found Billy. Considering how similar he was to Elmer Holmgren, and what he knew about my mother, I'm worried. He's not, sadly, the sort of person that a whole posse of folks would miss. Billy, if you're alive, call me.

31

GUARDIAN ANGEL

I'd never heard the word *grifter* till my family was arrested. Then I heard and read it everywhere. The New York tabloids loved the detective-novel feel of the word, and it kept appearing in boldface attached to Mom's and Kenny's names.

I grew to hate the term. It was useful shorthand, but inadequate. I didn't think that *grifter* or *con artist* quite captured the tangle of my mother's psyche or the confused motives of my little brother. Part of Mom was detached and calculated, dead to feeling the way con artists were supposed to be when they separated people from their money. But her desperation and emotional volatility and need for chaos weren't the hallmarks of a seasoned, professional crook. If she were such a great grifter, she wouldn't have been broke and scrambling for money in her early sixties. She wouldn't have blown her big score, Ken Kimes.

Because the word *grifter* had been burned into my brain, I began to notice it everywhere, even after the initial press furor about my family had died down. When Kenny and Mom were in jail awaiting trial, I came across a film called *The Grifters*. I was in a video rental place and the title jumped out at me. When I read the back of the box, I realized the movie was about a mother-and-son team of con artists. I decided I had to rent it.

The Grifters turned out to be an entertaining, hard-boiled crime flick set in 1930s Los Angeles. It starred Anjelica Huston and John Cusack, and I quickly got caught up in the convoluted plot and stopped taking notes about the parallels between my family and theirs.

At the climax of the movie, though, I got a jolt of too much reality. Mother and son are arguing, and the mom accidentally jabs a broken glass into her offspring's jugular. He bleeds to death in front of her. She's as shocked as the viewer and starts to cry, and then the con half of her brain takes over. Her grief evaporates, and she makes the best of the situation. She picks up a bag of money and walks out the door.

In that scene I saw what my mother had done to my little brother. She'd sacrificed him, and I knew she felt no guilt about it. I saw her as a grifter for an instant. I saw her the way the rest of the world does, now that she's famous.

It had been almost a year since the Macaroni Grill incident when I got that phone call from my friend Carl in July 1998 and saw my mother on page four of the Vegas paper. During the year before the Silverman disappearance, I'd seen Mom and Kenny very little. I was trying to stay true to my no-contact vow, but I accepted the occasional phone call, and a few days after Easter of 1998 I relented and let Mom see her grandkids.

Our encounter reminded me of court-ordered visitations after a divorce. Mom and Kenny met me and my three children, ages two to thirteen, for dinner at a local restaurant called the Lone Star. Throughout the meal, I cut off my mother's and brother's attempts at conversation. I told them to talk to the kids, not to me. But my mother still managed to make me laugh.

The place served free peanuts and encouraged customers to throw the shells on the floor. Five-year-old Carson loved flinging them around, so Mom handed him basket after basket, until the floor was no longer visible.

Our college-girl waitress sighed and pouted as the mound around the table grew deeper. When she couldn't take it anymore, she complained, as politely as she could. "You guys are making a bit of a mess, aren't you?"

Mom attacked. With mock sweetness, she said, "I know — why don't you get a broom and sweep the shells up?" She paused. "And then, when you're done, you can ride the broom right on out of here!"

When Mom and Kenny did call me, it was liable to be from anywhere. I was accustomed to Mom's travels, but they tended to be from one fixed point to another in her known world — Hawaii to Vegas to Santa Barbara to the Bahamas and back. Now she was popping up in places like Louisiana and Utah and

Cuba and Bahrain. Something was up, and I had my suspicions that soon enough I'd get a call from jail on a fraud beef, shoplifting again, grand larceny, even arson. That was crime Sante style, which now meant Kenny style too. I waited for the phone to ring.

What finally happened was unexpected. Despite the Jeff David plot in 1981 and the drunken confession about Elmer Holmgren in 1992, I hadn't considered murder a possibility. When the news came, however, I was like Anjelica Huston in *The Grifters*. Soon after the initial shock had faded, I was assembling the facts in my mind with a certain detachment. The pieces of the puzzle fit.

I knew before I finished reading the first newspaper article that Mom and Kenny weren't innocent bystanders. It was murder, and it was over the top, but it sounded just like them. I knew they were guilty right away because I knew them so well.

I didn't know what they'd done, however, other than what I read in the paper. I could fill in some of the blanks, and I could guess the motivation for their activities. They'd been rich, and now, by Mom's standards, they were poor. She had a desperate need for cash.

For a year after their arrest I lived in fear that Mom would somehow find a way to implicate me in her crimes or otherwise draw me into the vortex. She wanted my attention and my help, and that would be her way of getting it. A horrified fascination, a concern for my wife and my children, as well as worries about Mom and Kenny, drove me to suck up every factoid I could find about the Silverman case. I was a latecomer to the internet, but by August of 1998 I was spending four hours every weekday and parts of weekends surfing the web via my slow, creaky modem, learning about my mother and brother. As I understand it, based on that research and my own background knowledge, here's what my mother and brother were doing when I was (mostly) not looking.

On September 4, 1996, Mom and Kenny were staying at their house in the Bahamas, the four-bedroom green-and-white rental on Nassau two blocks from the Radisson called Rainbows by the Sea. That night they met a business associate for dinner at the nearby Androsia Steak and Seafood Restaurant, where Mom's face was well known. The three of them sat at a table behind a screen at the rear of the restaurant.

Mom and Kenny's dinner guest worked for one of Ken's

offshore banks. Forty-eight-year-old Syed Bilal Ahmed, a real East Indian with past positions at banks in Bahrain and Qatar, was an executive at First Cayman Bank, an Arab-backed institution based in the Cayman Islands. Ken had an account that police estimate at $850,000 at a First Cayman subsidiary called Gulf Union Bank.

Mom was trying to get Ken's money out of the bank. She and Kenny had visited the Caymans, the offshore banking haven in the western Caribbean near Jamaica, in March. They'd met with Ahmed and the bank's principal, Sheikh Jabor Mohammed "Khalifa" Al-Thani of Qatar. They also seemed to know the Pakistani to whom Al-Thani had sold or was trying to sell the bank, Sheikh Adus Shimveel Querishi. Mom and Kenny rented a house near him in Florida in 1997. Mom schmoozed them with some of her longevity hoo-ha, talking up her antiaging formula and flashing some of those Princess Sante business cards.

In order to get the money, Mom and Kenny had been sending faxes with Ken's forged signature to the bank offices, demanding, pleading that the money be shipped to this or that address in the United States. As the assistant general manager of the bank, Ahmed was also the head auditor. He and Mom and Kenny and Sheikh Al-Thani had apparently flown together from the Caymans to the Bahamas six days before the Androsia meeting. After their dinner and a few drinks, Mom and Kenny and Ahmed walked out of the restaurant at about 10 P.M. on the fourth. Ahmed hasn't been seen since. It makes sense that Ahmed, as the auditor, had figured out there was something fishy about the faxes, and with the right Social Security number, birth date, and name, it wouldn't have taken him too many phone calls to learn that Ken Kimes was long dead.

Somebody besides Ahmed must have known about the phony faxes, because the Bahamas police heard about them after Ahmed vanished. Local cops investigating his disappearance also discovered that a few days before the Androsia dinner, a couple who looked like Mom and Kenny had tried and failed to get the Radisson Hotel staff to cough up Ahmed's room key.

The Bahamians staked out Rainbows by the Sea. Mom and Kenny hunkered down in the house. Mom was used to waiting out the authorities, and all she had to do was follow her own rules of many years' standing: Don't answer the phone. Don't answer the door. When they saw their chance, she and Kenny fled the two hundred miles back to Florida.

The police ransacked the empty house. They dug in the sand in and under the house, in the basement, under the floor. They looked for Ahmed's body under the Gulf Union branch itself. They sent divers into the waters near the house and the bank, and never found anything.

But I found a little something. Interspersed on that tape of Dieter the German slave, the one from the box in my driveway, are snippets of conversation between Mom and an executive from Al-Thani's bank. The tape dates from the summer of 1996, right before Syed Bilal Ahmed's disappearance.

In it, Mom presses "Saddam" for information on Khalifa Al-Thani. She and Kenny had hatched some kind of longevity business scheme called Voyager. What product or service they planned to sell remains a mystery, but Kenny had picked out office space in Havana and Delaware. They'd courted Al-Thani relentlessly, calling and sending him packets of info, trying to get him to go to Havana with them to research Voyager. Kenny had even designed a web page for Al-Thani to butter him up.

Khalifa, it turns out, is in London and not expected back for a week. Saddam reassures Mom a half dozen times that Khalifa fully intends to accompany them to Cuba. But then Mom keeps Saddam on the phone, so she can ask questions about another subject.

> **SANTE**: And what happened, what happened, um, um, Saddam, do you think everything is okay? That other guy from . . .
> **SADDAM**: (*Thinking she's still worried about Khalifa*) Yes, he is perfectly agreed in that.
> **SANTE**: No, but for your sake, that other guy — (*having trouble with Syed Bilal Ahmed's name*) Bowman? Khalifa's not bringing him to Nassau?
> **SADDAM**: No, Bilal, I can speak to that, Bilal will not be coming to Nassau. Bilal will be staying in the Cayman Islands as the assistant manager over there. But you know, he is a person [who] just wants to have his show only. Khalifa met you and me and we had some good times together. He was inclined to us. He was interested in good ideas and modern life and modern thinking. Bilal is an Indian man from the south of India and very

traditionally . . . you know, he doesn't want anyone else to come in.

SANTE: Uh-huh.

SADDAM: So we have to combat that and we can do it. We are quite capable of doing that. You are close to Khalifa, and I am in the driver's seat in the Nassau office. I can do that. Khalifa is happy with me. Khalifa kept [*sic*] with me and he also confided certain things of a bank matter . . . he wanted the bank to come up. We had new ideas, we are doing something. We are going to recover the bad amounts, the bad loans from the defaulters. He is in close touch. He will be coming regularly to Nassau now. Go ahead with those plans. Ask him to start a company in Cuba, and then we can look after the affairs and each other and do business with each other.

SANTE: Do you think now that your chances are very good to become manager?

SADDAM: Well, I think so.

SANTE: (*Brightly*) Great! Because I told you [Khalifa] said that he was going to let Syed [Bilal Ahmed] go very soon. So that means you would become the manager.

SADDAM: (*Chortling, like a fat little boy who's been tickled*) General manager!

SANTE: Yes.

SADDAM: Ah, Sante.

SANTE: (*Still having trouble with the rest of Syed Bilal Ahmed's name*) Now, so Bow . . . Bow . . . Boward will not be coming up there. You will be the new general manager.

SADDAM: I hope so.

SANTE: Oh, honey, that would be wonderful.

SADDAM: That would be great. We will have a better way of working, independent and confident work.

SANTE: Oh, honey, that's great. Well, I wish I could find him, because I made all the reservations in Cuba. Maybe he'll call. But he told you he's going to go ahead with Voyager?

SADDAM: Yes, he said, "I would love to go with them to Cuba."

SANTE: I know you're going to be the next general manager.

SADDAM: We'll have real fun then.

SANTE: Perfect.

SADDAM: Give my love to Kenny.
SANTE: Love to your family. We'll see you this week.
Okay, honey, kisses, bye.

Both Saddam and Mom seem to fear Bilal and to want to
keep him far from the Bahamas. But Syed Bilal Ahmed did go to
Nassau, and he disappeared. After he was gone, the faxes from
the dead Ken Kimes kept arriving at the Gulf Union offices. On
December 3, 1996, Mom and Kenny tried to get the bank to send
a check for forty thousand dollars to their bookkeeper Nan
Wetkowski. Three faxes over two days in April demanded a
total of $165,320.

But Mom got none of the money, because the bank was
being liquidated. In part because of Ahmed's disappearance,
investors had gotten nervous and the Caymans government
had moved in. They thought perhaps Ahmed had absconded
with some of the money, because five million dollars was missing from the faltering bank's ledgers. If Mom murdered
Ahmed, she made Ken's money that much harder to get. It was
another example of the supposedly nimble grifter shooting herself in the foot.

In October 1997, the bank collapsed. Creditors were out
thirty million dollars. Investors seemed to be out of luck,
because offshore banks don't have deposit insurance. I don't
have a clue whether any of my stepdad's supposed six figures
is accessible or still existent because I haven't asked. Mom must
not have known much more than me, because she kept sending
phony faxes after the Bahamian government had shuttered the
bank.

During the police investigation of Ahmed's apparent murder, Mom was hovering around the Bahamas without entering
the country. She was hopping from one address to another
across the water in Florida. At one point she tried to send a
proxy to Nassau, a Shade Tree recruit named Donna Lawson.
The woman had no passport and tried to get one with stolen
identification. Caught by the State Department, Lawson
squealed, accusing Mom of sending her to the Bahamas to
"clean a house."

Lawson steered the feds to Mom and Kenny's low-rent one-
bedroom Fort Lauderdale apartment. It wasn't a cushy bungalow at the Miramar Hotel. The mighty had fallen, but they

weren't yet going to be caught. The feds found only dirty dishes, groceries, and legal documents—the last a sure sign of Mom's decorating sensibility. This was in May 1997, about the same time Mom and Kenny called me from Miami begging for help with their department store bust. I never heard a peep about the passport snafu, just the shoplifting. They also didn't tell me that they'd spent a year beating their heads against the wall, trying to get a dead man's money out of a dying bank.

After the fact, it was easy to figure out why Sante wanted Syed Bilal Ahmed gone. In life, though, I didn't know the man. I'm sorry for his loss, and I feel for his family, and for his son, who canceled his wedding in India and flew to the Caribbean to search for his missing dad. I hope that someday he finds out what happened to his father's body, so he can have a measure of peace. But since I didn't know Ahmed, his apparent murder at the hands of my mother and brother had less impact on me than the realization that my twelve-year-old daughter, Kristina, could have been there. If not for the stun-gun incident at the Vegas airport, I might have let my daughter go with them. They were on their way to the Bahamas with that stun gun to zap the nosy auditor. Mom often used her favorite grandchild as bait when she was in the Caribbean. She'd learn that someone she needed to manipulate had a kid Kristina's age and she'd set up a play date. I thank God she didn't have the chance to use my child in her schemes in September 1996.

Similarly, the death of Syed Bilal Ahmed didn't have the same effect on me as what happened to Dave Kazdin a year and a half later. I had known Dave Kazdin for twenty years.

Back in the days of Ed and Sandy Walker, Mom cheated on her mate with his knowledge. Her lovers would be Ed's business associates, and Dad would keep working with the men and welcoming them into his home despite their betrayal. I think something similar happened with Kazdin. I'm certain that Mom and Kazdin had a few assignations in the seventies and eighties and that Ken Kimes knew, yet Dave was an honored guest at our homes in Hawaii and Vegas.

Mom called Dave a "guardian angel" and a "savior" because he'd helped out the family. I found him to be a soft-spoken but sharp-edged guy from Brooklyn who could beat me at eight ball. We'd shoot pool and exchange amused, exasperated glances as my mother jabbered on and on. He thought

Mom was full of it, but he talked to her often during her prison years. I used to relay her calls to him in California via my office phone.

I liked the man in spite of his crustiness, and from what I've heard about him he was warm and generous to his family and friends. That said, I have to sound an ugly note. Sante Kimes got people to do her bidding by flattery, by lying, by overwhelming weak personalities. But a lot of her success had to do with creating the possibility of profit. New friends saw Mom's tacky displays of wealth and wondered, *What's in it for me?* Mom explicitly encouraged this thinking. After a little schmoozing and a few free trips to the Bahamas or Honolulu, it wasn't hard to float a scheme and get an otherwise upstanding citizen to go along with it. There was also that old standby, sex.

If you were an intelligent professional, involved in real estate or insurance, you couldn't be around my mother off and on for twenty years and not know what she was about. Kazdin was complicit in some shady title switching on the Geronimo house. In December 1992 he agreed to let my parents put the property in his name to hide it from an attorney named Doug Stewart whom Ken had stiffed. Stewart had won a judgment against Mom and Ken for his unpaid bills and wanted to seize the house. Kazdin also signed a secret quitclaim, which my parents held on to, which would allow them to reassert their ownership of the property in the event that Kazdin tried to sell it or mortgage it.

Before Ken died, around the time he and Mom were driving us crazy on Almart Circle, Ken decided he wanted to file an insurance claim on the Geronimo house because of some supposed damage to the property. To get the money, he'd have to convince the titular owner of the house, Kazdin, to meet with the insurance people. The last time I saw Dave was when Mom and Ken asked him for this "little favor." He declined, perhaps sensing that this bid for a settlement was as, um, questionable as most of the others filed by my parents. Ken would now have to whip out the quitclaim and become the owner of 2121 Geronimo Way again if he wanted the cash. Kazdin assumed he'd done just that.

In 1996 I saw Kazdin's name on one of the dummy corporations Mom invented to camouflage the Santa Maria acreage. Soon after, by chance, I answered the phone when he called looking for Mom. "I hope you know what you're doing," I warned. I figured he knew a lot about the Santa Maria situation. But Kazdin didn't have a clue what I was talking about. I told him his name was on the paperwork, and he began to curse. "What *is* it with this woman?" he groused.

Not long afterward, frantic to raise cash, Mom tried to arm-twist me into buying the Geronimo house. I liked the house and could afford it but had no intention of doing business with Mom. She came back with a different offer: I should take out a loan on the house, give her half, and keep the house and the other half of the cash. I'd be buying it for half price. "It would really help me out, and I would love to do it for you and the kids. You could turn around and sell it and make a quick hundred-seventy-five grand!" She sold me hard, but I knew better. It was 1997, when her behavior and Kenny's had become too scary for me to tolerate. I no longer felt safe from their "projects."

They decided to victimize Kazdin instead of me. On January 23, 1998, he got two nasty surprises in the mail. He learned that he was still the owner of the Geronimo property and that he'd just taken out a thirty-year mortgage worth $280,000. He hadn't even gotten that great a rate—it was 9.37 percent, more than a point above prime.

My mother and brother had apparently been busy in Florida. Somehow, someone who was not Dave Kazdin had talked the Ocwen Federal Bank in West Palm Beach into parting with the money.

Kazdin called up the bank to yell. It was too late. Mom had already cashed a check for $180,000 and squirreled it away offshore. Kazdin told the bank it had been bilked and gave them the name of the number one suspect.

A few weeks later, Kazdin got still more bad news. His unwanted second home in Las Vegas had burned. But he wouldn't be the beneficiary of any settlement, because the house didn't belong to him. As soon as the mortgage check cleared, evidently, Mom had used Kazdin's quitclaim to transfer the property to one of her Shade Tree lackeys, Robert McCarren. Then she'd taken out a spanking new insurance policy with the aptly named Fireman's Fund. On January 31, with the policy only nine days old, someone—Mom or Kenny or one of the Shade Tree flunkies—had torched the house.

Mom had used Kazdin's willingness to participate in the asset-hiding plan of 1992 against him. Now, however, Kazdin was going to be a problem. He had given the bank the whole scenario and identified the signature on the mortgage form as a fraud. Mom sent one of her Shade Tree women to California to scare him. She wanted to set up a meeting. She started calling Kazdin herself and drafting angry faxes in which she accused him of knowing all about the bogus mortgage beforehand and reneging on a deal. "I will give you five days to stop all these lies," she wrote in late February 1998. "You know you endorsed the loan. Why are you doing this?"

By that time Mom and Kenny, with the Geronimo house torched and my home off-limits, had moved within a half hour's drive of Kazdin. In February, Sandy and Manny Guerin, aka Mom and Kenny, had plopped down eight thousand dollars in cash for a six-month stay in a house at 3221 Elvido Drive in Bel Air, next to Beverly Hills. The eccentric woman who'd advertised for a roommate got more than she bargained for. Mom brought Kenny and Robert McCarren, her servant, whom she called Robert Carro. She told the landlady that she was a millionaire and her son was a student at UCLA. She ordered McCarren to pretend to be unable to speak. Other Shade Tree types turned up at the house, and the landlady got scared.

On March 13, a Friday, Carolene Davis recalls, Mom and Kenny came to visit her in Santa Barbara near noon. Carolene was recuperating from cancer surgery, and Mom and Kenny had been in and out for the past several weeks, cementing their bond with Carolene, their connection for any title they wanted around the country and for the paperwork on the Santa Maria property. Carolene remembers that soap operas were on the television when Mom and Kenny arrived. Mom stayed, Kenny left, and when he returned he was very agitated.

Early that morning, Kenny and one of the drifters, Sean Little, had paid a visit to David Kazdin's house in Granada Hills, north of Studio City in the San Fernando Valley. Little waited in the car while Kenny went inside. Little claims he heard a lone shot from inside the house, after which Kenny came back out to the car and told him what had happened. There had been an argument, and Kenny had had to shoot Kazdin.

Kazdin was killed with a single .22-caliber bullet to the back of the neck. It suggests ambush and/or execution. Little, an ex-

con, tells a tale in which he doesn't know what's going to happen and doesn't see it happen, but whoever pulled the trigger,
the murder was premeditated. The motive and the likely suspects, as in the Ahmed case, are clear.

Little says that after the shooting, Kenny asked for help
moving the evidence, and the two of them carried the 175-
pound body down to Kazdin's garage and stowed it in the
trunk of Kazdin's own green Jaguar. One of them drove
Kenny's car and the other drove the Jaguar, clipping Kazdin's
retaining wall and leaving flakes of green paint and dislodged
bricks in the driveway as they fled the scene. An hour south,
they hoisted Kazdin's body into a Dumpster behind a black
iron fence in an alley near the Los Angeles airport. A homeless
man found Dave there the next morning while he rifled
through the trash looking for food. Dave was shoeless, wearing
jeans and a shirt, and stripped of all identification.

I never knew he was dead until I read the stories about
Irene Silverman four months later. An upstanding middle-class
citizen had been shot to death and hadn't made the papers in
his hometown, much less Las Vegas. Because I was aware of the
quitclaim deed and the way Mom and Ken had slapped his
name on things from Vegas to Santa Maria, and because I'd
heard about the mortgage and had seen the burned-out house, I
connected the dots as soon as I read that he'd been murdered.
That alone would have been enough to sell me on my mother's
guilt, but I also couldn't forget that she'd tried the loan scam on
me. I had been the original fall guy, but Dave had been my
guardian angel and taken the hit instead. Would Mom and
Kenny have killed me, like Kazdin, if I'd complained?

The cops knew who was to blame within days of Kazdin's
death, because a friend of Kazdin's told them about the troubles
Dave had been having with Sante Kimes. The so-called cunning
grifter had left her fingerprints all over the incident. She and
whoever might have aided her were the lone suspects, and this
time there was a body, unlike the Holmgren case.

By the middle of March 1998 my mother and brother were
wanted for two murders. They were still on the loose in Southern California, but their paranoid habits were about to get them
booted from their rental in Bel Air. They wouldn't park their car
in front of the house, they whispered and acted furtive, and
they had an odd, shabby, mute manservant. They refused to

have a phone installed in the house, but they did screw dead bolts on the inside of their bedroom doors. Their landlady began to get the willies.

The simple and perhaps innocent act of buying a car proved my mother and brother's undoing. In February Mom had become Sante Kimes again long enough to place a call to an automobile dealership in Cedar City, Utah. My stepdad had been a loyal customer of Parkway Motors, which was in the southwest corner of the state, a four-hour drive from Vegas. He'd bought a series of behemoths there, Caddies and Lincolns, always a year or two old, because when he wasn't gambling or paying lawyers he was tight with a buck.

Mom told the dealer, Jim Blackner, that Papa was away doing business in Japan and that she needed a car. She wanted a dark green 1997 Lincoln with tinted windows delivered to the Regent Beverly Wilshire Hotel on Rodeo Drive in Beverly Hills.

Blackner sent a truck driver and his wife to the hotel on February 27. They were to pick up a check for fifteen thousand dollars and Mom's trade-in, a 1993 silver Lincoln that Ken had purchased from Parkway just before his death.

Mom and Kenny met them in the lobby and proceeded to wine and dine the couple. They fed them the usual crap about how they simply had to come visit them at their estate in the Bahamas, et cetera. Just in case that didn't work, Mom doped their drinks. After two cocktails the man felt very funny, and his wife, who'd opted for an alcohol-free beverage, felt strange as well. They were too disoriented to protest when Mom gave them the ID of her bookkeeper, Nan Wetkowski, instead of her own, used bogus names on the car's paperwork, and handed them a check from Nan's account.

I don't think my mother knew that she was passing a bad check. Authorities had frozen Nan's account because, during the investigation of the Geronimo fire, they'd determined that some of the cash from the ersatz Kazdin mortgage had passed through it. Mom probably expected the check to clear.

When it bounced, Jim Blackner of Parkway Motors listened to Mom's excuses for a month or so over the phone before taking action. Meanwhile, Mom's nervous landlady on Elvido Drive had hired a private investigator, who'd contacted Parkway about the mysterious tenants driving the big Lincoln from out of state. Between them, the private eye and the car dealer figured out that Sante's husband was never coming back from his business trip.

The landlady decided it was time for the Guerins to go. Mom was steps ahead of her. She and Kenny cleared their belongings out in a rush. She had just convinced one of her stooges, a woman she'd met in December, to fetch her motor home from Vegas and drive it to L.A. The woman's name was Dawn Guerin—she hadn't yet deduced that Mom was using her last name. Mom and Kenny and Dawn and faithful mute manservant Robert McCarren convened at a restaurant to figure out their next move.

Robert McCarren suddenly found his voice and his will and ran away, leaving the rest of the crew at their table. Mom had a cult leader's knack for finding drifters and marginal people and binding them to her, but eventually she always squeezed too hard. Now a potential witness against her was at large. McCarren was probably the firebug in the Geronimo blaze.

The landlady was rid of Sante. Now the car dealer wanted to be rid of her. Jim Blackner tried to set up a sting in which he would pretend to let her swap the green car for yet another used model. In fact, his representatives, one of whom was a Cedar City cop, had been told to repossess the green Lincoln and leave Mom carless. Her antennae must have been raised, though, because she didn't show up for the "swap." Blackner gave up, and an arrest warrant was issued. That warrant would ultimately prove her undoing.

In the cash-poor pre-Kimes era, when it was just me and Mom, there was fraud and theft, but the violence was restricted to punches and property destruction. When Mom pulled a gun on my dad, she was firing blanks. Now Mom was playing a much more desperate game than she'd played back in Palm Springs, and she was playing it badly. Cops in three states wanted to talk to her.

Mom and Kenny were homeless now, operating out of an RV. By early April they were crashing at the Vegas residence of Dawn Guerin. Before Dawn's husband kicked them out, my mother and brother convinced Dawn and yet another stooge named Stan Patterson, a sometime pizza deliveryman, to buy them two handguns at a pawn shop, a 9-millimeter Glock and a .22.

Armed and dangerous, living out of a motor home and

working their cell phones, Mom and Kenny headed east. With them went Sean Little, the purported witness in the Kazdin shooting. They drove through the Southwest and Texas and across the Gulf Coast to Florida. They were back within hankering distance of all that inaccessible cash in the Caymans and the Bahamas.

Perhaps it was an urge to stay close to the money that led them to the Palm Beach Polo and Country Club. They rented a town house there in mid-May from the ex-wife of the guy who'd tried to buy the Gulf Union Bank, Sheikh Querishi. The Sheikh also lived in the complex, in another unit.

But they couldn't get to the money, and Mom resorted to golden-oldie measures. She got the necessary info on a ninety-year-old Palm Beach resident—birthday, Social Security number, mother's maiden name—and ordered up a bogus MasterCard. It wasn't anything she hadn't done before, in her pre-Kimes life. Again, though, Mom screwed up. Max Schorr may have been ninety, but he was an attorney, and he still went to work daily. He noticed the fraudulent credit card bills.

While roosting in Florida, Mom and Kenny tried another of their long-distance motor vehicle scams. Just as they had with Parkway Motors, they got a dealer in another state to deliver a vehicle to a high-toned location. Dixie Motors of Hammond, Louisiana, near New Orleans, must have figured that anyone who wanted to take delivery of a motor home at the Ritz Carlton in Palm Beach had to be loaded. It was the Regent Wilshire redux.

Again Mom had arranged a trade-in. The Dixie rep drove the new RV the thousand miles to Palm Beach, expecting to get an old RV and a check for seventy thousand dollars in return from a woman named Nan Wetkowski. Mom met him outside the hotel and told him the buyer was inside. She ducked into the hotel and came back with two checks. The first was on the account of L. M. Carpeneto, a real person who'd reported his checks stolen in Vegas. The other was drawn on the empty account of a certain S. A. Kahn, one of Mom's aliases. Dixie turned down the two checks and asked for something certified. Sante came right back at them with a check marked Certified. Such rubber stamps are on sale everywhere.

Mom had arranged the handoff for a weekend, and when the checks proved rubbery come Monday, she couldn't be found. Three weeks later, Florida cops stumbled on the RV in a parking lot, its vehicle identification number scratched out and its Dixie Motors decal scraped off. It had been parked and waiting for Mom and Kenny when they needed it next.

By the time the cops found the grifted RV, the grifters were gone. Mom and Kenny were motoring north in the hot Lincoln, and they'd hired Jose Alvarez, a fast-food cook in West Palm Beach, as their replacement for Sean Little, who'd run off just like Robert McCarren before him. Alvarez was a South Florida, recent-Cuban-immigrant version of Mom and Kenny's Vegas losers, or a fusion of those Shade Tree skels and the Latina maids. Alvarez spoke little English, and he was just barely employed when my family found him. He'd left a big pile of unpaid parking tickets behind him, but as far as I know, that's the worst thing he'd ever done in his life. He didn't know what Mom and Kenny were planning when the three of them set off, Jose at the wheel, for New York City. Mom and Kenny already had their next victim picked out.

3 2

IRENE

During the era of my mother and brother's wanderings, Carolene Davis probably heard from them more than I did. Just after Ken's death, Mom had used Carolene to turn the paperwork on the Santa Maria property into an unrecognizable mess. In 1997 and 1998, Mom called the Santa Barbara office of First American Title. "Is Carolene there?" she'd ask. "This is her mom."

Carolene's "mom" wanted her "daughter" to pull titles on various properties and houses. Sante and Kenny would be in California or Florida and have their eyes on something owned by someone vulnerable. Sante had plied Carolene with so much swag—plane tickets, stacks of casino chips, dresses, a heavy glass-and-iron table—that Carolene would do whatever "Mom" wanted. If she needed to see if there were any liens or mortgages on a property and what the chain of ownership was, Carolene would drop everything and find out.

Carolene claims innocence as to Mom's motives. Only once in Carolene's life had she ever seen Sante with her teeth bared, a time when the dread word *widow* had turned up in the Santa Maria paperwork. Other than that it had been a few years at the trough for Carolene, a good example of how Mom could manipulate with kindness. So Carolene didn't ask questions when Sante asked her to fax documents to women named Nancy or Sandy or Linda at a succession of hotels. "Could you fax that to Linda?" Mom would mew. "She'll pick it up for me." The women were all my mother, using aliases to collect data on properties she coveted, but Carolene says she never caught on.

One day in May 1998, two months before she was arrested, Sante called First American Title from the East Coast. She wanted information again, this time about a mansion in Manhattan. Carolene was out sick, bedridden and drugged because of her ongoing battle with cancer. She delegated the job to another woman in the Santa Barbara office, who discovered that it would cost seventy-five dollars to get their branch in New York to pull the papers. Mom was mad. She wanted the data free of charge, like her long-distance phone call, which was probably billed to my sales office or to a phony credit card. Mom decided to get the information by other means. She became a real estate broker named Joy Landis, and it was Joy Landis who obtained the paperwork on 20 East 65th Street.

Mom had met and schmoozed a Prudential-Bache executive, either at an investment seminar in Florida or at an antiaging conference in Vegas. She wanted him to give her the names of high-end rental apartments in exclusive neighborhoods in Manhattan. The exec didn't refer her to a real estate agent or a homeowner but to a butcher. Paul Vaccari, owner of an Italian meat store at 633 Ninth Avenue called Piccinini Brothers, had told the man about an interesting, outgoing old lady who'd been his customer for years. The woman, whose name was Irene Silverman, rented out apartments in a multimillion-dollar mansion on the Upper East Side. She was eighty-two and her house was on 65th Street between Fifth and Madison Avenues, steps from Central Park. She accepted tenants for short-term or long-term stays, and she lived in the most elegant zip code in the richest city in the world. Mom pounced.

In April, posing as a secretary named Eva, Mom called Irene Silverman, probably via cell phone from the mobile home or the town house in Florida, and inquired about renting a flat. Eva's boss, Manny Guerin, aka little brother Kenny, would arrive in June and take up residence in Apartment 1B.

So here again, as in Bel Air, was the worldly, maybe eccentric woman with the big house in the fabulous neighborhood, the right address in her town, who for money or company rented out rooms for a high price. Kenny arrived, cash in hand, deploying the scent of money and entitlement.

But Mom and Kenny's act worked best on people who'd never been around money before. For Kay Frigiano and our other Vegas friends, Mom was a window into a world of possibility. Without her, they never would have gone to Mexico or

Hawaii or eaten every night at expensive restaurants. They'd
overlook the fake rock on her finger and the bullshit in her pat-
ter because the airline tickets and the meals were real.

Mom acted Jackie Susann, Jackie Collins rich. I'd already
seen how people who were more comfortable with their wealth
behaved, and I'd seen how they reacted to Mom. With some
education and polish, you'd be skeptical about the things Mom
did. She drove everybody away eventually, even her only lifelong friend, Ruth Tanis. The more sophisticated they were, the
faster they ran.

There had always been plenty of people who sensed right
off that there might be something nasty underneath Mom's
domineering eccentricity. Vegas had probably been the right
playpen for her, since there were lots of people there prone to
vulgar displays of wealth, people who behaved as if they'd
found their money in a bag on the street. Because of the slots
and the blackjack tables, many mooks there were rich for a
week or two at a time. Vegas was the apogee of Okie-wins-lotto,
or street kid hits the jackpot, either of which could be applied to
my mother and stepfather.

Transposed to the more sophisticated venue of Bel Air,
Mom's gaudy front had failed. Mom and Kenny's landlady had
a private eye on their backs within weeks. Four months later, on
the Upper East Side of Manhattan, her poorly schooled protégé
fared even worse. Kenny skulked around the Silverman mansion acting strange, arousing suspicion, and he and Mom got
found out just as quickly. Their victim saw them coming.

WHENEVER I READ ABOUT Irene Silverman, the woman
my mother killed, I feel compelled to make an observation that
some people might find in bad taste. Irene and Sante had a lot
in common besides humble beginnings. I don't think they
would ever have been friends, but Irene's story and Mom's are
similar.

Irene was born the same year as Ken, 1916. My mom
claimed to be the daughter of an Indian immigrant and a prostitute and to have been abandoned on the streets of Los Angeles
before my grandparents adopted her and took her north to Carson City at the age of thirteen. Irene Silverman claimed to have
been born above a New Orleans whorehouse and to have spent

her childhood living next to a second one. Her parents were a Greek immigrant seamstress and a gambler named Zambelli, who'd grown up in an orphanage. George Zambelli left the family when Irene Zambelli was sixteen, and she moved north with her mother to New York.

Her mother, also named Irene, sewed for a living, while little Irene, five feet tall and less than a hundred pounds, caught on as one of the thirty-six dancers with the Radio City Music Hall Ballet Corps. She danced hard for low wages, but she and her mom were getting by in the Depression.

I don't know what passed between mother and daughter, or whether the two Irenes ever had the kind of discussions I had with my mother in Palm Springs in the sixties, but it sounds as if in later years Irene was frank about her affection for money and status. She and Mom both had a habit of flashing hundred-dollar bills. When I was a boy, Sante—at that time Santee—was open with me about her designs on a rich man. She ran through a string of real estate types, moving mostly up the economic scale, until she landed Ken Kimes in the early seventies. She was pushing forty by the time she found her Papa.

At age twenty-five, in 1941, Irene Zambelli married a millionaire who'd been hanging around the Radio City stage door trying to meet her. Like Ken Kimes, Sam Silverman was a divorced father of two who would serve in the army during World War II. Like Ken, he made his millions in the real estate business. Ken was a motel builder; Sam was a mortgage broker. Sam affected a false Ivy League pedigree and had left a legal career in Florida under a cloud—he was shading the details of his past, à la Mom.

Sam and Irene were like an Upper East Side version of my mother and stepfather. Both pairs were considered odd couples, composed of an extrovert and an introvert, an eccentric, vivacious female with attention-getting clothes and dyed hair, and a rich, natty, proper, very reserved but devoted male. Neither new wife got along with the two kids from her husband's first marriage. My mother the bigot used to kid Ken that his hooked nose looked Jewish, and Ken, equally bigoted, would bristle. Sam Silverman was a Jew who could pass for a WASP.

Perhaps their paths crossed on Oahu in the late seventies. The Silvermans had a condo on Waikiki, and Ken and Sante had the Portlock house, and both of them were associates of the Ho family, well-known Hawaiian real estate developers. We hit

Hawaii in 1975, five years before Sam Silverman passed away in 1980.

After their spouses died, the Widow Silverman and the Widow Kimes took the same approach to replacing the lost income. Mom rented rooms (and gouged tenants), filling her house with Shade Tree types. Irene and Sam Silverman had rented apartments in their five-story 65th Street town house for many years before Sam's death. In 1985, with Big Irene and Sam gone, Irene Silverman chopped the apartments in half, creating ten rentable units, and began to focus on short-term tenants.

Silverman decorated every unit in her own idiosyncratic style. My mother's taste in clothes has inspired some mirth among observers since she became a public figure, but Irene shared her belief that turbans were classy headgear. You could argue that Mom and Irene had similarly nouveau riche sensibilities. Exotic flowers filled Irene's town house, especially white ones, the color my mother first wore for Ken and continued wearing after he was gone. Irene had a huge painting of herself from her ballerina days hanging on the main floor of the house. She'd edited it slightly to make the hips smaller — she was planning to get plastic surgery before she disappeared. Her pink ballet slippers had been set up in a kind of shrine.

For all their superficial similarities, however, Irene lacked the glitch in her soul that has made Mom's life a catastrophe. Maybe it was her long, close relationship with her mother, who was there with her only child when she nearly died of typhus at fourteen, who moved in when she married Silverman and never left, but Irene sounds like a healthy, settled, benevolent version of Sante. She sounds like Sante with the kinks ironed out, and with a bigger score.

Irene lived at 20 East 65th Street, a Parisian-looking limestone town house built in 1880, from 1957 until her death. The ballroom, swathed in oak, marble, and gilt, was a replica of the Petit Trianon at Versailles. Besides the condo in Hawaii, she had two homes in and near the real Paris. She tried to compensate for dropping out of high school by taking courses at Columbia and inviting professors to dinner. She had a wide circle of long-term friends. Irene Silverman had a real marriage ceremony and benefited from a real will when her husband died. He didn't hide money from her. He left her $3.2 million and the house with the junipers out front. It was valued at more than $7 million by the time Irene disappeared.

She was a domineering presence in her household, intrusive in the lives of her tenants, but in a motherly, busybody kind of way. Her employees were devoted, including her version of Mom's Latina maids. Most of her tenants liked her too. She didn't lock them in the house, and they weren't down-and-outers from the shabby dream capital of the West, like Mom's zombie renters. They tended to be fabulous, the minor boldface names of the entertainment world. Jennifer Grey, Chaka Khan, Daniel Day-Lewis, society bandleader Peter Duchin, the Jordanian royal family. They were the kind of contacts my mother might have wanted, and could have had, were she not so helplessly destructive.

When Kenny and Mom entered her life, Irene Silverman was eighty-two and getting ready to die. Mom's response to fading health and advancing age was selfish. She pursued "longevity," hoping to put off the inevitable and scam a few more people in the process. Irene plowed her money into a nonprofit foundation that would honor her mother, something called the Coby Foundation, dedicated to the decorative art of embroidery and the women who labor at it.

But she shared something with my mother that was her undoing. She liked money, even if it was all going into the Coby coffers. She'd sleep in the basement on a cot sometimes so that she could rent out her own apartment in the town house.

Normally Irene had a woman at Feathered Nest realty check out her prospective tenants. The applicants were supposed to supply references, and Feathered Nest vetted them.

In June, a thin-lipped, well-dressed young man with a big nose that looked as if it had been broken rang her doorbell. He was the Manny Guerin whose secretary had been calling Irene's office, and he didn't want to deal with the real estate agent. He offered to pay a month's rent up front, six thousand dollars. He pulled out a roll of hundreds and started to count them. He was willing to pay in cash, on the spot. Irene decided to forgo the reference check and let the young man move into 1B. She gave him a key.

Everybody, no matter how smart or sophisticated they are, has a weakness. My mother is correct in assuming that for most people, it's money.

33

JULY 5

I would have been a better protégé for Mom than Kenny. I can manipulate people—if not with Sante's ardor and finesse, then often enough. I can keep a low profile. I can make detached, rational decisions. And I can tell, usually, where my (or Mom's) fantasies end and the outside world begins.

For those very reasons, though, I chose not to be my mother's soldier. In the short run, I had a weakness for money and I could be seduced by the scent of an easy score. But in the long run, as hard as she pulled, and as often as I wavered, I declined the offer. I knew better, because of that moral core of unknown origin, a certain worldliness, and simple fear.

Kenny had some of the right skills. He could be charming. He dressed well. He could lie with confidence, which is job one for a confidence man. Kenny's problem was that he really didn't know how he came across. He could embarrass you in a room full of people, like the time I went to the steakhouse with him and Mom and he abused the wait staff.

Part of that was the uncomplicated smugness of youth. Jet-setting around the islands in his expensive suits, cigar clamped between his teeth and money in the bank, he felt sophisticated. The cigars and the web-page design were part of his self-conscious trendiness; he'd been a follower of fashion since his alternative rock days as a preteen.

But most of the problem was that Kenny was too much my mother's son, and too much the spawn of Ken Kimes. Nothing had tempered his mood swings, his hyperactive demand for instant gratification. He jittered and chattered and flashed his big-toothed grin to grab attention. If he saw a camera, he'd jump in front of it, mugging.

He was over the top by nature and nurture. Sometimes, to be a good con artist, one really needs to be invisible. Quite often, in fact. Kenny, like his mother, couldn't manage it.

From his first days at 20 East 65th, Manny Guerin attracted too much attention. He put his hands over his face and ducked his head when he came through the black iron front doors and walked down the marble hall to 1B. He didn't want to be seen on Irene Silverman's security camera. The moves made him as conspicuous as the grimacing gargoyle that hung over the mansion's front door.

Kenny stood at the peephole of 1B and stared out at passersby, and they could see the shadow of his feet in the crack under the door. He added a dead bolt to his bedroom door. He wouldn't let the maids clean his room. He brought in Mom and Jose Alvarez, "sneaking" them past the security camera with the duck-and-cover move. Everyone was aware that he was keeping this older woman in his room, because sometimes it was the woman's voice that shooed away the maids.

Kenny's behavior put the whole house on alert. Silverman realized within days that she'd made a mistake. The strange new tenant wouldn't sign his rental agreement form, but instead asked if he could look at the penthouse and offered to pay thirty thousand dollars in cash for a month's stay. He was snooping around other floors of the mansion and asking the staff alarming questions, like "What's Irene Silverman's Social Security number?"

"He smells like jail," griped Silverman. She told friends and employees that there was something amiss with her new tenant and that she was thinking of calling an attorney to get him out. Like Mom, she wrote things down. She sketched Kenny, with his big and unmistakable Roman nose, barely altered by his failed plastic surgery, and she took notes on his activities. When she confronted him about the rental agreement, and he blathered about having given it to a lawyer to review and then to one of Silverman's employees, she cut him off. "That's a lie," she said. His ears turned red. When she saw him at the peephole of his door, the eighty-two-year-old would flip him the bird.

Irene Silverman had made Kenny as a con artist. She knew he wanted something from her, but I doubt she guessed the scale on which her unwelcome boarder was working. Silver-

man was irate and ready to evict Kenny because he'd disman-
tled an antique chest in his room, worth thousands, but Mom
and Kenny planned to take over the entire mansion, worth millions. One of her employees warned Irene to leave the house
and protect herself from the weird guy with the blazing blue-
green eyes in 1B. She retorted, "This is my house. I'll stay in my
house, and *he'll* have to leave."

My mother had written out a step-by-step procedure for
stealing the home of someone old, wealthy, and vulnerable. She
and Kenny had a list of names when they arrived in Manhattan.
Their first prospect, an old woman many blocks north whose
name they seem to have procured in the Bahamas, refused to
accept Kenny as a tenant.

Silverman was their second try. Once Kenny was inside, he
and Mom got busy. To get the house, they needed Silverman's
Social Security number and signature on a whole series of documents, culminating with a fake deed.

Kenny tapped Irene's phones and kept a diary of her behavior ("Thursday night, stayed up. Went upstairs to sleep. *By Herself*"). Mom was Mrs. Outside in the scheme. When she wasn't
bunking at 1B, she lived in the nearby high-end hotels like the
Plaza Athénée, at three hundred dollars and up a night, piling
many of the charges on the credit card of the old man from
Florida. She had shoved her son out front, the way she used to
urge me through windows in Newport Beach. She might have
figured that she was too hot because of her rap sheet and the
Utah Lincoln, she might have been training Kenny, or she could
have been hanging back because her highest good was always
and forever self-preservation. Better Kenny than Sante if the
cops came.

When Kenny failed to weasel Silverman's Social Security
number out of the maids, Mom called Irene Silverman directly.
Pretending to be the promotions director for a casino, Mom told
Irene that she'd won a free trip to Vegas, complete with a complimentary stack of chips. All she had to do was cough up that
magic nine-digit number.

Mom had misjudged her mark. Mom's idea of glamour was
lowbrow — big cars, big jewels, big steaks, and Frank Sinatra.
Ken Kimes would have jumped at the free trip to Vegas. Irene
Silverman preferred Paris, ballet, and the opera. Mom had a
house next to a golf course; Irene's Paris house abutted a theater, and she boasted about how she could hear the actors

through her wall. She didn't fall for Mom's Vegas scam, or for three other calls offering her island cruises.

Lacking a real Social Security number, Mom and Kenny generated a fake one. By the end of June they had a number and all the documents they needed. Mom had a tax form, a power of attorney, a rental agreement, a transfer form, and she'd obtained a copy of the deed — she'd had to buy it, since Carolene Davis couldn't get her a freebie. She forged Irene Silverman's name on all the papers, tracing over the lone shaky signature that Kenny had cadged out of the landlady, on his rental receipt. Mom was ready to spend real money to complete the deal. She had her offshore banks send her checks for seventy-five hundred dollars, the amount that would be owed in taxes upon sale.

With the papers ready, Mom and Kenny had to find a notary who'd stamp them without witnessing Silverman's signature. On July 1 at 11:20 P.M., having renamed himself Mr. Win, Kenny arranged to meet a part-time notary named Don Aoki at the bar of the Plaza Athénée. He escorted Aoki to the Silverman mansion a few yards away, and into apartment 1B.

Aoki saw a scene from *Little Red Riding Hood*. In the dim bedroom of the apartment lay an elderly woman in a nightgown, red wig, and hat. Mr. Win told Aoki that this feeble old Grandma, with the covers pulled up to her chin and the paperwork beside her, was Irene Silverman. It was, of course, Sante Kimes in disguise.

The Manhattanites were proving more difficult than the suckers in Vegas. It was New York nature to mistrust an easy smile and be suspicious of a slick story. Despite the fact that Kenny had offered to pay him several hundred dollars, far above his normal fee, Aoki refused to notarize Grandma Silverman's documents. He declined because they were already signed. He asked the old lady, who wouldn't get out of bed, to autograph a separate piece of paper so he could make a comparison. She demurred, and then staged an argument with Mr. Win so that Aoki wouldn't have time to ask why. Aoki took a cab home.

The next day, July 2, another notary, a woman named Noel Sweeney, did what Aoki wouldn't. Mom and Kenny had succeeded. They had a signed, sealed, and delivered deed to the property. For $396,000, Irene Silverman had transferred her $7.5 million home to the Atlantis Group Ltd., a corporation based on the Caribbean island of Antigua. The nominal president of the Atlantis Group was one of Mom's Shade Tree drifters, Manuel Guerrero (not Manny Guerin). Back in Nevada, Guerrero had no clue that he was a corporate president.

Everything was in order for the final phase of the operation. It's the part I have the hardest time accepting, though I don't deny that it happened, and it was almost certainly premeditated. Before July 5, 2000, Mom and Kenny between them had apparently killed at least three people. In each case, Mom could invoke the Kimes family logic and paint the victim as an enemy — a traitor or a threat who had to be eliminated. Holmgren, Kazdin, and the Caribbean banker all could have put Mom in prison with a phone call. Mom framed their murders, in her mind and to her youngest son, as self-defense. That's the way she's wired.

Killing Irene Silverman, however, was a crime of a different order. Making her disappear seems to have been implicit from the minute Kenny rang her doorbell. I wonder whether even Sante Kimes could convince herself that Irene Silverman deserved to die.

I've told myself sometimes that Mom meant to bully the woman into signing papers and something went wrong, or she was going to dope her up and keep her hidden until she could take out a whopping mortgage on the mansion and flee with the cash. Too bad the evidence says otherwise.

Mom had called one of her Vegas minions several times before July 5 to offer him a new job. She told Stan Patterson, a pizza deliveryman/jack-of-all-trades who lived in a trailer park, that he should fly to New York to manage a fancy East Side apartment house. He was supposed to fire Silverman's employees and then start restaffing. Mom contacted a homeless shelter in Queens and asked a man there to be the building's new superintendent.

She was trying to re-create her Geronimo house on a grandiose, delusional scale. She would hire homeless people, as always, and mistreat and abuse them, and she would milk her rich tenants for cash. It was the luxury boardinghouse of which she'd long dreamed. She told Patterson that there'd be a crazy old ballerina living there, dancing through the halls with no panties, but in reality the plan required, sooner or later, the absence of Irene Silverman.

Locals flee New York City on July Fourth weekend. They go to the beach or the country, and the richer precincts of town are especially empty of people. Mom and Kenny had learned that Irene was going to slap Kenny with an eviction order on Monday, July 6.

At noon on July 5, Silverman dialed a pal to chat. She scribbled out a note about her suspicious tenant, Manny Guerin. He'd skulked up to the door of her first-floor suite and asked her if she had the latest issue of the *Wall Street Journal* or *Barron's*. She'd brushed him off and written down the details. Neither paper publishes on the weekend.

Irene was last seen alive sitting in her suite with the door open around the time of that phone call. At one-thirty, a friend called Irene's apartment and got no answer. Around that time, Manny Guerin, who'd refused maid service for three weeks, twice badgered a maid named Marta to clean up his room, offering the enticement of a major tip. She said no. She then watched on the security camera as a furtive man in a white shirt left the building by the basement entrance. Marta assumed he was Manny, the weirdo in 1B, because all the other tenants were gone for the weekend.

Several hours later, a person named Lucy called Marta and told her that if any officials or tax people came to the door over the next few days, she should say nothing. Lucy also asked Marta to take Irene's bulldog, Georgie, home with her when she left for the day. The requests alarmed Marta, and the voice sounded too deep and masculine to belong to anyone named Lucy. Rattled, Marta rushed from the basement to her boss's ground-floor apartment. Irene Silverman was gone.

Between noon and seven, Mom and Kenny disposed of Irene Silverman so completely that not one drop of blood has ever been found. According to the police, they zapped her with a 50,000-volt stun gun, strangled her with a clothesline or smothered her with a pillow, then shoved her into a duffel bag and made her go poof. Dogs sniffing the house, the sidewalk, and every inch of the Lincoln came up empty. Cops dug up the swamps of New Jersey and chased down countless tips in vain. Cell phone records, restaurant receipts, and a parking garage ticket prove that Mom never left the island of Manhattan; if Kenny had, it wasn't for more than a few hours. As far as anyone could tell, Silverman's tiny body, less than five feet tall and

115 pounds, might have been consigned to a Dumpster across the street. This time, however, no homeless person stumbled across it.

Mom and Kenny, on the other hand, were all too noticeable. Marta had contacted a friend of Irene's, the same buddy to whom Irene had been kvetching about her bizarre tenant. The friend called the rental agent, the rental agent buzzed the 19th Precinct, and all parties converged on the mansion in a rush. It wasn't hard to sell the cops on the idea that Silverman wasn't out for a walk. The victim herself had made a police sketch of the suspect, with little arrows pointing out his distinguishing features.

Irene Silverman was the wrong victim. Old and rich didn't mean addled and vulnerable. This wasn't some lonely, isolated dowager in a transient town like Vegas. Her friends and employees noticed her missing within three hours. If they hadn't, the tenants would have. Mom had homeless drifters for tenants on Geronimo Way; that July, *Nanny* producer Peter Jacobson was staying at Mrs. Silverman's. Mom had picked a building full of the kind of people who call the police, their lawyers, and maybe the media too when something goes wrong.

Still, I wonder if Mom and Kenny might have slipped away from New York and onto an interstate to elsewhere, with zip to show for the Silverman scam but *free*, were it not for Mom's repeated calls to her gofer Stan Patterson. When Kazdin's body turned up in a trash bin, a joint task force of the LAPD and the FBI had started searching for Sante and Kenny. They'd connected my mother and brother to the Utah Lincoln and the fake credit card from Florida, and they'd busted Patterson for buying guns in Nevada. Rather than facing charges of procuring firearms under false pretenses for Mom the convicted felon, Patterson agreed to turn snitch. The cops urged him to accept the invite to New York from the woman he knew as Ellen.

Sante bought Patterson a ticket on the America West redeye from Vegas to JFK. Cops met him at the gate. He was so scared of being caught in the crossfire between the law and my family, or of being executed by Mom and Kenny for snitching, that he wore a bulletproof vest under his shirt in the dead of summer. The police made him take it off, and slapped a black baseball cap on his head. Stan was the bait in a sting.

That afternoon, Mom and Stan went barhopping in midtown while the cops watched. Mom downed several of her late husband's favorite drinks, Seven-and-Sevens, at the bar of the New York Hilton on 53rd Street and Sixth Avenue, and then wine at a restaurant a block away called Ciao Europa.

Stan sat next to her, listening to her ramble, sweating under his cap. He and his invisible escort of cops had waited six hours in the Hilton lobby for Sante, and when she finally arrived it had been without Kenny. The sting dragged on from the afternoon into early evening, and still Kenny hadn't materialized.

Mom and Patterson wandered out into one of Manhattan's ubiquitous street fairs. Vendors clogged the sidewalks of Sixth Avenue, and traffic was rerouted. It was the only crowd to be found in Manhattan on a quiet summer Sunday. Mom carried a big vinyl purse, the same kind that had swung from her arm since Palm Springs, thirty years before. Had I been there, I would have expected to see some of the cheap junk from the sidewalk tables disappear into the bag.

Mom liked shopping. She'd chosen the fair so she could browse, and because the throng provided cover for her reunion with Kenny. He didn't appear till almost seven P.M., and he hung back several yards from Mom and Stan when he did, so he could make sure he wasn't being followed.

My brother and mother hugged. Stan pulled off his baseball cap. Kenny pissed his pants when the police grabbed and cuffed the three of them. My mother and little brother were in custody.

It was only Kenny's second or third arrest, but Mom had stopped counting. She didn't panic. From the second a cop's hand touched her, Mom was spinning. "That's not my purse," she said, without blinking, of the mammoth bag attached to her side.

In the bag that didn't belong to her, Mom was carrying $10,580, as well as checks, payroll stubs, five bank books, and seven different passports. She'd stolen Silverman's passport and pasted her own picture over her victim's face. Kenny had Silverman's American Express charge plates and her fake Social Security card.

At FBI headquarters Kenny and Mom blustered and stalled, denying everything. They thought, and the cops didn't contradict them, that the bust might be about nothing more than the Utah car, and they had an explanation for that. They'd written the bad check in good faith.

They also benefited from police brainlock on a massive scale, the sort of unmissable but missed connections that makes you wonder how anybody gets arrested except people who turn themselves in. Mom and Kenny had bags and pockets full of the name Irene Silverman. They were practically wearing T-shirts with their victim's picture on the front. The police had been hunting them because they killed a man to hide a real estate fraud. Stan Patterson had told the feds that Sante wanted him in New York so he could manage a building she was taking over. Yet, incredibly, neither the NYPD nor the FBI, supposedly the finest police agencies in the land, bothered to add one plus one. Nobody tried to make a single call to find out who this Irene Silverman lady might be and whether she was upset that her passport was missing. They seemed to buy Mom's excuse that the Silverman documents belonged to a friend. At some point, Mom or Kenny or both of them must have realized — they don't know. They don't know!

Using a ticket stub from Kenny's pocket, the task force traced the Lincoln to a garage on 44th Street in midtown Manhattan. Inside, on the floor of the front seat, they could see a discarded cardboard stun-gun container. The backseat was obscured by a mound of plastic bags, topped by a quilt. The spare tire and the jack had been dumped in the backseat, leaving the trunk empty. The FBI moved the car to its downtown headquarters without searching the bags, not making the link between the vacant trunk and Irene Silverman, still not aware of who they had in custody.

The next evening, unbeknownst to the Kazdin task force, the lead cop investigating the disappearance of Irene Silverman scheduled a press conference for 8 P.M. Deputy Inspector Joseph Reznick appealed to the public for information. All the city's TV news outlets broadcast the department's sketch of the mysterious Manny Guerin.

A member of the Kazdin task force — an NYPD officer, not a fed — happened to be watching TV that night. He heard the name Irene Silverman and glimpsed the sketch. At six A.M. Tuesday morning, he phoned a detective working the Silverman case and told him "Manny Guerin" was already in custody. Mom and Kenny's luck had run out.

Now the New York cops scoured the Lincoln. They understood why the jack was in the backseat and the trunk was empty. They sifted through the contents of the garbage bags in the backseat. Besides clothes, they cataloged pepper spray, a tape recorder, the semiautomatic Glock handgun Patterson had purchased in Vegas, unused hypos, handcuffs, license plates from Nevada, Florida, and Georgia, a container of the date-rape drug Rohypnol, and thirteen notebooks in which Mom outlined every step of the Silverman caper. In apartment 1B, police collected garbage bags and duct tape. They found Kenny's fingerprint on a piece of tape.

I don't see Mom killing Irene Silverman, though she's capable of it. Instead, I'm sure she delegated the task to Kenny. The tranquilizer, the stun gun, the pistol—by whatever means Silverman was dispatched, she wound up with duct tape on her mouth, wrapped in garbage bags, shoved into a duffel bag, and carted into the beyond atop a shower curtain in the trunk of the Lincoln.

You're reading this, and you're disgusted by my family. I can't argue with you, because so am I. But my anger and revulsion are complicated by shame. I'm ashamed of my mother, and I feel guilty about my little brother. In the retelling he seems as monstrous as Mom, an eager, precocious young murderer. I have to stop myself from wallowing in if-onlys. Chief among them, if only I'd done more to save him from Mom.

I'm also struck by different things than you might be when I hear about Mom and Kenny's deeds. Details affect me. For example, the ancient container of the date-rape drug makes me think of the time Mom doped my wife. It was probably from the same jar. The pepper spray, like the brass knuckles and knife from Kenny's pocket, and his scribbled plans to order how-to books on money laundering and homemade silencers, reminds me of the scary stuff I used to find in his room. He'd made the leap from *The Anarchist Cookbook* to murder. And the name that Mom gave the police, and the manner in which she did it, makes me sad. "Want to know my real name?" Mom had asked the cops, as if sharing a secret. "It's Sandra Louise Walker." That was her name when she was married to my dad, back in Palm Springs in the sixties. We'd come full circle.

After the cops made the connection between Manny and Kenny, my mother and brother became larger than life. They became tabloid headlines, the kind with the ink so heavy it stains your fingers black. While I scanned those stories in the *New York Post* and elsewhere, I was thinking something very different from what you might have been thinking. Number one, I thanked God they'd been nailed for the New York murder before the task force had a chance to extradite them to Los Angeles. In California, they would have faced the death penalty. Number two, based on everything that had transpired in the first thirty-six years of my life, as of July 8, 2000, I thought Mom and Kenny had a better than even chance of somehow, some way, getting away with murder.

34

HOLDING
THE BAG

I could tell that the two men in the parking lot were cops before they got within fifty feet of my office building. When you're the son of Sante Kimes you don't need to see a badge, you don't need to check the shoes. You have a sixth sense about law enforcement, and I made this pair of short-haired, stern-faced suits as cops as soon as I spied them through my window. By the time they'd reached the front door, where they asked for the manager, I'd already instructed one of my employees to usher them straight back to my private office.

It was a week after Mom and Kenny's arrest across the continent in New York, and they were already national celebrities. I'd been expecting and dreading this kind of visit. Now the requisite tag team had arrived and it would be over soon. If they did their homework they'd get bored with me fast. They'd determine I had nothing to do with Silverman, Kazdin, the Caribbean banker, the Lincoln, or anything else. My only worry was that Mom or Kenny had used my name in some new, unknown, and unfortunate way, something more serious than fake utility bills, and I'd have to go to court to protect myself.

The suits sat in two chairs facing my big wooden desk. One was older and after he said hello didn't open his mouth again till he said good-bye. He scribbled notes on a spiral pad. The younger one, whose name was Victor, talked. He was in charge.

"Some serious crimes have been committed by two people in New York City," intoned Victor with much gravity. "These people have been under investigation for six months."

I nodded, and bit the inside of my cheek to keep from smirking. The people he was talking about were in the room. If either one of these guys could unstiffen their necks and turn their heads just a little, they'd see framed photos of Mom and Kenny all over the walls. A glossy of Mom was right behind the note taker.

Victor continued. "We're here on behalf of the NYPD, the LAPD, the FBI. . . ." He spilled an alphabet soup of acronyms. He and his senior partner were here to interrogate me on behalf of the joint task force investigating Mom and Kenny's crime spree in half a dozen states, and that sounded efficient to me. Instead of many cops and many interviews it would be one-stop shopping. I kept nodding.

"In my twenty years of law enforcement, I've never seen a more thorough investigation than this one." His claim, as I would come to learn, might have been true. New York City alone would have seventeen detectives on the case for a full year.

"While Sante Kimes and her son have been incarcerated, we've noticed that they've called this number a great deal." Victor fixed me with a stare. "Do you have any idea why that might be?"

These guys had to be FBI. Who else would ask a question to which they already knew the answer in such a formal, button-down way?

I said my line. "My name's Kent Walker."

They had blank looks on their faces. That scared me. I repeated myself, in case they'd gone deaf on the shooting range. "My name is Kent Walker."

"You said that before,"countered Victor, getting impatient. "We want to know why they call you so much."

"I'm Sante Kimes's son," I nearly shouted, slow and aston-ished.

I thought the stenographer was going to drop his pen. He and Victor really had no clue. Fifty-five different media organi-zations on several continents had been in my face within days of the arrest, and the police investigating the crimes didn't rec-ognize my name. I was glad I had Dominic Gentile watching my back.

Maybe there were just too many cops on the case to keep the facts straight. The NYPD knew who I was right away. I'll never forget two calls they made, one to my house and one to my office, in the first weeks after the arrest.

I'd been trying to chase down my mother's lawyer, Jose Muniz, on the phone. I kept lobbing messages at Jose's office in New York, and I wasn't hearing back. Mom and Kenny had rung me again and again at the office, proclaiming their innocence, and I wanted a cold assessment of reality from their lawyer instead. What were their chances?

My wife phoned me from home one morning in tears. Somebody claiming to be with the NYPD had called the house and crawled through the phone line to browbeat her. I had informed the police via Gentile that I wouldn't say a word without immunity, though I'd done nothing and knew very little. It seemed the prudent course. That pissed off the New York cops, and they took it out on Lynn. They yelled and threatened until she broke down and cried.

Later that day I was at work when the phone rang. "Jose for you," announced my secretary, and as I walked past her toward my private office I grabbed the receiver and said, "Hold on a second, Jose, all right?" I handed the receiver back without waiting for an answer and then went into my office. I wanted the call to be private.

As soon as I picked up the handset in the other room, the person on the other end was shouting. "Okay, Mr. Kent-Walker-I-don't-want-to-get-involved," blared a New York voice, with an edge of gotcha. "Who the fuck do you think I am?"

"If you're a cop or a reporter," I yelled back, recovering fast, "you're breaking some kind of law. Who the fuck *are* you?"

"I got Jose Alvarez right here next to me, Mr. Kent Walker." The cop thought he'd scored. "The one you supposedly don't know, Mr. I-don't-want-to-get-involved."

Now I had him. "Hey, jerkoff," I retorted. "What's the first name of my mother's attorney?"

He realized his mistake. Very quickly, I told him he'd actually made two mistakes in one. At that point only the police had the name of Mom and Kenny's Cuban driver. The media couldn't drag anything out of the NYPD other than that the accomplice was a Latino male. The abusive cop, forgetting that my mom's lawyer was named Jose, had inadvertently told me the name of the mystery chauffeur. As far as I knew, Alvarez hadn't been apprehended yet, and the cop who called me had nobody sitting beside him. He was bluffing. Alvarez was on the lam, and I could throw a glitch in the manhunt with one phone call.

"Suppose I tell the *New York Post* that you're looking for a guy named Jose Alvarez?" The cop started saying no, but I didn't stop to listen. "Don't call my wife again, you fucking asshole. Call my attorney if you need to speak to me."

The cop apologized. I didn't rub it in. I didn't call the *Post*. When I thought about it, calmly, for a second, I had some empathy for the guy. The NYPD was investigating a trail that had gone cold. The police commissioner asked his captains about it every day, and the officers on the case were still missing crucial pieces of evidence.

They couldn't find the body. It didn't look like they ever would. It's nearly impossible to file murder charges without a corpse or a confession. Lacking either of those, they couldn't find the other single most important proof that there'd been a murder plot. Mom and Kenny's motive for the killing was obtaining the deed to Silverman's $7.5 million mansion. The police had plenty of incriminating documents, but they didn't have the centerpiece, the forged and falsely notarized deed.

That there was such a document, I had no clue at the time. What was clear was that Mom desperately needed me to come to New York and do something for her in the first few weeks after the arrest. That's why she'd called me so much that it inspired the task force to pay a visit to my vacuum-cleaner business. Mom begged me in call after call to drop everything and fly across the country to rescue her. I thought it was the maids trial all over again. She wanted me to make her defense my career. I would have to spend the next few years the way I'd spent the late eighties, working every day at finding witnesses and documents, and calling lawyers, but this time there would be no Ken to pay the bills. She begged me to come to New York, and I didn't.

If I had, I might have gotten her off the hook for the Silverman murder. She needed someone to destroy evidence for her, though she never told me that's why she wanted me to come. She wouldn't have told me that when I arrived either. She simply would have demanded that I go to the Plaza Hotel and fetch her bag.

On the afternoon of July 5, Mom had checked a black canvas bag with a bellhop at the Plaza Hotel, a ten-minute walk from the Silverman mansion. Mom wasn't a guest at the hotel, but she looked rich, so nobody asked questions.

After the arrest, Mom badgered Muniz to send his private investigator to the Plaza to pick up the bag. For some reason the private eye, Lawrence Frost, dragged his feet for weeks. Meanwhile the cops were combing hotels and bus lockers and anyplace they could think of in search of the missing pieces of evidence.

On July 23, Frost finally went to the Plaza and signed for the satchel. Five minutes later the hotel's head of security, a former New York cop, learned of the exchange and alerted the investigators. The cops flew after Frost, lest he or Muniz have a notion to disappear the evidence. It wasn't going to be like O. J.'s notorious bag of a few years before, the one he apparently handed off to his buddy Robert Kardashian.

Muniz surrendered the bag to the NYPD, and my mother never forgave him. Muniz seemed to think he could finagle some Fifth Amendment protection for his clients because the incriminating evidence had been supplied voluntarily by the counsel for defense. His strategy didn't work, and when examined, the contents of the bag proved very incriminating indeed.

Inside the black bag police found a loaded .22-caliber Beretta, a white turban, cosmetics, syringes, and another notebook full of Mom's notes. They also found a manila folder that held the long-sought-after deed. On the outside of the folder, Mom or Kenny had scrawled the words *Final Dynasty*. I guess they'd grown tired of the word *empire*.

The clumsy pincer had finally closed. Throughout the summer and the fall, District Attorney Robert Morgenthau held Mom and Kenny on lesser charges. First he used the Utah car theft to hold them without bail and then he switched to the Florida credit-card fraud. On December 16, he finally presented an indictment. The charges ran to seventy-three pages and included eighty-four counts. New York had reached for the kitchen sink. Prosecutors weren't going to take a chance that the mother-and-son grifters could wriggle free. Some of the charges had to stick.

Mom and Kenny faced trial for possession of weapons, forged documents, and stolen property, as well as robbery, attempted robbery, burglary, grand larceny, attempted grand larceny, forgery, and eavesdropping. At the top of the list, though, was second-degree murder. Forged deed in hand, the prosecutors felt they could make their circumstantial case. Body or not, my mother and brother were looking at spending their lives in prison.

35

BAD VIBRATIONS

Mom and Kenny rang my phone off the hook from the moment of their arrest till months afterward. All of Mom's calls were the same.

My mother's phone calls were just like her letters, which were single-spaced, every margin crammed with extra sideways words, textbook manic. When she talked she filled every square centimeter of air. Her voice rose to high-pitched, girlish outrage every time she mentioned the courts or the police. "We've been framed," she'd howl, a dozen times in a fifteen-minute conversation. "This is the greatest injustice in the history of the American judicial system. They've made a terrible mistake. Your brother is innocent. He hasn't done anything." And so on. She seized on whatever in the outside world she could use in her defense. I cringed when she compared herself to Abner Louima and Amadou Diallo, the latter shot and killed by police without provocation, the former sodomized with a broomstick. Mom felt she was their equal as a martyr.

While she droned on, I remembered what life was like during the maids case, when I had no life, except shuffling papers and listening to hours of collect calls, her prayer wheel of lies and excuses and order after order that had to be completed *now*. Do this. Do that. Come to New York. Move here. Help me. Help us. Save your brother. I listened and said "Uh-huh" and never left home. I didn't come to her rescue, though Mom lobbied and begged. None of the orders she issued to me from her holding cell at Rikers Island ever got carried out. She grew angry and suspicious when I wouldn't cooperate, but she didn't give up.

During the first few months in jail, Mom and Kenny were defiant. Kenny in particular didn't understand how high the stakes were. It's hard to admit you've been caught, and when there's no corpse you have that much more reason to believe you'll see freedom again. In August 1998 Kenny wrote me a letter dripping with jaunty denial, tasteless humor, and misplaced bravado:

> Well, as you clearly know, our popularity has gone up quite a bit in the past two months. Here is a brief summation of what's been going on. We have fallen victim to a police conspiracy in which the authorities have made various charges with no evidence and no proof. We are being victimized in every way! . . . know that we will emerge victorious, and that fantastic things are coming. You all must stay strong and keep your heads held high. Do not let anyone gain power over you by seeing any conflict or weakness, sadness or so on.

He was Mom's echo, right down to her turns of phrase.

> The California [Kazdin] investigation has stopped. Nothing will happen there. Nassau [Bilal Ahmed] is nothing, and nothing in NV. The whole battle is in NY. The Utah [car] case is about to fail. . . . In about two weeks we will be facing credit card charges [Florida] only! But we have a 60 percent chance of getting a M[urder] case filed. Here is the reason why:
> —The NYPD to date have spent $15 million in investigations on charges, they have devoted 300 investigators to the case and NADA! The NYPD have to file in order to save face. . . . [They] will be unable to prove anything, and we will be able to dismiss the case on those grounds alone. We also have many other defenses. . . .
> The civil cases from this alone are worth $300 million in damages (not counting movie and book rights!). Also, if I get an acquittal, they pay $150.00 per day. HA HA. When we get out we will all go on a nice 1–2 month cruise around the globe for some stress relief!

He'd forgotten to deny killing the old lady. He was, in effect, boasting about how well he'd disposed of the body. In the sad, cold detachment of my voice when we talked on the phone, he could tell what I knew. "Kent," he finally blurted one day, "you don't think I did this, do you?" I couldn't tell him the truth, because I didn't want to take away his hope. I responded instead, as if I were a lawyer myself, "Listen to your lawyers. Do what they say."

When I wasn't talking to my mother and brother, I was waiting for calls from the police and, at least for the first few weeks, fending off the media. I had some experience.

My mother has been in the news a great deal in her sixty-six years. The Wagner scandal, the Ambassador embarrassment, the Caruso scam, the furs case. In the sixties and seventies she dealt with bad publicity by leaving town and taking us with her. Then came the maids case. Mom was the only one who left home that time, for three years of federal detention in California.

I came back to Vegas for the maids case and stayed put, and that was my initial encounter with the modern American media. I'd been a baby in Sacramento, and had only read the clippings about the other debacles. During the maids trial, I talked to reporters and stared down TV cameras for the first time.

Probably everybody in our media-saturated culture knows what you're supposed to do when a mike appears in your face and a stranger says, "Why'd your mother do it?" If you're starved for attention, you go on Barbara Walters and cry. If you want to be left alone, you say, "No comment," and hope they get bored with you.

But before the maids case I wasn't prepared for my visceral reaction to the actual fact of the mikes and cameras. I'd inherited some of the Sante Kimes temper, and reporters inspired an instinctive fight-or-flight response in me.

I ducked the camera crews in my driveway and said, "No comment," like you're supposed to. One afternoon, however, at Dominic Gentile's office in downtown Las Vegas, I got on the elevator and turned around and there was a TV camera. It was just the two of us in the little box, me and the man with the big machine on his shoulder. He was filming me as I stood there silent.

"Turn the camera off," I said. He didn't. I tried to move away from him in the elevator, and somehow in the maneuvering he bumped my chin with the black plastic end of his machine and I snapped. I slugged him, or actually I slugged the camera. He turned it off.

The maids case was like a county fair compared with the Silverman disappearance, which had happened in the media capital of the world. It had happened within blocks of the studios of the three major networks and the *New York Times*. The tabloids reveled in the rich narrative of the case, and Mom and Kenny became notorious throughout the Western Hemisphere.

Most crimes are pedestrian and tawdry. Though each perpetrator has his own rap sheet and motivation and banged-up psyche, the crime blotter is very repetitive. A wife beater kills his wife. A crack addict uses a gun to get money for his habit. Liquor-store holdups, domestic abuse, drug dealer shoot-outs, DWIs, and so on.

This one had a story line you could reduce to a movie pitch. Mother/Son Grifters Held in Millionaire's Disappearance! My mother's over-the-top persona, Kenny's shady polish, and the ridiculous rumors of mother-son incest gave the media a narrative it couldn't resist. Mom and Kenny were the smart, interesting, evil criminals with the elaborate, diabolical plan who exist in fiction and rarely in real life.

The media landed on my life with elephant feet. I was under siege as soon as I returned to my office after my family's excursion to Newport Beach. The deluge started at 10 A.M. on July 8, 1998. I kept a list in a drawer of the media outlets that called or dropped by our little one-story L-shaped office building on Decatur. It was a tabloid clusterfuck. Every network, newspaper, local news station, and wire service sent troops. *Dateline* and *20/20* competed to see who could get a Kimes segment on-air first. *Dateline* did two shows about Mom and Kenny.

I developed a strategy for dealing with reporters. My unusual training in the media arts as the son of Sante, and as a de facto paralegal in the maids case, meant that I had a better idea of how to deal with reporters than my staff did. They might find it exciting that someone wanted to talk to them, and forget to stop at "No comment." I knew better.

So I hid from the camera crews in a back room, so there'd be no pictures, and I handled the calls myself. I told my secretary not to bother asking who was on the line and to transfer all comers back to me. I would get the name and affiliation of the reporter, write down the info on my roster, and then say, "No comment." If they came to the office door, I'd meet them, say, "No, thanks," and send them away. The rebuffed reporters could tell their bosses that they'd reached me and I refused to talk. I felt like I was taking my name off a mailing list.

That wasn't good enough for some of the reporters. I noticed that the folks from the high-end outlets were more professional and polite about taking no for an answer, but they were also slicker. One day a producer from ABC's *20/20* flew in from New York and dropped by the office. He came to the back door, where vacuums are brought for repairs, and started chatting with my service manager, Jerry. Before I knew what had happened, he was inside the building, a few yards from the room where I was hiding, having an in-depth discussion with Jerry about the merits of various vacuum-cleaner models. Jerry gave him a twenty-minute pitch, and along the way scattered a few details about me. I came out of my hiding place and pulled my friend aside. "Jerry," I said, deadpan, "he didn't come here from New York to buy a vacuum cleaner." I chased the producer away.

The most obnoxious pests were from the tabloids. There was some British weasel who wouldn't go away, and there was some guy who said he was from the *New York Post,* a rag I'd never heard of before July 8. The *Post,* with its hyperventilating headlines, loved my mother and brother.

The supposed *Post* guy got in the building somehow and refused to leave. He yammered at me for several minutes, trying not to understand "No comment." I found myself, at six-foot-three and two hundred plus pounds, backed up against a wall by a little man with a pen and a briefcase. He was almost standing on my toes. I was flashing back to the camera that hit me in Vegas, afraid I'd have that uncontrollable impulse again and do something lawsuit-worthy to him. I grabbed his briefcase, ran to the door, and threw it across the parking lot. It almost reached Decatur. He left. But he still wrote a half-page story about me, woven out of hot air and a few details probably cadged from some sucker in my office.

I had to be circumspect, because my feelings were so mixed and because I thought Mom and Kenny might get away with it. Part of me thought the only barrier to Kenny's cruise idea

would be the price of the tickets. My mother had gotten away
with so much for so long that I thought she and Kenny might
really walk free. I thought they might get bail and then skip, or
that they'd beat the charges altogether, because who'd ever
heard of a murder trial without a body? For every one of Mom's
arrests, she'd committed a hundred crimes that went unre-
ported; for every conviction, there were many more arrests, and
the convictions rarely led to many consequences. Mom was
relentless. She would prevail. She would flip New York City
upside down and shake out its pockets.

And if she and Kenny got out and didn't have any money,
they'd come to my doorstep. I kept silent out of fear, and cold-
blooded calculation. Self-preservation. I was screwed anyway.
Tell the media, "They're guilty," and I'd be a traitor, one at risk
of reprisal from my mother or her proxies. She has always had,
and will always have, proxies. She has them right now, making
phone calls on her behalf.

I didn't want to hurt my mother and brother, and I didn't
want to help them. I didn't want to be my brother's keeper, but
I didn't relish being his executioner either.

If I told the media, "They're innocent," I'd be a liar. I
wouldn't say the words, which perplexed my friends. I had
associates who were offering me support because they thought
Mom was guilty and I was in on it with her. There were many
more, however, who assumed that the larger-than-life, efferves-
cent, ostentatiously wealthy woman they'd met at my parties or
in the office couldn't possibly be guilty of violence. She didn't
need the money. Kenny was a mere boy, behind the pumped-
up muscles a prissy boy to boot.

So my friends would say, "Raw deal, huh?" and I wouldn't
answer right. I'd dodge the question. Or they'd dance around
another question that perplexed them: Why wasn't I in New
York? Wasn't I furious? Didn't I want to fight for them? Visit
them, at least? I stayed in Vegas, and I never said, "They didn't
do it." But I also never said, "Oh yes, they did." I did what I
thought was right and prudent, and it strained my relationship
with a few friends.

Some people began to avoid me altogether. I was the
spawn of a killer, raised by a murdering con artist and brother
to another, and how could I be any different? My friendly
exterior, my generosity, which were probably an overcompen-
sation because of my mother, became evidence against me. I

was a glad-handing grifter too, a phony, a murderer. My mother's son.

I've described how I reestablished contact with Evelyn, the woman in Palm Springs who'd been my surrogate mother when I was between six and twelve. After Ken's death, while Mom's behavior grew stranger and more destructive, I'd been seized by nostalgia for the simple childhood days I'd spent apart from her, playing Cowboys and Indians and riding horses with Evelyn. Maybe I idealized those interludes in my memory, but the time I'd spent with her was free of stress and buried agendas and was the closest thing to a normal childhood I'd known. If not for her, I thought, I might have been Kenny.

We'd agreed to keep in touch, and we had. Some time after my mother's arrest, though, when I called Evelyn's house, her husband answered the phone. He was brusque. He said, "Why do you keep calling here?" Evelyn saw me as the quiet little boy she'd loved and mothered, but her husband had decided that as Sante's son I was tainted. He laid down the law. Soon I got a letter from Evelyn. "I'm so sorry it turned out this way," she wrote. "I had hoped that by the time this all was finished, we could be like family, but it is not to be. . . . You will be in my thoughts always." Her husband had ordered her to cut off contact. I haven't heard from her since.

You can't always control what people think of you. Soon enough I discovered that people in the office were gossiping about the case. A direct sales business is a high-pressure, high-turnover proposition. You hire people in droves, they quit in droves. You have to field-test a lot of candidates to find out who can sell. There are always new faces in the halls, and those who arrived in the months right before or after Mom and Kenny's arrest hadn't really had a chance to get close to me. I was merely their new boss, and they were hearing things about some case in New York involving my family.

With each retelling and fresh wave of employees, the stories in the office got stranger. I heard a rumor that my mother and I had killed my stepfather for his life insurance and had used the settlement to open my distributorship. It was a poisonous game of Telephone.

Day by day I withdrew from my business. Direct sales is all about recruitment and motivation. Find the sales force, train the sales force, charge them up, send them out. They call from the field with questions and needing pep talks, and as the big chief

you motivate them. They endure rejection after rejection
between each sale. It takes emotional armor to handle so much
negativity. My job was to supply the armor.

Instead of doing that, each morning after our sales meeting
I retreated into my office and scoured the internet for news
about Mom and Kenny. I raced across town several times a
week to a bookstore that carried out-of-town papers, to see
what the New York media was saying. I ended each day
depressed, exhausted, and resentful, exactly the way I had back
in the days of the maids case.

I became a better person because of it. Before, I dismissed as
wimps those who wallowed in their unhappy pasts and blamed
their parents or anybody but themselves for their problems. I
thought that as a hard-boiled stoic I would carry the secrets of
my own upbringing to my grave. Now, as I read about my family or saw our private lives on TV, I felt like I'd been dumped
naked on a street corner for the whole world to see. I wondered
what new shameful revelations about the fires, the furs, the
maids, the Ambassador et al., would hit the media, and what
people would think of me. I obsessed over things I used to
ignore or deny. At thirty-six I finally stopped judging other
people as weaklings and let myself be weak and vulnerable too.

But my business took a nosedive. I couldn't hire new people or keep the ones I had. Sales dropped fast. The phones went
quiet. A year into the ordeal, I had to sell my sailboat, which
had been my refuge. I could go out to Lake Mead and sit and
read a book if I wanted, or sail away from the shore. It had to
go, because I needed the money.

And when I got home from a dismal, defeated day at work,
things were worse. As a pilot, I'd experienced firsthand one of a
helicopter's scariest quirks. A tremor in any part of the craft can
be picked up by the whirring blades and amplified, and once
the rotor has started shaking the chopper can literally beat itself
to death. Now all the bad vibrations from New York had
crossed the country and entered my home, and my family had
begun to shake very hard.

Mom had spoiled my children for years. She had treated
Kristina like a princess. Though those trips to the Bahamas and
elsewhere had ulterior motives, and Kristina had been trauma-
tized by the stun-gun ordeal at the airport, she adored my
mother. Babish was her hero. Now Babish was in prison, and
the kids at school giggled about it. Kristina, never a good stu-

dent, began to have more serious problems in the classroom. She sank into a depression.

My younger daughter, Brandy, made me laugh once when Mom called the house. "Babish," asked Brandy, as soon as she had the receiver in her hands, "are you still in jail?" We laughed, but I wondered if Brandy was troubled. On the way to a birthday party, in a van full of other kids, she blurted, "My uncle Kenny's in jail." It was like me in 1969 telling Evelyn, "My mother burns houses." It was everything I'd tried to keep away from my kids.

My wife, meanwhile, hounded and hated by Sante, couldn't make up her mind how to feel about her mother-in-law's predicament. Sometimes Lynn doubted Mom's guilt, and even when she didn't, she might lapse into rooting for Mom's escape. Thinking about Kenny made her cry. And she was angry with me, first because I tried to convince her they were guilty, which she didn't want to accept, and second because my evidence for their guilt was everything I'd never told her. She'd been aware of half of what Mom had done, but I'd concealed the rest. Now I told her the whole truth, and she hated me for it. I had thought I was protecting her. Secrecy had been my best friend. Whenever I'd told the truth before, people had thought I was lying, so I'd learned to keep my mouth shut.

My life, in short, fell apart. So I did what my mother always used to do when she got in trouble. I moved.

Lynn and I had talked about relocating to San Diego for years. Though business in Las Vegas had been good, Lynn had wanted to return to her hometown because her family was there and my mother wasn't, and because it was a better place to raise kids. We'd abandoned the plan out of resignation. In the early nineties, we'd mentioned to Mom and Ken that we were considering a move, and within days they'd rented an apartment in La Jolla in anticipation. There was no such thing as moving away from them. They'd follow us, because they were obsessed with me. They couldn't bear the thought that the only audience for their spats might strike his tent and steal away.

I had been trapped in Vegas. Now there was nothing holding me back except the hope, which was really more of a fear, that Mom might get out. So Lynn and the kids and I fled Vegas, leaving the glitz and the heat and twenty years of bad memories behind.

I'm still in San Diego today. I'm close to the ocean again, the way I was in Hawaii, when I lived with John and his father and was the president of the student body. It was by the ocean in Hawaii and San Diego that I met and married my wife. If I ever have any money again, I'll buy a new sailboat.

36

POISON PEN

Jury selection in my mother and brother's trial for second-degree murder and eighty-three other counts started in the Manhattan Criminal Courts Building on January 27, 2000. My mother didn't have her first official courtroom outburst till April 28.

"Your Honor!" she yelled at Judge Rena Uviller. "How can we have some fairness?"

Mom had tried to make her first courtroom speech at the arraignment fifteen months before, in January 1999. "Your Honor," she said, "I plead not guilty, and I pray to be treated equally as any other —" The judge, Justice Herbert Altman, cut her off. "That will be enough!"

My mother and brother stayed defiant throughout their long pretrial incarceration. Professional wrestlers have a term called *kayfabe*, which means being in character, whether hero or heel. Mom and Kenny never, ever broke kayfabe. They maintained a public stance of outraged innocence from the moment of their arrest.

That was nothing more than what the tabloid press in New York expected. Con artists are supposed to stay in character. But what added fever to the media's love affair with my mother and brother was that Mom and Kenny seemed to be in love with each other. They held hands and whispered at the arraignment. A story circulated that witnesses had spied Mom and Kenny sleeping in the same motel bed during their final months of freedom in 1998. The media began to whisper, and then gossip aloud, about the possibility of incest.

What my mother has always said to me, when she's in jail and can't touch me physically, is "I'm holding your hand." To her, holding hands means maternal love; on another level, it means maternal control. Anyone unfamiliar with the quirks of our family might not understand that, or know that Kenny had shared a bed with his father till he was fourteen. I never believed the incest rumors about my mother and brother. They might've shared beds in hotels and at Irene's—an emotionally unhealthy habit, I grant you—but they didn't have sex. The truth was deeply neurotic, but PG rated.

Had my mom wanted to duck the press, she couldn't have. Her lawyers ran toward the cameras. She'd hired Jose Muniz and then a Manhattan showboat named Mel Sachs, with strangely smooth skin and a host of annoying affectations, from his bow ties to his card tricks. Sachs agreed to participate in on-line interviews about the case. He and his private investigator, ex-NYPD cop Les Levine, traveled to the Caymans and Las Vegas on what became a media junket. Sachs had promised exclusives to a gaggle of competing outlets, and angry reporters and producers from Fox and *20/20* tripped over one another at the Grand Cayman airport's baggage carousel.

As proof that he cared more about soaking up the limelight than protecting his client, Sachs and his co-counsel, Matthew Weissman, allowed *60 Minutes* to interview Mom and Kenny on March 11, 1999. Against a backdrop of bookshelves full of law books, dressed sensibly and neatly, instead of in white lace and wigs, Mom looked like a partner in a law firm. "All we are praying for is a trial, because we are innocent," Mom told reporter Steve Kroft. "We don't know where [Irene Silverman] is. Wherever she is, I pray to God she's all right." Even *I* gasped at the bit about praying for Irene.

Mom and Kenny spieled on, holding hands, expressing their distaste for the term *grifter,* with Kenny sniffing, "It's so derogatory," and Mom professing, "I don't even know where the word comes from." Kroft let the hot air flow for half an hour before confronting Kenny. He flourished Kenny's college records. "I see from your transcripts that you got an A in acting." Matthew Weissman yelled, "Cut!" and the interview had ended.

But Mom and her lawyers continued to try the case in the media. They used the press to test their red herrings. Like O. J. Simpson and his legal team, Mom suggested that there were shady figures in Irene Silverman's life who might have wanted her dead. She laid out her theory for Juan Gonzalez of the *Daily News* in a jailhouse tête-à-tête.

No one ever said Mom wasn't brazen. She told Gonzalez that on July 3, 1998, two days before Silverman disappeared, Sante and her "friend" Irene had been sipping champagne together in the old woman's apartment. Mom had done her friend's hair, and Irene had told Mom how glad she was to be getting rid of her $7.5 million mansion for less than four hundred thousand dollars.

What Mom said next might have brought a libel charge, had the person libeled still been breathing. It made me shudder. She described the Silverman beaux arts mansion as a whorehouse. "At night," she assured Gonzalez, "you would see all kinds of men going in there."

The evening of the Fourth, Mom claimed, she and Kenny had declined an invitation to a small party on the second floor. When the party started, they heard an argument upstairs. "There were three or four men, Latin types. You could hear it through the walls." According to Mom, Irene was mad because her maid wasn't around to serve drinks. The maid had supposedly gone out for a few hours to pick up a friend at the airport. The lie was pure Sante. Mom would have been livid if *her* maid wasn't toting a drinks tray around a cocktail party. That's why when *her* maids slipped out for a few hours, they never came back.

Mom kept up her media blitz. She had her lawyers fax a statement to the newsrooms of the New York dailies. "I am an American mother fighting for justice for my innocent young son. We have been framed and wrongly indicted when no one knows where the missing Irene Silverman is and there is no evidence against us." It was a print version of what she said to me every time she called. Her brain had turned into a tape loop.

Mom and Kenny kept blustering while their situation got worse and worse. From my office, combing the web sites of the New York newspapers, and comparing what I read with what my mother told me in her telephone monologues, I could see the future dimming.

First the New York judge ruled that the famous black bag from the Plaza Hotel, the one Muniz had handed to the cops, would be allowed into evidence. It held the most damning evidence against my mother and brother—the fake deed. Then, in

August 1999, L.A. prosecutors filed murder charges against Mom and Kenny for the death of David Kazdin. Eight months after the March 1998 murder, Kenny's alleged accomplice, Sean Little, had ratted him out. The criminal complaint fingered Kenny as the gunman, and said he'd been "lying in wait" for Kazdin. It was the language of a premeditated, first-degree murder charge, and prosecutors reserved the right to ask for Mom's and Kenny's lives. "I'm thrilled," Dave's daughter Linda told the press. "Believe me, I'd like to see them both go down for the death penalty."

I had been a walking, talking bundle of ambivalence for a full year by then. I had no doubt that my mother and brother were guilty, only questions about relative guilt—how much was Kenny's idea and how much Mom's? I also couldn't resolve my feelings about their upcoming murder trials. I didn't want them to die, but did I want them to walk free? After thirty-plus years of watching my mother slip the noose time and again, I still couldn't convince myself that she might be finished. In the nineties alone, she'd been hit with more than a million dollars in civil judgments and hadn't paid a cent. She was practically a Teflon Con.

With the Kazdin charge I began to come around. If she beat the rap in New York they'd just put her on Con Air to California, and she'd have to spend another year or two spinning hysterical lies and fighting for her life. I began to wonder, in guilty privacy, about the value of Kenny's life versus that of my mother. Sometimes I thought my little brother should try to buy himself a few years of freedom at the end of his days by snitching on Mom and cutting a deal.

But from the instant of his arrest, when Kenny had pissed his black jeans, he'd been looking to my mother for guidance. He'd yelled to her through the walls of the interrogation room in Manhattan that first night, "Mom, what should I do?" Later Mom had tried to pass him a note on toilet paper that said "Don't tell all" and ordered him to contact various people.

Now he and Mom were standing trial together, and they would walk free or go down together. At their arraignment, even the judge had asked Kenny whether it might not be a good idea to retain his own counsel. Eventually Mel Sachs became Kenny's lawyer, and Mom hired a well-known civil rights attorney named Michael Hardy, but Mom and Kenny still wouldn't be divided. They wouldn't do what most defendants do, which is ask that their trials be severed and then snitch on their accomplice.

Mom and Kenny kept their game faces right up through the opening statements of their trial on Valentine's Day, 2000. Mom, in her sensible going-on-trial-for-murder business suits, took notes throughout. It was a compulsion. She continued scribbling in her latest notebook even while lead prosecutor Connie Fernandez was telling the jurors that the evidence for the murder was spelled out in fourteen other notebooks.

Kenny, on the other hand, began to get it right away. Color drained from his face as he listened to Fernandez outline the evidence to be presented. Brick by brick, the DA's team built a circumstantial case that only an O. J. juror could ignore. And Mom and Kenny didn't have half a city cheering their white Bronco toward the finish line. Instead, they had the entire population of the nation's biggest city rooting for their conviction.

Over fifteen weeks of testimony, the DA presented 130 witnesses and 430 exhibits. Sachs and Hardy could counter with only a single defense witness, an expert who disputed that Silverman's signature on the phony deed was forged. It wasn't like Mom's courtroom dramas of years past, where she could troll her address book and the bars of Washington for a supporting cast. In New York all her lawyers could do was try to raise doubts about the credibility of the state's battalion of witnesses.

By the end of March, halfway through the grueling trial, cracks appeared in the defense. The prosecution called a witness who testified that Kenny had opened a stock account in Bermuda. On cross-examination, Sachs inadvertently opened the door wider for questions about the criminal origin of the funds. It was apparently the proceeds of the bogus Kazdin mortgage.

Mom's enraged lawyer, Michael Hardy, responded by threatening to call Kenny as a hostile witness so he could protect his client. Both Hardy and Sachs then filed severance motions, trying to split the trial in half. It was too late. Judge Uviller denied both motions.

My mother lasted another four weeks before the strain got to her. She made her "fairness" remark to Judge Uviller in front of the jury. She began champing at the bit to commit legal suicide. She made it known that she desperately wanted to testify on her own behalf. The prosecution prepared to tear the Dragon Lady to pieces.

On May 5, Judge Uviller ruled that if Mom took the stand, the prosecution couldn't ask her about the Kazdin or Ahmed murders. It could, however, bring up her 1986 conviction for keeping slaves. The DA's office indicated that it would also like to question her about the Shoot-out in Washoe Valley, the ambush in which Mom and Clyde fired guns at my father. Thirty years later, Ed Walker was having his revenge.

If the jury, three quarters nonwhite, heard about the slavery case, they'd hate Mom. They wouldn't be impressed by her gunplay either. Still, over the advice of Muniz and Hardy, Mom was determined to testify. Her whole life she'd "fixed" things by talking, like the time she'd almost talked me into juvenile hall over those surfboards in Newport Beach. Kenny could see that Mom was delusional, and he broke down in tears at the defense table. Finally his begging prevailed, and she agreed not to testify. First, though, she had to have her Joan of Arc moment.

After the lunch recess, Judge Uviller had informed Mom that she had to make her decision about whether to testify. Mom wanted permission to talk to the media and for TV cameras to enter the courtroom. The judge said no. When Mom countered by accusing her of giving the prosecution unfair access to the press, the judge had had enough. "Be seated," she ordered.

"No, I'm not going—you don't want me to talk," Mom yelped. "More than anything in the world, I wanted to take that stand. I am this boy's mother, and we are innocent, and I wanted to take that stand."

"You *are* free to take the stand," observed Judge Uviller.

"I'm afraid of you," Mom told the judge. "I'm afraid of this corrupt system, I'm afraid of the gossip, the lies, that have been fed about my son and me. I'm afraid of this! That everybody in New York believes this!"

Mom then wheeled around to the courtroom crowd and flashed the front page of the New York *Daily News* from six weeks earlier. It read "POLL: COPS OUT OF CONTROL—NEED FEDERAL MONITORS." She shouted to the reporters and spectators. "This is a corrupt system! We're innocent! For God's sake, help us!" Mom had worked herself into outrage mode, red-faced and sobbing. A bailiff forced her to turn back around and face the judge.

New York didn't rally to her defense. The *Daily News* headline the next day cackled: "GRIFTER TURNS ON WATERWORKS." On May 15 Mom tried again. Against court order, she slipped a note to a reporter in which she claimed that she'd purchased Silverman's mansion legally and that Silverman's employees were to blame for the old lady's disappearance. The judge warned Mom that she'd be handcuffed if the stunt were repeated.

No one was buying. By the time Mom passed the note, the jury was already in its second day of deliberations. They came back with a verdict on the fourth day, May 18. My little brother rapped the defense table with his knuckles, knocking on wood, as the forewoman stood up to read.

It took her twenty minutes to pronounce 118 guilty verdicts. Mom and Kenny had been convicted on every count. Halfway through, Kenny leaned over to Mom and mouthed, "It'll be okay." When it was over, he told her, "Stay strong." According to the tabloids, she responded, "Is this the end of everything for us?" The line sounds like invented melodrama, or a clip from the gangster flick *Little Caesar* ("Is this the end of Rico?"). Knowing that melodrama is Mom's bread and butter, though, I don't doubt she said it.

To my mind, two things clinched the case. First, my mother's own words convicted her, just as they had in the maids case fourteen years earlier. Writing everything down was stupid, and a better crook would have learned her lesson the first time. But Mom didn't, or couldn't, learn lessons. She was in the grip of something bigger and more irrational than mere crime. She will always have to write it down.

I have one of Mom's famous notebooks at my house in San Diego. I found it when I threw her out of my Vegas place. Most of it dates from 1996, and consists of instructions for Billy Lovekamp re the Santa Maria property. There are the usual emphatic orders about secrecy and control. She tells him to tape-record every conversation with Santa Maria city officials. There are also entries about longevity and names of Cuban officials, which seems to indicate that when she and Kenny were schmoozing Arab bankers on that tape I found, they were planning to launch a longevity business in Havana. The most interesting entry, however, sits nearly alone on a white page near

the end. It's the phone number for the direct line to the Oval
Office in the White House. If she couldn't reach the president
there, she also had a number for Air Force One scribbled in yet
another notebook confiscated from the RV in Florida. Did
Princess Sante have an appointment with Bill Clinton? He
would have been the third president she met.

Two years later Mom's Irene Silverman notebooks, all fourteen of them, were a step-by-step manual for the commission of
the murder. They even included a statement of purpose:
"Goal=Get house and not get screwed." Some of the instructions were repeated in book after book, like the daily reminders
to get Irene's Social Security number and "copy her sig[nature]."
Jurors couldn't ignore notes like "easy marks/elderly with
money" or "give no one information/none . . . if P come—
nothing." "P" meant police.

There were scripts for Kenny to use with Irene's employees,
and there were homicidal shopping lists. Mom would write
down the groceries she needed, like onions, soup, and
Cremora, right next to items needed to complete her plan, like
garbage bags, Band-Aids, and a shower curtain, and what
she should steal from Irene when she was dead ("Take *satin*
pillowcase"). For June 27, Mom's to-do list read "get layout/
SS/garbage bags/notary/carbon/get Lincoln/park closely."
Two days before Silverman's disappearance, Mom wrote,
"pack all in Lincoln/IS . . . put shower curtain on couch."
Police looked for Irene's body in the Meadowlands because a
page of the notebooks said "get layout—what streets to New
Jersey?"

The jurors were up front about the impact of Mom's writing. "I put the pieces together with the notebooks," said one.
"There was so much information." A second agreed: "There
was other evidence, but the notebooks played a great part."

I think, however, that the other clincher was Irene Silverman. The jury liked her, and they liked her because of her
employees. *My* mother had told her maids that she was going
to be their "Mama," and then she'd treated them like slaves. In
New York, a multicultural parade of workers, including Latina
maids, took the stand to say that Irene Silverman really *had*
treated them like family. Her Ethiopian maintenance man cried
as he talked about how he'd come to work for her. He'd made a
pact with Silverman: "If you'll be like a mother to me, I'll be like
a son to you."

An hour after the verdicts, Mom had gathered herself, just as she'd rallied after Ken's death. She told a TV reporter that the verdicts were "a temporary setback," and she again appealed to the public. "I want to cry out for help to anyone in the country who believes in justice to help us."

By the date of her sentencing, Mom was ready for her close-up. On June 27, after her attorney had begged the judge to show mercy on the grounds that Mom wasn't as bad as, say, Hitler, Mussolini, or Jack the Ripper, Mom gave a speech. Or rather, she ranted, her face turning red with righteous indignation as she blamed every living thing on earth for her fate except herself. She donned the cloak of martyrdom like a veteran.

"It's the first time that a mother and a son have been convicted with no crime, no witnesses, and no DNA," said Mom. "All of our precious civil and constitutional rights were trampled. . . . Much like the witch-hunts of old Salem, the police planted and planted and planted evidence to fool the jury. No one has been told the truth in this case."

But there weren't any marks in the audience. People tittered at Mom's grande dame flourishes and her appeals for justice. As she rambled on, the laughter grew more bitter. Some in the packed courtroom gasped when she rehashed her claim of being Irene Silverman's friend. When she said there was no crime, because "no one knows where that woman is!" Silverman's building superintendent had had enough. "*You* know!" yelled Ramon Casales, who'd worked for the old woman for two decades.

Exasperated, Judge Uviller suggested that Mom get to the point. Mom kept talking. Her own lawyer urged her to shut up, but the words continued to flow. "The only murderers in this case are the prosecutors, for murdering the Constitution. . . . Get the transcripts. Read the Constitution."

Mom jabbed her finger at the DA's table. "You know. You know. They planted evidence. They made many allegations. But there was no evidence. . . . My attorney let me down. I begged him to let me take the stand. I was stopped from taking the stand in my own defense."

Finally my little brother couldn't take it anymore. He interrupted. "Mom, don't talk!"

Mom continued. "They seem to feel I should not say too much."

"Mom! Mom!" wailed Kenny. "Stop!"

She didn't. Kenny clapped his hands over his ears as Mom told Judge Uviller, "The attorney advises me I do not want to say anything that will upset Your Honor. . . . The real criminals are still out there. They know where [Silverman] is."

And then, at the umpteenth repetition of this lie, the judge ended the show. "Your performance," she barked, "I mean your statement, is over." The last two words of the judge's order were drowned out by hooting and cheering. Laughter forced the bailiffs to demand, "Quiet!"

It was Kenny's turn to speak. His lawyer took a different tack. Sachs said that Kenny felt remorse, unlike his mother, and was a victim of manipulation. It was a spin that might have helped Kenny had Sachs used it during the trial, instead of after. Kenny, however, would never have permitted it.

When Kenny spoke, all pretense of remorse was forgotten. His speech was shorter and saner than Mom's, but it didn't help him. A dozen of the detectives who'd investigated the case for more than a year were seated in the jury box so they could watch as sentence was passed. Kenny explained how Mom feared cops, and then addressed the policemen in the jury box. "No offense," he said, "but you're spooky." He talked about how he was going to present only the facts and then reprised Mom's protests of innocence, lashing out at the same imaginary enemies.

The judge wasn't impressed. Four hours into the marathon, Judge Uviller pronounced sentence. She told my mother and brother what she thought of them. "Sante Kimes is surely the most degenerate defendant who has ever appeared in this courtroom." She called Mom a sociopath of "unremitting malevolence."

Kenny had inspired some pity in her, at first. But his behavior during the trial had convinced her that Mom had transformed this "vacuous dupe" into "a remorseless predator."

Judge Uviller hit my mother and brother with the maximum sentences possible. She gave Mom 120 years, to be served consecutively. She gave Kenny still more time, 125 years. They wouldn't even be eligible for parole till the twenty-second century. As court officers led Mom and Kenny back to their holding cells, one of the cops in the jury box had the last word. "You have plenty of time," yelled Detective Anthony Vasquez, "to tell us where Irene Silverman is."

During the twenty-three months between arrest and sentencing, I'd done everything in my power not to darken a New York courtroom. Despite Mom's pleas, I hadn't rescued her. I didn't want to, and I couldn't have. I didn't rush to her side in an army uniform. I stayed at home.

The only time I thought about moving a muscle was the day of their sentencing. My mother's life was over, and I knew it. I thought, however, that I might be able to make a strong case for my brother. I didn't buy the idea that he was Mom's mindless puppet; he was a grown man, fully conscious of his actions. But then I'd remember myself at twenty-three, and how easily Mom had run my life. Kenny was twenty-three when he made Irene Silverman vanish, and at that age Mom had reached out from a Nevada jail cell and ended my army career. I don't know what would have happened after that if I hadn't had other forces pulling me in a different direction—my wife and family. As a child, I'd had Evelyn to show me what the real world was like. Kenny's childhood world ended at the high wall around the house.

I wanted to ask for mercy, but I didn't. The thought of a courtroom stuffed with reporters and the angry friends of Irene Silverman sobered me. I stayed put and read about the shocking sentences on-line.

The only time I raised my head out of my foxhole, I did it for selfish reasons. Out of the dozens of demands for TV interviews, I accepted two. I let a reporter from the syndicated newsmagazine *Extra* ask me leading questions for two hours. I also flew to New York to appear on *Good Morning America*, checking into my hotel late the night before the broadcast. The next morning, I chatted with Diane Sawyer on-air for a few minutes, then fled to the airport after less than twelve hours in the city where my family's name was mud.

I did *Extra* for the money, because Mom and Kenny's case had devastated my business; I did *Good Morning America* for the credibility. Both interviews were a way of establishing, for the benefit of the authorities, that I wasn't involved in any crimes. They were also a message to Mom and Kenny. You have to read between the lines of what I said on TV. The reporters asked me if Mom was capable of murder, and I answered, "She's capable of anything. . . . She's crazy like a fox." I knew it would get back to Mom and Kenny, and I knew they would understand that I considered them guilty.

With the sentence imposed and Mom locked up for good, my wife finally began to feel safe. She stopped assuming that her phone was bugged. She began keeping a diary for the first time in fifteen years, because for the first time there was little danger someone else would read it. When we saw a report in the New York papers that Mom, riding back to Rikers Island after the sentencing, had tried to enlist another inmate in an escape plan, part of Lynn rooted for Mom to get away, but most of her was petrified.

After the sentencing, Mom kept lobbing phone calls and letters at me in the hope that I'd believe her or help her. She exploited the guilt I felt about my little brother. Sometimes she'd write to my wife instead and talk about Kenny because Lynn and my brother were once so close, but I was the real target.

Any mental health professional could look at those letters and see that they're the product of a disturbed personality. You don't need to read English to recognize the signs. She ended half her sentences with exclamation points, capitalized whole paragraphs, and filled the margins with frantic sideways handwriting. Little white space was left. But she never strayed from her message. She begged for clothes, toiletries, and a hot pot, and professed innocence. She always hammered away at our pity for Kenny, in hopes that we would crack.

To protect Lynn and the kids, I changed my home phone number in San Diego. I refused to give the new one to my mother. I didn't want her calling and upsetting my children or trying to manipulate members of my family. Kenny got through in the summer of 2000 and started working on Kristina, and I was livid. Mom and Kenny didn't just want love and support. They had errands they wanted us to run.

When my mother wanted to talk to me, she had to call my office. Like all inmates, she called collect, and I accepted most of the time. She always knew which buttons to push, like my concern for Kenny, but safe in San Diego I let her push them. I noted, with detachment, that she retained her uncanny skill for wrapping a grain of truth in a pound of bullshit. I didn't do what she asked.

She called three times in July 2000, a month after the sentencing. She'd been remanded to the women's prison in Bedford Hills, New York. She wanted to know if Kenny had been transferred to his final destination yet, since she'd lost track of him. I tape-recorded the phone calls. They were all essentially the same call, and I've cut and pasted them together below.

As you read the script that follows, imagine my voice as a low monotone, deepened further still by my bad habit of smoking Benson & Hedges menthol 100s. Insert the slightest overtone of weary skepticism where appropriate, but don't let it verge into anger, no matter how ridiculous the conversation becomes.

For my mother, set the volume on high and the pitch higher. Assume that there's an exclamation point at the end of each sentence, even where none is indicated. Realize that the conversations in their unedited form are circular, with Mom returning to the same themes again and again in every possible order—her upcoming appearance on the Larry King show, innocence, Kenny, Larry King, the Creeps, innocence, crooked cops, the Creeps, Kenny, Larry King, and crooked lawyers. Multiply the length by ten. If you don't find the results exhausting and relentless, you're not imagining hard enough.

"Hello?"

"Hi, Mom."

"Honey, have you heard from him?"

"No, I haven't. He hasn't called here yet."

"Oh, my goodness."

"He might still be in processing. Don't let it alarm you too much."

"I'm really worried, Kent. It's been too long. I hope he's all right."

"I'm sure he's okay." My role hadn't changed in fifteen years—I was supposed to reassure her.

"I hope so, honey," said Mom. "I pray so. Oh, honey, this is hell. Anything could happen to him. *Know that.* You don't have the slightest idea."

"What do you mean by that?"

"I mean anything could happen to that boy. I don't have good feelings about it!"

"He's got to be okay, Mom. If there was anything wrong, somebody would've contacted me by now. How are *you* doing?"

"I'm a little shook, because it's been a big change, but I'm okay. It's not too bad. I'm getting ready to work on the appeal.

Did you see the Larry King show? They interviewed us at Rikers."

"Wow, that's incredible. I hope that will help you guys." The show hadn't aired yet.

"I liked him very much. He wants to help us. He's ordering the transcripts of the trial. It's so unfair what they did, but at least now we can get our hands into something. Before it was just gossip and allegations. Now the trial transcript proves that every constitutional right was violated, you know—our sellout attorney, the judge wouldn't let me take the stand, all these horrible things—it's proof. Now we have something we can work with! Before we were just fighting gossip and lies. Larry King is doing six shows on this!"

"Six shows on *this*?"

"Yes! They're calling it the worst injustice in U.S. history—"

"Who is, Mom?"

"In Britain. This magazine. We didn't have a prayer. You can't even imagine what they did. It was political! We were just railroaded! We are totally innocent! And the transcripts will prove it! Anyway, it's sure good to hear your voice. It's very important to be supportive and to write Kenny, bless his heart, because believe me, honey, he's going through hell."

"I can't even imagine what you guys are going through. It must be incredible."

"*And he's innocent!* Larry King is going to read the court transcripts. They don't have any proof. They manufactured it. They had us for two years on that little car thing. I didn't even write the check, [my bookkeeper] wrote the check. They know they made a mistake. They manufactured a crime and they didn't have any evidence! It's the first time in U.S. history that people have been convicted of a crime when there is no crime. It's kind of earthshaking. It's a precedent-setting case. We have to fight really hard. Now we have something in our hands. Before, they were getting away with it. Even though we lost in the lower trial, the unfairness now is in black and white. That's how you win. We have to get to a higher court. See what I mean?"

"Have they said anything about the Kazdin case in Los Angeles?"

"No, I don't know what's going to happen. You know, Kenny needs your help. You're all he's got, honey. I've lived my life, honey, but he's just a kid. He hasn't done anything! He hasn't done one thing! That's the horror. They made a mistake! It got out of hand. The New York police are the ones that caused all of that. And in L.A.—we haven't done anything! David Kazdin was my best friend! Kenny didn't even know him! He never met him in his life! You have no idea of the horror we're going through, but we've got to fight hard, and it sure helps to hear your voice."

"Well, just hang in there, Mom. Do the best you can." I didn't ask her why her son had never met her best friend.

"They want to kill Kenny!" she continued. "And he hasn't done anything! I've lived my life, honey, if I die tomorrow. I know that we're innocent. We didn't do any of these things. We've been framed by one of the most ruthless . . . the feds just took over the entire New York police system for corruption. It's just like L.A. You know how in L.A., they have a scandal?"

"Right." In the business of sales, we call that qualifying a customer. Mom had just gotten me to agree with her. Never mind that the feds had not taken over the NYPD.

"Well, here it's worse," insisted Mom. "They just do whatever they want to do. We never had a chance. They held us for two years, they lied to the press, they framed us, they planted stuff. We didn't have anything on us that they said had on us. There were four days of mystery where nothing was even vouchered. It's all in the trial transcript. Just listen to Larry King. They said Kenny did really well. I hope you'll tape it."

"I promise I will." I did plan to tape it.

"I liked him very much and he told me to write him and they're doing five more shows and maybe even more. Larry King is a wonderful man. He believes in justice. You could tell. He said, 'You hang in there. We'll see what we can do.' "

I watched the single episode a week later. King had interviewed my mother and brother separately, each for an hour, on Rikers. He'd cut together an hour-long show from the tape, and nowhere in it is there the faintest hint that he believes a word she says.

But my mom needed to think otherwise. "More and more people are becoming for us," she assured me. "Honey, the judge gave us over a hundred years. Mass murderers only get twenty-five. It was totally political."

"It was definitely a political deal," I agreed. "There's not a doubt about it." That was another of the truth grains in her rap. There are always a few. It *had* been a big deal, and the cops had been under heavy pressure to solve it.

"Okay, listen, honey," commanded Mom, "you need to know this. The Creeps are very busy. They're trying to get everything. I don't know if you ever had a chance to sit back and think about what happened to my little life. You got affected because you were my child. From the time I met Papa, you know what I went through with them. I was kind of hysterical fleeing to get away from them. I'm sure you remember that."

"I remember everything," I said with a smirk. "Believe me." Mom missed the irony.

"That's what started it all. My actions were a little unusual, maybe. But you know what they did, they followed us to Hawaii. What the Creeps did is behind a lot of my terror and my fright. They were behind the maids case. They came over there. They've been after me since I met Papa and we fell in love. It's my personal horror story. They're back full strength now. That son-of-a-bitch dyke Linda, she's the one that caused it all. She tried to steal Kenny off the beach! My life was terror because of those people. I was terrified! That's why I am the way I am! And they're back! They're trying to get everything!"

"Here we go again." I sighed. Once more, Mom either ignored the sarcasm, or it flew over her head.

"She got herself appointed as executor of the probate," seethed Mom, "which should never have happened. It's all illegal. When you're down, everybody in the world takes advantage. But if you don't know what happened in the trial, watch Larry King."

"I will."

"The world doesn't know what happened to you or your mother because of the Creeps. Kent, I lived a life of terror because of them. You know how Ken's mother was and all that crap. Andrew was on drugs and there was blood on the doors. I'm trying to find Sandy Spears to help me prove it. She lived the terror with me. She saw the blood all over the doors. She saw the rattlesnakes. I was almost psychiatric because I had to run from the Creeps. You were young. You don't realize. They were trying to kill me! Remember when Andrew threw you against the wall?"

"I don't remember that." It was easier to say that than "It never happened."

"In Newport Beach?"

"I remember meeting him two or three times," I said, "and he was nice to me."

"That's okay, honey, I remember it well. Don't let them hurt Kenny, honey. I mean I've made mistakes in my life but not really big ones. I haven't done anything bad or hurt anybody. I never could, honey. We're being framed."

"It's a hell of a ride, that's for sure." And the circles repeated themselves, for hours more. We revisited Mom's obsessions and I listened, but I didn't lie to her.

Over time Mom began to introduce a new theme to our one-sided conversations. According to her, there was almost a billion dollars of Ken's money in the hands of her last Las Vegas attorney, Ned Rohmer, who she also suggested had something to do with setting her up for the Silverman murder. In prison for the rest of her life, Mom had taken Ken's net worth at its peak, which might have been as high as twenty million, and enlarged it fiftyfold. The fantasy sustained her. She intended the fantasy to be contagious.

"I've got to find Ned Rohmer," she told me. "The California State Bar disbarred him in 1996. They may have something on him. I've got to start a civil lawsuit to get back over three hundred million . . ."

"I thought it was nine hundred million."

"Three hundred million and then land. Three hundred fifty million in CDs. Remember I said that? *And there's land right on the Vegas strip!* There's stuff you don't know anything about. That's not including land and everything else. [Rohmer's] a son-of-a-bitch rogue offshore attorney who was at Nevada Corporate Services. He's got the money, so if anything happens to me, he's a redheaded Canadian attorney, an offshore genius. I trusted him. I never got the chance to talk to you about it. *He's taken everything!*"

"For that kind of money," I pointed out, suppressing the urge to laugh, "you could *probably* get an attorney to sue him for a contingency fee. Trust me."

"Someone has got to try to get my money for me. Kent, *it's a fortune!*"

"You have to understand where I'm coming from," I said

patiently. "Before all this happened, you were telling me how broke you were."

"Because it was all tied up! There are reasons for that! I'll explain it in a letter. Trust me, [Ned Rohmer] has over three hundred million!"

"Why were you asking me for money all the time?"

"I couldn't get it from him! He said it was all invested! He said we would lose all of our interest. He's an offshore evil genius! *He's a crook!* There's got to be a paper trail. You saw the CDs! You were there! We didn't realize they were cash. When we got those CDs in the bank, those were cash!"

"I don't remember that."

"Think back, Kent."

"That's what I've been doing for the last two fucking years." Oops. That was anger.

Mom blathered on. "After Papa died, we went to the bank and you waited for me. I went in. You've *got* to remember that."

"I remember safety-deposit boxes." They were full of junk.

"There were all kinds of papers in there that we didn't pay any attention to. I showed them to you! They were in a huge box!" She was trying to con me the way she'd always conned people. She could talk them into revising their own memories.

"You put stuff in a bag," I said. "You never showed it to me."

"I want you to think about this. There were papers from when you form a corporation, and there were CDs. Most of them were for three hundred thousand. There were two hundred and fifty to three hundred of them!"

"The California State Bar must know where Rohmer is."

"It's a fortune! Ken was an extremely wealthy man. You have no idea! The Creeps don't know about the CDs. They're after the land." Mom had flubbed her fake math. Three hundred times three hundred thousand still only added up to ninety million. Whatever.

"By California law," I said, "that should be yours." It was so much less fatiguing to agree with her than to argue with her, so I agreed with her when I could. What I said was, as far as I knew, true. Ken and Mom had been together for more than twenty years, and he'd introduced her to people as his wife since about 1975.

"We've got to find it! Kent, think about all this!"

"I'm thinking."

"You'll remember all of this!" she insisted. "Honey, listen, promise me that you'll never stop trying to get the money. If anything happens to me, you'll get that money from Ned Rohmer. I should probably be signing things over to you." Mom had showed me the nine hundred million dollars and now she was waving it under my nose. It was the purpose of her phone calls, that and finding out where Kenny had been transferred. She wanted to conjure the mirage of money into being so that I'd have some reason to work for her again, collecting documents, calling attorneys, and searching for money. But I wasn't tempted to lift a finger, because I knew the money was gone.

Within days of this call, my mother was making similar overtures to Carolene Davis in Santa Barbara. She still identified herself as Mom when she called Carolene. Most of the time Carolene dodged her, but sometimes Sante got through. She even had a stalking horse named Cookie, a former cellmate from Rikers, calling California on her behalf.

And she could always write Carolene letters. They were exactly like the ones I received. Mom asked for a long list of personal items for herself and for Kenny. Then she issued orders about the Santa Maria property and made her ludicrous accusations against Rohmer. Carolene, the daughter she'd never had, would be the sole beneficiary of her will when the hundreds of millions of dollars of Ken's money were finally found. So much for me and the grandkids.

On the phone with my mother, when she dangled the fake money in my face, I demurred. I stalled her on the idea of "signing things over" to me. There wasn't anything to sign. "I don't know about that," I said. "I should talk to an attorney."

"Be sure it's a good attorney, someone that does probate. Don't go to that asshole."

"What asshole?"

"You know who I mean."

"Dominic?"

"Go to a probate attorney. Ask them to sign it over." Then, finally, she stopped talking about money. "Kent, honey, I love you," she said. "I love you, honey."

"I love you too, Mom." There was no anger or sarcasm in my voice. Then I said what I used to say to my mother fifteen years ago, when she was in federal prison, except that now I had to make it plural. "I hope you guys are going to be all right."

"I've got to be strong, Kent. When I hear that Kenny's all right, I will be. I love you. I love you all."

"Hang in there."

"I will. Kent, I love you with all my heart. Don't let them get Kenny. He hasn't done anything. It's up to you! We've got to get my money back! The enemy is the Creeps and of course my attorneys, who sold us out. That's what people are saying. It's Larry King, he's got the documents. They've got it in black and white! Our attorney has gone to the other side!"

"We pray for you every night, Mom. I've got to go, Mom. I have to take care of some business right now."

"I send love to everybody."

"Okay, Mom."

"I'm holding your hand, Kent."

"We're praying for you, Mom."

"I'm with you, honey. Just remember your little brother, they're trying to kill him and he *hasn't done anything*!"

"Try to stay strong."

"Tell everybody I love them, and don't worry, I'm adjusting over here. I'm going to fight like you've never seen. You know how strong I can be."

"I know how strong you can be."

"I'm fighting for you and for all of us. When I'm through with this and we win this I'm going to own New York! I love you, honey."

"I love you too, Mom."

"Okay, I just hope Kenny's all right."

"Me too."

And on and on and on.

The state of New York sends its convicts, most of whom are blacks and Latinos from a few poor neighborhoods in New York City, to far-flung prisons in cold rural counties up by the Canadian border, over by snowy Buffalo, and along the Hudson River. It's where the phrase *up the river* comes from. Mom and Kenny had been close to each other on Rikers Island in Long Island Sound off Queens. Now she was in a women's prison in Westchester County, an hour from the city, and Kenny was on the moon. Not long after the last of those July phone calls I learned he'd been transferred to Clinton, a prison in an Adirondack Mountain hamlet called Dannemora, half an hour south of Canada.

On the phone, I told my mother that Kenny had to be all right, but I really didn't know. I did know that he was changing. He still asked for books — Anne Rice, Shakespeare, and science fiction — but he'd stopped requesting designer outfits. Instead of Perry Ellis and Geoffrey Beene, he focused on prison necessities, like a hot pot and warm clothes. He'd stopped calling me or writing me at all, since I wasn't reciprocating. After my TV interviews he'd accepted the fact that I wasn't buying the frame-up story. "I am saddened by the fact that you haven't even sent a simple letter," he said in a terse note in August 2000. "I guess I won't hear from you." He started canvassing my friends and in-laws, searching for surrogate supporters.

He'd been in custody for two years. His cockiness was history. Cunning, articulate, well-groomed criminals like my brother are mostly the stuff of movies. In the real world of incarceration, the average inmate is likely to be illiterate, disturbed, violent, and from an impoverished urban background. My brother the white college boy was a ready-made target. In the city lockup, another inmate had opened a gash on the back of Kenny's head. The cut took eight stitches to close. He shrugged off the assault, but not the alienation. "Please," he implored in his letters, begging for books, "all the guys just watch cartoons and Jerry Springer. Quote, 'I came to jail as a twenty-three-year-old and left being a seven-year-old!' "

As the end of the year 2000 approached I thought more and more about visiting Kenny. He'd stopped listening to me after Kona, and he'd been living my mother's delusions ever since, but in Dannemora reality had to be sinking in. Maybe with time, as he got older and the long days without my mother passed, he'd become more approachable. He'd get some perspective on his situation. I could visit him, and he would start to tell me the truth.

It was depressing, then, to read an article in early October 2000 that seemed to show I was dead wrong. A writer for *Details* magazine interviewed my little brother, and over the course of many visits, Kenny wouldn't break character. He still professed innocence, crying victim and frame-up. Most disturbing, though, were Kenny's diary entries, excerpted in the piece. "Dreamy images of me and Mom," he'd written, "walking down the beach together hand in hand, walking into the sunset.

But that was before our trouble." He seemed to think people
were jealous of him and his mother. "Two cops start saying to
me, . . . 'Were you fucking her?' It's not my fault that she looks
young and beautiful at her age." Kenny told the author of the
story that rather than rat out Mom in return for a lesser sentence, as his attorneys had suggested, he'd vowed, "I'd rather
have my legs torn off."

It depressed me to read about his mother love. When I
skimmed the diaries myself, I turned up two dozen more disturbing, obsessive references to how much he missed his "little
mom" and wanted to hold her hand. ("Mom was wearing a
cute little black hat today.") I didn't think the bond was sexual,
but if it wasn't a pose, it was childish and sick. It looked as if it
would be a long time before I could visit Kenny and have a real
conversation with him. There was a murder trial in California
looming, and with it the strong possibility of a death sentence. I
didn't want my little brother strapped down to a gurney with a
needle in his arm because he couldn't bring himself to tell the
truth. It didn't seem, however, like there was much chance I
could convince my brother to look out for himself rather than
Mom. He and Mom were still in contact, via daily letters and, I
presume, illegal three-way phone calls.

On October 10, 2000, I was about to leave my San Diego
office and grab some lunch when the phone rang. I sat back
down in my chair and picked up the receiver.

"Hello."

"Kent, it's Larry. Listen, I have some incredible news about
your brother."

My friend Larry had played a practical joke on me a few
months before. He'd called and told me that Sante had escaped
from prison. The blood had drained out of my face and I'd
started thinking about where I could hide my wife and kids
before Larry laughed and said, "I'm kidding!"

"Don't you ever do that to me again," I'd warned him. It
wasn't funny. Now I was wondering whether he planned on
being a comedian a second time.

"Your brother," said Larry, "has taken a reporter hostage.
He's holding a pen to her throat. I'm not kidding. Just turn on
the TV."

I skipped lunch. My brother's stunt was all over the cable
dial. Court TV, MSNBC, and CNN, among others, had gone to

live coverage. Though they didn't have footage of my brother and his hostage, they provided updates minute by minute. I was twenty-five hundred miles away and helpless. I worried that my little brother might hurt someone, and I worried that I'd missed my chance to help him, or even to see him alive again.

A freelance reporter for Court TV named Maria Zone had entered the Clinton visiting room at 10:00 A.M. EST for an interview with Kenny. A petite, pretty thirty-five-year-old Latina raised in New Jersey, Zone was producing a documentary for Court TV on my mother and brother. She'd already conducted one lengthy interview with my brother, and they seemed to have a rapport.

Zone faced my brother across a table in the visiting room. They were watched by the cameraman and the sound engineer and a single corrections officer. Four hours and fifteen minutes into the interview, Zone got up to buy some bottled water from the vending machine in the visiting room. Kenny rose from his chair to walk to the bathroom. They passed within inches of each other.

My brother took a black Papermate that he'd borrowed from a guard and pressed it to Zone's carotid artery. He slipped his arm around her neck and yelled "Back off!" at the three men in the room. Slowly Kenny pushed Zone's shoulders down till the two of them were sitting entwined on the concrete floor.

They crouched there, uncomfortable, sweating on each other. "This is your biggest story now," said Kenny.

"I don't want this story," said Zone, trying to remain composed. "I want to go home to my two kids."

Zone was telling herself it was just a pen, but she was a 115-pound woman in the grip of a six-foot man with nothing to lose. No matter how polite and preppie her captor seemed, he'd been convicted of killing one person and was a suspect in at least two other murders. He reminded her what was at stake. "Maria, they're going to kill me."

Kenny began to make demands. The one that got the most play in the media was his insistence that Mom not be extradited to California. He wanted someone to send a fax to California to make the death penalty go away. Mom was too old to be executed, he said. When I heard that, I thought, *No, Kenny, you're too young.* He wanted some things for himself too, like a blanket, handcuffs, and a ride to Canada. He might have gotten it in his head that Canada wouldn't extradite someone facing the death penalty.

While the negotiators tried to get Kenny to let Zone go, and Zone coaxed Kenny into reciting the Lord's Prayer, I was on the telephone, trying desperately to roust someone in the New York State corrections department who could put me through to my brother. I finally reached the secretary of the media relations director and left a message.

That was all anyone would let me do. They wouldn't put me through at the Clinton switchboard, and they never called me back from Albany. I was impotent and desperate. I'm sure they figured I wasn't really Kenny's brother, just an unscrupulous reporter, or that anyone claiming to be the brother of a grifter was probably a shady character too. At the time I didn't know that negotiators almost never let family members speak to hostage takers. It tends to make matters worse.

Four hours and twenty-one minutes into the drama, the negotiators distracted Kenny, and corrections officers tackled him. Zone was unhurt. Prison guards drove her to her home in Syracuse, and the next morning she was retelling her story for the national morning news shows.

I was relieved that Zone and Kenny had emerged alive and unhurt. I should have been angry at my brother, I guess, but I was mad at the prison officials. What were they thinking? They'd allowed a man who was never getting out of prison, and who was looking at a lethal injection in California, to pass unshackled within reach of a potential hostage.

Humiliated, afraid of a lawsuit, the Clinton staff put Kenny in twenty-three-hour-a-day lockdown, pending a hearing. The worst punishment, however, came from New York's governor, George Pataki. A week after Kenny pulled his hostage stunt, begging not to be sent back to California, Pataki made sure he would. He signed the extradition papers that had been sitting on his desk. New York wanted to be rid of Kenny.

I paid close attention to the reports from the East. It looked as if Mom and Kenny would be headed to California any day. Though it would be a short drive to visit them in Los Angeles, the media would be on my doorstep as soon as I did. I dreaded Mom and Kenny's return to the West Coast. And I wondered about Kenny's state of mind. Maybe he'd snapped. Hostage taking might have been his bid to get the authorities to kill him fast rather than kill him slow. I began to think it might make sense to sneak in and visit both Mom and Kenny sooner rather than later—before they left New York.

I was still hemming and hawing in late October when I saw two news reports in the New York papers. Kenny wasn't the only one in my family prepared to use a pen as a weapon. A search of my mother's cell in Bedford Hills had turned up a pen melted and sharpened into the shape of a knife. At sixty-six she might have been the oldest woman in a New York prison ever to carry a shank. Had Mom and Kenny coordinated some desperate act?

Prison officials responded by putting Mom in lockdown for six months. She would have no access to collect phone calls. Two weeks after the hostage incident, the corrections system decided on Kenny's official punishment. He would be in solitary confinement for eight whole years. If it had been me, I would have preferred a bullet from a guard.

But I also locked onto something that other readers of the newspapers and the corrections department's press releases might have ignored. Kenny's phone privileges had been suspended—and he wasn't allowed to contact Mom in any way. Because of her shank, Mom was also enjoined from contact with Kenny, lest they be hatching an escape plot.

Kenny was in solitary confinement a continent away from me, but he was finally where I could reach him. Mom couldn't tell him what to do. She couldn't talk or write, and he couldn't listen to her. There was silence, at last. Without that voice in his ear, maybe he'd listen to me instead. It was time to visit. On forty-eight hours' notice, I booked a flight to New York.

37

SHOWDOWN

These days they build prisons far from town. You're driving in some rural area and you see a few discreet signs on the highway for a "correctional facility," and then up on a hill in the distance, surrounded by razor wire and green fields, there's a windowless modern hulk full of felons.

The Clinton Correctional Facility isn't like that. It dates from 1855. The second-oldest prison in New York State dominates the little mountain town of Dannemora like a feudal castle. As you drive up into the Adirondacks from Lake Champlain, Highway 3 turns into Dannemora's Main Street, and for a quarter mile the whole right side of Main Street is the dirty white wall of the prison.

As I stood on Main Street in my heavy winter coat on the last Friday in October 2000 and looked at the town, I thought, *What a horrible place to live.* And as I turned and surveyed the high stone ramparts of the prison itself, and the guards with their rifles in the corner towers, I understood why my mother's letters were so desperate. If my brother was unlucky, he'd be executed in California. If he was lucky, he was going to spend the rest of his life here in this cold, ancient fortress, where it was winter seven months a year.

I walked toward a hole in the great wall that said VISITORS. A guard buzzed me through the heavy steel door, and after I showed the friendly guy behind the front desk my driver's license he handed me a pen and a form to fill out.

When I passed the paper back a minute later, the guard

asked, "Who are you here to see, Mr. Walker?" He hadn't looked at what I'd written. "My brother, Kenny," I answered.

I saw him turn to the Ws in his book and cut him off. "I'm visiting Kenneth Kimes," I said. "I'm his half brother."

On the phone in the hectic forty-eight hours before my visit, the officers at Clinton prison had been flustered. Kenny's hostage stunt had landed them in hot water, with whispers of a lawsuit. Kenny had been shut up in solitary as punishment, with no visitors allowed except family, which meant that no one could see him except me, but still, none of the guards wanted to go on record as the guy who let the hostage-taking celebrity have a visitor. They'd never heard about Kenny Kimes having a brother till now, and I could guess what they were thinking. One, I was posing as Kenny's kin—I was either a reporter who wanted to interview him or a dirtbag who wanted to spring him. Two, I was really his brother and therefore I was a dirtbag who wanted to spring him.

In order to prove who I was, I had to bring my birth certificate. It's never hard to find a birth certificate in a Kimes household; the problem is making sure that whatever you find is authentic. The first one I came across was a Xerox copy that Mom had home-notarized. I didn't find the real thing till the afternoon before my flight.

Now that I was at the prison and I could prove who I was, complete with birth certificate, the guy behind the front desk was nonplussed. His attitude turned chilly.

I put the contents of my pockets in a locker, along with a Bible and a stack of letters from Lynn and the kids to Kenny. It had been a waste to bring them; the front-desk guy wouldn't let me deliver them. He ran me through a huge, antique metal detector twice, once with my shoes and once without.

He gave me a yellow stub and marked my hand with a fluorescent stamp, like a bouncer at a nightclub. "Don't lose that stub and don't wash your hands too well," he warned, "or we might not let you out." Then he pointed toward the rear door and told me to walk. I left the reception area and entered the prison courtyard. I was inside the thirty-foot-high walls, on a neat grass lawn, and unescorted. Prisoners milled behind a razor-wire fence as I strolled across the lawn. They played basketball and lifted barbells. I could've sidled over and said hello.

But I walked where the Boss Man had told me to walk.

When I reached the designated building, I presented my papers at another big desk, and got a second icy response. After I signed in, the female sergeant told me to have a seat. Before I sat down, I stole a peek at the past entries in the visitors' book, looking for the name Maria Zone. The page for October 10 was missing.

Within three minutes, five guards had entered the little building to gawk at the brother of the hostage taker. They stood and stared, and I think they were sizing me up, to see how many guards they'd need to take me if I tried something.

First they made me wait. After a few minutes a scared, skinny, beardless adolescent appeared in front of the receiving desk. He was a new inmate, a first-time offender ready for intake. "How old are you?" barked a guard who'd crept up behind him. The kid jumped, and answered, softly, "Seventeen." He wasn't giving any attitude. "Boy," chortled the officer, "you're in for a rude awakening." And then he continued hazing the kid. I thought maybe some of his coworkers would be disgusted by his petty show of power, but no one said a word. They seemed to like it. I guess working in a prison warps your idea of fun.

They didn't have any reason to bully the kid, other than habit, but I understood their wariness of me a bit better. The guard who escorted me out of the reception room, down a hall with polished floors and filthy walls, walked behind me. I didn't know where I was going, but when I tried to slow down so the guard could take the lead, I got a firm hand in my back. "You stay in front of me," said the officer.

We passed several cubicles that looked like factory break rooms, empty except for vending machines and tables lined with chairs. I heard the footsteps behind me stop when we got to a different kind of space.

A long, worn wooden counter bisected the room. Atop it, a thick Plexiglas partition reached the ceiling. There were three guards on my side of the bulletproof wall and a little mesh hole down by the tabletop to speak through. On the other side was another guard and my baby brother.

I'd seen plenty of pictures of Kenny since his arrest. I knew, and didn't much like, the dapper con man in the expensive suit from *60 Minutes*. More recently I'd seen pictures of a crew-cut hostage taker in a prison uniform, a desperate, cold-eyed convict I barely recognized.

The young man behind the Plexiglas was wearing a blue prison smock with someone else's name on it, but this was my brother. At twenty-five, Kenny was trying hard to grow a beard, and mostly succeeding, although there were still patches high on his jaw that wouldn't cooperate. Behind the beard, I saw a face that was beginning to merge with my memory of my stepfather. Kenny was growing into a dead ringer for his brown-haired, hawk-nosed dad. The new thing was the look in his green eyes, sheepish, impish, fearful, and resolute, all at once.

I put my palm up against the Plexiglas. It was something I'd always done with Mom when she was in the Vegas and D.C. jails. I'd lay my hand against the partition and she'd match it with hers and we'd pretend to touch. It was the best we could do. From his chair, Kenny raised his hands six inches off the counter, enough to show me why he couldn't lift them any further. After the Zone debacle, the guards weren't going to let Kenny talk to anyone without shackles on his ankles and wrists.

"Hey, bro," said Kenny.

"Hey, tiger," I answered. He'd been calling me "bro" since he was a teenager, and I'd been calling him "tiger" since he could crawl.

Part of me wanted to bolt for the door. It was disconcerting to feel so uncomfortable in the presence of my own brother. In his wannabe grown-up beard he looked so innocent, and I knew he wasn't. But I had to stay, and when I couldn't take it anymore I avoided his gaze.

For an awkward half hour, we stuck with the basics. He asked me how I'd been and how Lynn and the kids were and whether they remembered him. The sound of his voice alone was enough to choke me up. Minus an Okie twang and a half century of drinking, it was Ken senior's.

We had to press our faces down toward the mesh to talk, and before long our necks were hurting. Through the heavy mesh Kenny looked like a ghost, or a priest behind a screen in a confession booth.

We talked, and finally we forgot about the soreness in our necks, the shackles, the barrier that muffled the sound, and the guards sitting five feet away listening to our every word. We became brothers again, and Kenny let his defenses down. The first emotion to escape was anger.

"If you're mad at me, tell me now," I ventured, "because I'm mad at you."

"What the fuck, Kent," he grumbled. "You didn't write me, not a card or anything. You get on TV and say that me and Mom are capable of anything." He scowled. "What the fuck was I supposed to think?"

"I had to protect myself," I countered. "You guys put my name all over the Geronimo house. There was plenty for me to be afraid of. That's why I did the interviews. You should've figured that one out."

Kenny wasn't going to let me off the hook. "You wouldn't let me talk to the kids. You abandoned me in here."

"I didn't think you wanted to listen to what I had to say," I explained. "Before the shit hit the fan, it was you and Mom against me. Based on what I was hearing from you right after you were arrested, I had no reason to believe anything had changed."

"Maybe if you had come to New York, I would've listened," he said. He was trying to shift some of the blame to me, but I let it pass, because for the first time I glimpsed an opening. We were circling around the big question—why Kenny was on his side of the Plexiglas and I was on mine—but it meant he was open to talking about it. I decided to file that subject till later.

I could tell from Kenny's body language that his attitude had changed. He'd lost the last shred of teenage hyperactivity. The manic note in his voice, which he'd inherited from Mom, had been replaced by a softer tone, like his dad's. We talked about Mom and life in Vegas, and we laughed about a few things. He still tried to work the Boss Man when he came in the room. "Hello, Officer Lopez!" said Kenny. My brother was trying to make small talk with the supervisor who, seventeen days before, had spent more than four hours trying to talk him out of stabbing a reporter. The need to influence people hadn't left him. But I thought I could read in Kenny's eyes and his demeanor that he was defeated. He had resigned himself to the reality of his situation and what the rest of his life was going to be.

Every family has its nonverbal vocabulary. In mine a lot of the signals were developed so you'd know when someone was lying and when they were telling the truth. When Kenny wanted to tell you, without saying a word, that you'd stumbled on the truth, he'd tilt his head forward, stare at you from under his massive brow, and give you a wry smirk.

I was making a very educated guess about the state of Kenny's mind. The rest of what he told me that day was conveyed directly, often through his quirky nonverbal cues. The first revelation was delivered via the downward tilted head and the upward glance.

We'd come back around to the Maria Zone incident, and I'd asked him, "What were you thinking?"

His eyes twinkled.

"Okay," I said, "what's going on?"

"I had to get in here." He meant solitary confinement.

"You did it on purpose," I said.

He gave me the look. He never came out and told me, point-blank, that the whole thing was a setup. He said everything but.

"I wanted to be put in solitary. In fact"—he smirked again—"Maria Zone knew exactly what was going to happen."

"You mean it was a setup," I stated, more for my benefit than his.

"She was supposed to get me a lawyer for my appeal. It hasn't hurt her career, has it?"

I nodded my head.

"There you have it," he concluded.

He wanted me to think that the Court TV reporter had agreed to the whole ordeal in advance and that she'd double-crossed him by not hooking him up with an attorney. If Kenny's allegation was true, it meant the end of Maria Zone's credibility.

I had my doubts about that part of Kenny's bombshell. Why would a sane person agree to let a convicted killer hold her hostage? How would they arrange it? As for Kenny wanting to be put in solitary, that was easier to buy. There was the incident with the fellow prisoner back in Manhattan's Tombs who'd opened a gash on his head. Kenny didn't appreciate the illiterate, impoverished ghetto black and brown felons, the bikers and backwoods whites, beating his college-boy ass. But he hadn't complained. He'd grown stoic about physical pain, surprisingly, just like his close-mouthed dad. What really bothered him was the sheer boredom of living with his new neighbors.

"Bro," he explained, "I've got nothing in common with anyone in that population." He was referring to General Population, meaning everyone else in Clinton. "I know I'm this hardened criminal now and stuff, but I have nothing to talk to them about. I'm an outsider here." He wanted to sit by himself in his windowless compartment and read science fiction. He wouldn't even come out of his cell for his allotted one hour a day in the exercise yard.

I got up to stretch my neck and to buy lunch out of the vending machine, a chicken cordon bleu sandwich that had been at Clinton longer than my brother. We ate together, he on his side of the Plexiglas, me on mine. In his blue smock and white T-shirt, he had to hunch over and eat like a squirrel, his head bent low to snatch bites from the sandwich in his shackled hands. And for him, this was freedom, a brief escape from the monotony of his little box. I worried about his mental health. How could he stand eight years of solitary? The Kenny I'd known would have cracked after eight days of it.

We had, by then, already broken the ice on the subject of Kenny's fate. During our discussion of the hostage incident he'd told me about all the other demands he'd made, the ones the media didn't report. They'd emphasized his plea for Sante's life, which he hadn't made till ninety minutes into the ordeal, because it fit the public image of an obsessed mama's boy. As he pointed out, he'd been trying to stop his own extradition as well.

He'd told me he was scared of dying in the California gas chamber. A few minutes later, he'd talked about slitting his own throat. "How can you talk about suicide?" I'd demanded. "You were just telling me how afraid you were of execution."

"I don't want *them* to do it to me," Kenny had said.

Now we were tiptoeing back around to the heavy stuff again. I'd outlined a simple plan in my mind on the cross-country flight the night before.

"Kenny," I began, "I don't give a fuck about Mom at this point. I love her, but this joined-at-the-hip shit has to stop."

He was listening.

"I don't want to have to tell my children that you've been executed. I don't know how to explain that to them."

I was trying to sound hard. These were the first few lines of a little speech I'd rehearsed, in which I was going to try to get Kenny to cop a plea. To save his own life, he'd have to confess

to killing Dave Kazdin, and in the process he'd have to implicate Mom.

I expected to meet stiff resistance, but there was none.
Kenny was a step ahead of me.

"I'm ready to cooperate," he said. It was a murder confession.

After ten years of trying to pry my brother loose from my
mother's grasp, he seemed to be slipping free with a simple tug.
He was looking out for himself, and what he wanted in return
was better living conditions. Kenny intimated that there were
aspects of the Kazdin case that made it federal, and that he
thought he could parlay a confession into a ticket out of the
state prison system.

He had to be smug about it, though. "There is a lot of stuff
they don't know," Kenny whispered into the steel mesh. We
both had our heads nearly flush with the tabletop. We were
grabbing at an illusion of secrecy. "The idiots don't even know
how much we got away with. I can tell them everything they
want to hear and a lot more. I have a shot at being put into the
federal system. Anything would be better than this." He
wanted to be with his peers, educated white-collar criminals.

"Who knows," he concluded, smiling, "maybe if I'm a good
boy I can get out on furlough once in a while and get laid."

He was wishing his 125-year sentence away. "They have a
conviction here," I stressed. I should have been gentle, but I
wasn't. "They don't have to bargain with you."

"Mom's notes are what got me convicted," he insisted.
"They never should've been able to use those on me. We have a
strong appeals case." I'd been relieved not to hear a word of
those fairy tales about innocence that Mom had been peddling
for two years, but he was still hanging on to one delusion.

"I don't see the appeals working," I said. "You can't rely on
that."

But again, Kenny thought he smelled another way out.
"Every day at the trial," he recalled, "when they took me back
to Rikers, the cops would say, 'Tell us where the body is, and
we'll make California go away.' Every day, Kent."

Nervously, I asked a simple question. "Are you ready to do
that?"

He gave a curt nod. And with that, he'd confessed to the
tabloid crime of the decade in New York. I had known that the

Larry King Live and *Details* interviews were mere performances, but it still hurt to get confirmation of the Kazdin and Silverman killings from Kenny himself.

Finally Kenny had put himself in a position where I could help him. "What do you want me to do?" I asked.

"I need you to go to Manhattan to the Federal Building and get hold of Special Agent Blasse." That sounded like the name of the FBI agent who'd first interrogated him in July 1998. "But I'm not giving anything to anybody," he emphasized, "till I know for sure that they'll put me in a federal prison. They can make me a snitch, whatever it takes, but I have to have guarantees."

I had to be sure of what Kenny was saying. I didn't want him blaring "I killed Irene" to the roomful of guards, but I didn't want to leave room for doubt. "If I go to the FBI," I told Kenny, "they're not going to want to hear these harebrained schemes like the Silverman mansion was a whorehouse and that kind of made-up stuff. They'll want the truth and nothing else. The truth includes specific details."

"I'll do that." He'd said it again.

"They want to know everything. The only thing that's going to get their attention is if you tell them where the body is."

"I'll get their attention."

My brother compared himself to Sammy "the Bull" Gravano, the Mafia turncoat who'd ratted out his godfather, John Gotti, in exchange for a short sentence and the safety of the federal witness protection program. It sounded grandiose, but the parallels existed, and I liked the feel of them. He and Mom were racketeers, sort of, with criminal enterprises in many states. They hadn't killed seventeen people, like Gravano, but from Kenny's hints and nods, it might be more than the official body count of three. Yet the feds had let Gravano skate in return for the trophy they really wanted, Gotti. If I closed my eyes and squinted, I could see Mom as Gotti, the boss. That meant that Kenny was the underboss, and he was ready to hand the feds her head.

It had been so much easier than I anticipated. The next of my goals, though, would be the hardest to achieve.

"Mom is going to die in prison, Kenny. Nothing's going to change that." I half shouted the words through the mesh screen.

"So am I, Kent," he said, without emotion. "All I can hope for is an easier time. I need your help with that."

"I'll help you, but as far as Mom is concerned—you have to cut everything off. It won't work unless you do."

Kenny nodded. Just like that, two years too late, he was telling me he was free. He had figured out where Mom ended and he began. It looked as if my cross-country trip had been a complete success.

We spent much of the time after lunch talking about our family. It felt good to compare notes with the only other person on earth who knows what it is to be Sante's son. Many speculate, but only the two of us know. I had a private agenda, though, in mining the past. I was maneuvering my brother back to March 1994. A suspicion had nagged at me for six years.

"Did you know about Ken's death before we told you at Kona?" I asked.

Another nod. "Why do you think I came off the plane in a suit?" It made sense. He preferred to wear casual clothes when he flew.

"But how did you know?" I pressed.

"I just knew." It was a bullshit answer, but I let it go. I was too chicken to pursue the matter any further. The obvious follow-up question, one I'll probably never pose to Mom or Kenny directly, was, Did you have something to do with Ken's death?

That Kenny had just "known," somehow, about his father's death before Kona, despite all Mom's melodrama about keeping it a secret, suggested to me that I was right about the partnership between my mother and brother. It had started long before Ken's death, maybe in the Bahamas when his adolescent rebellion had fizzled out. He'd always been money hungry—it was a family affliction—and he and Mom could have hooked up then in pursuit of a common goal, Ken's fortune. Kenny was Mom's surest means of keeping the cash away from the Creeps.

Now that the partnership looked like it was over, I wanted to see if Kenny really understood about Mom. We shared the same memories, yes, but did he get it? Did he know, at last, that something had been askew in our house, and that Mom's poison influence was what had landed a preppy kid like him in a maximum-security prison?

What I got instead was ambiguous. Half the time he defended her.

"This is an exact repeat of everything Mom has ever done in her life," I told him. "Why didn't you listen to me?"

He shrugged his shoulders. "I wanted to be there for Mom. I remember that night when you told her she was going to die a lonely old woman. That really hurt her. I couldn't let that happen to her. I was all she had."

So I had inadvertently driven Kenny into Mom's camp. "Kenny," I said, sighing, "if I could have I would've done things a lot differently."

"I know you tried," he conceded, "but you asked me to turn on Mom, and I couldn't do that."

I was getting frustrated. "You had your own life," I snapped. "You had to know that things were screwed up. You and Mom fought for *years*!"

Another maddening shrug. "It's too late now."

Three years earlier, he would have lashed out at me if I'd said anything critical of Mom. At Dannemora, Kenny didn't come out and say, "Mom destroyed my life," and he made some of the same dumb excuses I'd made for Mom at his age. It sickened me to hear them coming out of another person's mouth. But I also read into his defeated posture, the shrugs and the sighs and the way he listened to me without protesting, that he knew the truth. He hid his emotions, but he told me, "I know what you went through." He even speculated aloud on when things went wrong. "I loved my dad more than anybody," he confided, "but [Ken] had his problems too. He did his best, but things were always messed up. It was pretty confusing sometimes."

"I loved him too," I said. "He had his hands full with Mom, but he also created a lot of his own enemies."

We had been speculating about what-ifs, like what would have happened if Mom had stayed in prison. I found myself wishing, guiltily, that Ken had died while Mom was locked up. But I didn't say it aloud. Instead I said, "I wish I'd taken you with me when Mom and Ken got arrested for the maids deal. We would've had a shot."

"They would've found us," replied Kenny. "Kent, we're all cursed, you, me, Mom, and Dad."

Then he revealed that there'd been one moment in his life when he hadn't been so fatalistic, and when he thought he could get away.

"You know, I almost escaped once," he mused.

"When?"

"Remember my girlfriend in Las Vegas? From junior year."

"Sure." I smiled. He was talking about the guidance counselor's daughter, the girl Mom had banned him from seeing.

"She had me talked into running off. I would've done it, but . . . you know."

I did know. I was the one who'd run *her* off instead, threatening her family, acting as Mom's muscle. I had run away twice in high school, once to Carson City, again to John Bower's house, and all that time away from Ken and Sante had probably saved my life. Kenny had tried to do the same thing, except he had an older brother shoving him back in line. That and maybe another time, he said, when he fantasized about joining the army, like me, were his only real shots at making a life separate from Mom.

When I left my little brother after four hours and twelve minutes, retracing my steps through the prison courtyard, collecting those unread letters from the battered locker near the front desk, I hoped that at the very least, I'd made him seem more like a human being to his captors. Kenny had kept a tight, stoic rein on his feelings during our visit, and hadn't been close to crying except in that last moment when we were saying good-bye, but the officers must have glimpsed something besides a grifter and a killer during our long conversation.

For me, though, the encounter had left a different aftertaste. I emerged into the wintry sunlight of Main Street feeling like shit. I wanted to kill my mother. I wanted to place my fingers around her throat and squeeze for what she'd done to my brother. All that was left of his life was locked up in this mountain dungeon.

And I was hating myself too, for not having tried harder. I was partly to blame for my brother's fate. He'd told me as much, and it hurt. I'd done the wrong thing again and again at my mother's command, and it had kept Kenny from running away. Now that I was finally able to help him, helping him meant contacting the feds so that Kenny could tell them where the bodies were buried.

For more than two years, I'd been asked more times than I could count, "With a mother like that, how'd you turn out okay?" My stock answer was: I made a choice to be okay, and my brother made a choice to do wrong. My visit with Kenny helped me understand that it wasn't that simple. Kenny was a victim. Worse, I had to confront the fact that Kenny had the added misfortune of an older brother who was a bad example. I had been the "do as I say, not as I do" guy. No matter what came out of my mouth, I stuck around a messed-up family, for love and profit. He probably thought that if he stuck around too, something good would come of it. But in October 2000, the point was moot. There beyond that wall was my brother, one poor bastard, and here was I, one lucky son of a bitch.

I crossed Main Street and entered one of the restaurants that form a gloomy strip in the shadow of the prison wall. It was two in the afternoon, and the guards who ate their lunch there every day had long since left. I sat at a table in the empty diner in my heavy coat with my sunglasses on and cried, as quietly as I could. The waitress knew enough to leave me alone. I'm sure any waitress working on Dannemora's Main Street has had plenty of customers just like me.

After a beer and a cigarette, I paid my check and got ready for the long drive ahead. Mom's new address was six hours south, in Bedford Hills. I planned to drop in on her unannounced first thing in the morning. It would give me a full day to tamp down my temper.

Before I climbed into my rental sedan, however, I reached into my suitcase and pulled out something I'd brought from home for the occasion. I stood on the sidewalk across from Clinton Correctional Facility with a little Global Positioning System gadget in my hand. It was a toy I'd rescued from the sailboat I'd had to sell. I entered the coordinates of Dannemora, New York, and I labeled the entry "Kenny." Now, wherever I was in the world, I could punch a few buttons and I would always know exactly how far I was from my little brother.

IT SHOULDN'T HAVE SURPRISED me that Mom got the better accommodations. Still, after seeing Kenny in his old stone crypt, it galled me to stand in the parking lot of the Bedford Hills Correctional Facility and gaze up through swirling autumn leaves at what looked like a corporate office park.

Everything about it was different from Clinton. It lay in a pretty glen near the northern edge of New York City's tony suburbs. There were children at the front gate and children in the visiting area, laughing and playing. The guards seemed more relaxed and friendly too, perhaps because it's a lot easier to manage female criminals than thousands of caged and angry males.

The atmosphere changed, though, when I told the guard at the front gate who I was there to see. For some reason my appearance at Bedford Hills was a bigger deal than my visit to Clinton. Minutes after I announced that I wanted to see Sante Kimes, the gatehouse at the foot of the prison's driveway filled with guards. They gawked at me and gossiped, and they didn't make much effort to hide it. "Is that him?" asked one. I overheard someone else say, "He must've been in on it."

They made me wait forty-five minutes, and then a guard approached me. "Come with me, Mr. Kimes," he ordered. "My name is *Walker*," I snapped. It seemed like an important distinction to me.

Four male guards escorted me to Mom's building. With all those female inmates, they must have been starved for a sense of danger. I made a lame attempt at small talk as we walked, something like "This is one of the nicest prisons I've ever been in." No one responded.

I'm not sure I would have recognized my mother if I'd seen her on the street. When I entered the side room where they were holding her, I saw, through double panes of glass, a middle-aged woman in a dumpy sweat suit, seated and shackled, who didn't look a thing like Liz.

Mom had grown heavy on prison food, and whoever had cut her salt-and-pepper hair had been trying to punish her. It was masculine, almost a crew cut. Her face still seemed young, but the body beneath her baggy prison clothes was aging. Wrinkles crept up past her neckline and stopped at her face-lift. With shackled hands she nudged a pair of bifocals higher up the bridge of her nose.

"Hi, honey!" she blared in the bright, sunny voice I'd been hearing all my life. "It's so good to see you. How're my babies?"

She meant my babies, of course, but no one ever said Sante didn't have boundary issues. "The kids miss you, Mom."

"Tell them Babish loves them. And how's Lynn?" she trilled.

She's your worst enemy, I could have said. She loves you and hates you. It tortures her just to think of where you've landed Kenny. She's a mess. "This has been really hard on her," I answered instead. "But I can't even imagine how hard it's been for you."

Before she could tell me how hard it had been, and she would, I mentioned Dannemora. "I saw Kenny yesterday."

As soon as Kenny put the pen to Zone's carotid, a phone had rung at Bedford. Officers had searched Mom's cell and found her shank. The guards had clapped her in solitary. She wasn't getting any information from the outside world, and she was left in her cell by herself, her mind whirring.

"Oh, honey, how is he?" She pouted. "I can't believe that nonsense about him taking a hostage. When will they stop telling lies about us?"

"He did it, Mom."

"No."

"He did it, Mom."

"No!"

"Believe me, Mom, it happened. *It happened.* He told me himself."

She kept shaking her head. She'd always ignored unpleasant facts.

"They've put him in solitary for eight years," I continued, watching her face for a reaction. "He'll be in a cell by himself for eight years." It didn't faze her.

And then she was off and running. She switched from upbeat to whining, the pitch and the volume on high, higher still to carry through the ring of sound holes punched in the plastic barrier. Because I didn't have to crane my neck to talk to her, as I had at Clinton, it meant I had to face her, and I searched the cinderblock walls of the cubicle for something to focus on besides her eyes. Her logic was more circular than ever, her tone more shrill, the lies more patent, and at the center of it was her eyes. She'd used them to command and intimidate me for years, but now there was nothing left in them but animal fear.

You've heard her routine before. Listening to her at Bedford Hills was the Larry King interview, her letters, her phone calls, her sentencing speech, all in one stale mash. My lawyer sold me out, I wasn't allowed to testify, I was framed, that attorney in Las Vegas stole a billion dollars and my diamonds, the Silverman deed in the black bag was forged and planted by the cops, Dave Kazdin was my best friend. She spewed forth all the innocence crap I hadn't had to endure from Kenny. She told me she'd lived her life, and all she cared about was justice for Kenny because he was so young and innocent, et cetera.

When it came out of the speakerphone in my office, I could at least get paperwork done and say, "Right," or, "Wow," every few minutes. In person, I parked my mind in neutral.

"We are going to win, honey," she was saying when I checked back in. "I just have to stay strong to save Kenny. We're so innocent of this." There was one guard on my side of the plastic and another on hers. Neither bothered rolling his eyes. All their inmates were innocent.

I tried to change the subject, but Mom wouldn't be moved. She could feel my attention flagging. "I swear we're innocent, Kent!" she wailed. And then, for dramatic effect, she said, "I swear on the life of Carson."

I leaped from my chair. I'd been away from Mom so long I hadn't remembered how angry she could make me. We both knew she was lying—with his own lips, Kenny had dispelled any whisper of a doubt—and yet Mom was invoking my eight-year-old son's name. "Don't you *ever* do that again," I shouted. "If you ever do that again—"

The guard behind me stood up, because he thought I might crash through the Plexiglas. Mom cowered. She apologized, but she didn't mean it. "Oops" was closer to her real emotion. She recognized that she'd made a tactical error.

"So, um, Kent," stammered Mom, sounding as if she were expecting a spanking, "is the media still after you?"

"Yeah." I sighed. "It heated up again after Kenny's hostage stunt."

"Well, honey, be careful," she warned. "If you do anything to hurt little Kenny, you'll have to live with it for the rest of your life."

Before I caught myself, I actually laughed. I think one of the guards snickered too. It was such a boneheaded statement, and Mom was so blind to its irony. She'd gone around the bend, I realized. She was marooned somewhere in her own brain, and she'd probably convinced herself that Irene Silverman was simply an old friend who'd wandered away from her house one day. It had always been one of her strengths as a criminal—she could make herself forget what she'd done and proclaim her innocence with the fervor of a true believer. It would do no good to yell at Mom.

"You're the last person," I stated, nice and slow, with a sad smile, hoping some part of her brain might get it, "who should say that."

Mom tried to recoup some points with me by telling me she was reading the Bible daily. She knew that I did, and I'd sent her a copy a year before. She related to the stories of persecution. "I'm reading the part now," she claimed, "where the disciples are being unjustly accused—you know, the stuff with Judas." She seemed vague. She hadn't bothered doing her homework.

"Read the Book of Matthew," I suggested gently. "It'll give you hope."

"I'm not sure mine has that one," said Mom. Again, I thought I heard a snort from a guard. "Trust me, Mom," I said, "it's in there."

I made one stab at breaking through the curtain of delusion. When Mom rebooted her innocence rap, I cut her off. "They want to execute you and Kenny in California," I said matter-of-factly.

"Oh, we'll win that one." Mom smiled.

"No, you won't."

"We're going to fight," vowed Mom.

"The price of that," I said, "is killing Kenny." Again, not a crack in the facade. As fiercely as my mother loved both Kenny and me—whatever way it was, exactly, that she loved us—she simply couldn't grasp the connection between her behavior and his fate. She never would.

I couldn't cope with the nonsense. I had to shift the conversation to something more positive. "The kids still love you, Mom," I said, repeating myself. I could talk in circles too. "And I have a lot of good memories. I wanted you to know it."

Her eyes welled up, and she wasn't acting. "My big brown-eyed boy," she cooed. "I've loved you the longest."

It was her old standby, what she'd always said to reel me back in, whenever I suspected she loved Ken or Kenny or sick thrills or money more. Since Newport Beach she'd been saying it, and it had always hit me in the heart. But something had changed. It didn't affect me anymore. I felt a crushing sense of loss instead.

Either my mother had lost her powers of persuasion, or my three years away from her had finally rendered me immune. It was probably both. I still cared what happened to her, I still loved her, but when I listened, I didn't hear any of the Sante

Kimes I remembered, the one I'd almost strangled in 1997. Her spirit was broken. There was nothing left of the charismatic, confident, seductive woman who was fun for everyone to be around, the loving mother I hid behind and followed from town to town. The woman whose skills I'd admired and exploited at times had been reduced to a scared grifter telling a lie, and telling it badly.

The gray-haired lady in the shapeless sweat suit behind the plastic wall had ruined my life. I'd rehearsed this day hundreds of times. I'd been hankering for this final showdown, where I told her what she was, and that I wasn't fooled. I wanted to say, "I was right, you were wrong. Here you are, a lonely old woman, like I predicted." I hoped to hear a single, sincere "I'm sorry," for myself or for Kenny.

I'd been reduced to the petty sin of vengeance. I'd been pining after it, and it wasn't worth it. We were never going to have that moment, my mother and I. Hours of screaming wouldn't have made a dent in her aura of persecuted innocence. She was going to die an enigma. She would never break character, she would never feel anything like remorse, she would never ask for forgiveness, not unless she saw an angle in it. I would never have the answer to that question that I've been asking and people have been asking me for years. Is Sante evil or crazy, or both?

After one hour and fifteen minutes, at most, with Mom's tape loop spooling again, I couldn't take it anymore. I'd flown cross-country to see her, and hadn't laid eyes on her since 1998, and should have stayed five more hours, but I could barely stop myself from running out of the room.

"I have to go, Mom." I grimaced.

"No!" she begged. "One more hour."

"I really have to go." I didn't bother giving an excuse. She knew I didn't have one. "Hang in there," I offered, "and we'll write, okay?"

She nodded as I got up to leave. My legs felt heavy. She'd be going back to solitary, where her paranoid brain would spin itself into new ruts. She'd be alone again, dreaming of vanished empires, and the greatest punishment for Sante Kimes was not having an audience. Despite the guilt, I kept walking.

When I reached the parking lot, I stole a glance back at the building that housed my mother and said what I hadn't had the courage to say to my mother's face: "Good-bye, Mom." I drove away fast, through the leafy suburbs of Westchester County toward Manhattan, without shedding a tear. I didn't enter the coordinates of Bedford Hills in my GPS.

I was through with Sante Kimes. She'd be in California in the spring to face murder charges, waiting in a jail two hours north of San Diego for me and the kids to visit, but we wouldn't be making the trip. I'd probably never see her again, and it felt as if a grifted piano had been plucked off my shoulders. It was the closest thing to closure I would ever get. I knew I'd made the right decision at the Macaroni Grill three years before.

And I'd made the right decision about not confronting Mom with what Kenny had told me. There had been a lack of drama in my showdown with Mom, but part of that had been intentional. She said she was going to fight on; I didn't want her to know that Kenny said he wasn't. I had to make sure that Kenny got in touch with the feds and made it apparent that he wanted to cut a deal before Mom could screw it up. It was worth forgoing revenge to be certain that Mom wouldn't have a chance to talk Kenny out of his plea bargain, or cut a deal herself. I'd been forced to choose between my mother and my brother, and it had been no contest.

Two hours after leaving Bedford, I was outside Federal Plaza in lower Manhattan, parked in a no-parking zone, chain-smoking cigarettes. I sat in the car and tried to summon the courage to walk into the building and ask for Special Agent Blasse, as Kenny had requested. He probably wasn't working on Saturday, but I didn't doubt he'd be at the office in a flash once he heard what I wanted.

The minute I said, "Kenny Kimes wants to deal," and told the feds that he would lead them to Silverman's body, I'd be swept up in a shitstorm of cops and reporters. I wouldn't be flying back to San Diego anytime soon.

As I sat and stewed and smoked, I thought better of it. As Sante's son, I'd had a lot of training in criminal law, and I knew you didn't bargain without a lawyer present—no matter how urgent the issue. I decided to gamble that I could find Kenny a lawyer before Mom found out what he was up to and talked him back into suicide. Instead of going to the feds, I went to a pay phone. I called Dominic Gentile.

38

ON ICE

I t took far longer to get my brother an attorney than I thought it would. Dominic sent a letter to the L.A. public defender within days of my phone call, but it was more than two months before a lawyer from that office called and told me she was ready to fly to New York to meet with my brother.

In the meantime, all hell had broken loose. I've come to use world events as bookmarks for my family history. TWA 800 went down around the time Kristina got abandoned at the Vegas airport. When Mom and Kenny were indicted for murder in New York, *Time* ran a story on them in an issue with Monica Lewinsky hugging the president on the cover. The Florida recount was the talk of the nation when my brother told the cops where to find the body of Irene Silverman.

It was November 15, 2000, and no attorney had yet signed on to help Kenny make the deal he and I had discussed at Dannemora. I read the news accounts of Kenny trying to trade the location of Irene's corpse for federal time, and my heart sank. He's blown it, I thought, because he's talking without a lawyer present. He's playing for his life, he only has a few chips, and he's just wasted one.

It got worse the more I read. Kenny had been shipped south to Albany on November 14 to meet with the L.A. prosecutor, three L.A. detectives, and one representative of the NYPD. There, according to the media, he'd hinted around about Irene being a half hour south of the Holland Tunnel in New Jersey, tossed in a ditch at a construction site near Highways 1 and 9. He said he couldn't recall the name of the street or the town, but he'd seen a billboard mockup of a residential high-rise. All the other details matched the police theory of the crime—she'd been wrapped in plastic, shoved in a duffel bag, stashed in the Lincoln's trunk, and carted across the river.

Kenny had already given them enough detail to find the body on their own, and he hadn't received anything in return. What tore at my guts, though, was that he seemed to be doing it to save Mom. All he would tell the police about her role in the killing was to insist she'd been in a Manhattan hotel the whole time. In one day he'd scotched his own appeal but handed Mom ammunition for hers. She could pin the whole thing on her son.

When your loved one is in solitary confinement in a maximum-security prison, it's very hard to exchange information. I'd been trading letters with Kenny since my visit to Dannemora, trying to keep him focused on his own fate instead of Mom's, and I'd thought it was working. Now he'd supposedly confessed in order to save her, but none of his letters before or after November 14 made any mention of it. I sent him an alarmed demand for an explanation. I got it back three weeks later, unread. I'd made the mistake of enclosing some news clippings about his interrogation in Albany, and Kenny's jailers had stopped delivery. I found out the hard way that you can't put anything in an envelope to a prisoner except a letter.

Valuable time had been wasted. I decided I'd better get my questions answered face-to-face. I made a second spur-of-the-moment trip to northernmost New York.

On January 6, 2001, I sat across from my shackled brother once again. This visit was different. There was no wary circling. His openness reminded me of the Kenny I'd known while Ken was alive, the one who'd confided in me and had potential to achieve good things. What had been lost became even more vivid.

"I didn't tell them shit," Kenny blared, as soon as I'd pulled a chair up to the Plexiglas. "I swear!" The first thing he needed to tell me was that he wasn't stupid enough to blab without a lawyer present. A week before his encounter with the cops, he'd received a copy of the letter that Dominic had sent the L.A. public defender, so he'd had plenty of proof that legal help was on the way.

"The cops came and got me at five in the morning," he explained, "and drove me to Albany. They told me that they heard I was ready to cooperate." How had they heard that? I wondered. Either the big-eared Dannemora guards had made a phone call, or someone in L.A. had loose lips.

According to Kenny, he'd demanded to have an attorney present before he said a word, but no one listened. When they ignored his demands, he'd shut his mouth for good. He seemed to enjoy his memory of defiance, real or imagined. "They tried to intimidate me into talking," he bragged, "but I wouldn't budge." The details of his so-called confession, he intimated, were nothing more than the educated guesses of the NYPD.

I left Dannemora more confused than ever about the events in Albany. My brother had lied to me before, but I'm afraid I had still less faith in the integrity of law enforcement. I remembered how they'd treated my wife during the Silverman investigation. *Anyone* familiar with the evidence and the timeline would have put my mother in Manhattan and picked Jersey as the dumping ground. If Kenny had really confessed, why did a judge refuse to approve the cops' request to drive Kenny around Jersey looking for the body?

But I also went home to San Diego less confused, and less optimistic, about my brother's chances. Optimism had always been one of my weaknesses when dealing with Mom. Now I had to accept that I'd made the same mistake with Kenny. I hadn't rescued him after all. If he ever had been willing to trade Mom's life for his, he'd reconsidered. I kept insisting that he needed to confess to the California authorities; he kept responding that he was ready to negotiate, but wouldn't consider anything that would hurt Mom. "Maybe I can get her in the federal system too!" he gushed. He'd tossed away another bargaining chip, by far his most valuable one.

I'm not ready to proclaim Mom the victor in the battle for Kenny. I'm still fighting, and the fate of both my mother and brother remains up in the air. Kenny's L.A. attorney tells me it's "guaranteed" that the prosecutor there will ask for a double death penalty. Yet at press time, both Mom and Kenny were still sitting in their New York prisons, waiting for extradition. Meanwhile, I think that solitary confinement is taking its toll. Locked up with nothing but his science fiction library for company, Kenny's mind has begun to wander. To my chagrin, we wasted a lot of that second visit talking about his latest enthusiasm: cryogenics. If he's going to be executed, he's decided, he wants to get his body and Mom's frozen afterward. "It may give us a second shot at life," Kenny explained. "You know that Mom only has a few years left." I winced, but said nothing. I didn't have the heart to rob him of hope. In his fantasies, he and Mom will wake up a hundred years from now and resume their walk down the beach, hand in hand, as if Irene Silverman and David Kazdin and Syed Bilal Ahmed had never existed.

I'VE LEARNED SOME SURPRISING things while writing this book. Thinking back on that letter to Judge Mc-Kibben sporting my forged signature, I have to laugh. I also consider it poetically just that Linda "Creep" Kimes has hired a private eye to search for Ken's assets. Mom's greatest fear has come true, all because of her own actions.

But most of my discoveries have been sad. It upset me to see "Kenny's idea" scrawled in Mom's notebook under a scheme for laundering money through an internet casino. Mom was so proud of her protégé's inventiveness. And for the first time I saw documents in which Ken tried to blame me for Mom's escape from the Vegas jail. No one took him seriously, but his attempt to make me the fall guy still hurts.

The most unsettling artifact is a 1987 medical report from Mom and Ken's favorite doctor, Nick Stavros. Ken wanted to postpone his deposition in the maids lawsuit; Stavros certified that Ken was in danger of an aortic aneurysm and couldn't han-dle the stress of testifying. I asked a doctor whether this diagno-sis sounded plausible, and he told me that any patient facing such a calamity would have been rushed straight to the ER. It seems like a scam, which makes it all the eerier that Ken died of an aortic aneurysm seven years later.

Learning the full extent of what my mother and brother did and writing about it has transformed me. I'll probably never watch another murder mystery on TV. My views on capital punishment have also changed. I was one of those eye-for-an-eye Old Testament guys, but knowing that I might have to explain to my kids why Babish and Uncle Kenny have been executed is more than I can bear. I now comprehend how some death row inmates could be victims of circumstance, as their defenders claim. My little brother is, and I pray that the Califor-nia courts have mercy on him and spare his life.

It's hard to imagine that anyone else *could* have the sort of childhood that Kenny and I endured, but if there is a son or daughter trapped in a remotely similar situation, my advice to you is: Hang in there. You might think I'd yell "Get out now!" but I know breaking the bonds isn't that easy. I've felt the turmoil and guilt you're feeling as you eye that exit sign. Instead, I urge you to stick to what you know is right and keep refusing to participate in wrongdoing till you have the strength to leave. When you do leave, run far and fast, but understand that it's not going to make everything better. It's damage control, pure and simple. Chances are, the only reward for doing the right thing will be knowing you did the right thing.

Once you've made the break, don't expect to be joining any support groups for family members of sociopaths. Get used to people disbelieving your stories, and get used to the sweet, safe, precious boredom of being a decent human being. Life among the marks is far less exciting than life among the cons.

Finally, prepare to ask forgiveness on behalf of yourself and your family. I do it now in the name of my mother and brother. I apologize to hundreds of maids whose names I don't recall. I apologize to the loved ones of Irene Silverman, David Kazdin, Syed Bilal Ahmed, Elmer Holmgren, and anyone else who might be among the missing.

I also ask forgiveness from all the people I victimized through my silence. Since Mom's and Kenny's arrests I've contacted many of my family's lost legion of friends, in part to jog my memory, in part to reassure myself that they're okay. To Evelyn, to Jeff David, and to countless others, I should have told you what my mother was, but I rarely did more than drop hints. I was a coward, and I apologize.

Most of all, I want forgiveness from my family. I ask my wife's forgiveness for hiding so much from her for so long. I ask my children's forgiveness. I should never have let them so much as meet their grandmother. I don't know how I could have prevented that, but I should have made the attempt. To Kenny, I'm sorry I didn't try harder. It's the greatest regret of my life. And to my mother, I'm sorry for absolutely everything, except what's in this book.

ACKNOWLEDGMENTS

E ven though my mother and brother will spend the rest of their lives in prison, some people still fear them. While I've changed some of the names in this book for legal reasons, I altered others because the people in question requested it. Many of my family's friends and associates were only too happy to help me in my research, provided I not use their real names. I'd like to thank them for their assistance. An even bigger thanks to those of you who provided a positive example to me in my youth and helped me avoid my brother's fate.

Throughout my life, my father, Ed Walker, has endured much for me. Our marathon interviews on the subjects of Sandy/Sante were painful for both of us, but, as always, he came through for me. I'm proud to be his son.

I'm fortunate to have lifelong friends in John and Sheelin Bower. I'm grateful for their support, and to John Senior — thanks for letting me live with you. Your kindness kept me on the right path.

Mark Schone deserves a medal. He kept me focused on the main goal — the truth. His empathy made it easier to relive the difficult parts of the past, and his talent as a writer made it worthwhile. Thanks for being a partner and a friend.

Thank God for Dominic Gentile, one hell of a lawyer and a wordsmith. He was there to help me every time I needed him. I drove him nuts, but his compassion was unfailing.

Thank you to Larry Garrison of Silvercreek Entertainment for his perseverance. You are truly one of a kind.

The world of big-league publishing was intimidating for

me, and Peter Steinberg was a great person to hide behind. Thanks to an agent's agent for making things smooth and enjoyable. Thanks to Michael Morrison and Trena Keating for believing in me and giving me a shot, and to David Hirshey for his hard work and the sparkling results.

My wife's family has been a true source of encouragement. To Lyla, Neil, Michele, Steve, Annette, Jenny, Debbie, and Aaron, thank you for the confidence you showed in me and for making me feel part of something good.

James and Phyllis Knight will always hold a special place in my heart. Thank you for being beacons of decency, and for reminding me to laugh once in a while.

Everyone should spend a day with Jimmy Iorio. His energy is endless and his ability to make people believe in themselves is unparalleled. Jimmy's insight was a source of strength and balance for me. Thank you for being a true friend and understanding better than any boss should. I think I'm ready for Golden Circle now.

For sticking by me and keeping the distributorship going, thank you Jerry, Gary, James, Edgar, Dan, Ray, Nancy, Rose, Wayne, Arik, and Dylan. I'm a lucky man to be able to work with friends.

For sharing their insight, thank you to Mike Stuhff, Jim Tanis, Kay Frigiano, Kathryn Etchart, Beverly Bates, and Doug Crawford. Their memories of my mother were invaluable and their honesty and openness very much appreciated. Thank you to Gloria Roberts and Karrie Roberts for sticking by me and sharing your insights of Ken and Sante. You provided a lot of answers. Thank you to some new friends, Pastor Al and Barbara Roundtree, for their encouragement. The love they show is an example I pray we can all follow. Thanks also to Kathy, Robin, Jeff, and Rick. Though you are two thousand miles away, your caring has always been there. Marina Hawkins is another person who listened and gave good advice and someone I'm fortunate to call a friend. Whenever I ran the risk of taking myself too seriously, I could count on Johnny Rubbico to bring me back down to earth—thanks.

"Thank you" doesn't seem like enough for Gil Lucas. He always seemed to call when I needed a shoulder to cry on, or just to vent. When things appeared to be their worst, he and Mara would point me back in the right direction. Thank you for having faith in me when I didn't have it in myself. George

Racha has been a positive example to me for twenty years, one I'll continue to rely on.

My wife, Lynn, has always been able to bring out the best in me and has taught me how to smile. Kristina, Carson, and Brandy make it wonderful to be a dad. I'm proud of each of you. I regret the tragedies my wife and kids have suffered through because of my "other" family. I have many things to be thankful for, but having my family stand by me is by far the most important. Because of you, I know the best is yet to come.

Finally, to my mother and my brother—I wish things could have been different. For what it's worth, I will miss the good times.

—K. W.

Thanks to Alan Light and Sia Michel, Craig Marks and Michael Hirschorn, Harriet Barlow and Benjamin Strader, Lisa Lerner and Dana Matthews, Alex Heard, Jay Stowe, Ilena Silverman, Frank DiGiacomo, Donn and Janet Cohen, Peter Herdrich and Karen Trott, David Peterkin and Nancy Jacobs, Larry Linsey and Margaret Furlong, Eric and Barbara Schone, Lynne Kirby and Neil Sieling, R. J. Smith and Jenny Burman, Peter Klein, Carolene Davis, Les Levine, Larry Garrison, Rebecca Boyd, Harlan and Anne Schone, and Harry and Margaret Rubin. Special thanks to Michael Morrison, Trena Keating, David Hirshey, and Peter Steinberg for making this happen; and to Kent Walker for his patience, hospitality, and honesty. Above all, thanks to Alice Rubin, for listening.

—M. S.